Artificial Neural Networks with Java

Tools for Building Neural Network Applications

Second Edition

Igor Livshin

Apress®

Artificial Neural Networks with Java: Tools for Building Neural Network Applications

Igor Livshin
Chicago, IL, USA

ISBN-13 (pbk): 978-1-4842-7367-8
https://doi.org/10.1007/978-1-4842-7368-5

ISBN-13 (electronic): 978-1-4842-7368-5

Managing Director, Apress Media LLC: Welmoed Spahr
Acquisitions Editor: Celestin Suresh John
Development Editor: Laura Berendson
Coordinating Editor: Aditee Mirashi

Cover designed by eStudioCalamar

Cover image designed by Freepik (www.freepik.com)

Distributed to the book trade worldwide by Springer Science+Business Media New York, 1 New York Plaza, Suite 4600, New York, NY 10004-1562, USA. Phone 1-800-SPRINGER, fax (201) 348-4505, e-mail orders-ny@springer-sbm.com, or visit www.springeronline.com. Apress Media, LLC is a California LLC and the sole member (owner) is Springer Science + Business Media Finance Inc (SSBM Finance Inc). SSBM Finance Inc is a **Delaware** corporation.

For information on translations, please e-mail booktranslations@springernature.com; for reprint, paperback, or audio rights, please e-mail bookpermissions@springernature.com.

Apress titles may be purchased in bulk for academic, corporate, or promotional use. eBook versions and licenses are also available for most titles. For more information, reference our Print and eBook Bulk Sales web page at http://www.apress.com/bulk-sales.

Any source code or other supplementary material referenced by the author in this book is available to readers on GitHub via the book's product page, located at www.apress.com/978-1-4842-7367-8. For more detailed information, please visit http://www.apress.com/source-code.

Printed on acid-free paper

To Asa and Sidney

Table of Contents

About the Author xi

About the Technical Reviewers xiii

Acknowledgments xv

Introduction xvii

Part I: Getting Started with Neural Networks 1

Chapter 1: Learning About Neural Networks 3

    Biological and Artificial Neurons 4

    Activation Functions 5

    Summary 7

Chapter 2: Internal Mechanics of Neural Network Processing 9

    Function to Be Approximated 9

    Network Architecture 10

    Forward Pass Calculation 12

    Input Record 1 13

    Input Record 2 14

    Input Record 3 14

    Input Record 4 15

    Back-Propagation Pass 16

    Function Derivative and Function Divergent 17

    Most Commonly Used Function Derivatives 18

    Summary 19

Chapter 3: Manual Neural Network Processing.. 21

Example: Manual Approximation of a Function at a Single Point................................ 21

Building the Neural Network... 22

Forward Pass Calculation 24

    Hidden Layers... 25

    Output Layer.. 25

Backward Pass Calculation... 26

    Calculating Weight Adjustments for the Output-Layer Neurons 26

    Calculating Weight Adjustments for Hidden-Layer Neurons................................... 30

Updating Network Biases... 35

    Back to the Forward Pass.. 36

Matrix Form of Network Calculation 39

Digging Deeper 40

Mini-Batches and Stochastic Gradient.. 42

Summary... 43

Part II: Neural Network Java Development Environment 45

Chapter 4: Configuring Your Development Environment 47

Installing the Java Environment and NetBeans on Your Windows Machine............................ 47

Installing the Encog Java Framework... 51

Installing the XChart Package... 52

Summary... 53

Chapter 5: Neural Networks Development Using the Java Encog Framework 55

Example: Function Approximation Using Java Environment 55

Network Architecture 57

Normalizing the Input Datasets.. 58

Building the Java Program That Normalizes Both Datasets... 58

Building the Neural Network Processing Program.. 69

Program Code 79

Debugging and Executing the Program 101

Processing Results for the Training Method 103

Testing the Network 104

Testing Results 108

Digging Deeper 109

Summary 110

Chapter 6: Neural Network Prediction Outside of the Training Range 111

Example: Approximating Periodic Functions Outside of the Training Range 111

    Network Architecture for the Example 116

    Program Code for the Example 116

    Testing the Network 134

Example: Correct Way of Approximating Periodic Functions Outside of the Training Range 136

    Preparing the Training Data 136

    Network Architecture for the Example 140

    Program Code for Example 141

    Training Results for Example 163

    Log of Testing Results for Example 3 164

Summary 166

Chapter 7: Processing Complex Periodic Functions 167

Example: Approximation of a Complex Periodic Function 167

    Data Preparation 170

    Reflecting Function Topology in the Data 172

    Network Architecture 178

    Program Code 179

    Training the Network 203

    Testing the Network 205

Digging Deeper 208

Summary 209

Chapter 8: Approximating Noncontinuous Functions 211

Example: Approximating Noncontinuous Functions 211

Network Architecture 215

Program Code 216

Code Fragments for the Training Process 230

Unsatisfactory Training Results 234

Approximating the Noncontinuous Function Using the Micro-Batch Method 237

Program Code for Micro-Batch Processing 239

Program Code for the getChart() Method 262

Code Fragment 1 of the Training Method 268

Code Fragment 2 of the Training Method 269

Training Results for the Micro-Batch Method 275

Testing the Processing Logic 281

Testing the Results for the Micro-Batch Method 285

Digging Deeper 287

Summary 294

Chapter 9: Approximation of Continuous Functions with Complex Topology 295

Example: Approximation of Continuous Functions with Complex Topology Using a
Conventional Neural Network Process 295

Network Architecture for the Example 298

Program Code for the Example 299

Training Processing Results for the Example 313

Approximation of Continuous Functions with Complex Topology Using the
Micro-Batch Method 317

Program Code for the Example Using the Micro-Batch Method 321

Example: Approximation of Spiral-like Functions 348

Network Architecture for the Example 352

Program Code for Example 353

Approximation of the Same Functions Using Micro-Batch Method 370

Summary 400

Chapter 10: Using Neural Networks for the Classification of Objects **401**

    Example: Classification of Records 401

        Training Dataset 403

        Network Architecture 407

        Testing Dataset 407

        Program Code for Data Normalization 408

        Program Code for Classification 414

        Training Results 444

        Testing Results 454

    Summary 455

Chapter 11: The Importance of Selecting the Correct Model **457**

    Example: Predicting Next Month's Stock Market Price 457

    Including the Function Topology in the Dataset 471

    Building Micro-Batch Files 479

    Network Architecture 484

    Program Code 485

    Training Process 519

    Training Results 521

    Testing Dataset 525

    Testing Logic 536

    Testing Results 546

    Analyzing Testing Results 553

    Summary 555

Chapter 12: Approximation Functions in 3D Space **557**

    Example: Approximation Functions in 3D Space 558

        Data Preparation 558

        Network Architecture 563

        Program Code 564

        Processing Results 580

    Summary 587

Part III: Introduction to Computer Vision...**589**

Chapter 13: Image Recognition **591**

Classification of Handwritten Digits... 592

Preparing the Input Data... 593

Input Data Conversion... 594

Building the Conversion Program 595

Summary... 606

Chapter 14: Classification of Handwritten Digits................................**607**

Network Architecture 607

Program Code 609

Programming Logic.. 622

Execution 624

Convolution Neural Network 625

Summary... 626

Index..**627**

About the Author

Igor Livshin has worked as senior J2EE architect at two large insurance companies, Continental Insurance and Blue Cross & Blue Shield of Illinois, developing large-scale enterprise applications. He published his first book, *Web Studio Application Developer 5.0*, in 2003. He currently works as a senior specialist at Dev Technologies Corp, specializing in developing neural network applications. Igor has a master's degree in computer science from the Institute of Technology in Odessa, Russia/Ukraine.

About the Technical Reviewers

Aakash Kag is a data scientist at AlixPartners and cofounder of the Emeelan application. He has six years of experience in big data analytics. He is a postgraduate in computer science with a specialization in big data analytics. He is passionate about social platforms, machine learning, and meetups where he often talks.

Sourav Bhattacharjee currently works as a senior engineer with Oracle Cloud Infrastructure. He earned his master's degree from Indian Institute of Technology Kharagpur, India. Previously he worked with IBM Watson Health Lab. He has developed many scalable systems, published research papers, and has a few patents under his name. He is passionate about building large-scale systems and machine learning solutions.

Acknowledgments

I would like to thank Celestin Suresh John, Apress executive editor, for helping me make this project a reality. Lots of thanks to Aditee Mirashi, Apress associate editor, and Sourav Bhattacharjee and Aakash Kag, technical reviewers. All contributed greatly to the technical accuracy and style of the book.

Introduction

Artificial intelligence is a rapidly advancing area of computer science. Since the invention of computers, we have observed intriguing phenomena. Tasks that are difficult for humans (such as heavy computations, searching, memorizing large volume of data, and so on) are easily done by computers, while tasks that humans are naturally able to do and do quickly (such as recognizing partially covered objects, intelligence, reasoning, creativity, invention, understanding speech, scientific research, and so on) are difficult for computers. It seems that each of us has a super computer in our head.

Artificial intelligence as a discipline was born in the 1950s. However, the neural network architecture known at that time used perceptions with a linear activation function, so it was unable to solve nonlinear problems. This reason and the lack of computing power made AI's early start unsuccessful. AI was revived in 1974–1980 but eventually failed again.

A new nonlinear network architecture developed after that second failure and a tremendous increase in the machines' computing power finally contributed to the phenomenal success of AI in 1990s. Gradually, AI became capable of solving many industrial-grade problems such as image recognition, speech recognition, natural language processing, pattern recognition, prediction, classification, self-driving cars, robotic automation, and so on.

Tremendous success of AI recently triggered all types of unwarranted speculations. You can read some discussions about robots of the near future matching and exceeding the intelligence of humans. We need to remember that currently AI is a set of clever mathematical and processing methods that let computers learn from the data they process and apply this knowledge to solving many important tasks. A lot of things that belong to humans such as intelligence, emotion, creativity, feeling, reasoning, and so on, are still outside of AI knowledge.

However, things are rapidly changing. In recent years, computers have become so good at playing chess that they reliably beat their human counterparts. That is not surprising, because their creators *taught* the program centuries of accumulated human experience in chess. Now, the world computer chess championship is established where the machines compete against each other. One of the best chess-playing programs called Stockfish 8 won the world computer chess championship in 2016.

Several years ago Google developed a chess playing program called AlphaZero, which defeated the Stockfish 8 program in the 2017 world computer chess championship. The amazing part of this is that no one taught AlphaZero the chess strategies, as had been done previously during development of other chess-playing programs. Instead, it used the latest machine learning principles to teach itself chess by playing against itself. It took the program four hours of learning chess strategies (while playing against itself) to beat Stockfish 8. Self-teaching is the new milestone achievement of artificial intelligence.

AI has many branches. This book is dedicated to one of them: neural networks. Neural networks enable computers to learn from observational data and make predictions based on that knowledge. This book is about neural networks training and using the training for function approximation, prediction, and image classification.

PART I

Getting Started with Neural Networks

CHAPTER 1

Learning About Neural Networks

The human brain consists of billions of interconnected neurons that form a neural network. Each neuron processes a small task, and then it activates the next neurons so that the processing continues. The main property of neural networks is their ability to learn from the surrounding environment. That is how human beings function.

The learning process is distributed throughout the network of neurons by increasing or decreasing synoptic connections so that the more relevant information gets stronger synaptic connections, while the less relevant information gets weaker. The artificial neural networks are built to mimic this process, and as you will learn later in this book, this is done by adjusting the weight of connections between neurons.

The artificial intelligence neural network architecture schematically mimics a brain network. It consists of layers of neurons being directionally connected. Figure 1-1 shows a schematic image of the human neuron.

© Igor Livshin 2022
I. Livshin, *Artificial Neural Networks with Java*, https://doi.org/10.1007/978-1-4842-7368-5_1

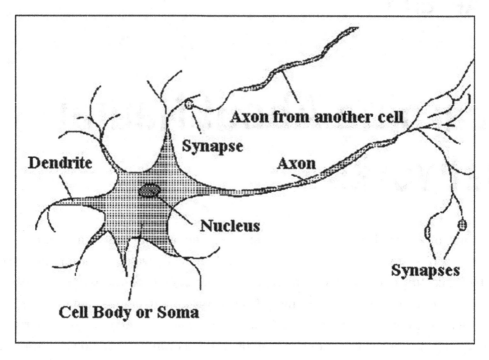

Figure 1-1. *Schematic image of a human neuron*

Biological and Artificial Neurons

A biological neuron (on a simplified level) consists of a cell body with a nucleus, axon, and synapses. Synapses receive impulses, which are processed by the cell body. The cell body sends a response over an axon to its synapses that are connected to other neurons. Mimicking the biological neuron, artificial neurons consist of a neuron body and connections to other neurons (see Figure 1-2).

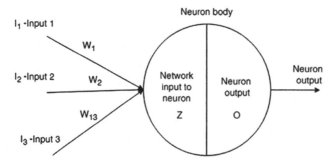

Figure 1-2. *Single artificial neuron*

Each input to a neuron is assigned a weight W. The weight assigned to a neuron indicates the impact this input makes in calculating the network output. If the weight assigned to neuron W_1 is greater than the weight assigned to neuron W_2, then the impact of input 1 on the network output is more significant than from input 2. We'll show how this works shortly.

The body of a neuron is depicted as a circle divided into two parts by a vertical line. The left part is called "Network input to neuron," and it is the part where the neuron body performs the calculation. This part is typically marked on network diagrams as Z. For example, the value of Z for the neuron shown in Figure 1-2 is calculated as a sum of each input to the neuron multiplied by the corresponding weight (W). That is the linear part of equation 1-1.

$$Z = W_1{}^*I_1 + W_2{}^*I_2 + W_3{}^*I_3 \qquad (1\text{-}1)$$

Activation Functions

To calculate the output, O, from the same neuron (Figure 1-2), we apply some special nonlinear function (called the *activation function*, σ) to the linear part of calculation Z (equation 1-2).

$$O = σ(Z) \qquad (1\text{-}2)$$

There are many activation functions that are used for the neural network. Their usage depends on the interval where they are well-behaved (not saturated), on how fast the function changes when its argument changes, and simply on preference. Let's look at one of the most frequently used activation functions, called *sigmoid*. The function has the formula shown in equation 1-3.

$$σ(Z) = \frac{1}{1+e^{-z}} \qquad (1\text{-}3)$$

Figure 1-3 shows the graph of the sigmoid activation function.

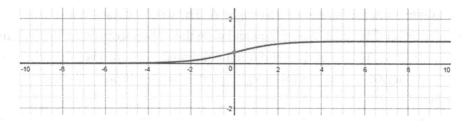

Figure 1-3. *Graph of the sigmoid function*

As shown in Figure 1-3, the sigmoid function (sometimes also called the *logistic* function) best behaves on the interval [-1, 1]. Outside of this interval, it quickly saturates, meaning that its value does not change when its argument changes. That is why (as you will learn later) the network's input data is typically normalized on the interval in [-1, 1].

Some activation functions are well-behaved on the interval [0, 1], so the input data for such activation functions is correspondingly normalized on the interval [0, 1]. Figure 1-4 shows the list of the most frequently used activation functions. It includes the function name, the plot, the equation, and the function's derivative. Figure 1-4 will be useful when calculating various parts within the network.

Name	Plot	Equation	Derivative
Identity		$f(x) = x$	$f'(x) = 1$
Binary step		$f(x) = \begin{cases} 0 & \text{for } x < 0 \\ 1 & \text{for } x \geq 0 \end{cases}$	$f'(x) = \begin{cases} 0 & \text{for } x \neq 0 \\ ? & \text{for } x = 0 \end{cases}$
Logistic (a.k.a Soft step)		$f(x) = \dfrac{1}{1 + e^{-x}}$	$f'(x) = f(x)(1 - f(x))$
TanH		$f(x) = \tanh(x) = \dfrac{2}{1 + e^{-2x}} - 1$	$f'(x) = 1 - f(x)^2$
ArcTan		$f(x) = \tan^{-1}(x)$	$f'(x) = \dfrac{1}{x^2 + 1}$
Rectified Linear Unit (ReLU)		$f(x) = \begin{cases} 0 & \text{for } x < 0 \\ x & \text{for } x \geq 0 \end{cases}$	$f'(x) = \begin{cases} 0 & \text{for } x < 0 \\ 1 & \text{for } x \geq 0 \end{cases}$
Parameteric Rectified Linear Unit (PReLU) [2]		$f(x) = \begin{cases} \alpha x & \text{for } x < 0 \\ x & \text{for } x \geq 0 \end{cases}$	$f'(x) = \begin{cases} \alpha & \text{for } x < 0 \\ 1 & \text{for } x \geq 0 \end{cases}$
Exponential Linear Unit (ELU) [3]		$f(x) = \begin{cases} \alpha(e^x - 1) & \text{for } x < 0 \\ x & \text{for } x \geq 0 \end{cases}$	$f'(x) = \begin{cases} f(x) + \alpha & \text{for } x < 0 \\ 1 & \text{for } x \geq 0 \end{cases}$
SoftPlus		$f(x) = \log_e(1 + e^x)$	$f'(x) = \dfrac{1}{1 + e^{-x}}$

Figure 1-4. *Activation functions*

Our preferred activation function is tanh. It is also well-behaved (like the sigmoid activation function) on the interval [-1, 1], but its rate of change on this interval is faster than that of the sigmoid function. It also saturates slower. We use tanh in almost all the examples of this book.

Summary

This chapter introduced you to artificial intelligence neural networks. It explained all the important concepts of a neural network such as layers, neurons, connections, weights, and activation functions. The chapter also explained the conventions used for drawing a neural network diagram. The following chapter shows all the details of neuron network processing by manually calculating all the network results. For simplicity, two terms, *neural network* and *network*, will be used interchangeably for the rest of this book.

CHAPTER 2

Internal Mechanics of Neural Network Processing

This chapter discusses the inner workings of neural network processing. It shows how a network is built, trained, and tested.

Function to Be Approximated

Let's consider the function $y(x) = x^2$ shown in Figure 2-1. However, let's pretend that the function formula is not known and that the function values are given to us by their values at four points.

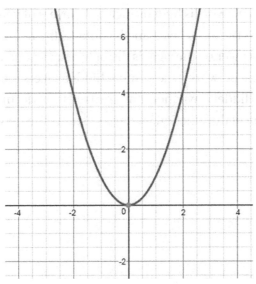

Figure 2-1. *Graph of the function*

© Igor Livshin 2022
I. Livshin, *Artificial Neural Networks with Java*, https://doi.org/10.1007/978-1-4842-7368-5_2

Table 2-1 shows the function values at the four points.

Table 2-1. *Function Values Given at Four Points*

x	f(x)
1	1
3	9
5	25
7	49

We want to build a formula (or procedure) that can be used for predicting the values of this unknown function at some arguments (x) that were not given to us (in statistical analysis such processing is called *regression*). To be able to get the value of the function at points that are not given, we need to approximate this function. When the approximation is done, we can then find the values of the function at any points of interest. That's what the neural network is used for, because the network is the universal approximation mechanism.

Network Architecture

How a network is built? A network is built by including layers of neurons (see Figure 2-2). The first layer on the left is the input layer, and it contains the neurons that receive input from the outside. The last layer on the right is the output layer, and it contains the neurons that carry the output of the network. One or more hidden layers are located between the input and output layers. Hidden-layer neurons are used to perform most calculations during the approximation of the function. Figure 2-2 shows the network diagram.

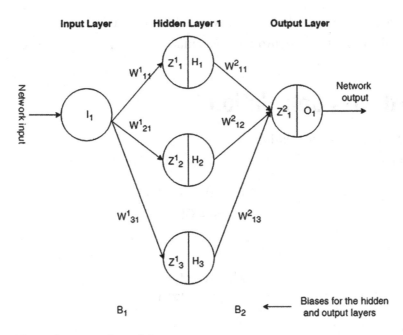

Figure 2-2. *Neural network architecture*

Connections are drawn from the neurons in the previous layer to the neurons in the next layer. Each neuron in the previous layer is connected to all neurons of the next layer. Such a network is called a *fully connected network*. Each connection carries a weight. Each weight is numbered by two indexes. The first index is the receiving neuron number, and the second index is the sending neuron number. For example, the connection between the second neuron in the hidden layer (H_2), and the only neuron in the input layer (I_1) is assigned the weight W^1_{21}. The superscript 1 indicates the layer number of the sending neuron. Each network layer is assigned a bias. The bias is similar to the weight assigned to a neuron, but applied to the entire layer.

When the network processing starts, the initial values for weights and biases are usually randomly set. Typically, to determine the number of neurons in a hidden layer, you double the number of neurons in the input layer and add the number of neurons in the output layer. In our case, it is ($1*2+1 = 3$), meaning three neurons. Determining the number of hidden layers to be used in the network depends on the complexity of the function to be approximated. Typically, one hidden layer is sufficient for a smooth continuous function, and more hidden layers are needed for more complex function topology. In practice, the number of layers and neurons in the hidden layers that leads to the best approximation results is typically determined experimentally.

The network processing consists of two passes: forward pass and backward pass.

11

In the forward pass, calculation moves from left to right. For each neuron, the network gets the input to the neuron and calculates the output from the neuron.

Forward Pass Calculation

Here is the forward pass calculation:

Neuron H_1

$$Z^1_1 = W^1_{11}*I_1 + B_1*1$$
$$H_1 = \sigma(Z^1_1)$$

Neuron H_2

$$Z^1_2 = W^1_{21}*I_1 + B_1*1$$
$$H_2 = \sigma(Z^1_2)$$

Neuron H_3

$$Z^1_3 = W^1_{31}*I_1 + B_1*1$$
$$H_3 = \sigma(Z^1_3)$$

The previous calculations give us the output from neurons H_1, H_2, and H_3. Those values are used as input when processing neurons in the next layer (in this case, the output layer).

Neuron O_1

$$Z^2_1 = W^2_{11}*H_1 + W^2_{12}*H_{2+} W^2_{13}*H_3 + B_2*1$$
$$O_1 = \sigma(Z^2_1)$$

The calculation made in the first pass gives us the output of the network (called the *network-predicted value*). When we train a network, we use the known output for the training points called the *actual* or *target* values. By knowing the output value that the network should produce for the given input, we can calculate the network error, which is the difference between the target value and the network-calculated value (predicted value). For the function we want to approximate on this example, the actual (target) values are shown in Table 2-2, column 2.

Table 2-2. *Input Dataset for the Example*

x	f(x)
1	1
3	9
5	25
7	49

The calculation is done for each record in the input dataset. For example, processing the first record of the input dataset is done by using the following formulas.

Input Record 1

Here is input record 1:

Neuron H_1

$$Z^1_1 = W^1_{11} * I_1 + B_1 * 1.00 = W^1_{11} * 1.00 + B_1 * 1.00$$
$$H_1 = \sigma(Z^1_1)$$

Neuron H_2

$$Z^1_2 = W^1_{21} * I_1 + B_1 * 1.00 = W^1_{21} * 1.00 + B_1 * 1.00$$
$$H_2 = \sigma(Z^1_2)$$

Neuron H_3

$$Z^1_3 = W^1_{31} * I_1 + B_1 * 1.00 = W^1_{31} * 1.00 + B_1 * 1.00$$
$$H_3 = \sigma(Z^1_3)$$

Neuron O_1

$$Z^2_1 = W^2_{11} * H_1 + W^2_{12} * H_2 + W^2_{13} * H_3 + B_2 * 1.00$$
$$O_1 = \sigma(Z^2_1)$$

The error for record 1 is as follows:

$$E_1 = \sigma(Z^2_1) - \text{Target value for Record 1} = \sigma(Z^2_1) - 1.00$$

Input Record 2

Here is input record 2:

Neuron H_1

$$Z^1_1 = W^1_{11}*I_1 + B_1*1.00 = W^1_{11}*3.00 + B_1*1.00$$
$$H_1 = \sigma(Z^1_1)$$

Neuron H_2

$$Z^1_2 = W^1_{21}*I_1 + B_1*1.00 = W^1_{21}*3.00 + B_1*1.00$$
$$H_2 = \sigma(Z^1_2)$$

Neuron H_3

$$Z^1_3 = W^1_{31}*I_1 + B_1*1.00 = W^1_{31}*3.00 + B_1*1.00$$
$$H_3 = \sigma(Z^1_3)$$

Neuron O_1

$$Z^2_1 = W^2_{11}*H_1 + W^2_{12}*H_{2+} W^2_{13}*H_3 + B_2*1.00$$
$$O_1 = \sigma(Z^2_1)$$

The error for record 2 is as follows:

$$E_1 = \sigma(Z^2_1) - \text{Target value for Record 2} = \sigma(Z^2_1) - 9.00$$

Input Record 3

Here is input record 3:

Neuron H_1

$$Z^1_1 = W^1_{11}*I_1 + B_1*1.00 = W^1_{11}*5.00 + B_1*1.00$$
$$H_1 = \sigma(Z^1_1)$$

Neuron H_2

$$Z^1_2 = W^1_{21}*I_1 + B_1*1.00 = W^1_{21}*5.00 + B_1*1.00$$
$$H_2 = \sigma(Z^1_2)$$

Neuron H_3

$$Z^1_3 = W^1_{31}*I_1 + B_1*1.00 = W^1_{31}*5.00 + B_1*1.00$$
$$H_3 = \sigma(Z^1_3)$$

Neuron O_1

$$Z^2_1 = W^2_{11}*H_1 + W^2_{12}*H_2 + W^2_{13}*H_3 + B_2*1.00$$
$$O_1 = \sigma(Z^2_1)$$

The error for the record 3 is as follows:

$$E_1 = \sigma(Z^2_1) - \text{Target value for Record 3} = \sigma(Z^2_1) - 25.00$$

Input Record 4

Here is input record 4:

Neuron H_1

$$Z^1_1 = W^1_{11}*I_1 + B_1*1.00 = W^1_{11}*7.00 + B_1*1.00$$
$$H_1 = \sigma(Z^1_1)$$

Neuron H_2

$$Z^1_2 = W^1_{21}*I_1 + B_1*1.00 = W^1_{21}*7.00 + B_1*1.00$$
$$H_2 = \sigma(Z^1_2)$$

Neuron H_3

$$Z^1_3 = W^1_{31}*I_1 + B_1*1.00 = W^1_{31}*7.00 + B_1*1.00$$
$$H_3 = \sigma(Z^1_3)$$

Neuron O_1

$$Z^2_1 = W^2_{11}*H_1 + W^2_{12}*H_{2+} W^2_{13}*H_3 + B_2*1.00$$
$$O_1 = \sigma(Z^2_1)$$

The error for the input record 4 is as follows:

$$E_1 = \sigma(Z^2_1) - \text{Target value for Record 4} = \sigma(Z^2_1) - 49.00$$

When all the records have been processed, such a point in processing is called the *epoch*. At that point, we take the average of the network errors for all records, as in E = (E1 + E2 + E3 + E4)/4, and that is the error at the current epoch. Obviously, the error at the first epoch (with randomly initially selected weights/biases) will be too large for a good function approximation; therefore, we need to reduce this error to the acceptable (desired) value called the *error limit*, which we set at the beginning of processing. Reducing the network error is done in the backward pass (also called *back-propagation*).

Back-Propagation Pass

How the network error can be reduced? Obviously, the initial weight and bias values were randomly set, and they are not good, which leads to a significant error for the epoch.

We need to adjust them so that their new values will lead to a smaller network-calculated error. Back-propagation does this by redistributing the error between all network neurons in the output and hidden layers and adjusting their initial weight values. Adjustment is also done for the layer biases.

To adjust the weight of each neuron, we calculate the partial derivative of the error function with respect to the neuron's output. For example, the calculated partial derivative for neuron O_1 is $\frac{\partial E}{\partial O_1}$. Because the partial derivative points to the direction of the increased function value (but we need to decrease the value of the error function), the weight adjustment should be done in the opposite direction.

$$\textit{Adjusted value of weight} = \textit{original value of weight} - \eta * \frac{\partial E}{\partial O_1}$$

Here, η is the learning rate for the network, and it controls how fast the network learns. Its value is typically set to be between 0.1 and 1.0.

A similar calculation is done for the bias of each layer. For bias B_1, the calculated partial derivative is $\frac{\partial E}{\partial B_1}$; then the adjusted bias is calculated as follows:

$$\textit{Adjusted value of bias } B_1 = \textit{original value of bias } B_1 - \eta * \frac{\partial E}{\partial B_1}$$

By repeating this calculation for each network neuron and each layer bias, we obtain a new set of adjusted weight/bias values. Having a new set of weight/bias values, we return to the forward pass and calculate the new network output using the adjusted weights/biases. We also recalculate the network output error.

Because the adjustment of weights/biases is done in the opposite direction from the gradient (partial derivatives), the newly network-calculated error should decrease. We repeat both forward and backward passes in a loop until the error becomes less than our limit error. At that point, the network is considered to be trained, and we save the trained network on disk. The trained network includes all weight and bias parameters that approximate the predicted function value to the needed degree of precision. In the next chapter, we will manually process some example and show all the detail calculations. However, before doing that, we need to refresh our knowledge of the function derivative and gradient.

Function Derivative and Function Divergent

A derivative of a function is defined as follows:

$$\frac{\partial f}{\partial x} = \frac{f(x+dx) - f(x)}{dx}$$

where ∂x is a small change in a function argument.

- $f(x)$: The value of a function before changing the argument

- $f(x + \partial x)$: The value of a function after changing the argument

The function derivative shows the rate of change of a single-variable function $f(x)$ at point x. The gradient is the derivative (rate of change) of a multivariable function $f(x, y, z)$ at the point (x, y, z). The gradient of a multivariable function $f(x, y, z)$ is a product of components calculated for each direction ($\frac{\partial f}{\partial x}$, $\frac{\partial f}{\partial y}$, $\frac{\partial f}{\partial z}$). Each component is called the *partial derivative* of function $f(x, y, z)$ with respect to the specific variable (direction) x, y, z.

The gradient at any function point always points to the direction of greatest increase of a function. At a local maximum or local minimum, the gradient is zero, because there is no single direction of increase at such locations. When we are searching for a function minimum (for example, for an error function), which we want to minimize, we move in the direction opposite to the gradient.

There are several rules for calculating derivatives.

- The power rule: $\frac{\partial}{\partial x}(u^a) = a*u^{a-1} * \frac{\partial u}{\partial x}$

- The product rule: $\frac{\partial(u*v)}{\partial x} = u*\frac{\partial v}{\partial x} + v*\frac{\partial u}{\partial x}$

- The quotient rule: $\dfrac{\partial f}{\partial x}\left(\dfrac{u}{v}\right) = \dfrac{v * \dfrac{\partial u}{\partial x} - u * \dfrac{\partial v}{\partial x}}{v^2}$

- The chain rule: This rule tells us how to differentiate a composite function.

  It states that $\dfrac{\partial y}{\partial x} = \dfrac{\partial y}{\partial u} * \dfrac{\partial u}{\partial x}$, where u = f(x).

  Here's an example: y = u^8 and u = x^2 + 5.

  According to the chain rule,

  $$\dfrac{\partial y}{\partial x} = \dfrac{\partial y}{\partial u} * \dfrac{\partial u}{\partial x} = 8u^7 * 2x = 16x*(x2 + 5)^7$$

Most Commonly Used Function Derivatives

Figure 2-3 shows the most commonly used function derivatives.

$$\frac{d}{dx}(a) = 0$$

$$\frac{d}{dx}(x) = 1$$

$$\frac{d}{dx}(au) = a\frac{du}{dx}$$

$$\frac{d}{dx}(u+v-w) = \frac{du}{dx} + \frac{dv}{dx} - \frac{dw}{dx}$$

$$\frac{d}{dx}(uv) = u\frac{dv}{dx} + v\frac{du}{dx}$$

$$\frac{d}{dx}\left(\frac{u}{v}\right) = \frac{1}{v}\frac{du}{dx} - \frac{u}{v^2}\frac{dv}{dx}$$

$$\frac{d}{dx}(u^n) = nu^{n-1}\frac{du}{dx}$$

$$\frac{d}{dx}(\sqrt{u}) = \frac{1}{2\sqrt{u}}\frac{du}{dx}$$

$$\frac{d}{dx}\left(\frac{1}{u}\right) = -\frac{1}{u^2}\frac{du}{dx}$$

$$\frac{d}{dx}\left(\frac{1}{u^n}\right) = -\frac{n}{u^{n+1}}\frac{du}{dx}$$

$$\frac{d}{dx}[f(u)] = \frac{d}{du}[f(u)]\frac{du}{dx}$$

$$\frac{d}{dx}[\ln u] = \frac{d}{dx}[\log_e u] = \frac{1}{u}\frac{du}{dx}$$

$$\frac{d}{dx}[\log_a u] = \log_a e\frac{1}{u}\frac{du}{dx}$$

$$\frac{d}{dx}e^u = e^u\frac{du}{dx}$$

$$\frac{d}{dx}a^u = a^u \ln a\frac{du}{dx}$$

$$\frac{d}{dx}(u^v) = vu^{v-1}\frac{du}{dx} + \ln u \; u^v\frac{dv}{dx}$$

$$\frac{d}{dx}\sin u = \cos u\frac{du}{dx}$$

$$\frac{d}{dx}\cos u = -\sin u\frac{du}{dx}$$

$$\frac{d}{dx}\tan u = \sec^2 u\frac{du}{dx}$$

$$\frac{d}{dx}\cot u = -\csc^2 u\frac{du}{dx}$$

$$\frac{d}{dx}\sec u = \sec u \tan u\frac{du}{dx}$$

$$\frac{d}{dx}\csc u = -\csc u \cot u\frac{du}{dx}$$

Figure 2-3. *Commonly used derivatives*

It is also helpful to know the derivative of the sigmoid activation function.

$$\sigma(Z) = 1/(1+\exp(-Z))$$

$$\frac{\partial \sigma(Z)}{\partial Z} = Z^*(1-Z)$$

The derivative of the sigmoid activation function gives us the rate of change of the activation function at any neuron.

Summary

This chapter explored the inner machinery of neural network processing by explaining how all the processing results are calculated. It introduced you to derivatives and gradients and described how these concepts are used in finding one of the error function minimums. The next chapter shows a simple example where the results are manually calculated. Simply describing the rules of calculation is not enough for understanding the subject, because applying the rules to a particular network architecture is really tricky.

CHAPTER 3

Manual Neural Network Processing

In this chapter, we show the internals of neural network processing by using a simple example. We provide a detailed step-by-step explanation of the calculations involved in processing the forward and backward propagation passes.

Note It is important to mention that all the calculations in this chapter are based on the information explained in Chapter 2. If you have any issues reading this chapter, consult Chapter 2 for an explanation.

Example: Manual Approximation of a Function at a Single Point

Figure 3-1 shows the vector shown in the 3D space.

© Igor Livshin 2022
I. Livshin, *Artificial Neural Networks with Java*, https://doi.org/10.1007/978-1-4842-7368-5_3

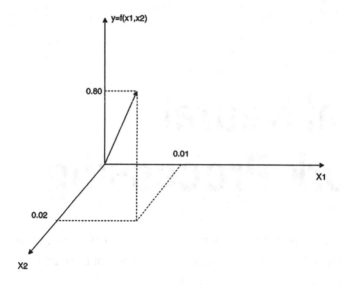

Figure 3-1. *Vector in 3D space*

It represents the value of the function y = f(x1, x2), where x1 = 0.01 and x2 = 0.02.

$$y(0.01, 0.02) = 0.80$$

Building the Neural Network

We want to build and train the network that for a given input (x1 = 0.01, x2 = 0.02) calculates the output result y = 0.80 (the target value for the network). Figure 3-2 shows the network diagram for the example.

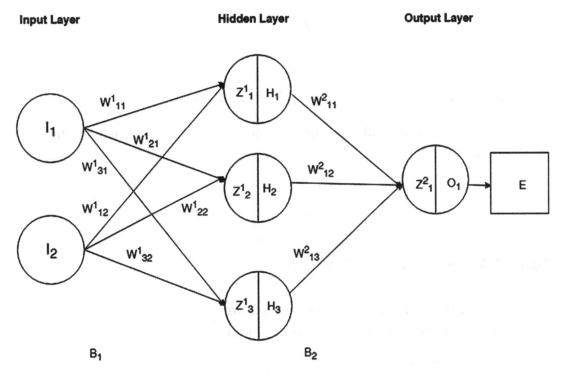

Figure 3-2. *Network diagram*

The network has three layers of neurons (input, hidden, and output). There are two neurons (I_1 and I_2) in the input layer, three neurons (H_1, H_2, H_3) in the hidden layer, and one neuron (O_1) in the output layer. Weights are depicted near arrows that show the links (connections) between neurons (for example, neurons I_1 and I_2 provide the input for neuron H_1 with the corresponding weights W^1_{11} and W^1_{12}).

The bodies of neurons in the hidden and output layers (H_1, H_2, H_3, and O_1) are shown as a circle divided in two parts (see Figure 3-3). The left part of the neuron body shows the value of the calculated network input for the neuron ($Z^1_1 = W^1_{11}*I_1 + W^1_{12}*I_2 + B_1*1$). The initial values for biases are typically set to 1.00. The right part shows the neuron's output calculation made by applying the activation function to the network input into the neuron.

$$H_1 = \sigma(Z^1_1) = 1/(1+\exp(-Z^1_1))$$

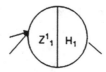

Figure 3-3. *Neuron presentation in the hidden and output layers*

The error function calculation is shown as a quadrant to distinguish it from a neuron (see Figure 3-4).

Figure 3-4. *Error function representation*

B_1 and B_2 are biases for the corresponding network layers.

Here is the summary of the initial network settings:

- Input to neuron $I_1 = 0.01$

- Input to neuron $I_2 = 0.02$

- T_1 - (The target output from neuron O_1) = 0.80

We also need to assign initial values to the weight and bias parameters. The values of the initial parameters are typically set randomly, but for this example we assign them the following values:

$W^1_{11} = 0.05$ $W^1_{12} = 0.06$ $W^1_{21} = 0.07$ $W^1_{22} = 0.08$ $W^1_{31} = 0.09$ $W^1_{32} = 0.10$

$W^2_{11} = 0.11$ $W^2_{12} = 0.12$ $W^2_{13} = 0.13$

$B_1 = 0.20$

$B_2 = 0.25$

Forward Pass Calculation

The forward pass calculation starts from the hidden layers.

Hidden Layers

Here are the hidden layers:

Neuron H_1:

a) Calculate the total net input for neuron H_1.

$Z^1_1 = W^1_{11} * I_1 + W^1_{12} * I_2 + B_1 * 1.00 = = 0.05*0.01 + 0.06*0.02 + 0.20*1.00 =$ 0.2017000000000000. (3-1)

b) Use the logistic function to get the output of H_1.

$H_1 = \delta(Z^1_1) = 1/(1+\exp(- Z^1_1)) = 1/(1+\exp(-0.2017000000000000)) =$ 0.5502547397403884. (3-2)

Neuron H_2:

$Z^1_2 = W^1_{21} * I_1 + W^1_{22} * I_2 + B_1 * 1.00 = 0.07*0.01 + 0.08*0.02 + 0.20*1.00 = 0.2023$
$H_2 = 1/(1+\exp(-0.2023)) = 0.5504032199355139$ (3-3)

Neuron H_3:

$Z^1_2 = W^1_{31} * I_1 + W^1_{32} * I_2 + B_1 * 1.00 = 0.09*0.01 + 0.10*0.02 + 0.20*1.00 =$ 0.20290000000000002
$H_3 = 1/(1+\exp(-0.20290000000000002)) = 0.5505516911502556$ (3-4)

Output Layer

The output-layer neuron O_1 calculation is similar to the hidden-layer neuron calculation, but with one difference. The input for the output neuron O_1 is the output from the corresponding hidden-layer neurons. Also, notice that there are three hidden-layer neurons contributing to the output-layer neuron O_1.

Neuron O_1:

a) Calculate the total net input for neuron O.

$Z^2_1 = W^2_{11} * H_1 + W^2_{12} * H_2 + W^2_{13} * H_3 + B_2 * 1.00 = 0.11*0.5502547397403884 +$ $0.12*0.5504032199355139 + 0.13*0.5505516911502556 + 0.25*1.00 =$ 0.44814812761323763 (3-5)

b)   Use the logistic function Ϭ to get the output from O_1.

$O_1 = Ϭ(Z^2_1) = 1/(1+\exp(- Z^2_1)) = 1/(1+\exp(-0.44814812761323763)) =$
0.6101988445912522   (3-6)

The calculated output from neuron O_1 is 0.6101988445912522, while the target output from neuron O_1 must be = 0.80; therefore, the squared error for the output for neuron O_1 is as follows:

$E = 0.5*(T_1 - O_1)^2 = 0.5*(0.80 - 0.6101988445912522) =$
0.01801223929724783   (3-7)

What is needed here is to minimize the network-calculated error to obtain good approximation results. This is done by redistributing the network error between the output- and hidden-layer neuron weights and biases, while taking into consideration that the impact of each neuron on the network output depends on its weight. This calculation is done in the backward propagation pass.

To redistribute the error toward all output- and hidden-layer neurons and adjust their weights, we need to understand how much the final error value changes when a weight for each neuron changes. The same is true for the biases for each layer. By redistributing the network error to all output- and hidden-layer neurons, we actually calculate adjustments for each neuron weight and each layer bias.

Backward Pass Calculation

Calculating weight and bias adjustments for each network neuron/layer is done by moving backward (from the network error to the output layer and then from the output layer to the hidden layers).

Calculating Weight Adjustments for the Output-Layer Neurons

Let's calculate the weight adjustment for the neuron W^2_{11}. As we already know, the partial derivative of a function determines the impact of a small change in the error function argument on the corresponding change of the function value. Applying it to the neuron W^2_{11}, we want to know how a change in W^2_{11} affects the network error E. To do this, we need to calculate the partial derivative of the error function E with respect to W^2_{11}, which is $\dfrac{\partial E}{\partial W^2_{11}}$.

Calculating Adjustment for W^2_{11}

Applying the chain rule for derivatives, $\partial E/\partial W^2_{11}$ can be expressed by the following formula:

$$\frac{\partial E}{\partial W^2_{11}} = \frac{\partial E}{\partial O_1} * \frac{\partial O_1}{\partial Z^2_1} * \frac{\partial Z^2_1}{\partial W^2_{11}} \tag{3-8}$$

Let's calculate separately each part of the equation using the derivative calculus.

$$E = 0.5*(T_1 - O_1)^2$$

$$\frac{\partial E}{\partial O_1} = 2*0.5*(T_1 - O_1)*\frac{\partial(0.5(T1 - O1))}{\partial O_1} = (T_1 - O_1)*(-1) = O_1 - T_1 =$$

$$0.80 - 0.6101988445912522 = -0.18980115540874787 \tag{3-9}$$

$\dfrac{\partial O_1}{\partial Z^2_1}$ is the derivative of the sigmoid activation function and is equal to

$$O_1*(1 - O_1) = 0.6101988445912522*(1 - 0.6101988445912522) = 0.23785621465075305 \tag{3-10}$$

$$Calculating\ \frac{\partial Z^2_1}{\partial W^2_{11}}$$

$$Z^2_1 = W^2_{11}*H_1 + W^2_{12}*H_2 + W^2_{13}*H_3 + B_2*1.00 \tag{3-11}$$

$$\frac{\partial Z^2_1}{\partial W^2_{11}} = H_1 = 0.5502547397403884 \tag{3-12}$$

Note that $\dfrac{\partial(W^2 12 * H2 + W^2 13 * H3 + B2 * 1.00)}{\partial W^2_{11}} = 0$, because this part does not depend on W^2_{11}.

Putting it all together, we have this:

$$\frac{\partial E}{\partial W^2_{11}} = -0.18980115540874787*0.23785621465075305*0.5502547397403884 =$$

$$-0.024841461722517316 \qquad (3\text{-}13)$$

To decrease the error, we need to calculate the new adjusted value for W^2_{11} by subtracting the value of $\dfrac{\partial E}{\partial W^2_{11}}$ (optionally multiplied by some learning rate η) from the original value of W^2_{11}.

$$\text{adjusted}W^2_{11} = W^2_{11} - \eta * \frac{\partial E}{\partial W^2_{11}}. \text{ For this example, } \eta = 1. \qquad (3\text{-}14)$$

$$\text{adjusted}W^2_{11} = 0.11 + 0.024841461722517316 = 0.13484146172251732$$

Calculating Adjustment for W^2_{12}

Applying the chain rule for derivatives, $\partial E/\partial W^2_{12}$ can be expressed by the following formula:

$$\frac{\partial E}{\partial W^2_{11}} = \frac{\partial E}{\partial O_1} * \frac{\partial O_1}{\partial Z^2_1} * \frac{\partial Z^2_1}{\partial W^2_{12}} \qquad (3\text{-}15)$$

Let's calculate separately each part of the equation using derivative calculus.

$$\frac{\partial E}{\partial O_1} = -0.18980115540874787 \text{ (see 1-3)} \qquad (3\text{-}16)$$

$$Calculating \ \frac{\partial O_1}{\partial Z^2_1}$$

$$\frac{\partial O_1}{\partial Z^2_1} = 0.23785621465075305 \text{ (see 1-4)} \qquad (3\text{-}17)$$

$$Calculating \ \frac{\partial Z^2_1}{\partial W^2_{12}}$$

$$Z^2_1 = W^2_{11}* H_1 + W^2_{12}* H_2 + W^2_{13}* H_3 + B_2*1.00 \qquad (3\text{-}18)$$

$$\frac{\partial Z^2_1}{\partial W^2_{11}} = H_2 = 0.5504032199355139 \text{ (see 1-3)} \qquad (3\text{-}19)$$

Putting it all together, we have this:

$$\frac{\partial E}{\partial W^2_{11}} = \text{-0.18980115540874787*0.23785621465075305*0.5502547397403884}$$
$$= \text{-0.024841461722517316} \tag{3-20}$$

To decrease the error, we need to calculate the new adjusted value for W^2_{11} by subtracting the value of $\frac{\partial E}{\partial W^2_{11}}$ (optionally multiplied by some learning rate η) from the original value of $W^2_{12.}$

$$\text{adjusted}W^2_{12} = W^2_{12} -\eta *\frac{\partial E}{\partial W^2_{12}}$$

$$\text{adjusted}W^2_{12} = 0.12 + 0.024841461722517316 = 0.1448414617225173 \tag{3-21}$$

Calculating Adjustment for W^2_{13}

$$\frac{\partial E}{\partial W^2_{13}} = \frac{\partial E}{\partial O_1} * \frac{\partial O_1}{\partial Z^2_1} * \frac{\partial Z^2_1}{\partial W^2_{13}}$$

$$\frac{\partial E}{\partial O_1} = \text{-0.18980115540874787 (see 1-13)} \tag{3-22}$$

$$\frac{\partial O_1}{\partial Z^2_1} = 0.23785621465075305 \text{ (see 1-14)} \tag{3-23}$$

$$Calculating \frac{\partial Z^2_1}{\partial W^2_{13}}$$

$$Z^2_1 = W^2_{11} * H_1 + W^2_{12} * H_2 + W^2_{13} * H_3 + B_2 * 1.00 \tag{3-24}$$

$$\frac{\partial Z^2_1}{\partial W^2_{13}} = H_3 = 0.5505516911502556 \text{ (see 1-4)} \tag{3-25}$$

Putting it all together, we have this:

$$\frac{\partial E}{\partial W^2_{13}} = \text{-0.18980115540874787*0.23785621465075305*0.5505516911502556}$$
$$= \text{-0.024854867708052567} \tag{3-26}$$

$$\text{adjusted}W^2_{13} = W^2_{13} -\eta *\frac{\partial E}{\partial W^2_{13}}. \text{ For this example, } \eta = 1.$$

$$\text{adjusted}W^2_{12} = 0.13 + 0.024841461722517316 = 0.1548414617225173 \tag{3-27}$$

Therefore, on the second iteration, we will use the following weight-adjusted values:

$$\text{adjustedW}^2{}_{11} = 0.08515853827748268$$
$$\text{adjustedW}^2{}_{12} = 0.09515853827748268$$
$$\text{adjustedW}^2{}_{13} = 0.10515853827748269$$

After adjusting weights for the output neurons, we are ready to calculate weight adjustments for the hidden neurons.

Calculating Weight Adjustments for Hidden-Layer Neurons

Calculating weight adjustments for the neurons in the hidden layer is similar to the corresponding calculations in the output layer, but with one important difference. For the neurons in the output layer, the input is now the output results from the corresponding neurons in the hidden layer.

Calculating Adjustment for $W^1{}_{11}$

Applying the chain rule for derivatives, $\partial E / \partial W^1{}_{11}$ can be expressed by the following formula:

$$\frac{\partial E}{\partial W^1{}_{11}} = \frac{\partial E}{\partial H_1} * \frac{\partial H_1}{\partial Z_1^1} * \frac{\partial Z_1^1}{\partial W^1{}_{11}} \tag{3-28}$$

$$\frac{\partial E}{\partial H_1} = \frac{\partial E}{\partial O_1} * \frac{\partial O_1}{\partial Z_1^1} = -0.18980115540874787 * 0.23785621465075305$$
$$= -0.04514538436186407 \text{ (see 1-13 and 1-14)} \tag{3-29}$$

$$\frac{\partial H_1}{\partial Z_1^1} = \sigma(H_1) = H_1 * (1 - H_1) = 0.5502547397403884 * (1 - 0.5502547397403884)$$
$$= 0.24747446113362584 \tag{3-30}$$

$$\frac{\partial Z_1^1}{\partial W^1{}_{11}} = \frac{\partial\left(W^1{}_{11} * I_1 + W^1{}_{12} * I_2 + B_1 * 1\right)}{\partial W^1{}_{11}} = I_1 = 0.01 \tag{3-31}$$

Putting it all together, we have this:

$$\frac{\partial E}{\partial W^1_{11}} = -0.04514538436186407 * 0.24747446113362584 * 0.01$$
$$= -0.0001117232966762273 \tag{3-32}$$

$$\text{adjusted}W^1_{11} = W^1_{11} - \eta * \frac{\partial E}{\partial W^1_{11}} = 0.05 - 0.0001117232966762273$$

$$= 0.049888276703323776 \tag{3-33}$$

$$\text{adjusted}W^1_{11} = W^1_{11} - \eta * \frac{\partial E}{\partial W^1_{11}} = 0.05 + 0.0001117232966762273$$

$$= 0.05011172329667623 \tag{3-34}$$

Calculating Adjustment for W^1_{12}

Applying the chain rule for derivatives, $\partial E/\partial W^1_{12}$ can be expressed by the following formula:

$$\frac{\partial E}{\partial W^1_{12}} = \frac{\partial E}{\partial H_1} * \frac{\partial H_1}{\partial Z^1_1} * \frac{\partial Z^1_1}{\partial W^1_{12}}$$

$$\frac{\partial E}{\partial H_1} = \frac{\partial E}{\partial O_1} * \frac{\partial O_1}{\partial Z^1_1} = -0.18980115540874787 * 0.23785621465075305$$
$$= -0.04514538436186407 \text{ (see 1-13 and 1-14)} \tag{3-35}$$

$$\frac{\partial H_1}{\partial Z^1_1} = 0.24747446113362584 \text{ (see 1-28)} \tag{3-36}$$

$$\frac{\partial Z^1_1}{\partial W^1_{12}} = \frac{\partial \left(W^1_{11} * I_1 + W^1_{12} * I_2 + B_1 * 1 \right)}{\partial W^1_{12}} = I_2 = 0.02 \tag{3-37}$$

Putting it all together, we have this:

$$\frac{\partial E}{\partial W^1_{12}} = -0.04514538436186407 * 0.24747446113362584 * 0.02$$
$$= -00022344659335245464 \tag{3-38}$$

$$\text{adjusted}W^1_{12} = W^1_{12} - \eta * \frac{\partial E}{\partial W^1_{12}} = 0.06 + 0.00022344659335245464$$

$$= 0.06022344659335245 \tag{3-39}$$

Calculating Adjustment for W^1_{21}

Applying the chain rule for derivatives, $\partial E/\partial W^1_{21}$ can be expressed by the following formula:

$$\frac{\partial E}{\partial W^1_{21}} = \frac{\partial E}{\partial H_2} * \frac{\partial H_2}{\partial Z^1_2} * \frac{\partial Z^1_2}{\partial W^1_{21}} \tag{3-40}$$

$$\frac{\partial E}{\partial H_2} = \frac{\partial E}{\partial O_1} * \frac{\partial O_1}{\partial Z^1_2} = -0.18980115540874787*0.23785621465075305$$

$$= -0.04514538436186407 \text{ (see 3-9 and 3-10)} \tag{3-41}$$

$$\frac{\partial H_2}{\partial Z^1_2} = H_2*(1 - H_2) = 0.5504032199355139* (1 - 0.5504032199355139)$$

$$= 0.059776553406647545 \tag{3-42}$$

$$\frac{\partial Z^1_2}{\partial W^1_{21}} = \frac{\partial\left(W^1_{21} * I_1 + W^1_{22} * I_2 + B_1 *1\right)}{\partial W^1_{21}} = I_1 = 0.01 \tag{3-43}$$

Putting it all together, we have this:

$$\frac{\partial E}{\partial W^1_{21}} = -0.04514538436186407*0.059776553406647545*0.01$$

$$= -0.000026986354793705983 \tag{3-44}$$

$$\text{adjusted}W^1_{21} = W^1_{12} - \eta * \frac{\partial E}{\partial W^1_{21}} = 0.07 + 0.000026986354793705983$$

$$= 0.07002698635479371 \tag{3-45}$$

Calculating Adjustment for W^1_{22}

$$\frac{\partial E}{\partial W^1_{22}} = \frac{\partial E}{\partial H_2} * \frac{\partial H_2}{\partial Z^1_2} * \frac{\partial Z^1_2}{\partial W^1_{22}} \tag{3-46}$$

$$\frac{\partial E}{\partial H_2} = \frac{\partial E}{\partial O_1} * \frac{\partial O_1}{\partial Z_2^1} = -0.04514538436186407 \text{ (see 3-9 and 3-10)} \qquad (3\text{-}47)$$

$$\frac{\partial H_2}{\partial Z_2^1} = H_2*(1 - H_2) = 0.5504032199355139* (1 - 0.5504032199355139)$$

$$= 0.059776553406647545 \qquad (3\text{-}48)$$

$$\frac{\partial Z_2^1}{\partial W_{22}^1} = \frac{\partial \left(W_{21}^1 * I_1 + W_{22}^1 * I_2 + B_1 *1\right)}{\partial W_{22}^1} = I_2 = 0.02 \qquad (3\text{-}49)$$

Putting it all together, we have this:

$$\frac{\partial E}{\partial W_{22}^1} = -0.04514538436186407*0.059776553406647545*0.02$$

$$= -0.000053972709587411966 \qquad (3\text{-}50)$$

$$\text{adjusted}W_{22}^1 = W_{22}^1 - \eta * \frac{\partial E}{\partial W_{22}^1} = 0.08 + 0.000053972709587411966$$

$$= 0.08005397270958742 \qquad (3\text{-}51)$$

Calculating Adjustment for W_{31}^1

$$\frac{\partial E}{\partial W_{31}^1} = \frac{\partial E}{\partial H_3} * \frac{\partial H_3}{\partial Z_3^1} * \frac{\partial Z_3^1}{\partial W_{31}^1} \qquad (3\text{-}52)$$

$$\frac{\partial E}{\partial H_3} = \frac{\partial E}{\partial O_1} * \frac{\partial O_1}{\partial Z_3^1} = -0.04514538436186407 \text{ (see 1-13 and 1-14)} \qquad (3\text{-}49)$$

$$\frac{\partial H_3}{\partial Z_3^1} = H_3*(1 - H_3) = 0.5505516911502556* (1 - 0.5505516911502556)$$

$$= 0.24744452652184917 \qquad (3\text{-}53)$$

$$\frac{\partial Z_3^1}{\partial W_{31}^1} = \frac{\partial \left(W_{31}^1 * I_1 + W_{32}^1 * I_2 + B_1 *1\right)}{\partial W_{31}^1} = I_1 = 0.01 \qquad (3\text{-}54)$$

Putting it all together, we have this:

$$\frac{\partial E}{\partial W^1_{22}} = -0.04514538436186407*0.24744452652184917*0.01$$
$$= -0.0001117097825806835 \tag{3-55}$$

$$\text{adjustedW}^1_{31} = W^1_{31} - \eta * \frac{\partial E}{\partial W^1_{31}} = 0.09 + 0.0001117097825806835$$
$$= 0.09011170978258068 \tag{3-56}$$

Calculating Adjustment for W¹₃₂

$$\frac{\partial E}{\partial W^1_{32}} = \frac{\partial E}{\partial H_3} * \frac{\partial H_3}{\partial Z^1_3} * \frac{\partial Z^1_3}{\partial W^1_{32}} \tag{3-57}$$

$$\frac{\partial E}{\partial H_3} = \frac{\partial E}{\partial O_1} * \frac{\partial O_1}{\partial Z^1_3} = -0.04514538436186407 \text{ (see 1-49)} \tag{3-58}$$

$$\frac{\partial H_3}{\partial Z^1_3} = H_3*(1 - H_3) = 0.5505516911502556* (1 - 0.5505516911502556)$$
$$= 0.24744452652184917 \text{ (see 1-50)} \tag{3-59}$$

$$\frac{\partial Z^1_3}{\partial W^1_{32}} = \frac{\partial \left(W^1_{31} * I_1 + W^1_{32} * I_2 + B_1 *1 \right)}{\partial W^1_{32}} = I_2 = 0.02 \tag{3-60}$$

Putting it all together, we have this:

$$\frac{\partial E}{\partial W^1_{32}} = -0.04514538436186407*0.24744452652184917*0.02$$
$$= -0.000223419565161367 \tag{3-61}$$

$$\text{adjustedW}^1_{32} = W^1_{32} - \eta * \frac{\partial E}{\partial W^1_{31}} = 0.10 + 0.000223419565161367$$
$$= 0.10022341956516137 \tag{3-62}$$

Updating Network Biases

We need to calculate the error adjustment for the biases B_1 and B_2. Again, using the chain rule:

$$\frac{\partial E}{\partial B_1} = \frac{\partial E}{\partial O_1} * \frac{\partial O_1}{\partial Z_1^1} * \frac{\partial Z_1^1}{\partial B_1} \tag{3-63}$$

$$\frac{\partial E}{\partial B_2} = \frac{\partial E}{\partial O_1} * \frac{\partial O_1}{\partial Z_1^2} * \frac{\partial Z_1^2}{\partial B_2} \tag{3-64}$$

Calculating three parts of the previous formula for both expressions, we get this:

$$\frac{\partial Z_1^1}{\partial B_1} = \frac{\partial\left(W^1{}_{11} * I_1 + W^1{}_{12} * I_2 + B_1 * 1\right)}{\partial B_1} = 1 \tag{3-65}$$

$$\frac{\partial Z_1^2}{\partial B_2} = \frac{\partial\left(W^2{}_{11} * H_1 + W^2{}_{12} * H_2 + W^2{}_{13} * H_3 + B_2 * 1\right)}{\partial B_2} = 1 \tag{3-66}$$

$$\frac{\partial E}{\partial B_1} = \frac{\partial E}{\partial H_1} * \frac{\partial H_1}{\partial Z_1^1} * 1 = \delta^1{}_1 \tag{3-67}$$

$$\frac{\partial E}{\partial B_2} = \frac{\partial E}{\partial H_2} * \frac{\partial H_2}{\partial Z_1^2} * 1 = \delta^2{}_1 \tag{3-68}$$

Because we use biases B_1 and B_2 per layer and not per neuron, we can calculate the average δ for the layer.

$$\delta^1 = \delta^1{}_1 + \delta^1{}_{2+} \delta^1{}_3 \tag{3-69}$$

$$\frac{\partial E}{\partial B_1} = \delta^1 \tag{3-70}$$

$$\frac{\partial E}{\partial B_2} = \delta^2 \tag{3-71}$$

$$\delta^2 = \frac{\partial E}{\partial O_1} * \frac{\partial O_1}{\partial Z_1^2} = -0.18980115540874787 * 0.23785621465075305$$

$$= -0.04514538436186407 \tag{3-72}$$

$$\delta^1{}_1 = \frac{\partial E}{\partial O_1} * \frac{\partial O_1}{\partial Z_2^1} = -0.04514538436186407 \tag{3-73}$$

$$\delta^1_2 = \frac{\partial E}{\partial O_1} * \frac{\partial O_1}{\partial Z^1_1} = -0.04514538436186407 \tag{3-74}$$

$$\delta^1_3 = \frac{\partial E}{\partial O_1} * \frac{\partial O_1}{\partial Z^1_3} = -0.04514538436186407 \tag{3-75}$$

Because a bias adjustment is calculated per layer, we take the average of the calculated bias adjustments for each neuron.

$$\delta^1 = (\delta^1_1 + \delta^1_2 + \delta^1_3)/3 = -0.04514538436186407 \tag{3-76}$$

$$\delta^2 = -0.04514538436186407$$

With the introduction of variable δ, we have this:

$$\text{adjusted } B_1 = B_1 - \eta^* \delta_1 = 0.20 + 0.04514538436186407 = 0.2451453843618641 \tag{3-77}$$

$$\text{adjusted } B_2 = B_2 - \eta^* \delta_2 = 0.25 _+ 0.04514538436186407$$
$$= 0.29514538436186405 \tag{3-78}$$

Now, that we have calculated all new weight values, we get back to the forward phase and calculate a new error.

Back to the Forward Pass

Recalculate the network output for the hidden and output layers using new adjusted weight/biases.

Hidden Layers

Here are the hidden layers:

Neuron H_1:

a)   Calculate the total net input for neuron H_1.

$$Z^1_1 = W^1_{11} * I_1 + W^1_{12} * I_2 + B_1 * 1.00 = 0.05011172329667623 * 0.01$$
$$+ 0.06022344659335245 * 0.02 + 0.2451453843618641 * 1.00$$
$$= 0.2468509705266979 \tag{3-79}$$

b) Use the logistic function to get the output of H_1.

$$H_1 = \delta(Z^1_1) = 1/(1+\exp(-Z^1_1)) = 1/(1+\exp(-0.2468509705266979))$$
$$= 0.561401266257945 \tag{3-80}$$

Neuron H_2:

$$Z^1_2 = W^1_{21} * I_1 + W^1_{22} * I_2 + B_1 * 1.00 = 0.07002698635479371 * 0.01$$
$$+ 0.08005397270958742 * 0.02 + 0.2451453843618641 * 1.00$$
$$= 0.24744673367960376 \tag{3-81}$$

$$H_2 = 1/(1+\exp(-0.24744673367960376)) = 0.5615479555799516 \tag{3-82}$$

Neuron H_3:

$$Z^1_2 = W^1_{31} * I_1 + W^1_{32} * I_2 + B_1 * 1.00 = 0.09011170978258068 * 0.01$$
$$+ 0.10022341956516137 * 0.02 + 0.2451453843618641 * 1.00$$
$$= 0.24805096985099312$$
$$H_3 = 1/(1+\exp(-0.24805096985099312)) = 0.5616967201480348 \tag{3-83}$$

Output Layer

Here is the output layer:

Neuron O_1:

a) Calculate the total net input for neuron O_1.

$$Z^2_1 = W^2_{11} * H_1 + W^2_{12} * H_2 + W^2_{13} * H_3 + B_2 * 1.00 = 0.13484146172251732 *$$
$$0.5502547397403884 + 0.1448414617225173 * 0.5504032199355139$$
$$+ 0.1548414617225173 * 0.5505516911502556 + 0.29514538436186405 * 1.00$$
$$= 0.5343119733119508 \tag{3-84}$$

b) Use the logistic function δ to get the output from O_1.

$$O_1 = \delta(Z^2_1) = 1/(1+\exp(-Z^2_1)) = 1/(1+\exp(-0.5343119733119508))$$
$$= 0.6304882485312977 \tag{3-85}$$

The calculated output from neuron O_1 is 0.6304882485312977, while the target output for O_1 is 0.80; therefore, the following is the squared error for the output for neuron O_1:

$$E = 0.5*(T_1 - O_1)^2 = 0.5*(0.80 - 0.6304882485312977)^2$$
$$= 0.014367116942993556 \tag{3-86}$$

Remember that on the first iteration the error was 0.01801223929724783 (see equation 1-7). Now, on the second iteration, the error has been reduced to 0.014367116942993556.

We continue these iterations until the network calculates the error that is smaller than the error limit that has been set. Let's look at the formulas for calculating the partial derivative of the error function E with respect to W^2_{11} and W^2_{12} for the node H_1.

$$\frac{\partial E}{\partial W^2_{11}} = \frac{\partial E}{\partial O_1} * \frac{\partial O_1}{\partial Z^2_1} * \frac{\partial Z^2_1}{\partial W^2_{11}} \tag{3-87}$$

$$\frac{\partial E}{\partial W^2_{12}} = \frac{\partial E}{\partial O_1} * \frac{\partial O_1}{\partial Z^2_1} * \frac{\partial Z^2_1}{\partial W^2_{12}} \tag{3-88}$$

$$\frac{\partial E}{\partial W^2_{13}} = \frac{\partial E}{\partial O_1} * \frac{\partial O_1}{\partial Z^2_1} * \frac{\partial Z^2_1}{\partial W^2_{13}} \tag{3-89}$$

You can see that all three formulas have a common part $\frac{\partial E}{\partial O_1} * \frac{\partial O_1}{\partial Z^2_1}$. This part is called *node delta* δ. Using δ we can rewrite the formulas in equation 3-87, equation 3-88, and equation 3-89.

$$\frac{\partial E}{\partial W^2_{11}} = \delta^2_1 * \frac{\partial Z^2_1}{\partial W^2_{11}} \tag{3-90}$$

$$\frac{\partial E}{\partial W^2_{12}} = \delta^2_1 * \frac{\partial Z^2_1}{\partial W^2_{12}} \tag{3-91}$$

$$\frac{\partial E}{\partial W^2_{13}} = \delta^2_1 * \frac{\partial Z^2_1}{\partial W^2_{13}} \tag{3-92}$$

Correspondingly, we can rewrite formulas for the hidden layer.

$$\frac{\partial E}{\partial W^1_{11}} = \delta^1_1 * \frac{\partial Z^1_1}{\partial W^1_{11}} \tag{3-93}$$

$$\frac{\partial E}{\partial W^1_{12}} = \delta^1_1 * \frac{\partial Z^1_1}{\partial W^1_{12}} \tag{3-94}$$

$$\frac{\partial E}{\partial W^1_{21}} = \delta^1_2 * \frac{\partial Z^1_2}{\partial W^1_{21}} \tag{3-95}$$

$$\frac{\partial E}{\partial W^1_{22}} = \delta^1_2 * \frac{\partial Z^1_2}{\partial W^1_{22}} \tag{3-96}$$

$$\frac{\partial E}{\partial W^1_{31}} = \delta^1_3 * \frac{\partial Z^1_3}{\partial W^1_{31}} \tag{3-97}$$

$$\frac{\partial E}{\partial W^1_{32}} = \delta^1_3 * \frac{\partial Z^1_3}{\partial W^1_{32}} \tag{3-98}$$

In general, calculating the partial derivative of error function E with respect to its weights can be done by multiplying the node's delta by the partial derivative of the error function with respect to the corresponding weight. That saves us from calculating some redundant data. That means that we can calculate δ values for each network node and then use the formulas in equation 3-93 and equation 3-98.

Matrix Form of Network Calculation

For the same network, we can express all the calculations using matrices. For example, by introducing the Z vector, W matrix, and B vector, we can get the same calculation results as we get when using scalars. See Figure 3-5.

$$\begin{vmatrix} Z^1_1 \\ Z^1_2 \\ Z^1_3 \end{vmatrix} = \begin{Vmatrix} W^1_{11} & W^1_{12} \\ W^1_{21} & W^1_{22} \\ W^1_{21} & W^1_{22} \end{Vmatrix} \begin{vmatrix} I_1 \\ \\ I_2 \end{vmatrix} + \begin{vmatrix} B1 \\ B1 \\ B1 \end{vmatrix} = \begin{Vmatrix} W^1 11^* I_1 + W_1 12^* I_2 + B_1 \\ W^1 11^* I_1 + W_1 12^* I_2 + B_1 \\ W^1 11^* I_1 + W_1 12^* I_2 + B_1 \end{Vmatrix}$$

Figure 3-5. *Matrix form of network calculation*

Using matrix or scalar calculations is a matter of preference. Using a good matrix library provides fast calculation, but the disadvantage is a high memory demand, since matrixes should be kept in memory.

Digging Deeper

When processing a neural network, we set the error limit (specifically indicating how close the trained network results should match the target data). The training process works iteratively by gradually moving in the direction toward the error function minimum, therefore reducing the error. The iterative process stops when the difference between the calculated network results and the target results becomes less than the preset error limit.

Could the network fail to reach the error limit being set? Unfortunately, yes. Let's discuss it in more detail. Of course, the approximation error depends on the network architecture being selected (the number of hidden layers and the number of neuron within each hidden layer). However, let's presume that the network architecture is being set correctly.

The approximation error also depends on the function topology. Again, let's presume that the function is monotone and continuous. Still, the network can fail to reach the network limit. Why? We already mentioned that back-propagation is an iterative process that looks for the minimum of error function. An error function is typically a function of many variables, but for simplicity we will show it as the 2D space chart. (See Figure 3-6.)

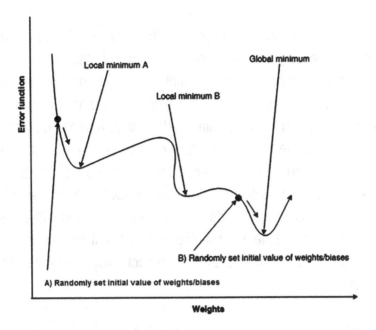

Figure 3-6. *Error function local and global minimums*

The goal of the training process is finding the minimum of the error function. The error function depends on the weight/bias parameters being calibrated during the iterative training process. The initial values of the weights/biases are typically set randomly, and the training process calculates the network error for this initial setting (point). Starting from this point the training process moves down to the function minimum.

As shown in Figure 3-6, the error function typically has several minimums. The lowest out of them is called the *global minimum,* while the rest of them are called the *local minimums.* Depending on the starting point of the training process, it can find some of the local minimums that are close to the starting point. Each local minimum works as a trap for the training process, because once the training process reaches a local minimum, any further move would not show changes in the gradient value; and the iterative process stops being stacked at the local minimum.

Consider starting points A and B in Figure 3-6. In the case of starting point A, the training process will find the local minimum A, which produces a much larger error than in case B. That's why running the same training process multiple times always produces different error results for each run (because for each run the training process starts at a random initial point).

Tip   How do we achieve the best approximation results? When programming neural network processing, always arrange the logic of starting the training process in a loop. After each call of the training method, the logic inside the training method should check whether the error is less than the error limit, and if it is not, it should exit from the training method with a nonzero error code. The control will be returned to the code that calls the training method in a loop. The code calls the training method again if the return code is not zero. The logic continues the loop until the calculated error becomes less than the error limit. Exit at this point with the zero return code, so the training method will no longer be called again. If this is not done, the training logic will just loop over the epochs, not being able to clear the error limit. Examples of such programming code are shown in later chapters.

Why is it hard to train the network sometimes? The network is considered to be a universal function approximation tool. However, there is an exception to this statement. The network can approximate only continuous functions well. If a function is noncontinuous (making sudden sharp up and down jumps), then the approximation results for such functions show low-quality results. The errors are so large that such approximation is practically useless.

The calculation shown here is done for a single function point. When we need to approximate a function of two or more variables at many points, the volume of calculations increases exponentially. Such a resource-intensive process puts high demand on computer resources (memory and CPU). That's why, as mentioned in the introduction to the book, earlier attempts to use artificial intelligence were unable to process serious tasks. Only later, due to dramatically increased computation power, did artificial intelligence achieve a huge success.

Mini-Batches and Stochastic Gradient

When the input dataset is very large (such as including millions of records), the volume of calculations becomes extremely high. Processing such networks takes a long time, and the network learning becomes very slow, because the gradient should be calculated for each input record.

To speed up this process, we can break a very large input dataset into a number of chunks called *mini-batches* and process each mini-batch independently. Processing all records in a single mini-batch file constitutes an epoch, the point where weight/bias adjustments are made.

Because of a much smaller size of the mini-batch file, processing all mini-batches will be faster than processing the entire dataset as a single file. Finally, instead of calculating the gradient for each record of the entire dataset, we calculate here the stochastic gradient, which is the average of gradients calculated for each mini-batch.

If the weight adjustment processed for the neurons in a mini-batch file m is W^m_n, then the weight adjustment for such a neuron for the whole dataset is approximately equal to the average of adjustments calculated independently for all mini-batches.

$$adjusted W^k_s \approx W^k_s - \frac{\eta}{m} \sum_{j}^{m} \frac{\partial E}{\partial W^j_s}.$$ where m is the number of mini-batches.

Neural network processing for large-input datasets is mostly done using mini-batches.

Summary

This chapter showed the internal neural network calculations. It explained why (even for a single point) the volume of calculations is quite high. The chapter introduced the δ variable that can reduce the calculation volume. The "Digging Deeper" section explained how to call the training method to achieve one of the best approximation results. The mini-batch approach was also explained here. The next chapter shows how to configure the Windows environment for using Java and the Java network processing framework.

PART II

Neural Network Java Development Environment

CHAPTER 4

Configuring Your Development Environment

This book is about neural network processing using Java. Before we can start developing any neural network program, we need to learn several Java tools. If you are a Java developer and are familiar with the tools discussed here, you can skip this chapter. Just make sure that all the necessary tools are installed on your Windows machine.

Installing the Java Environment and NetBeans on Your Windows Machine

As developers, we need both the Java JDK and NetBeans as development tools. Oracle provides the download that installs both environments during one execution.

Go to the following website:

```
https://www.oracle.com/technetwork/java/javase/downloads/jdk-netbeans-jsp-
3413139-esa.html
```

The screen shown in Figure 4-1 will be displayed.

© Igor Livshin 2022
I. Livshin, *Artificial Neural Networks with Java*, https://doi.org/10.1007/978-1-4842-7368-5_4

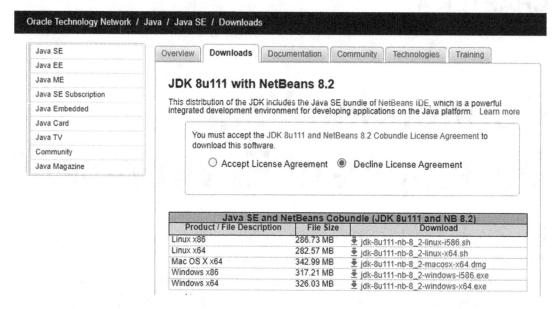

Figure 4-1. *Java downloads*

First accept the license agreement and then click to download the following file for Windows x64:

```
jdk-8u111-nb-8-windows-x64.exe
```

Right-click this executable and select Run. Follow the installation instructions. This will install the Java SE Development Kit for Windows (`jdk1.8.0_111`) and the NetBeans 8-2 development tool, both in the `C:\Program Files` directory. They will be in the following subdirectories:

```
C:\Program Files\Java\jdk1.8.0_111
C:\Program Files\NetBeans 8.2
```

Next, we need to set several environment variables that inform Windows 10 where the Java environment is installed. Enter **envir** into the Windows 10 search field and select "Edit the system environment variables."

The dialog shown in Figure 4-2 will appear.

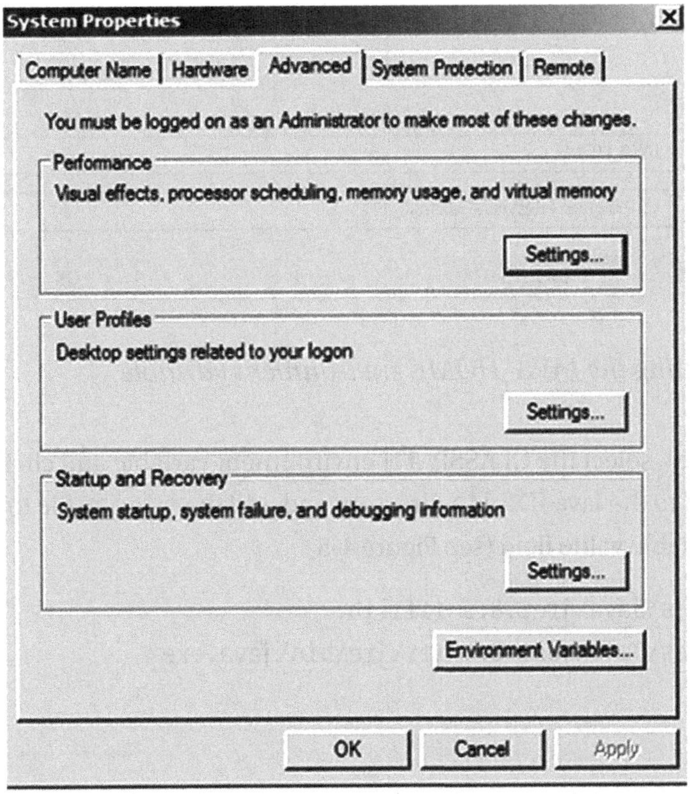

Figure 4-2. *System Properties dialog*

Click the Environment Variables button on the Advanced tab. Then, click New to open the dialog that allows you to enter a new environment variable (Figure 4-3).

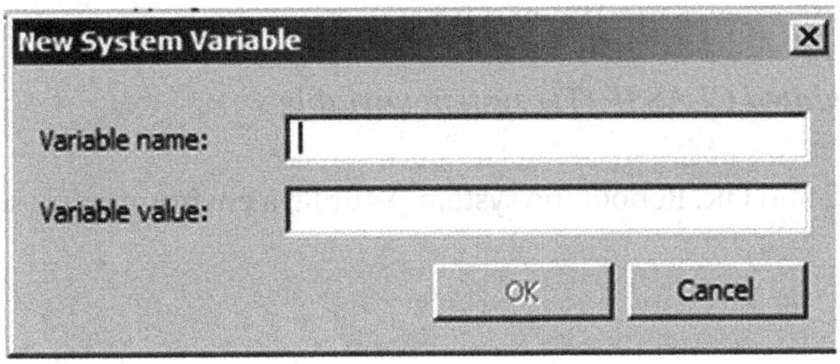

Figure 4-3. *New System Variable dialog*

Enter **JAVA_HOME** in the "Variable name" field. Enter the path to the installed Java environment in the "Variable value" field (Figure 4-4).

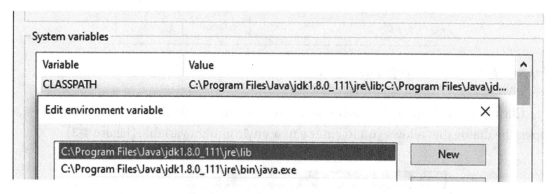

Figure 4-4. *Setting the JAVA_HOME environment variable*

Click OK. Next, select the CLASSPATH environment variable and click Update.

Add the path to the Java JDK lib directory and add the Java jar file to the CLASSPATH Variable value field (see Figure 4-5).

```
C:\Program Files\Java\jre1.8.0_111\lib;
C:\Program Files\Java\jdk1.8.0_111\jre\bin\java.exe
```

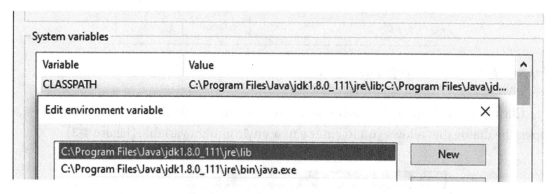

Figure 4-5. *Updated CLASSPATH system variable*

Click OK, OK, and OK. Reboot the system. Your Java environment is set.

Installing the Encog Java Framework

As you have seen from some of the previous examples of manually processing a neural network (Chapter 3), even a simple approximation of the function at a single point involves a large volume of calculations. For any serious work, you need to use one of the available frameworks.

At the time of writing this book, several frameworks are available. Here is a list of the most commonly used frameworks and the language they were written for:

- TensorFlow (Python, C++, and R)

- Caffe (C, C++, Python, and MATLAB)

- Torch (C++, Python)

- Keras (Python)

- Deeplearning4j (Java)

- Encog (Java)

- Neurop (Java)

Note   Frameworks implemented in Java are more efficient compared to those implemented in Python.

We are interested in a Java framework (for the obvious reason of developing an application on one machine and being able to run it anywhere). We are also interested in a fast Java framework and one that is convenient to use. After examining several Java frameworks, we selected Encog as the best framework for neural network processing. That is the framework we use in this book. The Encog framework was developed by Heaton Research, and it is free to use. All the Encog documentation can be found on its website.

To install Encog, go to `https://www.heatonresearch.com/encog`. Scroll down to the section called Encog Java Links and click the Encog Java Download/Release link. On the next screen, select these two files for Encog release 4.3:

```
encog-core-3.4.jar
encog-java-examples.zip
```

Unzip the second file. Keep these files in a directory you remember, and also add the following file to the CLASSPATH environment variable (also refer to the Java installation):

```
C:\encog-core-3.4\lib\encog-core-3.4.jar
```

Installing the XChart Package

During the data preparation and neural network development/testing, it is useful to be able to chart many results. We will be using the XChart Java charting library in this book. To download XChart, go to the following website:

```
https://knowm.org/open-source/xchart/
```

The screen in Figure 4-6 will appear. Click the Download 3.8.0 button.

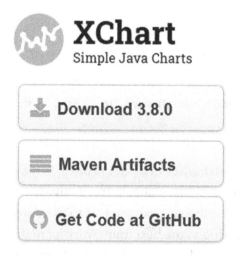

Figure 4-6. XChart home page

Unzip the downloaded zip file and double-click the executable installation file. Follow the installation instruction, and the XChart package will be installed on your machine. Add the following two files:

```
xchart-3.8.0.jar
xchart-demo-3.8.0.jar
```

to the CLASSPASS environment variable (see the way it was done for Java 8 earlier), as shown in Figure 4-7.

```
C:\Download\XChart\xchart-3.8.0\xcart-3.8.0.jar
C:\Download\XChart\xchart-3.8.0\xchart-demo-3.8.0.jar
```

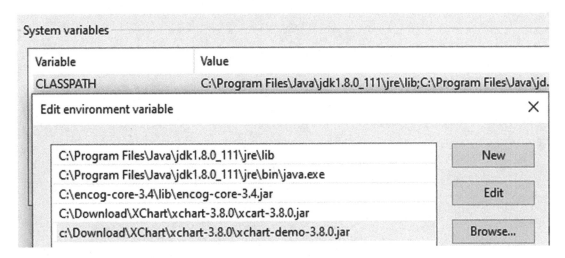

Figure 4-7. *CLASSPATH environment variable*

Update the PATH environment variable by adding the JDK binary directory to it.

```
C:\Program Files\Java\jdk1.8.0_111\bin
```

Finally, reboot the system. We are ready for neural network development.

Summary

We introduced you to the Java environment and explained how to download and install the set of tools necessary for building, debugging, testing, and executing neural network applications using Java. All the development examples in the rest of this book are done using this environment. The next chapter shows you the actual development of the neural network program using the Java Encog framework.

CHAPTER 5

Neural Networks Development Using the Java Encog Framework

To learn how to do network program development using Java, we will develop our first simple program using the function initially shown in the "Example: Manual Approximation of a Function at a Single Point" section of Chapter 3.

Example: Function Approximation Using Java Environment

Figure 5-1 shows the function, which is given to us with its values at nine points.

© Igor Livshin 2022
I. Livshin, *Artificial Neural Networks with Java*, https://doi.org/10.1007/978-1-4842-7368-5_5

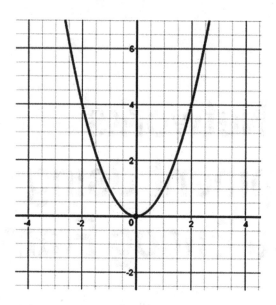

Figure 5-1. *Function to be approximated*

As previously mentioned, we will use the Encog software for neural network processing. Encog expects all the files it processes to be in the CSV format. This is actually a simplified Excel file format that includes comma-separated values in each record. CSV files have the extension `.csv`. Also, remember that Encog expects the first record in the processed files to be a label record. Accordingly, Table 5-1 shows the input (training) dataset with the given function values for this example.

Table 5-1. *Training Dataset*

xPoint	Function Value
0.15	0.0225
0.25	0.0625
0.5	0.25
0.75	0.5625
1	1
1.25	1.5625
1.5	2.25
1.75	3.0625
2	4

Next, Table 5-2 shows the dataset that we will use for testing the trained network. The xPoints in this dataset are different than the xPoints in the training dataset because (as you already know) the file used for testing should have different input data (not used in the training file).

Table 5-2. *Testing Dataset*

xPoint	Function Value
0.2	0.04
0.3	0.09
0.4	0.16
0.7	0.49
0.95	0.9025
1.3	1.69
1.6	2.56
1.8	3.24
1.95	3.8025

Network Architecture

Figure 5-2 shows the network architecture for the example. The network is set to have the input layer with a single neuron, seven hidden layers (each having five neurons), and the output layer with a single neuron.

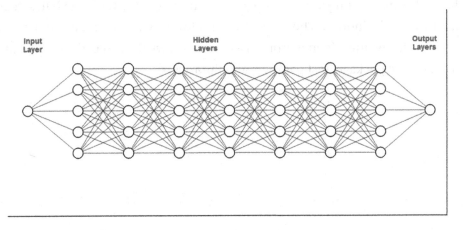

Figure 5-2. *Network architecture*

Normalizing the Input Datasets

Both training and testing datasets need to be normalized on the interval [-1, 1]. Let's build the Java program that normalizes those datasets. To normalize a file, it is necessary to know the max and min values for the fields being normalized. The first column of the training dataset has the min value 0.15 and the max value 2.00. The second column of the training dataset has the min value 0.0225 and the max value 4.00.

The first column of the testing dataset has the min value 0.20 and the max value 1.95. The second column of the testing dataset has the min value 0.04 and the max value 3.8025. Therefore, for simplicity, we select the min and max values for both training and testing datasets as min = 0.00 and max = 5.00.

The formula used to normalize the values the interval [-1, 1] is as follows:

$$f(x) = ((x - D_L)*(N_H - N_L))/(D_H - D_L) + N_L$$

Here,

x = the input data point.

D_L = the min (lowest) value of x in the input dataset.

D_H = the max (highest) value of x in the input dataset.

N_L = the left part of the normalized interval [-1, 1] = -1.

N_H = the right part of the normalized interval [-1, 1] = 1.

Building the Java Program That Normalizes Both Datasets

Click the NetBeans icon on your desktop to open the NetBeans IDE. The IDE screen is divided into several windows. The Navigation window is where you see your projects (Figure 5-3). Clicking the + icon in front of a project shows the project's components such as the source package, test package, and libraries.

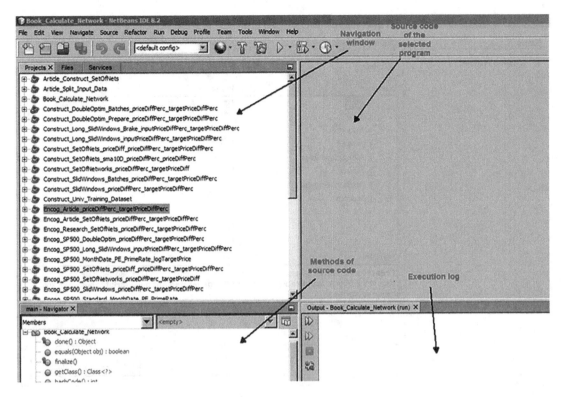

Figure 5-3. *The NetBeans IDE*

To create a new project, select File ➤ New Project. The window shown in Figure 5-4 appears.

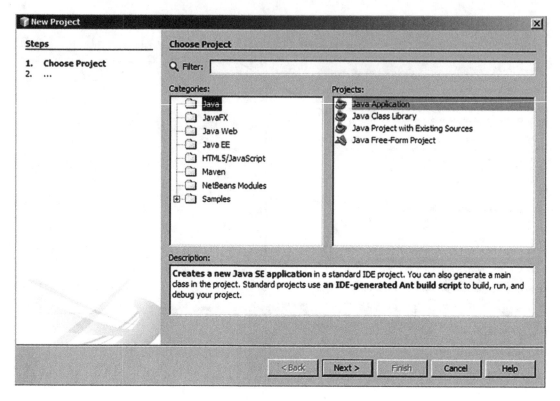

Figure 5-4. *Creating a new project dialog*

Click Next. The dialog shown in Figure 5-5 will appear.

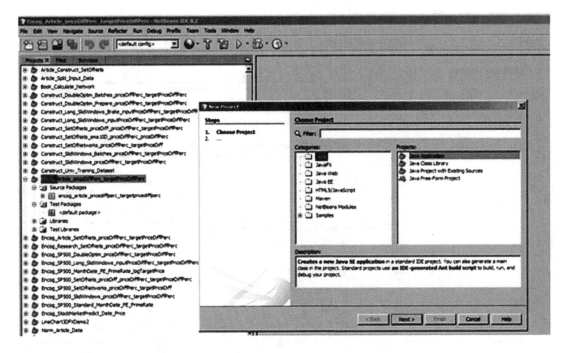

Figure 5-5. *Naming the new project*

Enter the project name **Sample1_Norm** and click the Finish button. Figure 5-6 shows the next dialog that appears.

Figure 5-6. *Sample1_Norm project*

The created project is shown in the Navigation window (Figure 5-7).

Figure 5-7. *Created project*

The source code is now visible in the source code window, as shown in Figure 5-8.

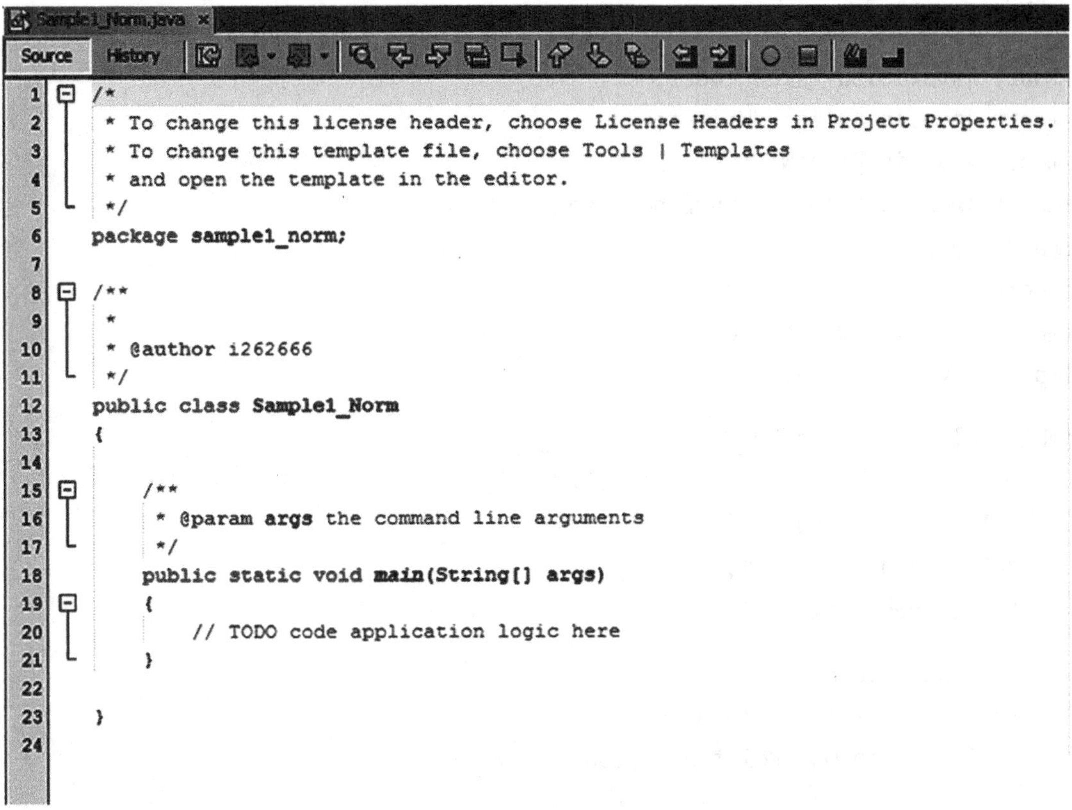

```
Sample1_Norm.java ×

Source   History   

1    /*
2     * To change this license header, choose License Headers in Project Properties.
3     * To change this template file, choose Tools | Templates
4     * and open the template in the editor.
5     */
6    package sample1_norm;
7
8    /**
9     *
10    * @author i262666
11    */
12   public class Sample1_Norm
13   {
14
15       /**
16        * @param args the command line arguments
17        */
18       public static void main(String[] args)
19       {
20           // TODO code application logic here
21       }
22
23   }
24
```

Figure 5-8. *The source code for the new project*

As you can see, NetBeans has generated a skeleton of the program. Next, add the normalization logic to the program. Listing 5-1 shows the source code for the normalization program.

Listing 5-1. Program Code That Normalizes Both Train and Test Datasets

```
// =========================================================================
// Normalize all columns of the input CSV dataset putting the result
// in the output CSV file.
// The first column of the input dataset includes the xPoint value and
// the second column includes the value of the function at the point X.
// =========================================================================
```

```java
package sample2_norm;

import java.io.BufferedReader;
import java.io.BufferedWriter;
import java.io.PrintWriter;
import java.io.FileNotFoundException;
import java.io.FileReader;
import java.io.FileWriter;
import java.io.IOException;
import java.nio.file.*;

public class Sample2_Norm
 {
   // Interval to normalize
   static double Nh =  1;
   static double Nl = -1;

   // First column
   static double minXPointDl = 0.00;
   static double maxXPointDh = 5.00;

   // Second column - target data
   static double minTargetValueDl = 0.00;
   static double maxTargetValueDh = 5.00;

   public static double normalize(double value, double Dh, double Dl)
    {
      double normalizedValue = (value - Dl)*(Nh - Nl)/(Dh - Dl) + Nl;

      return normalizedValue;
    }

   public static void main(String[] args)
    {
      // Configuration data (comment and uncomment the train or test
      configuration data)

      // Configuration for training
```

```
String inputFileName = "C:/My_Neural_Network_Book/Book_Examples/
Sample2_Train_Real.csv";
String outputNormFileName =
 "C:/My_Neural_Network_Book/Book_Examples/Sample2_Train_Norm.csv";

 //Configuration for testing
// String inputFileName = "C:/My_Neural_Network_Book/Book_Examples/
Sample2_Test_Real.csv";
// String outputNormFileName =
"C:/My_Neural_Network_Book/Book_Examples/Sample2_Test_Norm.csv";

  BufferedReader br = null;
  PrintWriter out = null;

  String line = "";
  String cvsSplitBy = ",";
  String strNormInputXPointValue;
  String strNormTargetXPointValue;
  String fullLine;
  double inputXPointValue;
  double targetXPointValue;
  double normInputXPointValue;
  double normTargetXPointValue;

  int i = -1;

  try
   {
    Files.deleteIfExists(Paths.get(outputNormFileName));

    br = new BufferedReader(new FileReader(inputFileName));
    out = new
     PrintWriter(new BufferedWriter(new FileWriter(outputNormFileName)));

    while ((line = br.readLine()) != null)
     {
        i++;
```

```java
      if(i == 0)
       {
         // Write the label line
         out.println(line);
       }
      else
      {
       // Brake the line using comma as separator
       String[] workFields = line.split(cvsSplitBy);

       inputXPointValue = Double.parseDouble(workFields[0]);
       targetXPointValue = Double.parseDouble( workFields[1]);

       // Normalize these fields
       normInputXPointValue =
          normalize(inputXPointValue, maxXPointDh, minXPointDl);
       normTargetXPointValue =
      normalize(targetXPointValue, maxTargetValueDh, minTargetValueDl);

       // Convert normalized fields to string, so they can be inserted
       //into the output CSV file
       strNormInputXPointValue = Double.toString(normInputXPointValue);
       strNormTargetXPointValue = Double.toString(normTargetXPointValue);

       // Concatenate these fields into a string line with
       //coma separator
       fullLine  =
          strNormInputXPointValue + "," + strNormTargetXPointValue;

       // Put fullLine into the output file
       out.println(fullLine);

      } // End of IF Else

    }    // End of WHILE

  } // End of TRY
```

```java
    catch (FileNotFoundException e)
     {
       e.printStackTrace();
       System.exit(1);
     }
    catch (IOException io)
     {
         io.printStackTrace();
         System.exit(2);
     }
    finally
     {
       if (br != null)
         {
             try
              {
                br.close();
                out.close();
              }
             catch (IOException e1)
              {
                  e1.printStackTrace();
                  System.exit(3);
              }
         }
     }

  }

} // End of the class
```

This is a simple program, and it does not need much explanation. We set the configuration to normalize either the training or the testing file by commenting and uncommenting the appropriate configuration sentences. We read the file lines in a loop. We break each line into two fields and normalize them. Next, we convert both fields back to strings, combine them into a line, and write the line into the output file.

Table 5-3 shows the normalized training dataset.

Table 5-3. *Normalized Training Dataset*

xPoint	Actual Value
-0.94	-0.991
-0.9	-0.975
-0.8	-0.9
-0.7	-0.775
-0.6	-0.6
-0.5	-0.375
-0.4	-0.1
-0.3	0.225
-0.2	0.6

Table 5-4 shows the normalized testing dataset.

Table 5-4. *Normalized Testing Dataset*

xPoint	Actual Value
-0.92	-0.984
-0.88	-0.964
-0.84	-0.936
-0.72	-0.804
-0.62	-0.639
-0.48	-0.324
-0.36	0.024
-0.28	0.296
-0.22	0.521

We will use these datasets as the input for the network training and testing.

Building the Neural Network Processing Program

To create a new project, select File ➤ New Project. The dialog shown in Figure 5-9 appears.

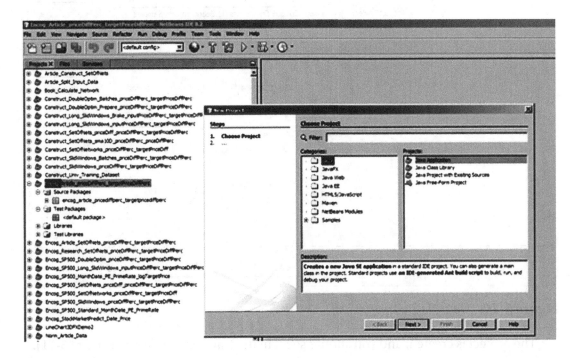

Figure 5-9. *NetBeans IDE*

Click Next. In the next dialog (shown in Figure 5-10), enter the project name and click the Finish button.

```
New Java Application                                                              ×

Steps                          Name and Location

1.  Choose Project             Project Name:      Sample1
2.  Name and Location
                               Project Location:  C:\Users\j262666\Documents\NetBeansProjects        Browse...

                               Project Folder:    C:\Users\j262666\Documents\NetBeansProjects\Sample1


                               ☐ Use Dedicated Folder for Storing Libraries

                                  Libraries Folder:                                                  Browse...

                                                   Different users and projects can share the same compilation
                                                   libraries (see Help for details).


                               ☑ Create Main Class  sample1.Sample1




                                            < Back     Next >      Finish     Cancel     Help
```

Figure 5-10. *New NetBeans project*

The project is created, and you should see it in the Navigation window (Figure 5-11).

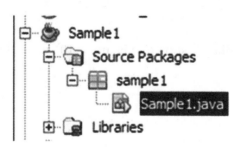

Figure 5-11. *Project Sample1*

The source code of the program appears in the source code window (Figure 5-12).

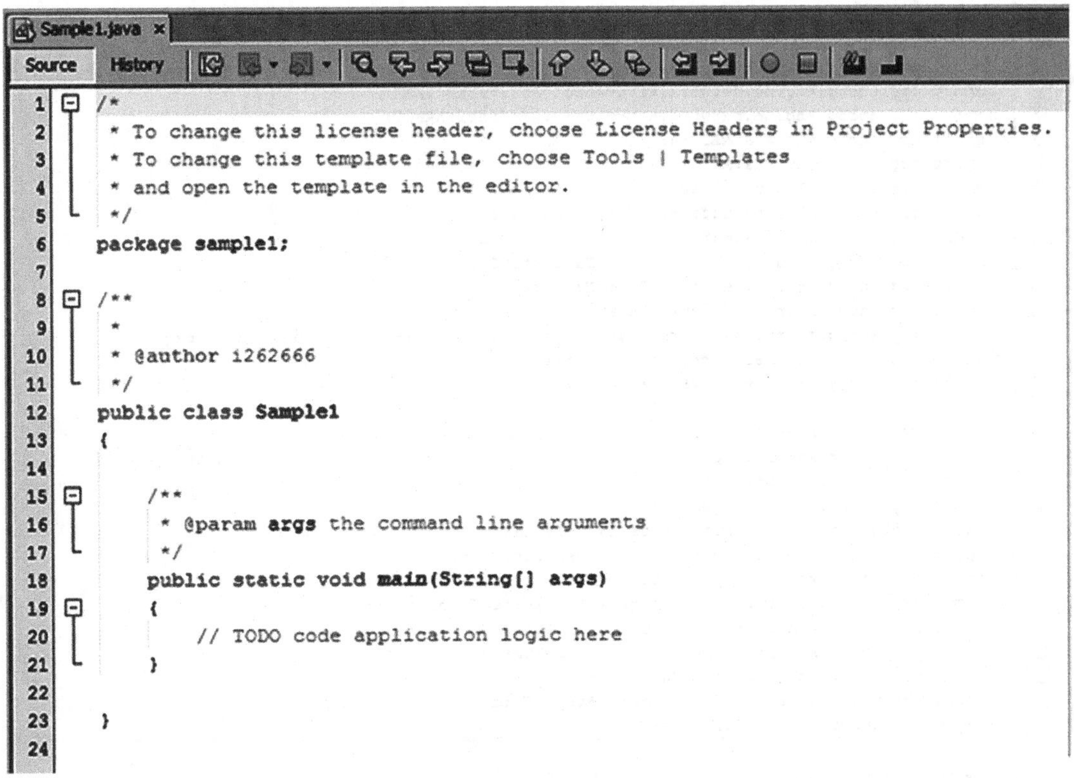

Figure 5-12. *Source code for program Sample1.java*

Again, this is just the automatically generated skeleton of the Java program. Let's add the necessary logic here. First, include all the necessary import files. There are three groups of import statements (Java imports, Encog imports, and XChart imports), and two of them (the one that belongs to Encog and the next that belongs to XChart) are marked as errors, because NetBeans is unable to find them (Figure 5-13).

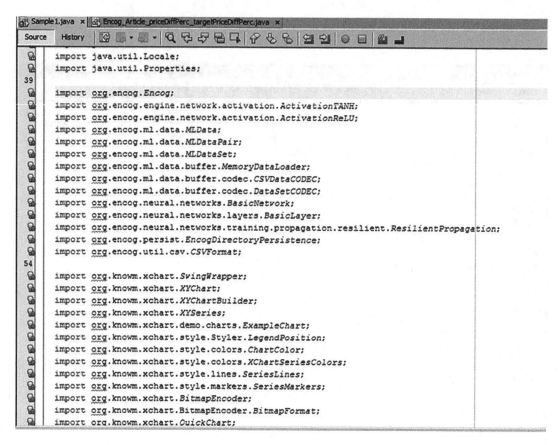

Figure 5-13. *Import statements marked as errors*

Here is how to fix this. Right-click the project and select Properties. The Project Properties dialog will appear (Figure 5-14).

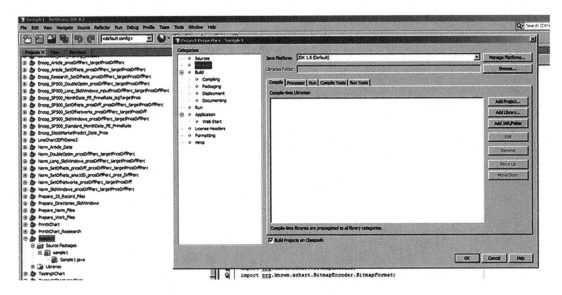

Figure 5-14. *Project Properties dialog*

On the left column of the Project Properties dialog, select Libraries. Click the Add Jar/Folders button located on the right of the Properties dialog. Click the down arrow of the Java Platform field (at the top of the screen) and go to the location where the Encog package is installed (Figure 5-15).

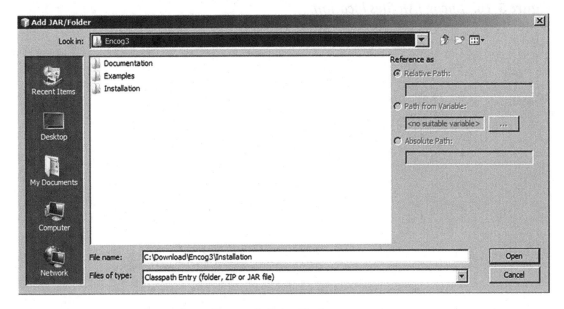

Figure 5-15. *Location where Encog is installed*

Double-click the Installation folder, and two JAR files will be displayed (Figure 5-16).

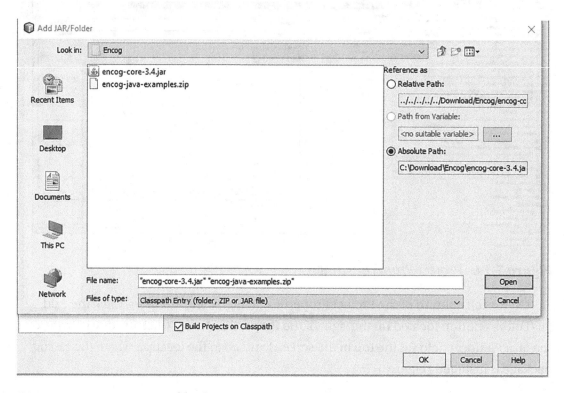

Figure 5-16. Encog JAR files location

Select both JAR files and click the Open button. They will be included in a list of JAR files to be added to NetBeans (Figure 5-17).

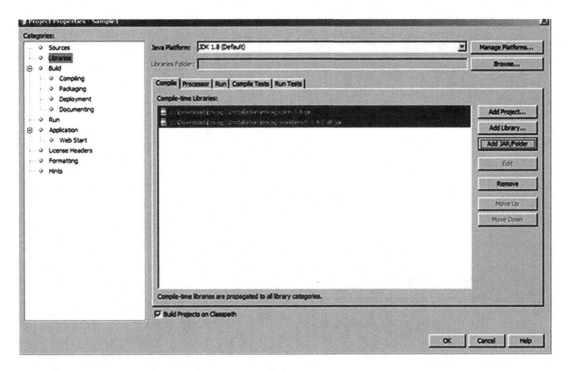

Figure 5-17. *List of Encog JAR files to be included in the NetBeans IDE*

Click the Add Jar/Folders button again. Click again the down arrow of the Java Properties field and go to the location where the XChart package is installed (Figure 5-18).

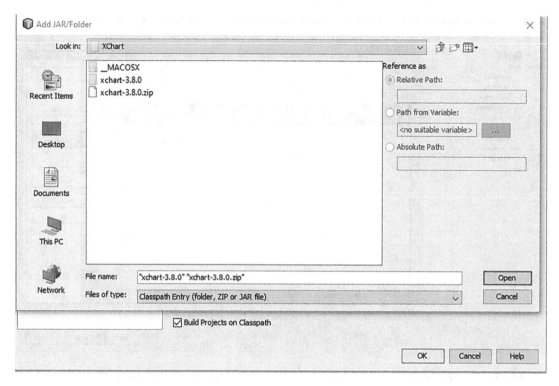

Figure 5-18. *XChart location*

Double-click the XChart-3.5.0 folder and select two XChart JAR files (Figure 5-19).

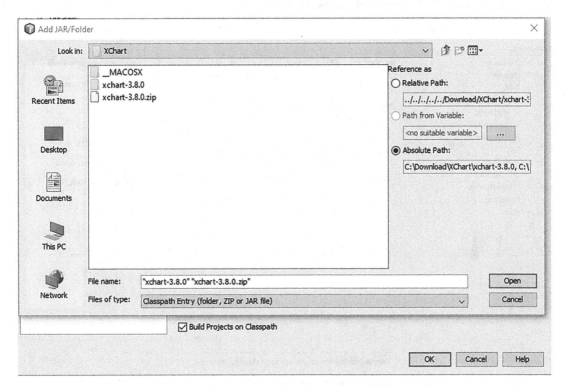

Figure 5-19. *XChart files*

Click the Open button. Now we have the list of four JAR files (from Encog and XChart) to be included in the NetBeans IDE (Figure 5-20).

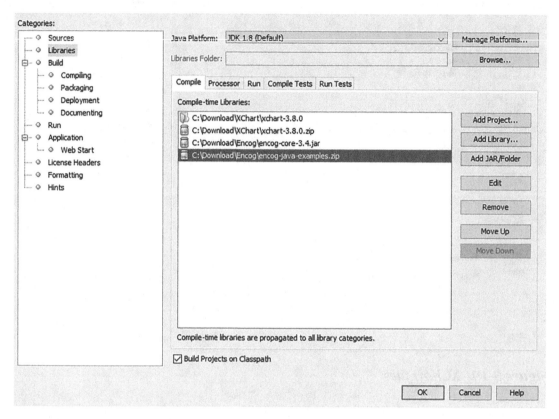

Figure 5-20. *List of JAR files to be included in the NetBeans IDE*

Finally, click OK, and all errors within the source file will disappear.

Instead of doing this for every new project, a better way is to set a new global library. From the main bar, select Tools ➤ Libraries. The screen shown in Figure 5-21 will appear.

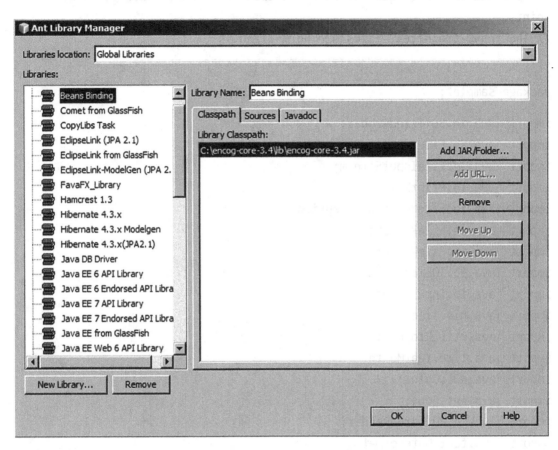

Figure 5-21. *Creating a global library*

Now, you repeat the same steps that were shown earlier on the project level. Do this by clicking the Add JAR/Folder button twice (for Encog and XChart) and add the appropriate JAR files for the Encog and XChart packages.

Program Code

Here, we will discuss all the important fragments of the program code using Encog. Just remember that you can find the documentation for all the Encog APIs and many examples of programming on the Encog website.

Listing 5-2. Network Processing Program Code

```java
// ================================================================
// Approximate the single-variable function which values are given at 9
points.
// The input train/test files are normalized.
// ================================================================

package sample2;

import java.io.BufferedReader;
import java.io.File;
import java.io.FileInputStream;
import java.io.PrintWriter;
import java.io.FileNotFoundException;
import java.io.FileReader;
import java.io.FileWriter;
import java.io.IOException;
import java.io.InputStream;
import java.nio.file.*;
import java.util.Properties;
import java.time.YearMonth;
import java.awt.Color;
import java.awt.Font;
import java.io.BufferedReader;
import java.text.DateFormat;
import java.text.ParseException;
import java.text.SimpleDateFormat;
import java.time.LocalDate;
import java.time.Month;
import java.time.ZoneId;
import java.util.ArrayList;
import java.util.Calendar;
import java.util.Date;
import java.util.List;
import java.util.Locale;
import java.util.Properties;
```

```java
import org.encog.Encog;
import org.encog.engine.network.activation.ActivationTANH;
import org.encog.engine.network.activation.ActivationReLU;
import org.encog.ml.data.MLData;
import org.encog.ml.data.MLDataPair;
import org.encog.ml.data.MLDataSet;
import org.encog.ml.data.buffer.MemoryDataLoader;
import org.encog.ml.data.buffer.codec.CSVDataCODEC;
import org.encog.ml.data.buffer.codec.DataSetCODEC;
import org.encog.neural.networks.BasicNetwork;
import org.encog.neural.networks.layers.BasicLayer;
import org.encog.neural.networks.training.propagation.resilient.
ResilientPropagation;
import org.encog.persist.EncogDirectoryPersistence;
import org.encog.util.csv.CSVFormat;

import org.knowm.xchart.SwingWrapper;
import org.knowm.xchart.XYChart;
import org.knowm.xchart.XYChartBuilder;
import org.knowm.xchart.XYSeries;
import org.knowm.xchart.demo.charts.ExampleChart;
import org.knowm.xchart.style.Styler.LegendPosition;
import org.knowm.xchart.style.colors.ChartColor;
import org.knowm.xchart.style.colors.XChartSeriesColors;
import org.knowm.xchart.style.lines.SeriesLines;
import org.knowm.xchart.style.markers.SeriesMarkers;
import org.knowm.xchart.BitmapEncoder;
import org.knowm.xchart.BitmapEncoder.BitmapFormat;
import org.knowm.xchart.QuickChart;
import org.knowm.xchart.SwingWrapper;

public class Sample2 implements ExampleChart<XYChart>
{
    // Interval to normalize
    static double Nh =  1;
    static double Nl = -1;
```

```java
// First column
static double minXPointDl = 0.00;
static double maxXPointDh = 5.00;

// Second column - target data
static double minTargetValueDl = 0.00;
static double maxTargetValueDh = 5.00;

static double doublePointNumber = 0.00;
static int intPointNumber = 0;
static InputStream input = null;
static int intNumberOfRecordsInTrainFile;
static double[] arrPrices = new double[2500];
static double normInputXPointValue = 0.00;
static double normPredictXPointValue = 0.00;
static double normTargetXPointValue = 0.00;
static double normDifferencePerc = 0.00;
static double denormInputXPointValue = 0.00;
static double denormPredictXPointValue = 0.00;
static double denormTargetXPointValue = 0.00;
static double valueDifference = 0.00;
static int returnCode  = 0;
static int numberOfInputNeurons;
static int numberOfOutputNeurons;
static int intNumberOfRecordsInTestFile;
static String trainFileName;
static String priceFileName;
static String testFileName;
static String chartTrainFileName;
static String chartTestFileName;
static String networkFileName;
static int workingMode;
static String cvsSplitBy = ",";
static List<Double> xData = new ArrayList<Double>();
static List<Double> yData1 = new ArrayList<Double>();
static List<Double> yData2 = new ArrayList<Double>();
```

```java
  static XYChart Chart;

@Override
public XYChart getChart()
 {

   // Create Chart
   Chart = new  XYChartBuilder().width(900).height(500).title(getClass().
          getSimpleName()).xAxisTitle("x").yAxisTitle("y= f(x)").build();

   // Customize Chart
   Chart.getStyler().setPlotBackgroundColor(ChartColor.
   getAWTColor(ChartColor.GREY));
   Chart.getStyler().setPlotGridLinesColor(new Color(255, 255, 255));
   Chart.getStyler().setChartBackgroundColor(Color.WHITE);
   Chart.getStyler().setLegendBackgroundColor(Color.PINK);
   Chart.getStyler().setChartFontColor(Color.MAGENTA);
   Chart.getStyler().setChartTitleBoxBackgroundColor(new Color(0, 222, 0));
   Chart.getStyler().setChartTitleBoxVisible(true);
   Chart.getStyler().setChartTitleBoxBorderColor(Color.BLACK);
   Chart.getStyler().setPlotGridLinesVisible(true);
   Chart.getStyler().setAxisTickPadding(20);
   Chart.getStyler().setAxisTickMarkLength(15);
   Chart.getStyler().setPlotMargin(20);
   Chart.getStyler().setChartTitleVisible(false);
   Chart.getStyler().setChartTitleFont(new Font(Font.MONOSPACED, Font.
   BOLD, 24));
   Chart.getStyler().setLegendFont(new Font(Font.SERIF, Font.PLAIN, 18));
   Chart.getStyler().setLegendPosition(LegendPosition.InsideSE);
   Chart.getStyler().setLegendSeriesLineLength(12);
   Chart.getStyler().setAxisTitleFont(new Font(Font.SANS_SERIF, Font.
   ITALIC, 18));
   Chart.getStyler().setAxisTickLabelsFont(new Font(Font.SERIF, Font.
   PLAIN, 11));
   Chart.getStyler().setDatePattern("yyyy-MM");
   Chart.getStyler().setDecimalPattern("#0.00");
```

```java
//Chart.getStyler().setLocale(Locale.GERMAN);

try
  {
    // Configuration (comment and uncomment the appropriate configuration)

     // Config for training the network
    workingMode = 1;
    intNumberOfRecordsInTrainFile = 10;
    trainFileName = "C:/My_Neural_Network_Book/Book_Examples/Sample2_
    Train_Norm.csv";
    chartTrainFileName = "Sample2_XYLine_Train_Results_Chart";

     // Config for testing the trained network
     // workingMode = 2;
     // intNumberOfRecordsInTestFile = 10;
     // testFileName = "C:/My_Neural_Network_Book/Book_Examples/
    Sample2_Test_Norm.csv";
     //   chartTestFileName = "XYLine_Test_Results_Chart";

     // Common configuration data
    networkFileName = "C:/Book_Examples/Sample2_Saved_Network_File.csv";
    numberOfInputNeurons = 1;
    numberOfOutputNeurons = 1;

     // Check the working mode to run

     // Training mode.
    if(workingMode == 1)
      {
         File file1 = new File(chartTrainFileName);
         File file2 = new File(networkFileName);

         if(file1.exists())
           file1.delete();

         if(file2.exists())
           file2.delete();

         returnCode = 0;     // Clear the return code variable
```

```
        do
         {
           returnCode = trainValidateSaveNetwork();

         } while (returnCode > 0);

       }

   // Test mode.
   if(workingMode == 2)
    {
      // Test using the test dataset as input
      loadAndTestNetwork();
    }

 }
catch (NumberFormatException e)
 {
     System.err.println("Problem parsing workingMode. workingMode = "
     + workingMode);
     System.exit(1);
 }
catch (Throwable t)
  {
      t.printStackTrace();
      System.exit(1);
  }
finally
  {
     Encog.getInstance().shutdown();
  }

   Encog.getInstance().shutdown();

    return Chart;

} // End of the method
```

```java
//-----------------------------------------------------------------
// Load CSV to memory.
// @return The loaded dataset.
// -----------------------------------------------------------------
public static MLDataSet loadCSV2Memory(String filename, int input, int
ideal, boolean headers,
  CSVFormat
      format, boolean significance)
  {
    DataSetCODEC codec = new CSVDataCODEC(new File(filename), format,
    headers, input, ideal,
      significance);
    MemoryDataLoader load = new MemoryDataLoader(codec);
    MLDataSet dataset = load.external2Memory();
    return dataset;
  }

// ==========================================================
//   The main method.
//   @param Command line arguments. No arguments are used.
// ==========================================================
public static void main(String[] args)
 {
   ExampleChart<XYChart> exampleChart = new Sample2();
   XYChart Chart = exampleChart.getChart();
   new SwingWrapper<XYChart>(Chart).displayChart();
 } // End of the main method

//==========================================================
// Training method. Train, validate, and save the trained network file
//==========================================================
static public int trainValidateSaveNetwork()
 {
   // Load the training CSV file in memory
   MLDataSet trainingSet =
```

```
  loadCSV2Memory(trainFileName,numberOfInputNeurons,
  numberOfOutputNeurons,
    true,CSVFormat.ENGLISH,false);

// create a neural network
BasicNetwork network = new BasicNetwork();

// Input layer
network.addLayer(new BasicLayer(null,true,1));

// Hidden layer
network.addLayer(new BasicLayer(new ActivationTANH(),true,5));
network.addLayer(new BasicLayer(new ActivationTANH(),true,5));
network.addLayer(new BasicLayer(new ActivationTANH(),true,5));
network.addLayer(new BasicLayer(new ActivationTANH(),true,5));
network.addLayer(new BasicLayer(new ActivationTANH(),true,5));
network.addLayer(new BasicLayer(new ActivationTANH(),true,5));
network.addLayer(new BasicLayer(new ActivationTANH(),true,5));

// Output layer
//network.addLayer(new BasicLayer(new ActivationLOG(),false,1));
network.addLayer(new BasicLayer(new ActivationTANH(),false,1));
//network.addLayer(new BasicLayer(new ActivationReLU(),false,1));
//network.addLayer(new BasicLayer(new ActivationSigmoid(),false,1));

network.getStructure().finalizeStructure();
network.reset();

// Train the neural network
final ResilientPropagation train = new ResilientPropagation(network,
trainingSet);

int epoch = 1;
returnCode = 0;

do
 {
    train.iteration();
    System.out.println("Epoch #" + epoch + " Error:" + train.getError());
```

```
    epoch++;

    if (epoch >= 500 && network.calculateError(trainingSet) >
    0.000000031)     // 0.000000091
      {
         returnCode = 1;

         System.out.println("Try again");
          return returnCode;
      }
  } while (network.calculateError(trainingSet) > 0.00000003);
  // 0.00000009

// Save the network file
EncogDirectoryPersistence.saveObject(new File(networkFileName),network);

System.out.println("Neural Network Results:");

double sumNormDifferencePerc = 0.00;
double averNormDifferencePerç = 0.00;
double maxNormDifferencePerc = 0.00;

int m = -1;
double xPointer = -1.00;

for(MLDataPair pair: trainingSet)
  {
      m++;
      xPointer = xPointer + 2.00;

      //if(m == 0)
      // continue;

       final MLData output = network.compute(pair.getInput());

      MLData inputData = pair.getInput();
      MLData actualData = pair.getIdeal();
      MLData predictData = network.compute(inputData);

      // Calculate and print the results
      normInputXPointValue = inputData.getData(0);
```

```
    normTargetXPointValue = actualData.getData(0);
    normPredictXPointValue = predictData.getData(0);

    denormInputXPointValue = ((minXPointDl -
      maxXPointDh)*normInputXPointValue - Nh*minXPointDl +
        maxXPointDh *Nl)/(Nl - Nh);

    denormTargetXPointValue = ((minTargetValueDl - maxTargetValueDh)*
      normTargetXPointValue - Nh*minTargetValueDl +
        maxTargetValueDh*Nl)/(Nl - Nh);

    denormPredictXPointValue =((minTargetValueDl - maxTargetValueDh)*
      normPredictXPointValue - Nh*minTargetValueDl +
        maxTargetValueDh*Nl)/(Nl - Nh);

    valueDifference = Math.abs(((denormTargetXPointValue -
      denormPredictXPointValue)/denormTargetXPointValue)*100.00);

    System.out.println ("xPoint = " + denormTargetXPointValue +
        "  denormPredictXPointValue = " + denormPredictXPointValue +
          "  valueDifference = " + valueDifference);

    sumNormDifferencePerc = sumNormDifferencePerc + valueDifference;

    if (valueDifference > maxNormDifferencePerc)
      maxNormDifferencePerc = valueDifference;

    xData.add(denormInputXPointValue);
    yData1.add(denormTargetXPointValue);
    yData2.add(denormPredictXPointValue);

}    // End for pair loop

XYSeries series1 = Chart.addSeries("Actual data", xData, yData1);
XYSeries series2 = Chart.addSeries("Predict data", xData, yData2);

series1.setLineColor(XChartSeriesColors.BLUE);
series2.setMarkerColor(Color.ORANGE);
series1.setLineStyle(SeriesLines.SOLID);
series2.setLineStyle(SeriesLines.SOLID);
```

```
     try
      {
        //Save the chart image
        BitmapEncoder.saveBitmapWithDPI(Chart, chartTrainFileName,
        BitmapFormat.JPG, 100);
        System.out.println ("Train Chart file has been saved") ;
      }
    catch (IOException ex)
      {
       ex.printStackTrace();
       System.exit(3);
      }

      // Finally, save this trained network
      EncogDirectoryPersistence.saveObject(new File(networkFileName),
      network);
      System.out.println ("Train Network has been saved") ;

      averNormDifferencePerc  = sumNormDifferencePerc/
      intNumberOfRecordsInTrainFile;

      System.out.println(" ");
      System.out.println("maxErrorDifferencePerc = " +
      maxNormDifferencePerc + "
          averErrorDifferencePerc = " + averNormDifferencePerc);

      returnCode = 0;
      return returnCode;

   }   // End of the method


//=======================================================
// Load and test the trained network at the points not used in training.
//=======================================================
static public void loadAndTestNetwork()
 {
   System.out.println("Testing the networks results");
```

```
List<Double> xData = new ArrayList<Double>();
List<Double> yData1 = new ArrayList<Double>();
List<Double> yData2 = new ArrayList<Double>();

double targetToPredictPercent = 0;
double maxGlobalResultDiff = 0.00;
double averGlobalResultDiff = 0.00;
double sumGlobalResultDiff = 0.00;
double maxGlobalIndex = 0;
double normInputXPointValueFromRecord = 0.00;
double normTargetXPointValueFromRecord = 0.00;
double normPredictXPointValueFromRecord = 0.00;

BufferedReader br4;
BasicNetwork network;

int k1 = 0;
int k3 = 0;

maxGlobalResultDiff = 0.00;
averGlobalResultDiff = 0.00;
sumGlobalResultDiff = 0.00;

// Load the test dataset into memory
MLDataSet testingSet =
loadCSV2Memory(testFileName,numberOfInputNeurons,numberOfOutputNeurons,
  true,CSVFormat.ENGLISH,false);

// Load the saved trained network
network =
 (BasicNetwork)EncogDirectoryPersistence.loadObject(new
 File(networkFileName));

int i = - 1;
double xPoint = -0.00;

for (MLDataPair pair:  testingSet)
 {
     i++;
     xPoint = xPoint + 2.00;
```

```java
        MLData inputData = pair.getInput();
        MLData actualData = pair.getIdeal();
        MLData predictData = network.compute(inputData);

        // These values are Normalized as the whole input is
        normInputXPointValueFromRecord = inputData.getData(0);
        normTargetXPointValueFromRecord = actualData.getData(0);
        normPredictXPointValueFromRecord = predictData.getData(0);

        //  De-normalize the obtained values
        denormInputXPointValue = ((minXPointDl - maxXPointDh)*
          normInputXPointValueFromRecord - Nh*minXPointDl +
            maxXPointDh*Nl)/(Nl - Nh);

        denormTargetXPointValue = ((minTargetValueDl - maxTargetValueDh)*
          normTargetXPointValueFromRecord - Nh*minTargetValueDl +
            maxTargetValueDh*Nl)/(Nl - Nh);

        denormPredictXPointValue =((minTargetValueDl - maxTargetValueDh)*
          normPredictXPointValueFromRecord - Nh*minTargetValueDl +
            maxTargetValueDh*Nl)/(Nl - Nh);

        targetToPredictPercent = Math.abs((denormTargetXPointValue -
          denormPredictXPointValue)/denormTargetXPointValue*100);

        System.out.println("xPoint = " + denormInputXPointValue +
          " denormTargetXPointValue = " + denormTargetXPointValue +
            " denormPredictXPointValue = " + denormPredictXPointValue +
              " targetToPredictPercent = " + targetToPredictPercent);

      if (targetToPredictPercent > maxGlobalResultDiff)
        maxGlobalResultDiff = targetToPredictPercent;

     sumGlobalResultDiff = sumGlobalResultDiff + targetToPredictPercent;

        // Populate chart elements
        xData.add(denormInputXPointValue);
        yData1.add(denormTargetXPointValue);
        yData2.add(denormPredictXPointValue);

  }  // End for pair loop
```

```
// Print the max and average results

System.out.println(" ");
averGlobalResultDiff = sumGlobalResultDiff/intNumberOfRecordsInTestFile;

System.out.println("maxErrorDifferencePercent = " + maxGlobalResultDiff);
System.out.println("averErrorDifferencePercent = " + averGlobalResultDiff);

// All testing batch files have been processed
XYSeries series1 = Chart.addSeries("Actual", xData, yData1);
XYSeries series2 = Chart.addSeries("Predicted", xData, yData2);

series1.setLineColor(XChartSeriesColors.BLUE);
series2.setMarkerColor(Color.ORANGE);
series1.setLineStyle(SeriesLines.SOLID);
series2.setLineStyle(SeriesLines.SOLID);

// Save the chart image
try
 {
   BitmapEncoder.saveBitmapWithDPI(Chart, chartTestFileName ,
   BitmapFormat.JPG, 100);
 }
catch (Exception bt)
 {
   bt.printStackTrace();
 }

System.out.println ("The Chart has been saved");

System.out.println("End of testing for test records");

  } // End of the method

} // End of the class
```

At the top, there is a set of instructions required by the XChart package, and the instructions allow us to configure how the chart should look (Listing 5-3).

Listing 5-3. Set of Instructions That Is Required by the XChart Package

```java
static XYChart Chart;

  @Override
  public XYChart getChart()
   {

    // Create Chart
    Chart = new  XYChartBuilder().width(900).height(500).title(getClass().
            getSimpleName()).xAxisTitle("x").yAxisTitle("y= f(x)").build();

    // Customize Chart
    Chart.getStyler().setPlotBackgroundColor(ChartColor.
    getAWTColor(ChartColor.GREY));
    Chart.getStyler().setPlotGridLinesColor(new Color(255, 255, 255));
    Chart.getStyler().setChartBackgroundColor(Color.WHITE);
    Chart.getStyler().setLegendBackgroundColor(Color.PINK);
    Chart.getStyler().setChartFontColor(Color.MAGENTA);
    Chart.getStyler().setChartTitleBoxBackgroundColor(new Color(0, 222, 0));
    Chart.getStyler().setChartTitleBoxVisible(true);
    Chart.getStyler().setChartTitleBoxBorderColor(Color.BLACK);
    Chart.getStyler().setPlotGridLinesVisible(true);
    Chart.getStyler().setAxisTickPadding(20);
    Chart.getStyler().setAxisTickMarkLength(15);
    Chart.getStyler().setPlotMargin(20);
    Chart.getStyler().setChartTitleVisible(false);
    Chart.getStyler().setChartTitleFont(new Font(Font.MONOSPACED, Font.
    BOLD, 24));
    Chart.getStyler().setLegendFont(new Font(Font.SERIF, Font.PLAIN, 18));
    Chart.getStyler().setLegendPosition(LegendPosition.InsideSE);
    Chart.getStyler().setLegendSeriesLineLength(12);
    Chart.getStyler().setAxisTitleFont(new Font(Font.SANS_SERIF, Font.
    ITALIC, 18));
    Chart.getStyler().setAxisTickLabelsFont(new Font(Font.SERIF, Font.PLAIN, 11));
    Chart.getStyler().setDatePattern("yyyy-MM");
    Chart.getStyler().setDecimalPattern("#0.00");
```

The program can be run in two modes. In the first mode (training, working Mode = 1), the program trains the network, saves the trained network on disk, prints the results, displays the chart results, and saves the chart on disk. In the second mode (testing, workingMode = 2), the program loads the previously saved trained network, calculates the predicted values at the points that were not used during the network training, prints the results, displays the chart, and saves the chart on disk.

Depending on the mode to run, we uncomment the config statements for the needed mode and comment them out for the opposite mode. *The program should always be run in the training mode first, because the second mode depends on the training results produced in the training mode.* The configuration is currently set to run the program in the training mode (see Listing 5-4).

Listing 5-4. Code Fragment of the Training Method Code

```
// ===================================================
// Configuration (comment and uncomment the appropriate configuration)
// ===================================================

// For training the network
workingMode = 1;
 trainFileName = "C:/Book_Examples/Sample1_Norm.csv";
 chartTrainFileName = "XYLine_Train_Results_Chart";

// For testing the trained network at non-trained points
//workingMode = 2;
//intNumberOfRecordsInTestFile = 3;
//testFileName = "C:/Book_Examples/Sample2_Norm.csv";
//chartTestFileName = "XYLine_Test_Results_Chart";

// Common configuration statements (stays always uncommented)
networkFileName = "C:/Book_Examples/Saved_Network_File.csv";
numberOfInputNeurons = 1;
numberOfOutputNeurons = 1;
```

With workingMode set to 1, the program executes the training method called trainValidateSaveNetwork(); otherwise, it calls the testing method called loadAndTestNetwork() (see Listing 5-5).

Listing 5-5. Checking the workingMode and Executing the Appropriate Method

```
// Check the working mode

if(workingMode == 1)
  {
      // Training mode.

      File file1 = new File(chartTrainFileName);
      File file2 = new File(networkFileName);

      if(file1.exists())
        file1.delete();

      if(file2.exists())
        file2.delete();

    trainValidateSaveNetwork();
  }

  if(workingMode == 2)
    {
        // Test using the test dataset as input
        loadAndTestNetwork();
    }

  }
catch (NumberFormatException e)
  {
      System.err.println("Problem parsing workingMode. workingMode = " +
      workingMode);
      System.exit(1);
  }
catch (Throwable t)
  {
      t.printStackTrace();
      System.exit(1);
  }
finally
```

```
{
    Encog.getInstance().shutdown();
  }
}
```

The next code fragment shows the training method logic. This method trains the network, validates it, and saves the trained network file on disk (to be used later by the testing method). The method loads the training dataset into memory. The first parameter is the name of the input training dataset. The second and third parameters indicate the number of input and output neurons in the network. The fourth parameter (true) indicates that the dataset has a label record. The rest of the parameters specify the file format and the language (see Listing 5-6).

Listing 5-6. Fragments of the Network Training Logic

```
MLDataSet trainingSet =
loadCSV2Memory(trainFileName,numberOfInputNeurons,numberOfOutputNeurons,
        true,CSVFormat.ENGLISH,false);
```

After loading the training dataset in memory, a new neural network is built by creating the basic network and adding the input, hidden, and output layers to it.

```
// create a neural network
BasicNetwork network = new BasicNetwork();
```

Now add the input layer:

```
network.addLayer(new BasicLayer(null,true,1));
```

The first parameter (null) indicates that this is the input layer (no activation function). Enter true as the second parameter for the input and hidden layers and false for the output layer. The third parameter shows the number of neurons in the layer. Next we add the hidden layer.

```
network.addLayer(new BasicLayer(new ActivationTANH(),true,2));
```

The first parameter specifies the activation function to be used (ActivationTANH()).
Alternatively, other activation functions can be used such as the sigmoid function, ActivationSigmoid(); logarithmic, ActivationLOG(); linear relay, ActivationReLU( ); so on. The third parameter specifies the number of neurons in this layer. To add the second hidden layer, simply repeat the previous statement.

Finally, add the output layer.

```
network.addLayer(new BasicLayer(new ActivationTANH(),false,1));
```

The third parameter here specifies the number of neurons in the output layer. The next two statements finalize the creation of the network.

```
network.getStructure().finalizeStructure();
network.reset();
```

To train the newly built network, we specify the type of back-propagation. Here, we specify resilient propagation as the most advanced propagation type. Alternatively, the regular back-propagation type can be specified here.

```
final ResilientPropagation train = new ResilientPropagation(network,
trainingSet);
```

While the network is trained, we loop over the network. On each step of the loop, we get the next training iteration number, increase the epoch number (see Chapter 2 for the epoch definition), and check whether the network error for the current iteration can clear the error limit being set to 0.00000046. When the error on the current iteration finally becomes less than the error limit, we exit the loop. The network has been trained, and we save the trained network on disk. The network also stays in memory.

```
int epoch = 1;

do
    {
        train.iteration();
        System.out.println("Epoch #" + epoch + " Error:" + train.
        getError());
        epoch++;
    } while (network.calculateError(trainingSet) > 0.00000046);

// Save the network file
EncogDirectoryPersistence.saveObject(new File(networkFileName),network);
```

The next section of the code retrieves input, meaning the actual data, and predicts values for each record in the training dataset. First, the inputData, actualData, and predictData objects are created.

```
MLData inputData = pair.getInput();
MLData actualData = pair.getIdeal();
MLData predictData = network.compute(inputData);
```

Having done that, we iterate over the `MLDataPair` pair object by executing the following instructions:

```
normInputXPointValue = inputData.getData(0);
normTargetXPointValue = actualData.getData(0);
normPredictXPointValue = predictData.getData(0);
```

A single field in the `inputData`, `actualData`, and `predictData` objects has a displacement of 0. In this example, there is only one input and output field in a record. Should the record have two input field, we would use the following statements to retrieve all input fields:

```
normInputXPointValue1 = inputData.getData(0);
normInputXPointValue2 = inputData.getData(1);
```

Conversely, should the record have two target field, we would use similar statements to retrieve all the target fields:

```
normTargeValue1 = actualData.getData(0);
normTargeValue2 = actualData.getData(1);
```

The predicted value is processed in a similar way. The predicted value predicts the target value for the next point. The values being retrieved from the network are normalized, because the training dataset that the network processes has been normalized. Getting those values retrieved, we denormalize them. Denormalization is done by using the following formula:

$$f(x) = ((D_L - D_H)*x - N_H*D_L + D_H \cdot N_L)/(N_L - N_H)$$

Here,

x = input data point.

D_L = min (lowest) value of x in the input dataset.

D_H = max (highest) value of x in the input dataset.

N_L = the left part of the normalized interval $[-1, 1]$ = -1.

N_H = the right part of the normalized interval $[-1, 1]$ = 1.

```
denormInputXPointValue = ((minXPointDl - maxXPointDh)*normInputXPointValue -
Nh*minXPointDl +
    maxXPointDh *Nl)/(Nl - Nh);

denormTargetXPointValue = ((minTargetValueDl - maxTargetValueDh)*normTarget
XPointValue -
    Nh*minTargetValueDl + maxTargetValueDh*Nl)/(Nl - Nh);

denormPredictXPointValue =((minTargetValueDl - maxTargetValueDh)*
normPredictXPointValue -
    Nh*minTargetValueDl +  maxTargetValueDh*Nl)/(Nl - Nh);
```

We also calculate the error percent as the difference percent between the denormTargetXPointValue and denormPredictXPointValue fields. We print the results, and we also populate the values denormTargetXPointValue and denormPredictXPointValue as the graph element for the currently processed record xPointer.

```
xData.add(denormInputXPointValue);
yData1.add(denormTargetXPointValue);
yData2.add(denormPredictXPointValue);

}   // End for pair loop // End for the pair loop
```

We save the chart file on disk and also calculate the average and maximum percent difference between the actual and predicted values for all processed records. After exiting the pair loop, we add some instructions needed by the chart to print a chart series and save the chart file on disk.

```
XYSeries series1 = Chart.addSeries("Actual data", xData, yData1);
XYSeries series2 = Chart.addSeries("Predict data", xData, yData2);
series1.setLineColor(XChartSeriesColors.BLUE);
series2.setMarkerColor(Color.ORANGE);
series1.setLineStyle(SeriesLines.SOLID);
series2.setLineStyle(SeriesLines.SOLID);

try
  {
    //Save the chart image
```

```
     BitmapEncoder.saveBitmapWithDPI(Chart, chartTrainFileName,
     BitmapFormat.JPG, 100);
     System.out.println ("Train Chart file has been saved") ;
  }
catch (IOException ex)
  {
     ex.printStackTrace();
     System.exit(3);
  }

 // Finally, save this trained network
 EncogDirectoryPersistence.saveObject(new File(networkFileName),network);
 System.out.println ("Train Network has been saved") ;

 averNormDifferencePerc  = sumNormDifferencePerc/4.00;
 System.out.println(" ");

  System.out.println("maxErrorPerc = " + maxNormDifferencePerc +
       "    averErrorPerc = " + averNormDifferencePerc);

}   // End of the method
```

Debugging and Executing the Program

When the program coding is complete, you can try executing the project, but it seldom works correctly. We need to debug the program. To set a breakpoint, simply click the program's source line number. Figure 5-22 shows the result of clicking line 180. The red line confirms that the breakpoint is set. If you click the same number again, the breakpoint will be removed.

Figure 5-22. *Setting the breakpoint*

Here, we set the breakpoint at the logic that checks which working mode to run. After setting the breakpoint, select Debug ➤ Debug Project from the main menu. The program starts executing and then stops at the breakpoint. Here, if you move the cursor on top of any variable, its value will be displayed in the pop-up window.

To advance execution of the program, click one of the arrow icons, depending on whether you want to advance execution by one line, go inside the executing method, exit the current method, and so on (see Figure 5-23).

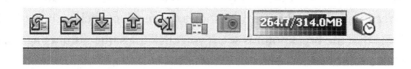

Figure 5-23. *Icons for advancing execution while debugging*

To run the program, select Run ➤ Run Project from the menu. The execution results are shown in the log window.

Processing Results for the Training Method

Listing 5-7 shows the training results.

Listing 5-7. Training Processing Results

```
RecordNumber = 0  TargetValue = 0.0224 PredictedValue = 0.022898  DiffPerc = 1.77
RecordNumber = 1  TargetValue = 0.0625 PredictedValue = 0.062009  DiffPerc = 0.79
RecordNumber = 2  TargetValue = 0.25   PredictedValue = 0.250359  DiffPerc = 0.14
RecordNumber = 3  TargetValue = 0.5625 PredictedValue = 0.562112  DiffPerc = 0.07
RecordNumber = 4  TargetValue = 1.0    PredictedValue = 0.999552  DiffPerc = 0.04
RecordNumber = 5  TargetValue = 1.5625 PredictedValue = 1.563148  DiffPerc = 0.04
RecordNumber = 6  TargetValue = 2.25   PredictedValue = 2.249499  DiffPerc = 0.02
RecordNumber = 7  TargetValue = 3.0625 PredictedValue = 3.062648  DiffPerc = 0.00
RecordNumber = 8  TargetValue = 4.0    PredictedValue = 3.999920  DiffPerc = 0.00

maxErrorPerc = 1.769902752691229
 averErrorPerc = 0.2884023848904945
```

The average error difference percent for all records is 0.29 percent, and the max error difference percent for all records is 1.77 percent.

The chart in Figure 5-24 shows the approximation results at nine points where the network was trained.

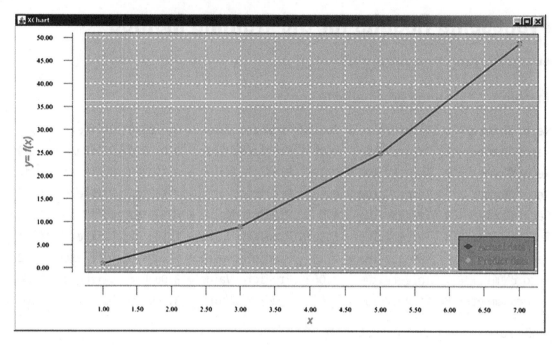

Figure 5-24. *The chart of the training results*

The actual chart (blue color) and the predicted (approximation) chart (orange color) are practically overlapped at the points where the network was trained.

Testing the Network

The test dataset includes records that were not used during the network training. To test the network, we need to adjust the program configuration statements to execute the program in the test mode. To do this, we commented out the configuration statements for the training mode and uncommented the configuration statements for the testing mode (Listing 5-8).

Listing 5-8. Configuration to Run the Program in Test Mode

```
// ===============================================
// Configuration (comment and uncomment the appropriate configuration)
// =======================================================

// For training the network
//workingMode = 1;
```

```
//intNumberOfRecordsInTrainFile = 4;
//trainFileName = "C:/Book_Examples/Sample1_Norm.csv";
//chartTrainFileName = "XYLine_Train_Results_Chart";

// For testing the trained network at non-trained points
workingMode = 2;
intNumberOfRecordsInTestFile = 3;
testFileName = "C:/Book_Examples/Sample2_Norm.csv";
chartTestFileName = "XYLine_Test_Results_Chart";

// Common configuration
networkFileName = "C:/Book_Examples/Saved_Network_File.csv";
numberOfInputNeurons = 1;
numberOfOutputNeurons = 1;
```

The processing logic of the test method is similar to the training method; however, there are some differences. The input file that the method processes is now the testing dataset, and the method does not include the network training logic, because the network was already trained and saved on disk during the execution of the training method. Instead, this method loads the previously saved trained network file in memory (Listing 5-9).

We load the testing dataset and the previously saved trained network file in memory.

Listing 5-9. Fragments of the Testing Method

```
// Load the test dataset into memory
MLDataSet testingSet =
loadCSV2Memory(testFileName,numberOfInputNeurons,numberOfOutputNeurons,
       true,CSVFormat.ENGLISH,false);

 // Load the saved trained network
network =
       (BasicNetwork)EncogDirectoryPersistence.loadObject(new
       File(networkFileName));
```

We iterate over the pair dataset obtaining from the network the normalized input and the actual and predicted values for each record. Next, we denormalize those values and calculate the average and the maximum difference percent (between the denormalized actual and predicted values). Getting those values, we print them and also

populate the chart element for each record. Finally, we add some code for controlling
the chart series and save the chart on disk.

```java
int i = - 1;
double xPoint = -0.00;

for (MLDataPair pair:  testingSet)
    {
        i++;
        xPoint = xPoint + 2.00;

        MLData inputData = pair.getInput();
        MLData actualData = pair.getIdeal();
        MLData predictData = network.compute(inputData);

        // These values are Normalized as the whole input is
        normInputXPointValueFromRecord = inputData.getData(0);
        normTargetXPointValueFromRecord = actualData.getData(0);
        normPredictXPointValueFromRecord = predictData.getData(0);

        denormInputXPointValue = ((minXPointDl - maxXPointDh)*
          normInputXPointValueFromRecord - Nh*minXPointDl +
            maxXPointDh*Nl)/(Nl - Nh);
        denormTargetXPointValue = ((minTargetValueDl - maxTargetValueDh)*
          normTargetXPointValueFromRecord - Nh*minTargetValueDl +
            maxTargetValueDh*Nl)/(Nl - Nh);
        denormPredictXPointValue =((minTargetValueDl - maxTargetValueDh)*
          normPredictXPointValueFromRecord - Nh*minTargetValueDl +
            maxTargetValueDh*Nl)/(Nl - Nh);

        targetToPredictPercent = Math.abs((denormTargetXPointValue -
          denormPredictXPointValue)/denormTargetXPointValue*100);

        System.out.println("xPoint = " + xPoint +
          " denormTargetXPointValue = " + denormTargetXPointValue +
            " denormPredictXPointValue = " + denormPredictXPointValue +
              " targetToPredictPercent = " + targetToPredictPercent);
```

```java
      if (targetToPredictPercent > maxGlobalResultDiff)
         maxGlobalResultDiff = targetToPredictPercent;

   sumGlobalResultDiff = sumGlobalResultDiff + targetToPredictPercent;

      // Populate chart elements
      xData.add(denormInputXPointValue);
      yData1.add(denormTargetXPointValue);
      yData2.add(denormPredictXPointValue);
 }  // End for pair loop

// Print the max and average results

System.out.println(" ");
averGlobalResultDiff = sumGlobalResultDiff/
intNumberOfRecordsInTestFile;

System.out.println("maxErrorPerc = " + maxGlobalResultDiff );
System.out.println("averErrorPerc = " + averGlobalResultDiff);

// All testing batch files have been processed
XYSeries series1 = Chart.addSeries("Actual", xData, yData1);
XYSeries series2 = Chart.addSeries("Predicted", xData, yData2);

series1.setLineColor(XChartSeriesColors.BLUE);
series2.setMarkerColor(Color.ORANGE);
series1.setLineStyle(SeriesLines.SOLID);
series2.setLineStyle(SeriesLines.SOLID);

// Save the chart image
try
 {
   BitmapEncoder.saveBitmapWithDPI(Chart, chartTestFileName ,
   BitmapFormat.JPG, 100);
 }
catch (Exception bt)
 {
   bt.printStackTrace();
 }
```

```
System.out.println ("The Chart has been saved");

System.out.println("End of testing for test records");
} // End of the method
```

Testing Results

Listing 5-10 shows the testing results.

Listing 5-10. Testing Results

```
xPoint = 0.20 TargetValue = 0.04000  PredictedValue =
0.03785  targetToPredictDiffPerc = 5.37
xPoint = 0.30 TargetValue = 0.09000  PredictedValue =
0.09008  targetToPredictDiffPerc = 0.09
xPoint = 0.40 TargetValue = 0.16000  PredictedValue =
0.15798  targetToPredictDiffPerc = 1.26
xPoint = 0.70 TargetValue = 0.49000  PredictedValue =
0.48985  targetToPredictDiffPerc = 0.03
xPoint = 0.95 TargetValue = 0.90250  PredictedValue =
0.90208  targetToPredictDiffPerc = 0.05
xPoint = 1.30 TargetValue = 1.69000  PredictedValue =
1.69096  targetToPredictDiffPerc = 0.06
xPoint = 1.60 TargetValue = 2.56000  PredictedValue =
2.55464  targetToPredictDiffPerc = 0.21
xPoint = 1.80 TargetValue = 3.24000  PredictedValue =
3.25083  targetToPredictDiffPerc = 0.33
xPoint = 1.95 TargetValue = 3.80250  PredictedValue =
3.82933  targetToPredictDiffPerc = 0.71

maxErrorPerc = 5.369910680518282
averErrorPerc = 0.8098656579029523
```

The max error (percent difference between the actual and predicted values) is 5.37 percent. The average error (percent difference between the actual and predicted values) is 0.81 percent. Figure 5-25 shows the chart for the testing results.

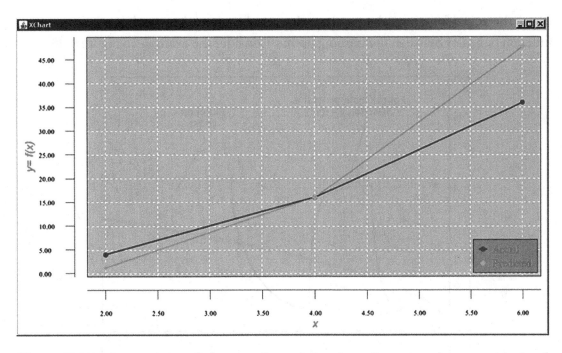

Figure 5-25. *Approximated chart at the points where the network was not trained*

The noticeable discrepancies between the actual and predicted values are due to the rough function approximation. Some improvement of the approximation precision can usually be done by tinkering with the architecture of the network (the number of hidden layers, the number of neurons in layers). However, the main problem here is a very small number of points and the correspondingly relatively large distance between points used to train the network. To get substantially better function approximation results, many more points (with a much smaller distance between them) should be used to approximate this function.

Should the training dataset include many more points (100, 1000, or even 10,000) and correspondingly much smaller distances between points (0.01, 0.001, or even 0.0001), the approximation results would be substantially more precise. However, that is not the goal of this first simple example.

Digging Deeper

Why are many more points needed for approximating this function? Function approximation controls the behavior of the approximated function at the points processed during training. The network learns to make the approximated results closely match the actual function values at the training points, but it has much less control of the function behavior between the training points. Consider the example in Figure 5-26.

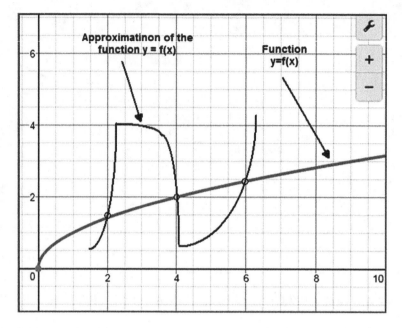

Figure 5-26. *Original and approximated functions*

In the graph in Figure 5-26, the approximation function values closely match the original function values at the training points, but not between points. The errors for testing points are deliberately exaggerated on Figure 5-26 to make the point clearer. If many more training points are used, then the testing points will always be much closer to one of the training points, and the testing results at the testing points will be much closer to the original function value at those points.

Summary

The chapter described how to develop neural network applications using the Java Encog framework. We used a step-by-step approach to explain all the details that are used when coding neural network applications using Encog. The examples in the rest of this book use the Encog framework.

CHAPTER 6

Neural Network Prediction Outside of the Training Range

Data preparation for neural network processing is typically the most difficult and time-consuming task. In addition to the enormous volume of data that could easily reach millions and even billions of rows, the main difficulty is in preparing the data in the correct format for the task in question. In this and the following chapters, we will demonstrate several techniques of data preparation/transformation.

The goal of this example is to show how to deal with the major restrictions of neural network approximation, which states that predictions should be used only inside of the training interval. This restriction exists for any function approximation mechanism (not only for approximation by neural networks but also using calculus). Getting function values outside of the training interval is called *forecasting* (rather than prediction). Forecasting function values is based on extrapolation, while the neural network processing mechanism is based on the approximation mechanism. Getting the function approximation value outside the training interval simply produces the wrong result. This is one of the important concepts to be aware of.

Example: Approximating Periodic Functions Outside of the Training Range

We will use for this example the tangent periodic function y = tan(x). We pretend that we don't know what type of periodic function is given to us; the function is given to us by its values at certain points. Table 6-1 shows the function values on the interval [0, 1.2]. We will use this data for network training.

© Igor Livshin 2022

I. Livshin, *Artificial Neural Networks with Java*, https://doi.org/10.1007/978-1-4842-7368-5_6

Table 6-1. *Function Values on the Interval [0, 1.2]*

Point x	y
0	10
0.12	10.12058
0.24	10.24472
0.36	10.3764
0.48	10.52061
0.6	10.68414
0.72	10.87707
0.84	11.11563
0.96	11.42836
1.08	11.87122
1.2	12.57215

Figure 6-1 shows the chart of the function values on the interval [0, 1.2].

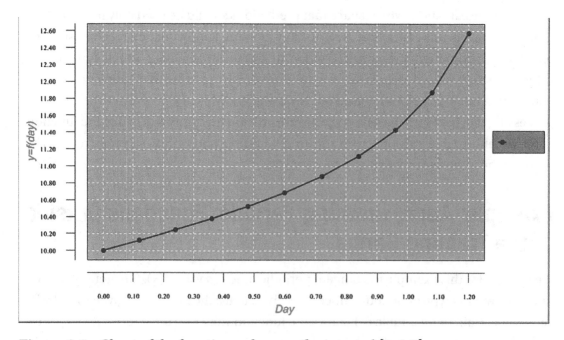

Figure 6-1. *Chart of the function values on the interval [0, 1.2]*

Table 6-2 shows the function values on the interval [3.141592654, 4.341592654]. We will use this data for testing the trained network.

Table 6-2. *Function Values on Interval [3.141592654, 4.341592654]*

Point x	y
3.141593	10
3.261593	10.12058
3.381593	10.24472
3.501593	10.3764
3.621593	10.52061
3.741593	10.68414
3.861593	10.87707
3.981593	11.11563
4.101593	11.42836
4.221593	11.87122
4.341593	12.57215

Figure 6-2 shows the chart of the function values on the interval [3.141592654, 4.341592654].

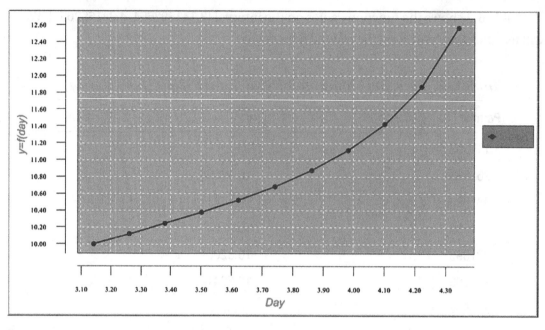

Figure 6-2. *Chart of the function values on the interval [3.141592654,*
4.341592654]

The goal of this example is to approximate the function on the given interval [0, 1.2]
and then use the trained network to predict the function values on the next interval
[3.141592654, 4.341592654].

For example, we will try to approximate the function in a conventional way, by using
the given data as it is. This data needs to be normalized on interval [-1, 1]. Table 6-3
shows the normalized training dataset.

Table 6-3. *Normalized Training Dataset*

Point x	Y
-0.666666667	-0.5
-0.626666667	-0.43971033
-0.586666667	-0.37764165
-0.546666667	-0.311798575
-0.506666667	-0.23969458

(*continued*)

Table 6-3. (*continued*)

Point x	Y
-0.466666667	-0.157931595
-0.426666667	-0.06146605
-0.386666667	0.057816175
-0.346666667	0.214178745
-0.306666667	0.43560867
-0.266666667	0.78607581

Table 6-4 shows the normalized testing dataset.

Table 6-4. *Normalized Testing Dataset*

Point x	y
0.380530885	-0.5
0.420530885	-0.43971033
0.460530885	-0.37764165
0.500530885	-0.311798575
0.540530885	-0.23969458
0.580530885	-0.157931595
0.620530885	-0.06146605
0.660530885	0.057816175
0.700530885	0.214178745
0.740530885	0.43560867
0.780530885	0.786075815

Network Architecture for the Example

Figure 6-3 shows the network architecture for this example. The network consists of a single neuron in the input layer, three hidden layers (each with five neurons), and the output layers with a single neuron.

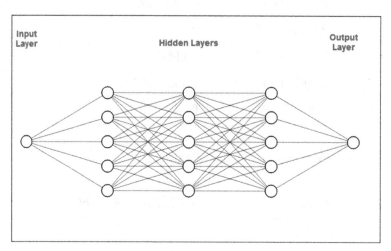

Figure 6-3. *Network architecture*

Program Code for the Example

Listing 6-1 shows the program code.

Listing 6-1. Program Code

```
// ========================================================
// Approximation of the periodic function outside of the training range.
// The input is the file consisting of records with two fields:
// - The first field is the xPoint value.
// - The second field is the target function value at that xPoint
// ========================================================

package sample3a;

import java.io.BufferedReader;
import java.io.File;
import java.io.FileInputStream;
import java.io.PrintWriter;
```

```java
import java.io.FileNotFoundException;
import java.io.FileReader;
import java.io.FileWriter;
import java.io.IOException;
import java.io.InputStream;
import java.nio.file.*;
import java.util.Properties;
import java.time.YearMonth;
import java.awt.Color;
import java.awt.Font;
import java.io.BufferedReader;
import java.text.DateFormat;
import java.text.ParseException;
import java.text.SimpleDateFormat;
import java.time.LocalDate;
import java.time.Month;
import java.time.ZoneId;
import java.util.ArrayList;
import java.util.Calendar;
import java.util.Date;
import java.util.List;
import java.util.Locale;
import java.util.Properties;

import org.encog.Encog;
import org.encog.engine.network.activation.ActivationTANH;
import org.encog.engine.network.activation.ActivationReLU;
import org.encog.ml.data.MLData;
import org.encog.ml.data.MLDataPair;
import org.encog.ml.data.MLDataSet;
import org.encog.ml.data.buffer.MemoryDataLoader;
import org.encog.ml.data.buffer.codec.CSVDataCODEC;
import org.encog.ml.data.buffer.codec.DataSetCODEC;
import org.encog.neural.networks.BasicNetwork;
import org.encog.neural.networks.layers.BasicLayer;
import org.encog.neural.networks.training.propagation.resilient.
ResilientPropagation;
```

```
import org.encog.persist.EncogDirectoryPersistence;
import org.encog.util.csv.CSVFormat;

import org.knowm.xchart.SwingWrapper;
import org.knowm.xchart.XYChart;
import org.knowm.xchart.XYChartBuilder;
import org.knowm.xchart.XYSeries;
import org.knowm.xchart.demo.charts.ExampleChart;
import org.knowm.xchart.style.Styler.LegendPosition;
import org.knowm.xchart.style.colors.ChartColor;
import org.knowm.xchart.style.colors.XChartSeriesColors;
import org.knowm.xchart.style.lines.SeriesLines;
import org.knowm.xchart.style.markers.SeriesMarkers;
import org.knowm.xchart.BitmapEncoder;
import org.knowm.xchart.BitmapEncoder.BitmapFormat;
import org.knowm.xchart.QuickChart;
import org.knowm.xchart.SwingWrapper;

public class Sample3a implements ExampleChart<XYChart>
{

    static double Nh =  1;
    static double Nl = -1;

   // First column
   static double maxXPointDh = 5.00;
   static double minXPointDl = -1.00;

   // Second column - target data
   static double maxTargetValueDh = 13.00;
   static double minTargetValueDl = 9.00;

   static double doublePointNumber = 0.00;
   static int intPointNumber = 0;
   static InputStream input = null;
   static double[] arrFunctionValue = new double[500];
   static double inputDiffValue = 0.00;
   static double predictDiffValue = 0.00;
   static double targetDiffValue = 0.00;
```

```java
static double valueDifferencePerc = 0.00;
 static String strFunctionValuesFileName;
static int returnCode  = 0;
static int numberOfInputNeurons;
static int numberOfOutputNeurons;
static int numberOfRecordsInFile;
static int intNumberOfRecordsInTestFile;
static double realTargetValue;
static double realPredictValue;
static String functionValuesTrainFileName;
static String functionValuesTestFileName;
static String trainFileName;
static String priceFileName;
static String testFileName;
static String chartTrainFileName;
static String chartTestFileName;
static String networkFileName;
static int workingMode;
static String cvsSplitBy = ",";
static double denormTargetDiffPerc;
static double denormPredictDiffPerc;

static List<Double> xData = new ArrayList<Double>();
static List<Double> yData1 = new ArrayList<Double>();
static List<Double> yData2 = new ArrayList<Double>();

static XYChart Chart;

@Override
public XYChart getChart()
 {

  // Create Chart

  Chart = new  XYChartBuilder().width(900).height(500).title(getClass().
          getSimpleName()).xAxisTitle("x").yAxisTitle("y= f(x)").build();

  // Customize Chart
```

```java
Chart.getStyler().setPlotBackgroundColor(ChartColor.
getAWTColor(ChartColor.GREY));
Chart.getStyler().setPlotGridLinesColor(new Color(255, 255, 255));
Chart.getStyler().setChartBackgroundColor(Color.WHITE);
Chart.getStyler().setLegendBackgroundColor(Color.PINK);
Chart.getStyler().setChartFontColor(Color.MAGENTA);
Chart.getStyler().setChartTitleBoxBackgroundColor(new Color(0, 222, 0));
Chart.getStyler().setChartTitleBoxVisible(true);
Chart.getStyler().setChartTitleBoxBorderColor(Color.BLACK);
Chart.getStyler().setPlotGridLinesVisible(true);
Chart.getStyler().setAxisTickPadding(20);
Chart.getStyler().setAxisTickMarkLength(15);
Chart.getStyler().setPlotMargin(20);
Chart.getStyler().setChartTitleVisible(false);
Chart.getStyler().setChartTitleFont(new Font(Font.MONOSPACED, Font.
BOLD, 24));
Chart.getStyler().setLegendFont(new Font(Font.SERIF, Font.PLAIN, 18));
Chart.getStyler().setLegendPosition(LegendPosition.InsideSE);
Chart.getStyler().setLegendSeriesLineLength(12);
Chart.getStyler().setAxisTitleFont(new Font(Font.SANS_SERIF,
Font.ITALIC, 18));
Chart.getStyler().setAxisTickLabelsFont(new Font(Font.SERIF,
Font.PLAIN, 11));
Chart.getStyler().setDatePattern("yyyy-MM");
Chart.getStyler().setDecimalPattern("#0.00");

// Configuration

// Training
workingMode = 1;
trainFileName = "C:/My_Neural_Network_Book/Book_Examples/Sample3a_Norm_
Tan_Train.csv";
functionValuesTrainFileName =
    "C:/My_Neural_Network_Book/Book_Examples/Sample3a_Tan_Calculate_
    Train.csv";
chartTrainFileName =
```

```
       "C:/My_Neural_Network_Book/Book_Examples/Sample3a_XYLine_Tan_Train_
       Chart";
numberOfRecordsInFile = 12;

// Test the trained network at non-trained points
// workingMode = 2;
// testFileName = "C:/My_Neural_Network_Book/Book_Examples/Sample3a_
Norm_Tan_Test.csv";
// functionValuesTestFileName =
       "C:/My_Neural_Network_Book/Book_Examples/Sample3a_Tan_Calculate_
       Test.csv";
 //chartTestFileName =
   "C:/My_Neural_Network_Book/Book_Examples/Sample3a_XYLine_Tan_Test_Chart";
 //numberOfRecordsInFile = 12;

 // Common configuration
 networkFileName =
    "C:/My_Neural_Network_Book/Book_Examples/Sample3a_Saved_Tan_Network_
    File.csv";
 numberOfInputNeurons = 1;
 numberOfOutputNeurons = 1;

 try
  {
      // Check the working mode to run

      if(workingMode == 1)
       {
         // Train mode
         loadFunctionValueTrainFileInMemory();

          File file1 = new File(chartTrainFileName);
          File file2 = new File(networkFileName);

          if(file1.exists())
            file1.delete();

          if(file2.exists())
            file2.delete();
```

```
                returnCode = 0;      // Clear the return code variable

                do
                 {
                    returnCode = trainValidateSaveNetwork();

                 } while (returnCode > 0);

            }   // End the train logic
          else
           {
             // Testing mode.

             // Load testing file in memory
             loadTestFileInMemory();

             File file1 = new File(chartTestFileName);

             if(file1.exists())
               file1.delete();

             loadAndTestNetwork();

           }
         }
       catch (Throwable t)
         {
               t.printStackTrace();
              System.exit(1);
          }
        finally
         {
             Encog.getInstance().shutdown();
         }
    Encog.getInstance().shutdown();

    return Chart;
```

```
}  // End of the method


// ----------------------------------------------------
// Load CSV to memory.
// @return the loaded dataset.
// ----------------------------------------------------
public static MLDataSet loadCSV2Memory(String filename, int input,
int ideal, boolean headers,
   CSVFormat format, boolean significance)
  {
     DataSetCODEC codec = new CSVDataCODEC(new File(filename), format,
     headers, input, ideal,
         significance);

     MemoryDataLoader load = new MemoryDataLoader(codec);
     MLDataSet dataset = load.external2Memory();
     return dataset;
  }

// ==================================================
//  The main method.
//  @param Command line arguments. No arguments are used.
// ==================================================
public static void main(String[] args)
 {
   ExampleChart<XYChart> exampleChart = new Sample3a();
   XYChart Chart = exampleChart.getChart();
   new SwingWrapper<XYChart>(Chart).displayChart();
 } // End of the main method

//=====================================
// Train, validate, and save the trained network file
//=====================================
static public int trainValidateSaveNetwork()
 {
   double functionValue = 0.00;
```

```
// Load the training CSV file in memory
MLDataSet trainingSet =
  loadCSV2Memory(trainFileName,numberOfInputNeurons,
  numberOfOutputNeurons,
    true,CSVFormat.ENGLISH,false);

// create a neural network
BasicNetwork network = new BasicNetwork();

// Input layer
network.addLayer(new BasicLayer(null,true,1));

// Hidden layer
network.addLayer(new BasicLayer(new ActivationTANH(),true,5));
network.addLayer(new BasicLayer(new ActivationTANH(),true,5));
network.addLayer(new BasicLayer(new ActivationTANH(),true,5));

// Output layer
network.addLayer(new BasicLayer(new ActivationTANH(),false,1));

network.getStructure().finalizeStructure();
network.reset();

// train the neural network
final ResilientPropagation train = new ResilientPropagation(network,
trainingSet);

int epoch = 1;
returnCode = 0;

do
 {
    train.iteration();
    System.out.println("Epoch #" + epoch + " Error:" + train.
    getError());

    epoch++;

    if (epoch >= 500 && network.calculateError(trainingSet) >
    0.000000061)
```

```java
        {
         returnCode = 1;

         System.out.println("Try again");
         return returnCode;
        }

  } while(train.getError() > 0.00000006);


// Save the network file
EncogDirectoryPersistence.saveObject(new File(networkFileName),network);

System.out.println("Neural Network Results:");

double sumDifferencePerc = 0.00;
double averNormDifferencePerc = 0.00;
double maxErrorPerc = 0.00;

int m = -1;
double xPoint_Initial = 0.00;
double xPoint_Increment = 0.12;
double xPoint = xPoint_Initial - xPoint_Increment;

realTargetValue = 0.00;
realPredictValue = 0.00;

for(MLDataPair pair: trainingSet)
  {
      m++;
      xPoint = xPoint + xPoint_Increment;

      //if(xPoint >  3.14)
      //    break;

       final MLData output = network.compute(pair.getInput());

      MLData inputData = pair.getInput();
      MLData actualData = pair.getIdeal();
      MLData predictData = network.compute(inputData);

      // Calculate and print the results
```

```
        inputDiffValue = inputData.getData(0);
        targetDiffValue = actualData.getData(0);
        predictDiffValue = predictData.getData(0);

        //De-normalize the values
        denormTargetDiffPerc = ((minTargetValueDl - maxTargetValueDh)*
        targetDiffValue -
            Nh*minTargetValueDl + maxTargetValueDh*Nl)/(Nl - Nh);
        denormPredictDiffPerc =((minTargetValueDl - maxTargetValueDh)*
        predictDiffValue -
            Nh*minTargetValueDl + maxTargetValueDh*Nl)/(Nl - Nh);

        valueDifferencePerc =
          Math.abs(((denormTargetDiffPerc - denormPredictDiffPerc)/
          denormTargetDiffPerc)*100.00);

      System.out.println ("xPoint = " + xPoint + "  realTargetValue = " +
          denormTargetDiffPerc + "  realPredictValue = " +
          denormPredictDiffPerc + "
              valueDifferencePerc = " + valueDifferencePerc);

        sumDifferencePerc = sumDifferencePerc + valueDifferencePerc;

        if (valueDifferencePerc > maxErrorPerc && m > 0)
          maxErrorPerc = valueDifferencePerc;

        xData.add(xPoint);
        yData1.add(denormTargetDiffPerc);
        yData2.add(denormPredictDiffPerc);

   }    // End for pair loop

   XYSeries series1 = Chart.addSeries("Actual data", xData, yData1);
   XYSeries series2 = Chart.addSeries("Predict data", xData, yData2);

   series1.setLineColor(XChartSeriesColors.BLUE);
   series2.setMarkerColor(Color.ORANGE);
   series1.setLineStyle(SeriesLines.SOLID);
   series2.setLineStyle(SeriesLines.SOLID);
```

```java
    try
     {
        //Save the chart image
        BitmapEncoder.saveBitmapWithDPI(Chart, chartTrainFileName,
        BitmapFormat.JPG, 100);
        System.out.println ("Train Chart file has been saved") ;
     }
    catch (IOException ex)
     {
      ex.printStackTrace();
      System.exit(3);
     }

     // Finally, save this trained network
     EncogDirectoryPersistence.saveObject(new File(networkFileName),network);
     System.out.println ("Train Network has been saved") ;

     averNormDifferencePerc  = sumDifferencePerc/numberOfRecordsInFile;

     System.out.println(" ");
     System.out.println("maxErrorPerc = " + maxErrorPerc +
        "   averNormDifferencePerc = " + averNormDifferencePerc);

     returnCode = 0;

     return returnCode;

  }    // End of the method
//=====================================================
// This method load and test the trained network at the points not
// used for training.
//=====================================================
static public void loadAndTestNetwork()
 {
   System.out.println("Testing the networks results");

   List<Double> xData = new ArrayList<Double>();
   List<Double> yData1 = new ArrayList<Double>();
```

```
List<Double> yData2 = new ArrayList<Double>();

double sumDifferencePerc = 0.00;
double maxErrorPerc = 0.00;
double maxGlobalResultDiff = 0.00;
double averErrorPerc = 0.00;
double sumGlobalResultDiff = 0.00;
double functionValue;

BufferedReader br4;
BasicNetwork network;
int k1 = 0;

// Process test records
maxGlobalResultDiff = 0.00;
averErrorPerc = 0.00;
sumGlobalResultDiff = 0.00;

MLDataSet testingSet =
loadCSV2Memory(testFileName,numberOfInputNeurons,numberOfOutputNeurons,
true,
  CSVFormat.ENGLISH,false);

// Load the saved trained network
network =
  (BasicNetwork)EncogDirectoryPersistence.loadObject(new
  File(networkFileName));

int i = - 1; // Index of the current record
int m = -1;

double xPoint_Initial = 3.141592654;
double xPoint_Increment = 0.12;
double xPoint = xPoint_Initial - xPoint_Increment;

realTargetValue = 0.00;
realPredictValue = 0.00;

for (MLDataPair pair:  testingSet)
  {
```

```
m++;
   xPoint = xPoint + xPoint_Increment;

   //if(xPoint >  3.14)
   //    break;

    final MLData output = network.compute(pair.getInput());

    MLData inputData = pair.getInput();
    MLData actualData = pair.getIdeal();
    MLData predictData = network.compute(inputData);

    // Calculate and print the results
    inputDiffValue = inputData.getData(0);
    targetDiffValue = actualData.getData(0);
    predictDiffValue = predictData.getData(0);

    // De-normalize the values
    denormTargetDiffPerc = ((minTargetValueDl - maxTargetValueDh)*
    targetDiffValue -
        Nh*minTargetValueDl + maxTargetValueDh*Nl)/(Nl - Nh);
    denormPredictDiffPerc =((minTargetValueDl - maxTargetValueDh)*
    predictDiffValue -
        Nh*minTargetValueDl + maxTargetValueDh*Nl)/(Nl - Nh);

    valueDifferencePerc =
      Math.abs(((denormTargetDiffPerc - denormPredictDiffPerc)/
      denormTargetDiffPerc)*100.00);

    System.out.println ("xPoint = " + xPoint + "  realTargetValue
    = " +
      denormTargetDiffPerc + "  realPredictValue = " +
      denormPredictDiffPerc + "
        valueDifferencePerc = " +
           valueDifferencePerc);

   sumDifferencePerc = sumDifferencePerc + valueDifferencePerc;

   if (valueDifferencePerc > maxErrorPerc && m > 0)
     maxErrorPerc = valueDifferencePerc;
```

```
                xData.add(xPoint);
                yData1.add(denormTargetDiffPerc);
                yData2.add(denormPredictDiffPerc);

    }  // End for pair loop

    // Print max and average results

    System.out.println(" ");
    averErrorPerc = sumDifferencePerc/numberOfRecordsInFile;

    System.out.println("maxErrorPerc = " + maxErrorPerc);
    System.out.println("averErrorPerc = " + averErrorPerc);

    // All testing batch files have been processed
    XYSeries series1 = Chart.addSeries("Actual", xData, yData1);
    XYSeries series2 = Chart.addSeries("Predicted", xData, yData2);

    series1.setLineColor(XChartSeriesColors.BLUE);
    series2.setMarkerColor(Color.ORANGE);
    series1.setLineStyle(SeriesLines.SOLID);
    series2.setLineStyle(SeriesLines.SOLID);

    // Save the chart image
    try
     {
       BitmapEncoder.saveBitmapWithDPI(Chart, chartTestFileName ,
       BitmapFormat.JPG, 100);
     }
    catch (Exception bt)
     {
       bt.printStackTrace();
     }

    System.out.println ("The Chart has been saved");

   } // End of the method
```

```
//=============================================
// Load Training Function Values file in memory
//=============================================
public static void loadFunctionValueTrainFileInMemory()
 {
    BufferedReader br1 = null;

    String line = "";
    String cvsSplitBy = ",";
    double tempYFunctionValue = 0.00;

     try
       {
         br1 = new BufferedReader(new FileReader(functionValuesTrainFile
         Name));

         int i = -1;
         int r = -2;

         while ((line = br1.readLine()) != null)
          {
             i++;
             r++;
           // Skip the header line
           if(i > 0)
             {
             // Brake the line using comma as separator
             String[] workFields = line.split(cvsSplitBy);

             tempYFunctionValue = Double.parseDouble(workFields[1]);
             arrFunctionValue[r] = tempYFunctionValue;
           }
      } // end of the while loop

      br1.close();

   }
  catch (IOException ex)
```

```
        {
          ex.printStackTrace();
          System.err.println("Error opening files = " + ex);
          System.exit(1);
        }

    }

//===================================
// Load testing Function Values file in memory
//===================================
public static void loadTestFileInMemory()
  {
     BufferedReader br1 = null;

     String line = "";
     String cvsSplitBy = ",";
     double tempYFunctionValue = 0.00;

      try
        {
          br1 = new BufferedReader(new FileReader(functionValuesTestFileName));

          int i = -1;
          int r = -2;

          while ((line = br1.readLine()) != null)
           {
             i++;
             r++;

            // Skip the header line
            if(i > 0)
              {
                // Brake the line using comma as separator
                String[] workFields = line.split(cvsSplitBy);

                tempYFunctionValue = Double.parseDouble(workFields[1]);
                arrFunctionValue[r] = tempYFunctionValue;
              }
```

```
      }  // end of the while loop

        br1.close();

      }
    catch (IOException ex)
      {
        ex.printStackTrace();
        System.err.println("Error opening files = " + ex);
        System.exit(1);
      }

    }

  } // End of the class
```

This code represents regular neural network processing and does not need any explanation.

Listing 6-2 shows the training processing results.

Listing 6-2. Training Processing Results

```
xPoint = 0.00  TargetValue = 10.00000  PredictedValue = 10.00027  DiffPerc = 0.00274
xPoint = 0.12  TargetValue = 10.12058  PredictedValue = 10.12024  DiffPerc = 0.00336
xPoint = 0.24  TargetValue = 10.24471  PredictedValue = 10.24412  DiffPerc = 0.00580
xPoint = 0.36  TargetValue = 10.37640  PredictedValue = 10.37629  DiffPerc = 0.00102
xPoint = 0.48  TargetValue = 10.52061  PredictedValue = 10.52129  DiffPerc = 0.00651
xPoint = 0.60  TargetValue = 10.68414  PredictedValue = 10.68470  DiffPerc = 0.00530
xPoint = 0.72  TargetValue = 10.87707  PredictedValue = 10.87656  DiffPerc = 0.00467
xPoint = 0.84  TargetValue = 11.11563  PredictedValue = 11.11586  DiffPerc = 0.00209
xPoint = 0.96  TargetValue = 11.42835  PredictedValue = 11.42754  DiffPerc = 0.00712
xPoint = 1.08  TargetValue = 11.87121  PredictedValue = 11.87134  DiffPerc = 0.00104
xPoint = 1.20  TargetValue = 12.57215  PredictedValue = 12.57200  DiffPerc = 0.00119

maxErrorPerc = 0.007121086942321541
averErrorPerc = 0.0034047471040211954
```

Figure 6-4 shows the chart of the training results.

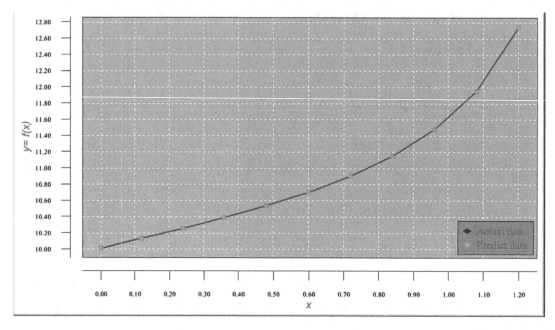

Figure 6-4. *Chart of the training results on the interval [0, 1.2]*

Testing the Network

While processing the test dataset, we extract the xPoint value (column 1) from the record, feed this value to the trained network, obtain from the network the predicted function value, and compare the results against the function values that we happen to know (see Listing 6-2, column 2).

Listing 6-3 shows the test processing results.

Listing 6-3. Test Processing Results

```
xPoint = 3.141594  TargetValue = 10.00000  PredictedValue =
12.71432  DiffPerc = 27.14318
xPoint = 3.261593  TargetValue = 10.12059  PredictedValue =
12.71777  DiffPerc = 25.66249
xPoint = 3.381593  TargetValue = 10.24471  PredictedValue =
12.72100  DiffPerc = 24.17133
xPoint = 3.501593  TargetValue = 10.37640  PredictedValue =
12.72392  DiffPerc = 22.62360
xPoint = 3.621593  TargetValue = 10.52061  PredictedValue =
12.72644  DiffPerc = 20.96674
```

134

```
xPoint = 3.741593  TargetValue = 10.68413  PredictedValue =
12.72849  DiffPerc = 19.13451
xPoint = 3.861593  TargetValue = 10.87706  PredictedValue =
12.73003  DiffPerc = 17.03549
xPoint = 3.981593  TargetValue = 11.11563  PredictedValue =
12.73102  DiffPerc = 14.53260
xPoint = 4.101593  TargetValue = 11.42835  PredictedValue =
12.73147  DiffPerc = 11.40249
xPoint = 4.221593  TargetValue = 11.87121  PredictedValue =
12.73141  DiffPerc = 7.246064
xPoint = 4.341593  TargetValue = 12.57215  PredictedValue =
12.73088  DiffPerc = 1.262565

maxErrorPerc = 25.662489243649677
averErrorPerc = 15.931756451553364
```

Figure 6-5 shows the chart of the test processing results on the interval [3.141592654, 4.341592654].

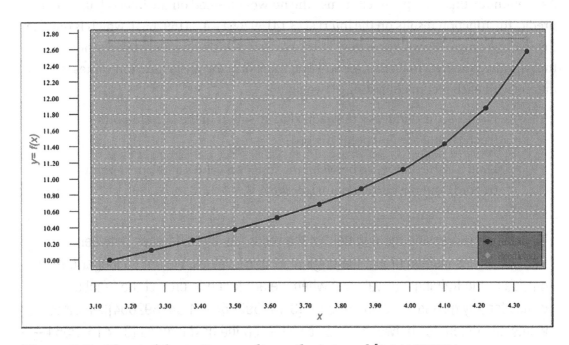

Figure 6-5. *Chart of the testing results on the interval [3.141592654, 4.341592654]*

Notice how different the predicted chart (yellow color) looks compared to the actual chart (blue color). The large errors of the test processing results, maxErrorPerc = 25.66% and averErrorPerc > 15.93% (see Listing 6-3), and the chart (Figure 6-5) show that such function approximation is simply useless. The network returns those values when it is fed the input xPoint values from the test records that are outside of the training range.

Example: Correct Way of Approximating Periodic Functions Outside of the Training Range

In this example, we show how with special data preparation it is possible for periodic functions to be correctly approximated outside of the network training range. As you will see later, this technique can also be used for more complex periodic functions and even some nonperiodic functions.

Preparing the Training Data

As a reminder, this example needs to use the network trained on the interval [0, 1.2] to predict the function results on the interval [3.141592654 – 4.341592654], which is outside the training range. We will show here how to sidestep this neural network restriction for the periodic function. To do this, we will first transform the given function values to a dataset with each record consisting of two fields:

- Field 1 is the difference between xPoint values of the current point (record) and the first point (record).

- Field 2 is the difference between the function values at the next point (record) and the current point (record).

Tip   When expressing the first field of the record as the difference between xPoint values instead of just the original xPoint values, we are no longer getting outside of the training interval even when we are trying to predict the function values for any next interval (in our case [3.141592654 – 4.341592654]). In other words, the difference between xPoint values on the next interval [3.141592654 – 4.341592654] becomes within the training range.

By constructing the input dataset in such way, we essentially teach the network to learn that when the difference in the function values between the current and the first xPoint is equal to some value a, then the difference in function values between the next and current points must be equal to some value b. That allows the network to predict the next day's function value by knowing the current day's function value. Table 6-5 shows the transform dataset.

Table 6-5. *Transformed Training Dataset*

Point x	y
-0.12	9.879420663
0	10
0.12	10.12057934
0.24	10.2447167
0.36	10.37640285
0.48	10.52061084
0.6	10.68413681
0.72	10.8770679
0.84	11.11563235
0.96	11.42835749
1.08	11.87121734
1.2	12.57215162
1.32	13.90334779

We normalize the training dataset on the interval [-1, 1]. Table 6-6 shows the results.

Table 6-6. *Normalized Training Dataset*

xDiff	yDiff
-0.968	-0.967073056
-0.776	-0.961380224
-0.584	-0.94930216
-0.392	-0.929267216
-0.2	-0.898358448
-0.008	-0.851310256
0.184	-0.77829688
0.376	-0.659639776
0.568	-0.45142424
0.76	-0.038505152
0.952	0.969913872

Table 6-7 shows the transformed testing database.

Table 6-7. *Transformed Testing Dataset*

xPointDiff	yDiff
3.021592654	9.879420663
3.141592654	10
3.261592654	10.12057934
3.381592654	10.2447167
3.501592654	10.37640285
3.621592654	10.52061084
3.741592654	10.68413681
3.861592654	10.8770679

(*continued*)

Table 6-7. (*continued*)

xPointDiff	yDiff
3.981592654	11.11563235
4.101592654	11.42835749
4.221592654	11.87121734
4.341592654	12.57215163
4.461592654	13.90334779

Table 6-8 shows the normalized testing dataset.

Table 6-8. *Normalized Testing Dataset*

xDiff	yDiff
-0.968	-0.967073056
-0.776	-0.961380224
-0.584	-0.94930216
-0.392	-0.929267216
-0.2	-0.898358448
-0.008	-0.851310256
0.184	-0.77829688
0.376	-0.659639776
0.568	-0.45142424
0.76	-0.038505136
0.952	0.969913856

We actually don't need the second column in the test dataset for processing. We just included it in the test dataset to be able to compare the predicted values against the actual values programmatically. Feeding the difference between the xPoint values at the current and previous points (Field 1 of the currently processed record) to the trained network, we will get back the predicted difference between the function values at the next point and the current point. Therefore, the predicted function value at the next point is equal to the sum of the target function value at the current point (record) and the network-predicted difference value.

Network Architecture for the Example

For this example, we will use the network with the output layer consisting of the single neuron, three hidden layers (each holding five neurons), and the output layer holding a single neuron. Again, we came up with this architecture experimentally (by trying and testing). Figure 6-6 shows the training architecture.

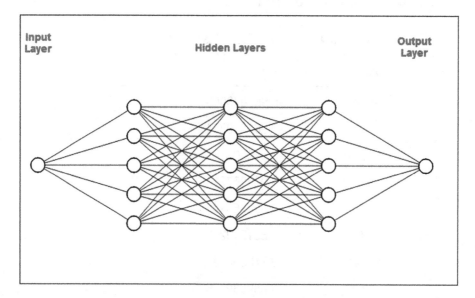

Figure 6-6. *Network architecture for the example*

Now we are ready to develop the network processing program and run the train and testing methods.

Program Code for Example

Listing 6-4 shows the program code.

Listing 6-4. Program Code

```
// ========================================================================
// Approximation of the periodic function outside of the training range.
// The input is the file consisting of records with two fields:
// - The first field holds the difference between the function values of
the
// current and first records.
// - The second field holds the difference between the function values of
the
// next and current records.
// ========================================================================
package sample3b;
import java.io.BufferedReader;
import java.io.File;
import java.io.FileInputStream;
import java.io.PrintWriter;
import java.io.FileNotFoundException;
import java.io.FileReader;
import java.io.FileWriter;
import java.io.IOException;
import java.io.InputStream;
import java.nio.file.*;
import java.util.Properties;
import java.time.YearMonth;
import java.awt.Color;
import java.awt.Font;
import java.io.BufferedReader;
import java.text.DateFormat;
import java.text.ParseException;
import java.text.SimpleDateFormat;
import java.time.LocalDate;
```

```
import java.time.Month;
import java.time.ZoneId;
import java.util.ArrayList;
import java.util.Calendar;
import java.util.Date;
import java.util.List;
import java.util.Locale;
import java.util.Properties;

import org.encog.Encog;
import org.encog.engine.network.activation.ActivationTANH;
import org.encog.engine.network.activation.ActivationReLU;
import org.encog.ml.data.MLData;
import org.encog.ml.data.MLDataPair;
import org.encog.ml.data.MLDataSet;
import org.encog.ml.data.buffer.MemoryDataLoader;
import org.encog.ml.data.buffer.codec.CSVDataCODEC;
import org.encog.ml.data.buffer.codec.DataSetCODEC;
import org.encog.neural.networks.BasicNetwork;
import org.encog.neural.networks.layers.BasicLayer;
import org.encog.neural.networks.training.propagation.resilient.
ResilientPropagation;
import org.encog.persist.EncogDirectoryPersistence;
import org.encog.util.csv.CSVFormat;

import org.knowm.xchart.SwingWrapper;
import org.knowm.xchart.XYChart;
import org.knowm.xchart.XYChartBuilder;
import org.knowm.xchart.XYSeries;
import org.knowm.xchart.demo.charts.ExampleChart;
import org.knowm.xchart.style.Styler.LegendPosition;
import org.knowm.xchart.style.colors.ChartColor;
import org.knowm.xchart.style.colors.XChartSeriesColors;
import org.knowm.xchart.style.lines.SeriesLines;
import org.knowm.xchart.style.markers.SeriesMarkers;
import org.knowm.xchart.BitmapEncoder;
```

```java
import org.knowm.xchart.BitmapEncoder.BitmapFormat;
import org.knowm.xchart.QuickChart;
import org.knowm.xchart.SwingWrapper;

public class Sample3b implements ExampleChart<XYChart>
{
    static double Nh =  1;
    static double Nl = -1;

  // First column
  static double maxXPointDh = 1.35;
  static double minXPointDl = 0.10;

  // Second column - target data
  static double maxTargetValueDh = 1.35;
  static double minTargetValueDl = 0.10;

  static double doublePointNumber = 0.00;
  static int intPointNumber = 0;
  static InputStream input = null;
  static double[] arrFunctionValue = new double[500];
  static double inputDiffValue = 0.00;
  static double predictDiffValue = 0.00;
  static double targetDiffValue = 0.00;
  static double valueDifferencePerc = 0.00;
  static String strFunctionValuesFileName;
  static int returnCode   = 0;
  static int numberOfInputNeurons;
  static int numberOfOutputNeurons;
  static int numberOfRecordsInFile;
  static int intNumberOfRecordsInTestFile;
  static double realTargetValue;
  static double realPredictValue;
  static String functionValuesTrainFileName;
  static String functionValuesTestFileName;
  static String trainFileName;
  static String priceFileName;
```

```java
  static String testFileName;
  static String chartTrainFileName;
  static String chartTestFileName;
  static String networkFileName;
  static int workingMode;
  static String cvsSplitBy = ",";
  static double denormTargetDiffPerc;
  static double denormPredictDiffPerc;

  static List<Double> xData = new ArrayList<Double>();
  static List<Double> yData1 = new ArrayList<Double>();
  static List<Double> yData2 = new ArrayList<Double>();

  static XYChart Chart;

@Override
public XYChart getChart()
 {

  // Create Chart


  Chart = new  XYChartBuilder().width(900).height(500).title(getClass().
          getSimpleName()).xAxisTitle("x").yAxisTitle("y= f(x)").build();

  // Customize Chart
  Chart.getStyler().setPlotBackgroundColor(ChartColor.
  getAWTColor(ChartColor.GREY));
  Chart.getStyler().setPlotGridLinesColor(new Color(255, 255, 255));
  Chart.getStyler().setChartBackgroundColor(Color.WHITE);
  Chart.getStyler().setLegendBackgroundColor(Color.PINK);
  Chart.getStyler().setChartFontColor(Color.MAGENTA);
  Chart.getStyler().setChartTitleBoxBackgroundColor(new Color(0, 222, 0));
  Chart.getStyler().setChartTitleBoxVisible(true);
  Chart.getStyler().setChartTitleBoxBorderColor(Color.BLACK);
  Chart.getStyler().setPlotGridLinesVisible(true);
  Chart.getStyler().setAxisTickPadding(20);
  Chart.getStyler().setAxisTickMarkLength(15);
  Chart.getStyler().setPlotMargin(20);
```

```java
Chart.getStyler().setChartTitleVisible(false);
Chart.getStyler().setChartTitleFont(new Font(Font.MONOSPACED, Font.
BOLD, 24));
Chart.getStyler().setLegendFont(new Font(Font.SERIF, Font.PLAIN, 18));
Chart.getStyler().setLegendPosition(LegendPosition.InsideSE);
Chart.getStyler().setLegendSeriesLineLength(12);
Chart.getStyler().setAxisTitleFont(new Font(Font.SANS_SERIF,
Font.ITALIC, 18));
Chart.getStyler().setAxisTickLabelsFont(new Font(Font.SERIF,
Font.PLAIN, 11));
Chart.getStyler().setDatePattern("yyyy-MM");
Chart.getStyler().setDecimalPattern("#0.00");

// Configuration

// Train
workingMode = 1;
trainFileName = "C:/My_Neural_Network_Book/Book_Examples/Sample3b_Norm_
Tan_Train.csv";
functionValuesTrainFileName =
      "C:/My_Neural_Network_Book/Book_Examples/Sample3b_Tan_Calculate_
      Train.csv";
chartTrainFileName =
      "C:/My_Neural_Network_Book/Book_Examples/Sample3b_XYLine_Tan_
      Train_Chart";
numberOfRecordsInFile = 12;

// Test
// workingMode = 2;
// testFileName = "C:/My_Neural_Network_Book/Book_Examples/Sample3b_
Norm_Tan_Test.csv";
// functionValuesTestFileName =
    "C:/My_Neural_Network_Book/Book_Examples/Sample3b_Tan_Calculate_
    Test.csv";
// chartTestFileName =
    "C:/My_Neural_Network_Book/Book_Examples/Sample3b_XYLine_Tan_Test_
    Chart";
```

```
// numberOfRecordsInFile = 12;

// Common configuration
networkFileName =
    "C:/My_Neural_Network_Book/Book_Examples/Sample3b_Saved_Tan_
    Network_File.csv";
numberOfInputNeurons = 1;
numberOfOutputNeurons = 1;

try
 {
    // Check the working mode to run

    if(workingMode == 1)
     {
       // Train mode
       loadFunctionValueTrainFileInMemory();

        File file1 = new File(chartTrainFileName);
        File file2 = new File(networkFileName);

        if(file1.exists())
          file1.delete();

        if(file2.exists())
          file2.delete();

        returnCode = 0;    // Clear the return code variable

        do
         {
           returnCode = trainValidateSaveNetwork();

         } while (returnCode > 0);

     }    // End the train logic
    else
     {
       // Testing mode.
```

```
        // Load testing file in memory
        loadTestFileInMemory();

        File file1 = new File(chartTestFileName);

        if(file1.exists())
          file1.delete();

        loadAndTestNetwork();

      }
   }
  catch (Throwable t)
    {
      t.printStackTrace();
      System.exit(1);
    }
  finally
    {
      Encog.getInstance().shutdown();
    }

 Encog.getInstance().shutdown();

 return Chart;

} // End of the method
// =======================================================
// Load CSV to memory.
// @return The loaded dataset.
// =======================================================
public static MLDataSet loadCSV2Memory(String filename, int input, int
ideal, boolean headers,
      CSVFormat format, boolean significance)
  {
    DataSetCODEC codec = new CSVDataCODEC(new File(filename), format,
    headers, input, ideal,
        significance);
```

```java
      MemoryDataLoader load = new MemoryDataLoader(codec);
      MLDataSet dataset = load.external2Memory();
      return dataset;
  }

// ==========================================================
//   The main method.
//   @param Command line arguments. No arguments are used.
// ==========================================================
public static void main(String[] args)
 {
    ExampleChart<XYChart> exampleChart = new Sample3b();
    XYChart Chart = exampleChart.getChart();
    new SwingWrapper<XYChart>(Chart).displayChart();
 } // End of the main method

//==========================================
// Train, validate, and saves the trained network file
//==========================================
static public int trainValidateSaveNetwork()
 {
    double functionValue = 0.00;

    // Load the training CSV file in memory
    MLDataSet trainingSet =
      loadCSV2Memory(trainFileName,numberOfInputNeurons,numberOfOutputNeurons,
        true,CSVFormat.ENGLISH,false);

    // create a neural network
    BasicNetwork network = new BasicNetwork();

    // Input layer
    network.addLayer(new BasicLayer(null,true,1));

    // Hidden layer
    network.addLayer(new BasicLayer(new ActivationTANH(),true,5));
    network.addLayer(new BasicLayer(new ActivationTANH(),true,5));
```

```java
network.addLayer(new BasicLayer(new ActivationTANH(),true,5));

// Output layer
network.addLayer(new BasicLayer(new ActivationTANH(),false,1));

network.getStructure().finalizeStructure();
network.reset();

// train the neural network
final ResilientPropagation train = new ResilientPropagation(network,
trainingSet);

int epoch = 1;
returnCode = 0;

do
 {
     train.iteration();
     System.out.println("Epoch #" + epoch + " Error:" + train.getError());

     epoch++;

     if (epoch >= 500 && network.calculateError(trainingSet) >
     0.000000061)
        {
          returnCode = 1;

          System.out.println("Try again");
          return returnCode;
        }

 } while(train.getError() > 0.00000006);

// Save the network file
EncogDirectoryPersistence.saveObject(new File(networkFileName),network);

System.out.println("Neural Network Results:");

double sumDifferencePerc = 0.00;
double averNormDifferencePerc = 0.00;
```

```
double maxErrorPerc = 0.00;

int m = -1;
double xPoint_Initial = 0.00;
double xPoint_Increment = 0.12;
//double xPoint = xPoint_Initial - xPoint_Increment;
double xPoint = xPoint_Initial;

realTargetValue = 0.00;
realPredictValue = 0.00;

for(MLDataPair pair: trainingSet)
  {
      m++;
      xPoint = xPoint + xPoint_Increment;

      final MLData output = network.compute(pair.getInput());

       MLData inputData = pair.getInput();
       MLData actualData = pair.getIdeal();
       MLData predictData = network.compute(inputData);

      // Calculate and print the results
      inputDiffValue = inputData.getData(0);
      targetDiffValue = actualData.getData(0);
      predictDiffValue = predictData.getData(0);

      // De-normalize the values
      denormTargetDiffPerc = ((minXPointDl -
      maxXPointDh)*targetDiffValue - Nh*minXPointDl +
          maxXPointDh*Nl)/(Nl - Nh);
      denormPredictDiffPerc =((minTargetValueDl - maxTargetValueDh)*
      predictDiffValue -
          Nh*minTargetValueDl + maxTargetValueDh*Nl)/(Nl - Nh);

      functionValue = arrFunctionValue[m+1];

      realTargetValue = functionValue + denormTargetDiffPerc;
      realPredictValue = functionValue + denormPredictDiffPerc;
```

```
    valueDifferencePerc =
      Math.abs(((realTargetValue - realPredictValue)/
      realPredictValue)*100.00);

    System.out.println ("xPoint = " + xPoint + "  realTargetValue = " +
      denormTargetDiffPerc + "  realPredictValue = " +
      denormPredictDiffPerc + "
          valueDifferencePerc = " +  valueDifferencePerc);

    sumDifferencePerc = sumDifferencePerc + valueDifferencePerc;

    if (valueDifferencePerc > maxErrorPerc && m > 0)
      maxErrorPerc = valueDifferencePerc;

    xData.add(xPoint);
    yData1.add(denormTargetDiffPerc);
    yData2.add(denormPredictDiffPerc);

}   // End for pair loop

XYSeries series1 = Chart.addSeries("Actual data", xData, yData1);
XYSeries series2 = Chart.addSeries("Predict data", xData, yData2);

series1.setLineColor(XChartSeriesColors.BLUE);
series2.setMarkerColor(Color.ORANGE);
series1.setLineStyle(SeriesLines.SOLID);
series2.setLineStyle(SeriesLines.SOLID);

try
 {
    //Save the chart image
    BitmapEncoder.saveBitmapWithDPI(Chart, chartTrainFileName,
    BitmapFormat.JPG, 100);
    System.out.println ("Train Chart file has been saved") ;
 }
catch (IOException ex)
 {
  ex.printStackTrace();
  System.exit(3);
 }
```

```
    // Finally, save this trained network
    EncogDirectoryPersistence.saveObject(new File(networkFileName),network);
    System.out.println ("Train Network has been saved") ;

    averNormDifferencePerc  = sumDifferencePerc/numberOfRecordsInFile;

    System.out.println(" ");
    System.out.println("maxErrorPerc = " + maxErrorPerc +
       "  averNormDifferencePerc = " + averNormDifferencePerc);

    returnCode = 0;

    return returnCode;

 }   // End of the method

//==================================================
// This method load and test the trained network at the points not
// used for training.
//==================================================
static public void loadAndTestNetwork()
 {
  System.out.println("Testing the networks results");

  List<Double> xData = new ArrayList<Double>();
  List<Double> yData1 = new ArrayList<Double>();
  List<Double> yData2 = new ArrayList<Double>();

  double sumDifferencePerc = 0.00;
  double maxErrorPerc = 0.00;
  double maxGlobalResultDiff = 0.00;
  double averErrorPerc = 0.00;
  double sumGlobalResultDiff = 0.00;
  double functionValue;

  BufferedReader br4;
  BasicNetwork network;
  int k1 = 0;
```

```
// Process test records
maxGlobalResultDiff = 0.00;
averErrorPerc = 0.00;
sumGlobalResultDiff = 0.00;

MLDataSet testingSet =
loadCSV2Memory(testFileName,numberOfInputNeurons,numberOf
OutputNeurons,true,
  CSVFormat.ENGLISH,false);

int i = - 1; // Index of the current record
int m = -1;

double xPoint_Initial = 3.141592654;
double xPoint_Increment = 0.12;
double xPoint = xPoint_Initial;

realTargetValue = 0.00;
realPredictValue = 0.00;

for (MLDataPair pair:  testingSet)
 {
   m++;
   xPoint = xPoint + xPoint_Increment;

   final MLData output = network.compute(pair.getInput());

   MLData inputData = pair.getInput();
   MLData actualData = pair.getIdeal();
   MLData predictData = network.compute(inputData);

   // Calculate and print the results
   inputDiffValue = inputData.getData(0);
   targetDiffValue = actualData.getData(0);
   predictDiffValue = predictData.getData(0);

   // De-normalize the values
   denormTargetDiffPerc = ((minXPointDl -
   maxXPointDh)*targetDiffValue - Nh*minXPointDl +
       maxXPointDh*Nl)/(Nl - Nh);
```

```
denormPredictDiffPerc =((minTargetValueDl - maxTargetValueDh)*predi
ctDiffValue -
     Nh*minTargetValueDl + maxTargetValueDh*Nl)/(Nl - Nh);

functionValue = arrFunctionValue[m+1];

realTargetValue = functionValue + denormTargetDiffPerc;
realPredictValue = functionValue + denormPredictDiffPerc;

valueDifferencePerc =
   Math.abs(((realTargetValue - realPredictValue)/
   realPredictValue)*100.00);

System.out.println ("xPoint = " + xPoint + "  realTargetValue = " +
realTargetValue + "  realPredictValue = " + realPredictValue +
"  valueDifferencePerc = " +
   valueDifferencePerc);

sumDifferencePerc = sumDifferencePerc + valueDifferencePerc;

if (valueDifferencePerc > maxErrorPerc && m > 0)
  maxErrorPerc = valueDifferencePerc;

xData.add(xPoint);
yData1.add(realTargetValue);
yData2.add(realPredictValue);

}  // End for pair loop

// Print max and average results

System.out.println(" ");
averErrorPerc = sumDifferencePerc/numberOfRecordsInFile;

System.out.println("maxErrorPerc = " + maxErrorPerc);
System.out.println("averErrorPerc = " + averErrorPerc);

// All testing batch files have been processed
XYSeries series1 = Chart.addSeries("Actual", xData, yData1);
XYSeries series2 = Chart.addSeries("Predicted", xData, yData2);

series1.setLineColor(XChartSeriesColors.BLUE);
```

```
      series2.setMarkerColor(Color.ORANGE);
      series1.setLineStyle(SeriesLines.SOLID);
      series2.setLineStyle(SeriesLines.SOLID);

      // Save the chart image
      try
       {
         BitmapEncoder.saveBitmapWithDPI(Chart, chartTestFileName ,
         BitmapFormat.JPG, 100);
       }
      catch (Exception bt)
       {
         bt.printStackTrace();
       }

      System.out.println ("The Chart has been saved");

} // End of the method

//==========================================
// Load Training Function Values file in memory
//==========================================
public static void loadFunctionValueTrainFileInMemory()
 {
    BufferedReader br1 = null;

    String line = "";
    String cvsSplitBy = ",";
    double tempYFunctionValue = 0.00;

     try
       {
         br1 = new BufferedReader(new FileReader(functionValuesTrainFileName));

         int i = -1;
         int r = -2;

         while ((line = br1.readLine()) != null)
          {
```

```
                i++;
                r++;

              // Skip the header line
              if(i > 0)
                {
                  // Brake the line using comma as separator
                  String[] workFields = line.split(cvsSplitBy);

                  tempYFunctionValue = Double.parseDouble(workFields[1]);
                  arrFunctionValue[r] = tempYFunctionValue;
                }
          }  // end of the while loop

         br1.close();

        }
      catch (IOException ex)
        {
            ex.printStackTrace();
            System.err.println("Error opening files = " + ex);
            System.exit(1);
        }

    }

//=====================================
// Load testing Function Values file in memory
//=====================================
public static void loadTestFileInMemory()
  {
    BufferedReader br1 = null;

    String line = "";
    String cvsSplitBy = ",";
    double tempYFunctionValue = 0.00;
```

```
    try
      {
        br1 = new BufferedReader(new FileReader(functionValuesTestFileName));

        int i = -1;
        int r = -2;

        while ((line = br1.readLine()) != null)
         {
           i++;
           r++;

          // Skip the header line
          if(i > 0)
            {
              // Brake the line using comma as separator
              String[] workFields = line.split(cvsSplitBy);

              tempYFunctionValue = Double.parseDouble(workFields[1]);
              arrFunctionValue[r] = tempYFunctionValue;
            }
        }  // end of the while loop

        br1.close();
      }
    catch (IOException ex)
      {
        ex.printStackTrace();
        System.err.println("Error opening files = " + ex);
        System.exit(1);
      }

   }

} // End of the class
```

As usual, some miscellaneous statements are present at the top of the program. They are required by the XChart package. The configuration part controls whether the training or testing method should be executed. If the workingMode field is equal to 1, we execute the training method; otherwise, the test method is executed.

Notice the quite unusual way of calling the training method trainValidateSaveNetwork. Actually, we already discussed it briefly in Chapter 2. Listing 6-5 shows how this technique can be programmed.

Listing 6-5. Calling the Training Method in a Loop

```
returnCode = 0;     // Clear the error Code

do
  {
      returnCode = trainValidateSaveNetwork();
  } while (returnCode > 0);
```

This logic calls the training method and then checks for the returnCode. If the returnCode field is not zero, the training method is called again in a loop. And each time the method is called, the initial weight/bias parameters are assigned different random values, which helps in selecting their best values when the method is repeatedly called in a loop.

Inside the called method, the logic checks for the error value after 500 iterations. If the network-calculated error is still larger than the error limit, the method exits with a returnCode of 1. And, as we just saw, the method will be called again. Finally, when the calculated error clears the error threshold, the method exits with returnCode 0 and is no longer called again. You select the error limit value experimentally, making it difficult for the network to clear the error code limit, but still making sure that after enough iterations the error will pass the error limit.

Listing 6-6 shows the beginning of the train method. It loads the training dataset in memory and creates the neural network consisting of the input layer (with a single neuron), three hidden layers (each with five neurons), and the output layer (with a single neuron). Then, we train the network using the most efficient ResilientPropagation as the back-propagation method.

Listing 6-6. Loading the Training Dataset and Building and Training the Network

```
// Load the training CSV file in memory
MLDataSet trainingSet =
    loadCSV2Memory(trainFileName,numberOfInputNeurons,numberOfOutputNeurons,
        true,CSVFormat.ENGLISH,false);

// create a neural network
BasicNetwork network = new BasicNetwork();

// Input layer
network.addLayer(new BasicLayer(null,true,1));

// Hidden layer (seven hidden layers are created
network.addLayer(new BasicLayer(new ActivationTANH(),true,5));
network.addLayer(new BasicLayer(new ActivationTANH(),true,5));
network.addLayer(new BasicLayer(new ActivationTANH(),true,5));

// Output layer
network.addLayer(new BasicLayer(new ActivationTANH(),false,1));

network.getStructure().finalizeStructure();
network.reset();

// train the neural network
final ResilientPropagation train = new ResilientPropagation(network,
trainingSet);
```

This is followed by the fragment that trains the network. We train the network by looping over epochs. On each iteration, we check whether the calculated error is less than the established error limit (in our case, 0.00000006). When the network error becomes less than the error limit, we exit the loop. The network is trained with the required precision, so we save the trained network on disk.

```
int epoch = 1;

returnCode = 0;
do
    {
        train.iteration();
```

```
    System.out.println("Epoch #" + epoch + " Error:" + train.getError());

    epoch++;

    if (epoch >= 500 && network.calculateError(trainingSet) > 0.000000061)
        {
            returnCode = 1;

            System.out.println("Try again");
            return returnCode;
        }

    } while(train.getError()0.00000006);

// Save the network file
EncogDirectoryPersistence.saveObject(new File(networkFileName),network);
```

Notice the logic shown in Listing 6-7 that checks whether the network error became less than the error limit.

Listing 6-7. Checking the Network Error

```
if (epoch >= 5000 && network.calculateError(trainingSet) > 0.00000006)
    {
        returnCode = 1;

        System.out.println("Try again");
        return returnCode;
    }
```

It checks whether after 500 iterations the network error is still not less than the error limit. If that is the case, the returnCode is set to 1, and we exit from the training method, returning to the point where the training method is called in a loop. There, it will call the training method again with a new random set of weight/bias parameters. Without that code, the looping would continue indefinitely if the calculated network error is unable to clear the error limit with the randomly selected set of the initial weight/bias parameters.

There are two APIs that can check the calculated network error. The results differ slightly depending on which method is used.

- `train.getError()`: The error is calculated before the training is applied.

- `network.CalculateError()`: The error is calculated after the training is applied.

The code fragment in Listing 6-8 loops over the pair dataset. The xPoint in the loop is set to be on the interval [0, 1.2]. For each record, it retrieves the input and actual and predicted values, denormalizes them, and, by having the function value, calculates the realTargetValue and realPredictValue, adding them to the chart data (along with the corresponding xPoint value). It also calculates the maximum and average value percent difference for all records. All this data is printed as the training log. Finally, the trained network and the chart image files are saved on disk. Notice that the return code is set to zero at that point, before we return from the train method, so the method will no longer be called again.

Listing 6-8. Looping Over the Pair Dataset

```
for(MLDataPair pair: trainingSet)
    {
        m++;
        xPoint = xPoint + xPoint_Increment;

        final MLData output = network.compute(pair.getInput());

        MLData inputData = pair.getInput();
        MLData actualData = pair.getIdeal();
        MLData predictData = network.compute(inputData);

        // Calculate and print the results
        inputDiffValue = inputData.getData(0);
        targetDiffValue = actualData.getData(0);
        predictDiffValue = predictData.getData(0);

        // De-normalize the values
        denormTargetDiffPerc = ((minXPointDl -
        maxXPointDh)*targetDiffValue - Nh*minXPointDl +
            maxXPointDh*Nl)/(Nl - Nh);
```

```
    denormPredictDiffPerc =((minTargetValueDl - maxTargetValueDh)*
    predictDiffValue -
        Nh*minTargetValueDl + maxTargetValueDh*Nl)/(Nl - Nh);

    functionValue = arrFunctionValue[m];

    realTargetValue = functionValue + targetDiffValue;
    realPredictValue = functionValue + predictDiffValue;

    valueDifferencePerc =
        Math.abs(((realTargetValue - realPredictValue)/
        realPredictValue)*100.00);

    System.out.println ("xPoint = " + xPoint + "  realTargetValue = " +
          realTargetValue + "  realPredictValue = " + realPredictValue);

    sumDifferencePerc = sumDifferencePerc + valueDifferencePerc;

    if (valueDifferencePerc > maxDifferencePerc)
          maxDifferencePerc = valueDifferencePerc;

    xData.add(xPoint);
    yData1.add(realTargetValue);
    yData2.add(realPredictValue);
  }    // End for pair loop

  XYSeries series1 = Chart.addSeries("Actual data", xData, yData1);
  XYSeries series2 = Chart.addSeries("Predict data", xData, yData2);

  series1.setLineColor(XChartSeriesColors.BLUE);
  series2.setMarkerColor(Color.ORANGE);
  series1.setLineStyle(SeriesLines.SOLID);
  series2.setLineStyle(SeriesLines.SOLID);

  try
   {
       //Save the chart image
       BitmapEncoder.saveBitmapWithDPI(Chart, chartTrainFileName,
       BitmapFormat.JPG, 100);
       System.out.println ("Train Chart file has been saved") ;
```

```
    }
catch (IOException ex)
   {
        ex.printStackTrace();
        System.exit(3);
     }

  // Finally, save this trained network
  EncogDirectoryPersistence.saveObject(new File(networkFileName),network);
  System.out.println ("Train Network has been saved") ;

  averNormDifferencePerc  = sumDifferencePerc/numberOfRecordsInFile;

  System.out.println(" ");
  System.out.println("maxDifferencePerc = " + maxDifferencePerc +
  "  averNormDifferencePerc = " +
     averNormDifferencePerc);

  returnCode = 0;
  return returnCode;

} // End of the method
```

The test method has a similar processing logic with the exception of building and training the network. Instead of building and training the network, it loads the previously saved trained network in memory. It also loads the test dataset in memory. By looping over the pair dataset, it gets the input, target, and predicted values for each record. The xPoint in the loop is taken from the interval [3.141592654, 4.341592654].

Training Results for Example

Listing 6-9 shows the training results.

Listing 6-9. Training Results

```
xPoint = 0.12  TargetValue = 0.12058  PredictedValue = 0.12072  DiffPerc = 0.00143
xPoint = 0.24  TargetValue = 0.12414  PredictedValue = 0.12427  DiffPerc = 0.00135
xPoint = 0.36  TargetValue = 0.13169  PredictedValue = 0.13157  DiffPerc = 9.6467E-4
xPoint = 0.48  TargetValue = 0.14421  PredictedValue = 0.14410  DiffPerc = 0.00100
```

xPoint = 0.60   TargetValue = 0.16353   PredictedValue = 0.16352   DiffPerc = 5.31138E-5
xPoint = 0.72   TargetValue = 0.19293   PredictedValue = 0.19326   DiffPerc = 0.00307
xPoint = 0.84   TargetValue = 0.23856   PredictedValue = 0.23842   DiffPerc = 0.00128
xPoint = 0.96   TargetValue = 0.31273   PredictedValue = 0.31258   DiffPerc = 0.00128
xPoint = 1.08   TargetValue = 0.44286   PredictedValue = 0.44296   DiffPerc = 8.16305E-4
xPoint = 1.20   TargetValue = 0.70093   PredictedValue = 0.70088   DiffPerc = 4.05989E-4
xPoint = 1.32   TargetValue = 1.33119   PredictedValue = 1.33123   DiffPerc = 2.74089E-4

maxErrorPerc = 0.0030734810314331077
averErrorPerc = 9.929718215067468E-4

Figure 6-7 shows the chart of the actual function values versus the validation results.

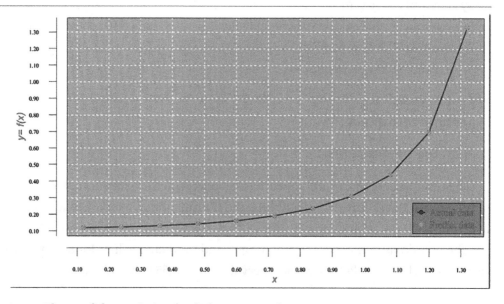

Figure 6-7. *Chart of the training/validation results*

As shown in Figure 6-7, both charts practically overlap.

Log of Testing Results for Example 3

Listing 6-10 shows the testing results on the interval [3.141592654, 4.341592654].

Listing 6-10. Testing Results on the Interval [3.141592654, 4.341592654]

```
xPoint = 3.26159  TargetValue = 10.12058  PredictedValue =
10.12072  DiffPerc = 0.00143
xPoint = 3.38159  TargetValue = 10.24472  PredictedValue =
10.24485  DiffPerc = 0.00135
xPoint = 3.50159  TargetValue = 10.37640  PredictedValue =
10.37630  DiffPerc = 9.64667E-4
xPoint = 3.62159  TargetValue = 10.52061  PredictedValue =
10.52050  DiffPerc = 0.00100
xPoint = 3.74159  TargetValue = 10.68414  PredictedValue =
10.68413  DiffPerc = 5.31136E-5
xPoint = 3.86159  TargetValue = 10.87707  PredictedValue =
10.87740  DiffPerc = 0.00307
xPoint = 3.98159  TargetValue = 11.11563  PredictedValue =
11.11549  DiffPerc = 0.00127
xPoint = 4.10159  TargetValue = 11.42836  PredictedValue =
11.42821  DiffPerc = 0.00128
xPoint = 4.22159  TargetValue = 11.87122  PredictedValue =
11.87131  DiffPerc = 8.16306E-4
xPoint = 4.34159  TargetValue = 12.57215  PredictedValue =
12.57210  DiffPerc = 4.06070E-4
xPoint = 4.46159  TargetValue = 13.90335  PredictedValue =
13.90338  DiffPerc = 2.74161E-4

maxErrorPerc = 0.003073481240844822
averErrorPerc = 9.929844994337172E-4
```

Figure 6-8 shows the chart of the testing results (actual function values versus the predicted function values) on the interval [3.141592654, 9.424777961].

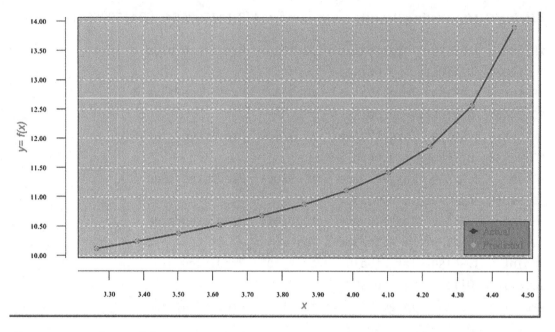

Figure 6-8. *Chart of the testing results*

Both actual and predicted charts practically overlap.

Summary

Again, the neural network is the universal function approximation mechanism. This means once you have approximated the function on some interval, you can then use such a trained neural network to predict the function values at any point within the training interval. However, you cannot use such a trained network for predicting the function values outside the training range. A neural network is not a function extrapolation mechanism.

The chapter explained how, for a certain class of functions (in this case, periodic functions), it is possible to get the predicted data outside of the training range. We continue exploring this concept in the next chapter.

CHAPTER 7

Processing Complex Periodic Functions

In this chapter, we continue discussing how to process periodic functions, concentrating on more complex periodic functions.

Example: Approximation of a Complex Periodic Function

Let's take a look at the function chart shown in Figure 7-1. The function represents some experimental data measured in days (x is the consecutive day of the experiment). This is a periodic function with a period equal to 50 days.

© Igor Livshin 2022
I. Livshin, *Artificial Neural Networks with Java*, https://doi.org/10.1007/978-1-4842-7368-5_7

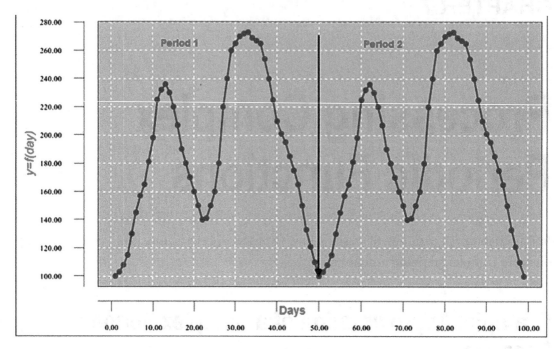

Figure 7-1. *Chart of the periodic function at two intervals, 1–50 and 51–100 days*

Table 7-1 shows the function values for two periods (1–50 and 51–100 days).

Table 7-1. *Function Values at Two Periods*

Day	Function Value (Period 1)	Day	Function Value (Period 2)
1	100	51	103
2	103	52	108
3	108	53	115
4	115	54	130
5	130	55	145
6	145	56	157
7	157	57	165
8	165	58	181
9	181	59	198
10	198	60	225

(continued)

Table 7-1. (*continued*)

Day	Function Value (Period 1)	Day	Function Value (Period 2)
11	225	61	232
12	232	62	236
13	236	63	230
14	230	64	220
15	220	65	207
16	207	66	190
17	190	67	180
18	180	68	170
19	170	69	160
20	160	70	150
21	150	71	140
22	140	72	141
23	141	73	150
24	150	74	160
25	160	75	180
26	180	76	220
27	220	77	240
28	240	78	260
29	260	79	265
30	265	80	270
31	270	81	272
32	272	82	273
33	273	83	269
34	269	84	267
35	267	85	265

(*continued*)

Table 7-1. *(continued)*

Day	Function Value (Period 1)	Day	Function Value (Period 2)
36	265	86	254
37	254	87	240
38	240	88	225
39	225	89	210
40	210	90	201
41	201	91	195
42	195	92	185
43	185	93	175
44	175	94	165
45	165	95	150
46	150	96	133
47	133	97	121
48	121	98	110
49	110	99	100
50	100	100	103

Data Preparation

We want to train the neural network using the function values at the first interval and then test the network by getting the network-predicted function values at the second interval. Similar to the previous example, to be able to determine the function approximation results outside of the training range, we will use the difference between xPoint values and the difference between the function values instead of the given xPoints and function values. However, in this example, we use the difference between xPoint values between the current and previous points as Field 1 and the difference between the function values between the next and current points as Field 2.

With these settings in the input file, we teach the network to learn that when the difference between the xPoint values is equal to some value a, then the difference in function values between the next day and the current day must be equal to some value b. That allows the network to predict the next-day function value by knowing the current-day (record) function value.

During the test, we calculate the function's next-day value in the following way. When at point x = 50, we want to calculate the predicted function value at the next point, x = 51. Feeding the difference between the xPoint values at the current and previous points (Field 1) to the trained network, we will get back the predicted difference between the function values at the next day and at the current day. Therefore, the predicted function value at the next point is equal to the sum of the actual function value at the current point and the predicted value difference obtained from the trained network.

However, this will not work for this example, simply because many parts of the chart may have the same difference and direction in function values between the current and previous days. It will confuse the neural network learning process when it tries to determine to which part of the chart such a point belongs (see Figure 7-2).

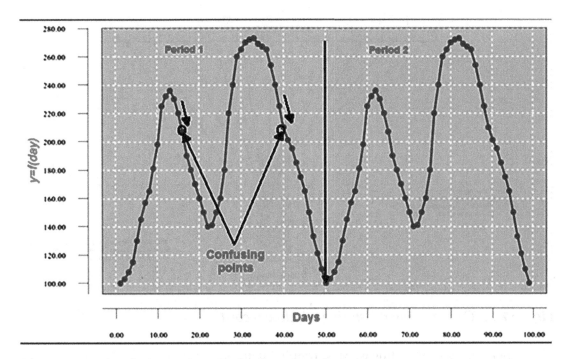

Figure 7-2. Confusing points on the function chart

Reflecting Function Topology in the Data

For this example, we need to use an additional trick. We are going to include the function topology in the data to help the network distinguish between confusing points. Specifically, our training file will use sliding windows as the input records. Each sliding window record includes the input function value differences (between the current and previous days) of the ten previous records. The target function value of the sliding window is the target function value difference (between the next and current days) of the original record number 11.

Essentially, by using such a record format, we teach the network to learn the following conditions. If the difference in function values for the ten previous records is equal to a1, a2, a3, a4, a5, a6, a7, a8, a9, and a10, then the difference in the next-day function value and the current-day function value should be equal to the target function value of the next record (record 11). Figure 7-3 shows a visual example of constructing a sliding window record.

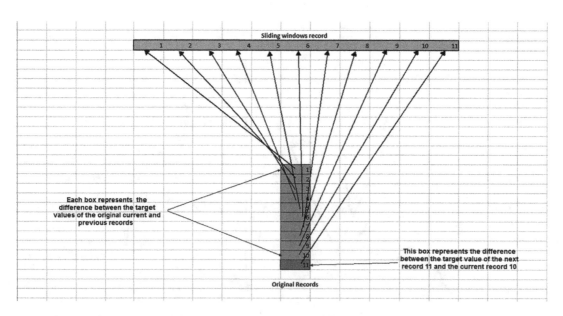

Figure 7-3. *Constructing the sliding window record*

Table 7-2 shows the sliding window training dataset.

Table 7-2. *Sliding Window Dataset on the Interval [1, 50]*

Sliding Windows										
-9	-6	-10	-10	-10	-15	-17	-12	-11	-10	3
-6	-10	-10	-10	-15	-17	-12	-11	-10	3	5
-10	-10	-10	-15	-17	-12	-11	-10	3	3	7
-10	-10	-15	-17	-12	-11	-10	3	3	7	15
-10	-15	-17	-12	-11	-10	3	3	7	15	15
-15	-17	-12	-11	-10	3	3	7	15	15	12
-17	-12	-11	-10	3	3	7	15	15	12	8
-12	-11	-10	3	3	7	15	15	12	8	16
-11	-10	3	3	7	15	15	12	8	16	17
-10	3	3	7	15	15	12	8	16	17	27
3	3	7	15	15	12	8	16	17	27	7
3	7	15	15	12	8	16	17	27	7	4
7	15	15	12	8	16	17	27	7	4	-6
15	15	12	8	16	17	27	7	4	-6	-10
15	12	8	16	17	27	7	4	-6	-10	-13
12	8	16	17	27	7	4	-6	-10	-13	-17
8	16	17	27	7	4	-6	-10	-13	-17	-10
16	17	27	7	4	-6	-10	-13	-17	-10	-10
17	27	7	4	-6	-10	-13	-17	-10	-10	-10
27	7	4	-6	-10	-13	-17	-10	-10	-10	-10
7	4	-6	-10	-13	-17	-10	-10	-10	-10	-10
4	-6	-10	-13	-17	-10	-10	-10	-10	-10	1
-6	-10	-13	-17	-10	-10	-10	-10	-10	1	9
-10	-13	-17	-10	-10	-10	-10	-10	1	9	10
-13	-17	-10	-10	-10	-10	-10	1	9	10	20
-17	-10	-10	-10	-10	-10	1	9	10	20	40

(continued)

Table 7-2. (*continued*)

				Sliding Windows						
-10	-10	-10	-10	-10	1	9	10	20	40	20
-10	-10	-10	-10	1	9	10	20	40	20	20
-10	-10	-10	1	9	10	20	40	20	20	5
-10	-10	1	9	10	20	40	20	20	5	5
-10	1	9	10	20	40	20	20	5	5	2
1	9	10	20	40	20	20	5	5	2	1
9	10	20	40	20	20	5	5	2	1	-4
10	20	40	20	20	5	5	2	1	-4	-2
20	40	20	20	5	5	2	1	-4	-2	-2
40	20	20	5	5	2	1	-4	-2	-2	-11
20	20	5	5	2	1	-4	-2	-2	-11	-14
20	5	5	2	1	-4	-2	-2	-11	-14	-15
5	5	2	1	-4	-2	-2	-11	-14	-15	-15
5	2	1	-4	-2	-2	-11	-14	-15	-15	-9
2	1	-4	-2	-2	-11	-14	-15	-15	-9	-6
1	-4	-2	-2	-11	-14	-15	-15	-9	-6	-10
-4	-2	-2	-11	-14	-15	-15	-9	-6	-10	-10
-2	-2	-11	-14	-15	-15	-9	-6	-10	-10	-10
-2	-11	-14	-15	-15	-9	-6	-10	-10	-10	-15
-11	-14	-15	-15	-9	-6	-10	-10	-10	-15	-17
-14	-15	-15	-9	-6	-10	-10	-10	-15	-17	-12
-15	-15	-9	-6	-10	-10	-10	-15	-17	-12	-11
-15	-9	-6	-10	-10	-10	-15	-17	-12	-11	-10
-9	-6	-10	-10	-10	-15	-17	-12	-11	-10	3

This dataset needs to be normalized on the interval [-1.1]. Table 7-3 shows the normalized dataset.

Table 7-3. *Normalized Training Dataset*

Normalized Sliding Windows										
-0.68571	-0.6	-0.71429	-0.71429	-0.85714	-0.91429	-0.77143	-0.74286	-0.71429	-0.34286	-0.34286
-0.6	-0.71429	-0.71429	-0.71429	-0.91429	-0.77143	-0.74286	-0.71429	-0.34286	-0.34286	-0.28571
-0.71429	-0.71429	-0.71429	-0.85714	-0.77143	-0.74286	-0.71429	-0.34286	-0.34286	-0.22857	-0.22857
-0.71429	-0.71429	-0.85714	-0.91429	-0.74286	-0.71429	-0.34286	-0.34286	-0.22857	0	0
-0.71429	-0.85714	-0.91429	-0.77143	-0.71429	-0.34286	-0.34286	-0.22857	0	0	0
-0.85714	-0.91429	-0.77143	-0.74286	-0.34286	-0.34286	-0.22857	0	0	-0.08571	-0.08571
-0.91429	-0.77143	-0.74286	-0.71429	-0.34286	-0.22857	0	0	-0.08571	-0.2	-0.2
-0.77143	-0.74286	-0.71429	-0.34286	-0.22857	0	0	-0.08571	-0.2	0.028571	0.028571
-0.74286	-0.71429	-0.34286	-0.34286	0	0	-0.08571	-0.2	0.028571	0.057143	0.057143
-0.71429	-0.34286	-0.34286	-0.22857	0	-0.08571	-0.2	0.028571	0.057143	0.342857	0.342857
-0.34286	-0.34286	-0.22857	0	-0.08571	-0.2	0.028571	0.057143	0.342857	-0.22857	-0.22857
-0.34286	-0.22857	0	0	-0.2	0.028571	0.057143	0.342857	-0.22857	-0.31429	-0.31429
-0.22857	0	0	-0.08571	0.028571	0.057143	0.342857	-0.22857	-0.31429	-0.6	-0.6
0	0	-0.08571	-0.2	0.057143	0.342857	-0.22857	-0.31429	-0.6	-0.71429	-0.71429
0	-0.08571	-0.2	0.028571	0.342857	-0.22857	-0.31429	-0.6	-0.71429	-0.8	-0.8
-0.08571	-0.2	0.028571	0.057143	-0.22857	-0.31429	-0.6	-0.71429	-0.8	-0.91429	-0.91429
-0.2	0.028571	0.057143	0.342857	-0.31429	-0.6	-0.71429	-0.8	-0.91429	-0.71429	-0.71429
0.028571	0.057143	0.342857	-0.22857	-0.6	-0.71429	-0.8	-0.91429	-0.71429	-0.71429	-0.71429

(continued)

Table 7-3. (continued)

Normalized Sliding Windows										
0.057143	0.342857	-0.22857	-0.31429	-0.6	-0.71429	-0.8	-0.91429	-0.71429	-0.71429	-0.71429
0.342857	-0.22857	-0.31429	-0.6	-0.71429	-0.8	-0.91429	-0.71429	-0.71429	-0.71429	-0.71429
-0.22857	-0.31429	-0.6	-0.71429	-0.8	-0.91429	-0.71429	-0.71429	-0.71429	-0.71429	-0.71429
-0.31429	-0.6	-0.71429	-0.8	-0.91429	-0.71429	-0.71429	-0.71429	-0.71429	-0.71429	-0.4
-0.6	-0.71429	-0.8	-0.91429	-0.71429	-0.71429	-0.71429	-0.71429	-0.71429	-0.4	-0.17143
-0.71429	-0.8	-0.91429	-0.71429	-0.71429	-0.71429	-0.71429	-0.71429	-0.4	-0.17143	-0.14286
-0.8	-0.91429	-0.71429	-0.71429	-0.71429	-0.71429	-0.71429	-0.4	-0.17143	-0.14286	0.142857
-0.91429	-0.71429	-0.71429	-0.71429	-0.71429	-0.71429	-0.4	-0.17143	-0.14286	0.142857	0.714286
-0.71429	-0.71429	-0.71429	-0.71429	-0.71429	-0.4	-0.17143	-0.14286	0.142857	0.714286	0.142857
-0.71429	-0.71429	-0.71429	-0.71429	-0.4	-0.17143	-0.14286	0.142857	0.714286	0.142857	0.142857
-0.71429	-0.71429	-0.71429	-0.4	-0.17143	-0.14286	0.142857	0.714286	0.142857	0.142857	-0.28571
-0.71429	-0.71429	-0.4	-0.17143	-0.14286	0.142857	0.714286	0.142857	0.142857	-0.28571	-0.28571
-0.71429	-0.4	-0.17143	-0.14286	0.142857	0.714286	0.142857	0.142857	-0.28571	-0.28571	-0.37143
-0.4	-0.17143	-0.14286	0.142857	0.714286	0.142857	0.142857	-0.28571	-0.28571	-0.37143	-0.4
-0.17143	-0.14286	0.142857	0.714286	0.142857	0.142857	-0.28571	-0.28571	-0.37143	-0.4	-0.54286
-0.14286	0.142857	0.714286	0.142857	0.142857	-0.28571	-0.28571	-0.37143	-0.4	-0.54286	-0.48571
0.142857	0.714286	0.142857	0.142857	-0.28571	-0.28571	-0.37143	-0.4	-0.54286	-0.48571	-0.48571
0.714286	0.142857	0.142857	-0.28571	-0.28571	-0.37143	-0.4	-0.54286	-0.48571	-0.48571	-0.74286

0.142857	0.142857	-0.28571	-0.28571	-0.37143	-0.4	-0.54286	-0.48571	-0.48571	-0.74286	-0.82857	-0.85714	-0.85714	-0.68571
0.142857	-0.28571	-0.28571	-0.37143	-0.4	-0.54286	-0.48571	-0.48571	-0.74286	-0.82857	-0.85714	-0.85714	-0.68571	-0.6
-0.28571	-0.28571	-0.37143	-0.4	-0.54286	-0.48571	-0.48571	-0.74286	-0.82857	-0.85714	-0.85714	-0.68571	-0.6	-0.71429
-0.28571	-0.37143	-0.4	-0.54286	-0.48571	-0.48571	-0.74286	-0.82857	-0.85714	-0.85714	-0.68571	-0.6	-0.71429	-0.71429
-0.37143	-0.4	-0.54286	-0.48571	-0.48571	-0.74286	-0.82857	-0.85714	-0.85714	-0.68571	-0.6	-0.71429	-0.71429	-0.71429
-0.4	-0.54286	-0.48571	-0.48571	-0.74286	-0.82857	-0.85714	-0.85714	-0.68571	-0.6	-0.71429	-0.71429	-0.71429	-0.85714
-0.54286	-0.48571	-0.48571	-0.74286	-0.82857	-0.85714	-0.85714	-0.68571	-0.6	-0.71429	-0.71429	-0.71429	-0.85714	-0.91429
-0.48571	-0.48571	-0.74286	-0.82857	-0.85714	-0.85714	-0.68571	-0.6	-0.71429	-0.71429	-0.71429	-0.85714	-0.91429	-0.77143
-0.48571	-0.74286	-0.82857	-0.85714	-0.85714	-0.68571	-0.6	-0.71429	-0.71429	-0.71429	-0.85714	-0.91429	-0.77143	-0.74286
-0.74286	-0.82857	-0.85714	-0.85714	-0.68571	-0.6	-0.71429	-0.71429	-0.71429	-0.85714	-0.91429	-0.77143	-0.74286	-0.71429
-0.82857	-0.85714	-0.85714	-0.68571	-0.6	-0.71429	-0.71429	-0.71429	-0.85714	-0.91429	-0.77143	-0.74286	-0.71429	-0.34286

Network Architecture

We will use the network shown in Figure 7-4 that consists of the input layer (holding 10 neurons), 4 hidden layers (each holding 13 neurons), and the output layer (holding a single neuron).

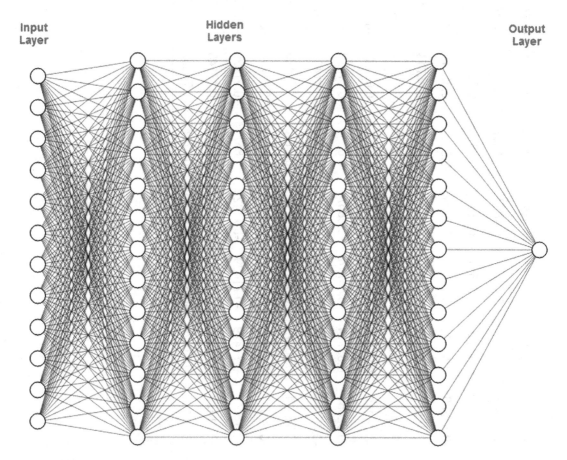

Figure 7-4. *Network architecture*

Each record in the sliding window training dataset contains ten input fields and one output field. We are ready to develop the neural network processing program.

Program Code

Listing 7-1 shows the program code.

Listing 7-1. Program Code

```
//========================================================================
//  Approximation of the complex periodic function. The input is training
//  or testing file with the records built as sliding windows. Each sliding
//  window record contains 11 fields.
//  The first 10 fields are the field1 values from the original 10 records
//     plus the field2 value from the next record, which is actually the
//  difference between the target values of the next original record
//  (record 11) and record 10.
//========================================================================

package sample4;

import java.io.BufferedReader;
import java.io.File;
import java.io.FileInputStream;
import java.io.PrintWriter;
import java.io.FileNotFoundException;
import java.io.FileReader;
import java.io.FileWriter;
import java.io.IOException;
import java.io.InputStream;
import java.nio.file.*;
import java.util.Properties;
import java.time.YearMonth;
import java.awt.Color;
import java.awt.Font;
import java.io.BufferedReader;
import java.text.DateFormat;
import java.text.ParseException;
import java.text.SimpleDateFormat;
import java.time.LocalDate;
import java.time.Month;
```

```java
import java.time.ZoneId;
import java.util.ArrayList;
import java.util.Calendar;
import java.util.Date;
import java.util.List;
import java.util.Locale;
import java.util.Properties;

import org.encog.Encog;
import org.encog.engine.network.activation.ActivationTANH;
import org.encog.engine.network.activation.ActivationReLU;
import org.encog.ml.data.MLData;
import org.encog.ml.data.MLDataPair;
import org.encog.ml.data.MLDataSet;
import org.encog.ml.data.buffer.MemoryDataLoader;
import org.encog.ml.data.buffer.codec.CSVDataCODEC;
import org.encog.ml.data.buffer.codec.DataSetCODEC;
import org.encog.neural.networks.BasicNetwork;
import org.encog.neural.networks.layers.BasicLayer;
import org.encog.neural.networks.training.propagation.resilient.
ResilientPropagation;
import org.encog.persist.EncogDirectoryPersistence;
import org.encog.util.csv.CSVFormat;

import org.knowm.xchart.SwingWrapper;
import org.knowm.xchart.XYChart;
import org.knowm.xchart.XYChartBuilder;
import org.knowm.xchart.XYSeries;
import org.knowm.xchart.demo.charts.ExampleChart;
import org.knowm.xchart.style.Styler.LegendPosition;
import org.knowm.xchart.style.colors.ChartColor;
import org.knowm.xchart.style.colors.XChartSeriesColors;
import org.knowm.xchart.style.lines.SeriesLines;
import org.knowm.xchart.style.markers.SeriesMarkers;
import org.knowm.xchart.BitmapEncoder;
import org.knowm.xchart.BitmapEncoder.BitmapFormat;
import org.knowm.xchart.QuickChart;
```

```java
import org.knowm.xchart.SwingWrapper;

public class Sample4 implements ExampleChart<XYChart>
{

    static double doublePointNumber = 0.00;
    static int intPointNumber = 0;
    static InputStream input = null;
    static double[] arrFunctionValue = new double[500];
    static double inputDiffValue = 0.00;
    static double targetDiffValue = 0.00;
    static double predictDiffValue = 0.00;
    static double valueDifferencePerc = 0.00;
    static String strFunctionValuesFileName;
    static int returnCode  = 0;
    static int numberOfInputNeurons;
    static int numberOfOutputNeurons;
    static int numberOfRecordsInFile;
    static int intNumberOfRecordsInTestFile;
    static double realTargetDiffValue;
    static double realPredictDiffValue;
    static String functionValuesTrainFileName;
    static String functionValuesTestFileName;
    static String trainFileName;
    static String priceFileName;
    static String testFileName;
    static String chartTrainFileName;
    static String chartTestFileName;
    static String networkFileName;
    static int workingMode;
    static String cvsSplitBy = ",";

    // De-normalization parameters
    static double Nh =  1;
    static double Nl = -1;

    static double Dh = 50.00;
    static double Dl = -20.00;
```

```java
    static String inputtargetFileName;
    static double lastFunctionValueForTraining = 0.00;
    static int tempIndexField;
    static double tempTargetField;
    static  int[] arrIndex = new int[100];
    static double[] arrTarget = new double[100];
    static List<Double> xData = new ArrayList<Double>();
    static List<Double> yData1 = new ArrayList<Double>();
    static List<Double> yData2 = new ArrayList<Double>();

    static XYChart Chart;

@Override
public XYChart getChart()
  {

  // Create Chart

  Chart = new  XYChartBuilder().width(900).height(500).title(getClass().
           getSimpleName()).xAxisTitle("Days").yAxisTitle("y= f(x)").build();

  // Customize Chart
  Chart.getStyler().setPlotBackgroundColor(ChartColor.
  getAWTColor(ChartColor.GREY));
  Chart.getStyler().setPlotGridLinesColor(new Color(255, 255, 255));
  Chart.getStyler().setChartBackgroundColor(Color.WHITE);
  Chart.getStyler().setLegendBackgroundColor(Color.PINK);
  Chart.getStyler().setChartFontColor(Color.MAGENTA);
  Chart.getStyler().setChartTitleBoxBackgroundColor(new Color(0, 222, 0));
  Chart.getStyler().setChartTitleBoxVisible(true);
  Chart.getStyler().setChartTitleBoxBorderColor(Color.BLACK);
  Chart.getStyler().setPlotGridLinesVisible(true);
  Chart.getStyler().setAxisTickPadding(20);
  Chart.getStyler().setAxisTickMarkLength(15);
  Chart.getStyler().setPlotMargin(20);
  Chart.getStyler().setChartTitleVisible(false);
  Chart.getStyler().setChartTitleFont(new Font(Font.MONOSPACED,
  Font.BOLD, 24));
```

```
Chart.getStyler().setLegendFont(new Font(Font.SERIF, Font.PLAIN, 18));
Chart.getStyler().setLegendPosition(LegendPosition.OutsideS);
Chart.getStyler().setLegendSeriesLineLength(12);
Chart.getStyler().setAxisTitleFont(new Font(Font.SANS_SERIF,
Font.ITALIC, 18));
Chart.getStyler().setAxisTickLabelsFont(new Font(Font.SERIF, Font.
PLAIN, 11));
Chart.getStyler().setDatePattern("yyyy-MM");
Chart.getStyler().setDecimalPattern("#0.00");

// Interval to normalize
double Nh =  1;
double Nl = -1;

// Values in the sliding windows
double Dh = 50.00;
double Dl = -20.00;

try
   {
      // Configuration

      //-----------------------------------------------------------
      // Train (using the train file contains all 1000 records)
      //-----------------------------------------------------------
      workingMode = 1;
      trainFileName = "C:/Book_Examples/Sample4_Norm_Train_Sliding_
      Windows_File.csv";
      functionValuesTrainFileName = "C:/Book_Examples/Sample4_Function_
      values_Period_1.csv";
      chartTrainFileName = "XYLine_Sample4_Train_Chart";
      numberOfRecordsInFile = 51;

      //-----------------------------------------------------------
      // Test the trained network at non-trained points
      //-----------------------------------------------------------
      // workingMode = 2;
```

```
// trainFileName = "C:/Book_Examples/Sample4_Norm_Train_Sliding_
   Windows_File.csv";
// functionValuesTrainFileName = "C:/Book_Examples/Sample4_
   Function_values_Period_1.csv";
// chartTestFileName = "XYLine_Sample4_Test_Chart";
// numberOfRecordsInFile = 51;
// lastFunctionValueForTraining = 100.00;

//------------------------------------------------------------
// Common configuration
//------------------------------------------------------------
networkFileName = "C:/Book_Examples/Example4_Saved_Network_
File.csv";
inputtargetFileName   = "C:/Book_Examples/Sample4_Input_File.csv";
numberOfInputNeurons  = 10;
numberOfOutputNeurons = 1;

// Check the working mode to run

// Training mode. Train, validate, and save the trained network file
if(workingMode == 1)
 {

   // Load function values for training file in memory
   loadFunctionValueTrainFileInMemory();

    File file1 = new File(chartTrainFileName);
    File file2 = new File(networkFileName);

    if(file1.exists())
      file1.delete();

    if(file2.exists())
      file2.delete();

    returnCode = 0;    // Clear the error Code

    do
     {
        returnCode = trainValidateSaveNetwork();
```

```
          } while (returnCode > 0);


       }    // End the train logic


     else
      {
        // Test mode. Test the approximation at the points where
        // neural network was not trained

        // Load function values for training file in memory
        loadInputTargetFileInMemory();

        //loadFunctionValueTrainFileInMemory();

        File file1 = new File(chartTestFileName);

        if(file1.exists())
          file1.delete();

        loadAndTestNetwork();

      }

   }
 catch (NumberFormatException e)
  {
      System.err.println("Problem parsing workingMode. workingMode = "
      + workingMode);
      System.exit(1);
   }
 catch (Throwable t)
   {
     t.printStackTrace();
     System.exit(1);
   }
  finally
   {
      Encog.getInstance().shutdown();
   }
```

```
  Encog.getInstance().shutdown();

  return Chart;

} // End of the method


// ===================================================
// Load CSV to memory.
// @return The loaded dataset.
// ===================================================
public static MLDataSet loadCSV2Memory(String filename, int input,
int ideal, boolean headers, CSVFormat
    format, boolean significance)
  {
    DataSetCODEC codec = new CSVDataCODEC(new File(filename), format,
    headers, input, ideal,
        significance);
    MemoryDataLoader load = new MemoryDataLoader(codec);
    MLDataSet dataset = load.external2Memory();
    return dataset;
  }

// ========================================================
//  The main method.
//  @param Command line arguments. No arguments are used.
// ========================================================
public static void main(String[] args)
 {
   ExampleChart<XYChart> exampleChart = new Sample4();
   XYChart Chart = exampleChart.getChart();
   new SwingWrapper<XYChart>(Chart).displayChart();
 } // End of the main method

//========================================================
// This method trains, Validates, and saves the trained network file
//========================================================
static public int trainValidateSaveNetwork()
```

```
{
  double functionValue = 0.00;
  double denormInputValueDiff = 0.00;
  double denormTargetValueDiff = 0.00;
  double denormTargetValueDiff_02 = 0.00;
  double denormPredictValueDiff = 0.00;
  double denormPredictValueDiff_02 = 0.00;

  // Load the training CSV file in memory
  MLDataSet trainingSet =
    loadCSV2Memory(trainFileName,numberOfInputNeurons,
    numberOfOutputNeurons,
      true,CSVFormat.ENGLISH,false);

  // create a neural network
  BasicNetwork network = new BasicNetwork();

  // Input layer
  network.addLayer(new BasicLayer(null,true,10));

  // Hidden layer
  network.addLayer(new BasicLayer(new ActivationTANH(),true,13));
  network.addLayer(new BasicLayer(new ActivationTANH(),true,13));
  network.addLayer(new BasicLayer(new ActivationTANH(),true,13));
  network.addLayer(new BasicLayer(new ActivationTANH(),true,13));

  // Output layer
  network.addLayer(new BasicLayer(new ActivationTANH(),false,1));

  network.getStructure().finalizeStructure();
  network.reset();

  // train the neural network
  final ResilientPropagation train = new ResilientPropagation(network,
  trainingSet);

  int epoch = 1;
  returnCode = 0;

  do
```

```
     {
          train.iteration();
          System.out.println("Epoch #" + epoch + " Error:" + train.
          getError());

     epoch++;

     if (epoch >= 11000 && network.calculateError(trainingSet) >
     0.00000119)
          {
          returnCode = 1;

          System.out.println("Error = " + network.
          calculateError(trainingSet));
          System.out.println("Try again");
          return returnCode;
          }

  } while(train.getError() > 0.000001187);

// Save the network file
EncogDirectoryPersistence.saveObject(new File(networkFileName),network);

double sumGlobalDifferencePerc = 0.00;
double sumGlobalDifferencePerc_02 = 0.00;

double averGlobalDifferencePerc = 0.00;
double maxGlobalDifferencePerc = 0.00;
double maxGlobalDifferencePerc_02 = 0.00;

int m = 0; // Record number in the input file
double xPoint_Initial = 1.00;
double xPoint_Increment = 1.00;
double xPoint = xPoint_Initial - xPoint_Increment;

realTargetDiffValue = 0.00;
realPredictDiffValue = 0.00;
```

```
for(MLDataPair pair: trainingSet)
  {
      m++;
      xPoint = xPoint + xPoint_Increment;

      if(xPoint >  50.00)
         break;

       final MLData output = network.compute(pair.getInput());

       MLData inputData = pair.getInput();
       MLData actualData = pair.getIdeal();
       MLData predictData = network.compute(inputData);

       inputDiffValue = inputData.getData(0);
       targetDiffValue = actualData.getData(0);
       predictDiffValue = predictData.getData(0);

       // De-normalize the values
       denormInputValueDiff     =((Dl - Dh)*inputDiffValue - Nh*Dl +
       Dh*Nl)/(Nl - Nh);
       denormTargetValueDiff = ((Dl - Dh)*targetDiffValue - Nh*Dl +
       Dh*Nl)/(Nl - Nh);
       denormPredictValueDiff =((Dl - Dh)*predictDiffValue - Nh*Dl +
       Dh*Nl)/(Nl - Nh);

       functionValue = arrFunctionValue[m-1];

       realTargetDiffValue = functionValue + denormTargetValueDiff;
       realPredictDiffValue = functionValue + denormPredictValueDiff;

       valueDifferencePerc =
         Math.abs(((realTargetDiffValue - realPredictDiffValue)/
         realPredictDiffValue)*100.00);

       System.out.println ("xPoint = " + xPoint +
       "  realTargetDiffValue = " + realTargetDiffValue +
         "  realPredictDiffValue = " + realPredictDiffValue);
```

189

```
                sumGlobalDifferencePerc = sumGlobalDifferencePerc +
                valueDifferencePerc;

                if (valueDifferencePerc > maxGlobalDifferencePerc)
                  maxGlobalDifferencePerc = valueDifferencePerc;

                xData.add(xPoint);
                yData1.add(realTargetDiffValue);
                yData2.add(realPredictDiffValue);

        }    // End for pair loop

        XYSeries series1 = Chart.addSeries("Actual data", xData, yData1);
        XYSeries series2 = Chart.addSeries("Predict data", xData, yData2);

        series1.setLineColor(XChartSeriesColors.BLUE);
        series2.setMarkerColor(Color.ORANGE);
        series1.setLineStyle(SeriesLines.SOLID);
        series2.setLineStyle(SeriesLines.SOLID);

        try
         {
            //Save the chart image
            BitmapEncoder.saveBitmapWithDPI(Chart, chartTrainFileName,
            BitmapFormat.JPG, 100);
            System.out.println ("Train Chart file has been saved") ;
         }
        catch (IOException ex)
         {
          ex.printStackTrace();
          System.exit(3);
         }

        // Finally, save this trained network
        EncogDirectoryPersistence.saveObject(new File(networkFileName),
        network);
        System.out.println ("Train Network has been saved") ;
```

```
    averGlobalDifferencePerc  = sumGlobalDifferencePerc/
    numberOfRecordsInFile;

    System.out.println(" ");
    System.out.println("maxGlobalDifferencePerc = " +
    maxGlobalDifferencePerc +
            "averGlobalDifferencePerc = " + averGlobalDifferencePerc);

    returnCode = 0;

    return returnCode;

}    // End of the method

//==========================================================
// Testing Method
//==========================================================
static public void loadAndTestNetwork()
 {
  System.out.println("Testing the networks results");

  List<Double> xData = new ArrayList<Double>();
  List<Double> yData1 = new ArrayList<Double>();
  List<Double> yData2 = new ArrayList<Double>();

  int intStartingPriceIndexForBatch = 0;
  int intStartingDatesIndexForBatch = 0;
 double sumGlobalDifferencePerc = 0.00;
  double maxGlobalDifferencePerc = 0.00;
  double averGlobalDifferencePerc = 0.00;
  double targetToPredictPercent = 0;
  double maxGlobalResultDiff = 0.00;
  double averGlobalResultDiff = 0.00;
  double sumGlobalResultDiff = 0.00;
  double maxGlobalInputPrice = 0.00;
  double sumGlobalInputPrice = 0.00;
  double averGlobalInputPrice = 0.00;
  double maxGlobalIndex = 0;
  double inputDiffValueFromRecord = 0.00;
```

```
double targetDiffValueFromRecord = 0.00;
double predictDiffValueFromRecord = 0.00;
double denormInputValueDiff    = 0.00;
double denormTargetValueDiff = 0.00;
double denormTargetValueDiff_02 = 0.00;
double denormPredictValueDiff = 0.00;
double denormPredictValueDiff_02 = 0.00;
double normTargetPriceDiff;
double normPredictPriceDiff;
String tempLine;
String[] tempWorkFields;
double tempInputXPointValueFromRecord = 0.0;
double tempTargetXPointValueFromRecord = 0.00;
double tempValueDiffence = 0.00;
double functionValue;
double minXPointValue = 0.00;
double minTargetXPointValue = 0.00;
int tempMinIndex = 0;
double rTempTargetXPointValue = 0.00;
double rTempPriceDiffPercKey = 0.00;
double rTempPriceDiff = 0.00;
double rTempSumDiff = 0.00;
double r1 = 0.00;
double r2 = 0.00;

BufferedReader br4;
BasicNetwork network;

 int k1 = 0;

// Process testing records
maxGlobalDifferencePerc  = 0.00;
averGlobalDifferencePerc = 0.00;
sumGlobalDifferencePerc = 0.00;
```

```
realTargetDiffValue = 0.00;
realPredictDiffValue = 0.00;

// Load the training dataset into memory
MLDataSet trainingSet =
    loadCSV2Memory(trainFileName,numberOfInputNeurons,numberOfOutput
    Neurons,true,
        CSVFormat.ENGLISH,false);

// Load the saved trained network
network =
  (BasicNetwork)EncogDirectoryPersistence.loadObject(new
  File(networkFileName));

int m = 0;   // Index of the current record

// Record number in the input file
double xPoint_Initial = 51.00;
double xPoint_Increment = 1.00;
double xPoint = xPoint_Initial - xPoint_Increment;

for (MLDataPair pair:  trainingSet)
 {
   m++;
   xPoint = xPoint + xPoint_Increment;

   final MLData output = network.compute(pair.getInput());

   MLData inputData = pair.getInput();
   MLData actualData = pair.getIdeal();
   MLData predictData = network.compute(inputData);

   // Calculate and print the results
   inputDiffValue = inputData.getData(0);
   targetDiffValue = actualData.getData(0);
   predictDiffValue = predictData.getData(0);

   if(m == 1)
     functionValue = lastFunctionValueForTraining;
   else
```

```
        functionValue = realPredictDiffValue;

        // De-normalize the values
        denormInputValueDiff       =((Dl - Dh)*inputDiffValue - Nh*Dl +
        Dh*Nl)/(Nl - Nh);
        denormTargetValueDiff = ((Dl - Dh)*targetDiffValue - Nh*Dl +
        Dh*Nl)/(Nl - Nh);
        denormPredictValueDiff =((Dl - Dh)*predictDiffValue - Nh*Dl +
        Dh*Nl)/(Nl - Nh);

        realTargetDiffValue = functionValue +  denormTargetValueDiff;
        realPredictDiffValue = functionValue + denormPredictValueDiff;

        valueDifferencePerc =
              Math.abs(((realTargetDiffValue - realPredictDiffValue)/
              realPredictDiffValue)*100.00);

        System.out.println ("xPoint = " + xPoint + "  realTargetDiffValue =
        " + realTargetDiffValue +
            "  realPredictDiffValue = " + realPredictDiffValue);

        sumGlobalDifferencePerc = sumGlobalDifferencePerc +
        valueDifferencePerc;

        if (valueDifferencePerc > maxGlobalDifferencePerc)
          maxGlobalDifferencePerc = valueDifferencePerc;

        xData.add(xPoint);
        yData1.add(realTargetDiffValue);
        yData2.add(realPredictDiffValue);

      }  // End for pair loop

    // Print the max and average results

    System.out.println(" ");
    averGlobalDifferencePerc = sumGlobalDifferencePerc/
    numberOfRecordsInFile;

    System.out.println("maxGlobalResultDiff = " +
    maxGlobalDifferencePerc);
```

```java
    System.out.println("averGlobalResultDiff = " +
    averGlobalDifferencePerc);

    // All testing batch files have been processed
    XYSeries series1 = Chart.addSeries("Actual", xData, yData1);
    XYSeries series2 = Chart.addSeries("Predicted", xData, yData2);

    series1.setLineColor(XChartSeriesColors.BLUE);
    series2.setMarkerColor(Color.ORANGE);
    series1.setLineStyle(SeriesLines.SOLID);
    series2.setLineStyle(SeriesLines.SOLID);

    // Save the chart image
    try
     {
       BitmapEncoder.saveBitmapWithDPI(Chart, chartTestFileName ,
       BitmapFormat.JPG, 100);
     }
    catch (Exception bt)
     {
       bt.printStackTrace();
     }

    System.out.println ("The Chart has been saved");

    System.out.println("End of testing for test records");
   } // End of the method
//-----------------------------------------------------------------------
// Load Function values for training file in memory
//-----------------------------------------------------------------------
public static void loadFunctionValueTrainFileInMemory()
 {
    BufferedReader br1 = null;

    String line = "";
    String cvsSplitBy = ",";
    String tempXPointValue = "";
```

```java
    double tempYFunctionValue = 0.00;

  try
    {
       br1 = new BufferedReader(new FileReader(functionValuesTrain
       FileName));

       int i = -1;
       int r = -2;

       while ((line = br1.readLine()) != null)
        {
           i++;
           r++;

          // Skip the header line
          if(i > 0)
            {
              // Brake the line using comma as separator
              String[] workFields = line.split(cvsSplitBy);

              tempYFunctionValue = Double.parseDouble(workFields[0]);
              arrFunctionValue[r] = tempYFunctionValue;

              //System.out.println("arrFunctionValue[r] = " +
              arrFunctionValue[r]);
            }
        } // end of the while loop

       br1.close();

    }
  catch (IOException ex)
    {
       ex.printStackTrace();
       System.err.println("Error opening files = " + ex);
       System.exit(1);
```

```java
        }

    }

//============================================
// Load Sample4_Input_File into 2 arrays in memory
//============================================
 public static void loadInputTargetFileInMemory()
    {
        BufferedReader br1 = null;

        String line = "";
        String cvsSplitBy = ",";
        String tempXPointValue = "";
        double tempYFunctionValue = 0.00;

         try
           {
             br1 = new BufferedReader(new FileReader(inputtargetFileName));

            int i = -1;
            int r = -2;

            while ((line = br1.readLine()) != null)
             {
               i++;
               r++;

              // Skip the header line
              if(i > 0)
                {
                   // Brake the line using comma as separator
                   String[] workFields = line.split(cvsSplitBy);

                   tempTargetField = Double.parseDouble(workFields[1]);

                   arrIndex[r] =  r;
```

```
                    arrTarget[r] = tempTargetField;
                 }

        }   // end of the while loop

         br1.close();

        }
      catch (IOException ex)
        {
          ex.printStackTrace();
          System.err.println("Error opening files = " + ex);
          System.exit(1);
        }

     }

} // End of the class
```

As always, we load the training file in memory and build the network. The built network has the input layer with 10 neurons, 4 hidden layers (each with 13 neurons), and the output layer with a single neuron. Once the network is built, we train the network by looping over the epochs until the network error clears the error limit. Finally, we save the trained network on disk (it will be used later by the testing method).

Notice that we call the training method in a loop (as we did in the previous example). When after 11,000 iterations the network error is still not less than the error limit, we exit the training method with the return code 1. That will trigger calling the training method again with the new set of weight/bias parameters (Listing 7-2).

Listing 7-2. Code Fragment at the Beginning of the Training Method

```
// Load the training CSV file in memory
MLDataSet trainingSet =
    loadCSV2Memory(trainFileName,numberOfInputNeurons,
    numberOfOutputNeurons,
       true,CSVFormat.ENGLISH,false);

// Create a neural network
 BasicNetwork network = new BasicNetwork();
```

```
// Input layer
network.addLayer(new BasicLayer(null,true,10));

// Hidden layer
network.addLayer(new BasicLayer(new ActivationTANH(),true,13));
network.addLayer(new BasicLayer(new ActivationTANH(),true,13));
network.addLayer(new BasicLayer(new ActivationTANH(),true,13));
network.addLayer(new BasicLayer(new ActivationTANH(),true,13));

// Output layer
network.addLayer(new BasicLayer(new ActivationTANH(),false,1));

network.getStructure().finalizeStructure();
network.reset();

// train the neural network
final ResilientPropagation train = new ResilientPropagation(network,
trainingSet);

int epoch = 1;
returnCode = 0;

do
    {
        train.iteration();
        System.out.println("Epoch #" + epoch + " Error:" + train.
        getError());

        epoch++;

        if (epoch >= 11000 && network.calculateError(trainingSet) >
        0.00000119)
          {
              // Exit the training method with the return code = 1

              returnCode = 1;
              System.out.println("Try again");
               return returnCode;
          }
    }
```

```
    } while(train.getError() > 0.000001187);
```

```
    // Save the network file
```

```
    EncogDirectoryPersistence.saveObject(new File(networkFileName),
    network);
```

Next, we loop over the pair dataset, getting from the network the input, actual, and predicted values for each record. The record values are normalized, so we denormalize their values. The following formula is used for denormalization:

$$f(x) = ((D_L - D_H)*x - N_H* D_L + N_L* D_H) /(N_L - N_H)$$

Here,

x = Input data point

D_L = Min (lowest) value of x in the input dataset

D_H = Max (highest) value of x in the input dataset

N_L = The left part of the normalized interval [-1, 1] = -1

N_H = The right part of the normalized interval [-1, 1] = 1

After denormalization, we calculate the realTargetDiffValue and realPredictDiffValue fields, print their values in the processing log, and populate the chart data for the current record. Finally, we save the chart file on disk and exit the training method with return code 0 (Listing 7-3).

Listing 7-3. Code Fragment at the End of the Training Method

```
int m = 0;
double xPoint_Initial = 1.00;
double xPoint_Increment = 1.00;
double xPoint = xPoint_Initial - xPoint_Increment;
realTargetDiffValue = 0.00;
realPredictDiffValue = 0.00;

for(MLDataPair pair: trainingSet)
    {
            m++;
            xPoint = xPoint + xPoint_Increment;

             final MLData output = network.compute(pair.getInput());
```

```
MLData inputData = pair.getInput();
MLData actualData = pair.getIdeal();
MLData predictData = network.compute(inputData);

// Calculate and print the results
inputDiffValue = inputData.getData(0);
targetDiffValue = actualData.getData(0);
predictDiffValue = predictData.getData(0);

// De-normalize the values
denormInputValueDiff    =((Dl - Dh)*inputDiffValue - Nh*Dl +
Dh*Nl)/(Nl - Nh);
denormTargetValueDiff = ((Dl - Dh)*targetDiffValue - Nh*Dl +
Dh*Nl)/(Nl - Nh);
denormPredictValueDiff =((Dl - Dh)*predictDiffValue - Nh*Dl +
Dh*Nl)/(Nl - Nh);

functionValue = arrFunctionValue[m-1];

realTargetDiffValue = functionValue + denormTargetValueDiff;
realPredictDiffValue = functionValue + denormPredictValueDiff;

valueDifferencePerc =
  Math.abs(((realTargetDiffValue - realPredictDiffValue)/
  realPredictDiffValue)*100.00);

System.out.println ("xPoint = " + xPoint +
"  realTargetDiffValue = " + realTargetDiffValue +
  "  realPredictDiffValue = " + realPredictDiffValue);

sumDifferencePerc = sumDifferencePerc + valueDifferencePerc;

if (valueDifferencePerc > maxDifferencePerc)
  maxDifferencePerc = valueDifferencePerc;

xData.add(xPoint);
yData1.add(realTargetDiffValue);
yData2.add(realPredictDiffValue);

}   // End for pair loop
```

```java
      XYSeries series1 = Chart.addSeries("Actual data", xData, yData1);
      XYSeries series2 = Chart.addSeries("Predict data", xData, yData2);

      series1.setLineColor(XChartSeriesColors.BLUE);
      series2.setMarkerColor(Color.ORANGE);
      series1.setLineStyle(SeriesLines.SOLID);
      series2.setLineStyle(SeriesLines.SOLID);

      try
       {
         //Save the chart image
         BitmapEncoder.saveBitmapWithDPI(Chart, chartTrainFileName,
         BitmapFormat.JPG, 100);
         System.out.println ("Train Chart file has been saved") ;
       }
    catch (IOException ex)
     {
      ex.printStackTrace();
      System.exit(3);
     }

      // Finally, save this trained network
      EncogDirectoryPersistence.saveObject(new File(networkFileName),
      network);
      System.out.println ("Train Network has been saved") ;

      averNormDifferencePerc  = sumDifferencePerc/numberOfRecordsInFile;

      System.out.println(" ");
      System.out.println("maxDifferencePerc = " + maxDifferencePerc +
      "  averNormDifferencePerc = " +
         averNormDifferencePerc);

      returnCode = 0;
      return returnCode;

}   // End of the method
```

So far, the processing logic of the training method is about the same as in the previous examples, disregarding that the format of the training dataset is different and includes sliding window records. We will see a substantial change in the logic of the testing method.

Training the Network

Listing 7-4 shows the training processing results.

Listing 7-4. Training Results

```
xPoint =  1.0  TargetDiff = 102.99999  PredictDiff = 102.98510
xPoint =  2.0  TargetDiff = 107.99999  PredictDiff = 107.99950
xPoint =  3.0  TargetDiff = 114.99999  PredictDiff = 114.99861
xPoint =  4.0  TargetDiff = 130.0      PredictDiff = 130.00147
xPoint =  5.0  TargetDiff = 145.0      PredictDiff = 144.99901
xPoint =  6.0  TargetDiff = 156.99999  PredictDiff = 157.00011
xPoint =  7.0  TargetDiff = 165.0      PredictDiff = 164.99849
xPoint =  8.0  TargetDiff = 181.00000  PredictDiff = 181.00009
xPoint =  9.0  TargetDiff = 197.99999  PredictDiff = 197.99984
xPoint = 10.0  TargetDiff = 225.00000  PredictDiff = 224.99914
xPoint = 11.0  TargetDiff = 231.99999  PredictDiff = 231.99987
xPoint = 12.0  TargetDiff = 236.00000  PredictDiff = 235.99949
xPoint = 13.0  TargetDiff = 230.0      PredictDiff = 230.00122
xPoint = 14.0  TargetDiff = 220.00000  PredictDiff = 219.99767
xPoint = 15.0  TargetDiff = 207.0      PredictDiff = 206.99951
xPoint = 16.0  TargetDiff = 190.00000  PredictDiff = 190.00221
xPoint = 17.0  TargetDiff = 180.00000  PredictDiff = 180.00009
xPoint = 18.0  TargetDiff = 170.00000  PredictDiff = 169.99977
xPoint = 19.0  TargetDiff = 160.00000  PredictDiff = 159.98978
xPoint = 20.0  TargetDiff = 150.00000  PredictDiff = 150.07543
xPoint = 21.0  TargetDiff = 140.00000  PredictDiff = 139.89404
xPoint = 22.0  TargetDiff = 141.0      PredictDiff = 140.99714
xPoint = 23.0  TargetDiff = 150.00000  PredictDiff = 149.99875
xPoint = 24.0  TargetDiff = 159.99999  PredictDiff = 159.99929
xPoint = 25.0  TargetDiff = 180.00000  PredictDiff = 179.99896
```

```
xPoint = 26.0  TargetDiff = 219.99999  PredictDiff = 219.99909
xPoint = 27.0  TargetDiff = 240.00000  PredictDiff = 240.00141
xPoint = 28.0  TargetDiff = 260.00000  PredictDiff = 259.99865
xPoint = 29.0  TargetDiff = 264.99999  PredictDiff = 264.99938
xPoint = 30.0  TargetDiff = 269.99999  PredictDiff = 270.00068
xPoint = 31.0  TargetDiff = 272.00000  PredictDiff = 271.99931
xPoint = 32.0  TargetDiff = 273.0      PredictDiff = 272.99969
xPoint = 33.0  TargetDiff = 268.99999  PredictDiff = 268.99975
xPoint = 34.0  TargetDiff = 266.99999  PredictDiff = 266.99994
xPoint = 35.0  TargetDiff = 264.99999  PredictDiff = 264.99742
xPoint = 36.0  TargetDiff = 253.99999  PredictDiff = 254.00076
xPoint = 37.0  TargetDiff = 239.99999  PredictDiff = 240.02203
xPoint = 38.0  TargetDiff = 225.00000  PredictDiff = 225.00479
xPoint = 39.0  TargetDiff = 210.00000  PredictDiff = 210.03944
xPoint = 40.0  TargetDiff = 200.99999  PredictDiff = 200.86493
xPoint = 41.0  TargetDiff = 195.0      PredictDiff = 195.11291
xPoint = 42.0  TargetDiff = 185.00000  PredictDiff = 184.91010
xPoint = 43.0  TargetDiff = 175.00000  PredictDiff = 175.02804
xPoint = 44.0  TargetDiff = 165.00000  PredictDiff = 165.07052
xPoint = 45.0  TargetDiff = 150.00000  PredictDiff = 150.01101
xPoint = 46.0  TargetDiff = 133.00000  PredictDiff = 132.91352
xPoint = 47.0  TargetDiff = 121.00000  PredictDiff = 121.00125
xPoint = 48.0  TargetDiff = 109.99999  PredictDiff = 110.02157
xPoint = 49.0  TargetDiff = 100.00000  PredictDiff = 100.01322
xPoint = 50.0  TargetDiff = 102.99999  PredictDiff = 102.98510

maxErrorPerc = 0.07574160995391013
averErrorPerc = 0.01071011328541703
```

Figure 7-5 shows the chart of the training results.

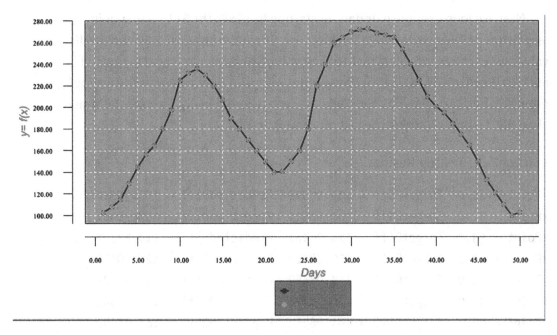

Figure 7-5. *Chart of the training/validation results*

Testing the Network

First, we change the configuration data to process the testing logic. We load the previously saved trained network. Notice here that we don't load the testing dataset. We will be determining the current function value in the following way. On the first step of the loop the current function value is equal to the `lastFunctionValueForTraining` variable, which was calculated during the training process. This variable holds the function value at the last point, 50. On all the following steps of the loop, we set the current record value to the function value calculated during the previous step of the loop.

Near the beginning of this example we explained how we intend to calculate the predicted values during the testing phase. We repeat this explanation here:

> *"During the test, we calculate the function's next-day value in the following way. When at training point x = 50, we want to calculate the predicted function value at the next point, x = 51. Feeding the difference between the function values at the current and previous points (Field 1) to the trained network, we will get back the predicted difference between the function values at the next and current points. Therefore, the predicted function value at the next point is equal to the sum of the actual function value at the current point and the predicted difference."*

Next, we loop over the pair dataset starting from xPoint 51 (the first point of the testing interval). At each step of the loop, we obtain the input, actual, and predicted values for each record, denormalize their values, and calculate realTargetDiffValue and realPredictDiffValue for each record. We print their values as the testing log and populate the chart elements with data for each record. Finally, we save the generated chart file. Listing 7-5 shows the test processing results.

Listing 7-5. Testing Results

```
xPoint = 51.0  TargetDiff = 102.99999  PredictedDiff = 102.98510
xPoint = 52.0  TargetDiff = 107.98510  PredictedDiff = 107.98461
xPoint = 53.0  TargetDiff = 114.98461  PredictedDiff = 114.98322
xPoint = 54.0  TargetDiff = 129.98322  PredictedDiff = 129.98470
xPoint = 55.0  TargetDiff = 144.98469  PredictedDiff = 144.98371
xPoint = 56.0  TargetDiff = 156.98371  PredictedDiff = 156.98383
xPoint = 57.0  TargetDiff = 164.98383  PredictedDiff = 164.98232
xPoint = 58.0  TargetDiff = 180.98232  PredictedDiff = 180.98241
xPoint = 59.0  TargetDiff = 197.98241  PredictedDiff = 197.98225
xPoint = 60.0  TargetDiff = 224.98225  PredictedDiff = 224.98139
xPoint = 61.0  TargetDiff = 231.98139  PredictedDiff = 231.98127
xPoint = 62.0  TargetDiff = 235.98127  PredictedDiff = 235.98077
xPoint = 63.0  TargetDiff = 229.98077  PredictedDiff = 229.98199
xPoint = 64.0  TargetDiff = 219.98199  PredictedDiff = 219.97966
xPoint = 65.0  TargetDiff = 206.97966  PredictedDiff = 206.97917
xPoint = 66.0  TargetDiff = 189.97917  PredictedDiff = 189.98139
xPoint = 67.0  TargetDiff = 179.98139  PredictedDiff = 179.98147
xPoint = 68.0  TargetDiff = 169.98147  PredictedDiff = 169.98124
xPoint = 69.0  TargetDiff = 159.98124  PredictedDiff = 159.97102
xPoint = 70.0  TargetDiff = 149.97102  PredictedDiff = 150.04646
xPoint = 71.0  TargetDiff = 140.04646  PredictedDiff = 139.94050
xPoint = 72.0  TargetDiff = 140.94050  PredictedDiff = 140.93764
xPoint = 73.0  TargetDiff = 149.93764  PredictedDiff = 149.93640
xPoint = 74.0  TargetDiff = 159.93640  PredictedDiff = 159.93569
xPoint = 75.0  TargetDiff = 179.93573  PredictedDiff = 179.93465
xPoint = 76.0  TargetDiff = 219.93465  PredictedDiff = 219.93374
xPoint = 77.0  TargetDiff = 239.93374  PredictedDiff = 239.93515
```

```
xPoint = 78.0  TargetDiff = 259.93515  PredictedDiff = 259.93381
xPoint = 79.0  TargetDiff = 264.93381  PredictedDiff = 264.93318
xPoint = 80.0  TargetDiff = 269.93318  PredictedDiff = 269.93387
xPoint = 81.0  TargetDiff = 271.93387  PredictedDiff = 271.93319
xPoint = 82.0  TargetDiff = 272.93318  PredictedDiff = 272.93287
xPoint = 83.0  TargetDiff = 268.93287  PredictedDiff = 268.93262
xPoint = 84.0  TargetDiff = 266.93262  PredictedDiff = 266.93256
xPoint = 85.0  TargetDiff = 264.93256  PredictedDiff = 264.92998
xPoint = 86.0  TargetDiff = 253.92998  PredictedDiff = 253.93075
xPoint = 87.0  TargetDiff = 239.93075  PredictedDiff = 239.95277
xPoint = 88.0  TargetDiff = 224.95278  PredictedDiff = 224.95756
xPoint = 89.0  TargetDiff = 209.95756  PredictedDiff = 209.99701
xPoint = 90.0  TargetDiff = 200.99701  PredictedDiff = 200.86194
xPoint = 91.0  TargetDiff = 194.86194  PredictedDiff = 194.97485

maxGlobalResultDiff = 0.07571646804925916
averGlobalResultDiff = 0.01071236446121567
```

Figure 7-6 shows the chart of the testing results.

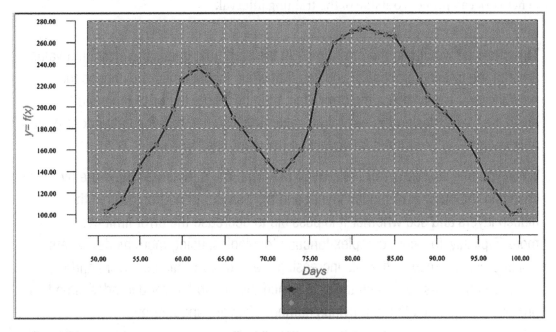

Figure 7-6. *The chart of the test result records*

Both charts practically overlap.

Digging Deeper

In this example, we learned that by using some special data preparation techniques, we are able to calculate the function value at the first point of the next interval by knowing the function value at the last point of the training interval. Repeating this process for the rest of the points in the testing interval, we get the function values for all points of the test interval.

Why do we always mention that the function needs to be periodic? Because we determine the function values on the next interval based on the results calculated for the training interval. This technique can also be applied to nonperiodic functions. The only requirement is that the function values on the next interval can be determined in some way based on the values in the training interval. For example, consider a function whose values in the next interval double from the training interval. Such a function is not periodic, but the techniques discussed in this chapter will work. Also, it is not necessary that each point in the next interval can be determined by the corresponding point in the training interval. As long as some rule exists for determining the function value at some point on the next interval based on the function value at some point on the training interval, this technique will work. That substantially increases the class of functions that the network can process outside of the training interval.

Tip   How do we obtain the error limit? At the start, just guess the error limit value and run the training process. If you see that while looping over the epochs the network error easily clears the error limit, then decrease the error limit and try again. Keep decreasing the error limit value until you see that the network error is able to clear the error limit; however, it must work hard to do this.

When you find such an error limit, try to play with the network architecture by changing the number of hidden layers and the number of neurons within the hidden layers and see whether it is possible to decrease the error limit even more. Typically, for more complex function topologies, using more hidden layers will improve the results. If while increasing the number of hidden layers and the number of neurons you reach the point when the network error degrades, stop this process and go back to the previous number of layers and neurons.

Summary

In this chapter, you saw an approximation of the complex periodic function. The training and testing datasets were transformed to the format of sliding window records to add the function topology information to the data. In the next chapter, we will discuss an even more complex situation that involves approximation of the noncontinuous function (which is currently considered a known problem for the traditional neural network approximation).

CHAPTER 8

Approximating Noncontinuous Functions

In this chapter, we will discuss the neural network approximation of noncontinuous functions. Currently, this is a problematic area for neural networks because network processing is based on the calculation of partial function derivatives (gradient descent algorithm), and our ability to calculate them for noncontinuous functions at the points where the function value suddenly jumps or drops is questionable. We will dig into this issue later in this chapter. The chapter includes method that I developed that solves this issue.

Example: Approximating Noncontinuous Functions

We will first attempt to approximate the noncontinuous function (shown in Figure 8-1) by using the conventional neural network processing and show that the results are of very low quality and practically useless. We will explain why this happens and then introduce the method that allows approximation of such functions with good precision results.

© Igor Livshin 2022
I. Livshin, *Artificial Neural Networks with Java*, https://doi.org/10.1007/978-1-4842-7368-5_8

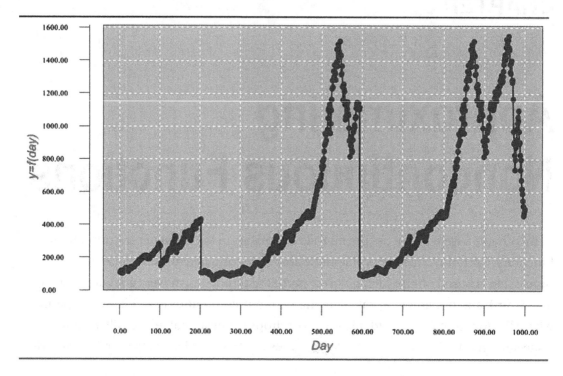

Figure 8-1.   *Chart of noncontinuous function*

As you remember from the preceding chapters, neural network back-propagation uses partial derivatives of the network error function to redistribute the error calculated in the output layer to all hidden-layer neurons. It repeats this iterative process by moving in the opposite direction of the function to find one of the local (possibly global) error function minimums. Due to the problem of calculating divergent/derivatives for noncontinuous functions, approximation such functions is problematic.

The function for this example is given by its values at 1,000 points. We are attempting to approximate this function using the traditional neural network back-propagation process. Table 8-1 shows the fragment of the input dataset.

Table 8-1. *Fragment of the Input Dataset*

xPoint	yValue	xPoint	yValue	xPoint	yValue
1	107.387	31	137.932	61	199.499
2	110.449	32	140.658	62	210.45
3	116.943	33	144.067	63	206.789
4	118.669	34	141.216	64	208.551
5	108.941	35	141.618	65	210.739
6	103.071	36	142.619	66	206.311
7	110.16	37	149.811	67	210.384
8	104.933	38	151.468	68	197.218
9	114.12	39	156.919	69	192.003
10	118.326	40	159.757	70	207.936
11	118.055	41	163.074	71	208.041
12	125.764	42	160.628	72	204.394
13	128.612	43	168.573	73	194.024
14	132.722	44	163.297	74	193.223
15	132.583	45	168.155	75	205.974
16	136.361	46	175.654	76	206.53
17	134.52	47	180.581	77	209.696
18	132.064	48	184.836	78	209.886
19	129.228	49	178.259	79	217.36
20	121.889	50	185.945	80	217.095
21	113.142	51	187.234	81	216.827
22	125.33	52	188.395	82	212.615
23	124.696	53	192.357	83	219.881
24	125.76	54	196.023	84	223.883
25	131.241	55	193.067	85	227.887

(*continued*)

Table 8-1. (*continued*)

xPoint	yValue	xPoint	yValue	xPoint	yValue
26	136.568	56	200.337	86	236.364
27	140.847	57	197.229	87	236.272
28	139.791	58	201.805	88	238.42
29	131.033	59	206.756	89	241.18
30	136.216	60	205.89	90	242.341

This dataset needs to be normalized on the interval [-1, 1]. Table 8-2 shows the fragment of the normalized input dataset.

Table 8-2. *Fragment of the Normalized Input Dataset*

xPoint	yValue	xPoint	yValue	xPoint	yValue
-1	-0.93846	-0.93994	-0.89879	-0.87988	-0.81883
-0.998	-0.93448	-0.93794	-0.89525	-0.87788	-0.80461
-0.996	-0.92605	-0.93594	-0.89082	-0.87588	-0.80936
-0.99399	-0.92381	-0.93393	-0.89452	-0.87387	-0.80708
-0.99199	-0.93644	-0.93193	-0.894	-0.87187	-0.80424
-0.98999	-0.94406	-0.92993	-0.8927	-0.86987	-0.80999
-0.98799	-0.93486	-0.92793	-0.88336	-0.86787	-0.8047
-0.98599	-0.94165	-0.92593	-0.88121	-0.86587	-0.82179
-0.98398	-0.92971	-0.92392	-0.87413	-0.86386	-0.82857
-0.98198	-0.92425	-0.92192	-0.87045	-0.86186	-0.80788
-0.97998	-0.9246	-0.91992	-0.86614	-0.85986	-0.80774
-0.97798	-0.91459	-0.91792	-0.86931	-0.85786	-0.81248
-0.97598	-0.91089	-0.91592	-0.859	-0.85586	-0.82594
-0.97397	-0.90556	-0.91391	-0.86585	-0.85385	-0.82698
-0.97197	-0.90574	-0.91191	-0.85954	-0.85185	-0.81042

(*continued*)

Table 8-2. (*continued*)

xPoint	yValue	xPoint	yValue	xPoint	yValue
-0.96997	-0.90083	-0.90991	-0.8498	-0.84985	-0.8097
-0.96797	-0.90322	-0.90791	-0.8434	-0.84785	-0.80559
-0.96597	-0.90641	-0.90591	-0.83788	-0.84585	-0.80534
-0.96396	-0.91009	-0.9039	-0.84642	-0.84384	-0.79564
-0.96196	-0.91962	-0.9019	-0.83644	-0.84184	-0.79598
-0.95996	-0.93098	-0.8999	-0.83476	-0.83984	-0.79633
-0.95796	-0.91516	-0.8979	-0.83325	-0.83784	-0.8018
-0.95596	-0.91598	-0.8959	-0.82811	-0.83584	-0.79236
-0.95395	-0.9146	-0.89389	-0.82335	-0.83383	-0.78716
-0.95195	-0.90748	-0.89189	-0.82719	-0.83183	-0.78196
-0.94995	-0.90056	-0.88989	-0.81774	-0.82983	-0.77096
-0.94795	-0.895	-0.88789	-0.82178	-0.82783	-0.77108
-0.94595	-0.89638	-0.88589	-0.81584	-0.82583	-0.76829
-0.94394	-0.90775	-0.88388	-0.80941	-0.82382	-0.7647
-0.94194	-0.90102	-0.88188	-0.81053	-0.82182	-0.76319

Network Architecture

The network for this example consists of the input layer with a single neuron, seven hidden layers (each with five neurons), and the output layer with a single neuron. See Figure 8-2.

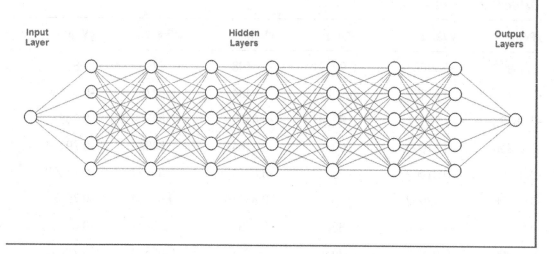

Figure 8-2. *Network architecture*

Program Code

Listing 8-1 shows the program code.

Listing 8-1. Program Code

```
// ===============================================================
// Approximation non-continuous function whose values are given
// at 999 points. The input file is normalized.
// ===============================================================

package sample5;

import java.io.BufferedReader;
import java.io.File;
import java.io.FileInputStream;
import java.io.PrintWriter;
import java.io.FileNotFoundException;
import java.io.FileReader;
import java.io.FileWriter;
import java.io.IOException;
import java.io.InputStream;
import java.nio.file.*;
```

```java
import java.util.Properties;
import java.time.YearMonth;
import java.awt.Color;
import java.awt.Font;
import java.io.BufferedReader;
import java.text.DateFormat;
import java.text.ParseException;
import java.text.SimpleDateFormat;
import java.time.LocalDate;
import java.time.Month;
import java.time.ZoneId;
import java.util.ArrayList;
import java.util.Calendar;
import java.util.Date;
import java.util.List;
import java.util.Locale;
import java.util.Properties;

import org.encog.Encog;
import org.encog.engine.network.activation.ActivationTANH;
import org.encog.engine.network.activation.ActivationReLU;
import org.encog.ml.data.MLData;
import org.encog.ml.data.MLDataPair;
import org.encog.ml.data.MLDataSet;
import org.encog.ml.data.buffer.MemoryDataLoader;
import org.encog.ml.data.buffer.codec.CSVDataCODEC;
import org.encog.ml.data.buffer.codec.DataSetCODEC;
import org.encog.neural.networks.BasicNetwork;
import org.encog.neural.networks.layers.BasicLayer;
import org.encog.neural.networks.training.propagation.resilient.
ResilientPropagation;
import org.encog.persist.EncogDirectoryPersistence;
import org.encog.util.csv.CSVFormat;

import org.knowm.xchart.SwingWrapper;
import org.knowm.xchart.XYChart;
```

```java
import org.knowm.xchart.XYChartBuilder;
import org.knowm.xchart.XYSeries;
import org.knowm.xchart.demo.charts.ExampleChart;
import org.knowm.xchart.style.Styler.LegendPosition;
import org.knowm.xchart.style.colors.ChartColor;
import org.knowm.xchart.style.colors.XChartSeriesColors;
import org.knowm.xchart.style.lines.SeriesLines;
import org.knowm.xchart.style.markers.SeriesMarkers;
import org.knowm.xchart.BitmapEncoder;
import org.knowm.xchart.BitmapEncoder.BitmapFormat;
import org.knowm.xchart.QuickChart;
import org.knowm.xchart.SwingWrapper;

public class Sample5 implements ExampleChart<XYChart>
  {
    // Interval to normalize
    static double Nh =  1;
    static double Nl = -1;

    // First column
    static double minXPointDl = 1.00;
    static double maxXPointDh = 1000.00;

    // Second column - target data
    static double minTargetValueDl = 60.00;
    static double maxTargetValueDh = 1600.00;

    static double doublePointNumber = 0.00;
    static int intPointNumber = 0;
    static InputStream input = null;
    static double[] arrPrices = new double[2500];
    static double normInputXPointValue = 0.00;
    static double normPredictXPointValue = 0.00;
    static double normTargetXPointValue = 0.00;
    static double normDifferencePerc = 0.00;
    static double returnCode = 0.00;
    static double denormInputXPointValue = 0.00;
```

```java
static double denormPredictXPointValue = 0.00;
static double denormTargetXPointValue = 0.00;
static double valueDifference = 0.00;
static int numberOfInputNeurons;
static int numberOfOutputNeurons;
 static int intNumberOfRecordsInTestFile;
static String trainFileName;
static String priceFileName;
static String testFileName;
static String chartTrainFileName;
static String chartTestFileName;
static String networkFileName;
static int workingMode;
static String cvsSplitBy = ",";

static List<Double> xData = new ArrayList<Double>();
static List<Double> yData1 = new ArrayList<Double>();
static List<Double> yData2 = new ArrayList<Double>();

static XYChart Chart;

@Override
public XYChart getChart()
 {
  // Create Chart

  Chart = new  XYChartBuilder().width(900).height(500).title(getClass().
          getSimpleName()).xAxisTitle("x").yAxisTitle("y= f(x)").build();

  // Customize Chart
  Chart.getStyler().setPlotBackgroundColor(ChartColor.
  getAWTColor(ChartColor.GREY));
  Chart.getStyler().setPlotGridLinesColor(new Color(255, 255, 255));
  Chart.getStyler().setChartBackgroundColor(Color.WHITE);
  Chart.getStyler().setLegendBackgroundColor(Color.PINK);
  Chart.getStyler().setChartFontColor(Color.MAGENTA);
  Chart.getStyler().setChartTitleBoxBackgroundColor(new Color(0, 222, 0));
  Chart.getStyler().setChartTitleBoxVisible(true);
```

```
Chart.getStyler().setChartTitleBoxBorderColor(Color.BLACK);
Chart.getStyler().setPlotGridLinesVisible(true);
Chart.getStyler().setAxisTickPadding(20);
Chart.getStyler().setAxisTickMarkLength(15);
Chart.getStyler().setPlotMargin(20);
Chart.getStyler().setChartTitleVisible(false);
Chart.getStyler().setChartTitleFont(new Font(Font.MONOSPACED, Font.
BOLD, 24));
Chart.getStyler().setLegendFont(new Font(Font.SERIF, Font.PLAIN, 18));
Chart.getStyler().setLegendPosition(LegendPosition.InsideSE);
Chart.getStyler().setLegendSeriesLineLength(12);
Chart.getStyler().setAxisTitleFont(new Font(Font.SANS_SERIF, Font.
ITALIC, 18));
Chart.getStyler().setAxisTickLabelsFont(new Font(Font.SERIF, Font.
PLAIN, 11));
Chart.getStyler().setDatePattern("yyyy-MM");
Chart.getStyler().setDecimalPattern("#0.00");
//Chart.getStyler().setLocale(Locale.GERMAN);

try
   {
      // Configuration

      // Training mode
      workingMode = 1;
      trainFileName = "C:/Book_Examples/Sample5_Train_Norm.csv";
      chartTrainFileName = "XYLine_Sample5_Train_Chart_Results";

      // Testing mode
      //workingMode = 2;
      //intNumberOfRecordsInTestFile = 3;
      //testFileName = "C:/Book_Examples/Sample2_Norm.csv";
      //chartTestFileName = "XYLine_Test_Results_Chart";

      // Common part of config data
      networkFileName = "C:/Book_Examples/Sample5_Saved_Network_File.csv";
      numberOfInputNeurons = 1;
```

```java
   numberOfOutputNeurons = 1;

   // Check the working mode to run

   if(workingMode == 1)
    {
      // Training mode
      File file1 = new File(chartTrainFileName);
      File file2 = new File(networkFileName);

      if(file1.exists())
        file1.delete();

      if(file2.exists())
        file2.delete();

      returnCode = 0;     // Clear the error Code

      do
       {
         returnCode = trainValidateSaveNetwork();
       }  while (returnCode > 0);
    }
   else
    {
      // Test mode
      loadAndTestNetwork();
    }
 }
catch (Throwable t)
  {
    t.printStackTrace();
    System.exit(1);
  }
 finally
  {
    Encog.getInstance().shutdown();
  }
}
```

```
  Encog.getInstance().shutdown();
  return Chart;

} // End of the method

// =========================================================
// Load CSV to memory.
// @return The loaded dataset.
// =========================================================
public static MLDataSet loadCSV2Memory(String filename, int input, int
ideal, boolean headers,
    CSVFormat format, boolean significance)
  {
    DataSetCODEC codec = new CSVDataCODEC(new File(filename), format,
    headers, input, ideal,
        significance);
    MemoryDataLoader load = new MemoryDataLoader(codec);
    MLDataSet dataset = load.external2Memory();
    return dataset;
  }

// =========================================================
//  The main method.
//  @param Command line arguments. No arguments are used.
// =========================================================
public static void main(String[] args)
 {
    ExampleChart<XYChart> exampleChart = new Sample5();
    XYChart Chart = exampleChart.getChart();
    new SwingWrapper<XYChart>(Chart).displayChart();
 } // End of the main method

//=============================================================================
// This method trains, Validates, and saves the trained network file
//=============================================================================
```

```java
static public double trainValidateSaveNetwork()
 {
   // Load the training CSV file in memory
   MLDataSet trainingSet =
     loadCSV2Memory(trainFileName,numberOfInputNeurons,
     numberOfOutputNeurons,
       true,CSVFormat.ENGLISH,false);

   // create a neural network
   BasicNetwork network = new BasicNetwork();

   // Input layer
   network.addLayer(new BasicLayer(null,true,1));

   // Hidden layer
   network.addLayer(new BasicLayer(new ActivationTANH(),true,5));
   network.addLayer(new BasicLayer(new ActivationTANH(),true,5));
   network.addLayer(new BasicLayer(new ActivationTANH(),true,5));
   network.addLayer(new BasicLayer(new ActivationTANH(),true,5));
   network.addLayer(new BasicLayer(new ActivationTANH(),true,5));
   network.addLayer(new BasicLayer(new ActivationTANH(),true,5));
   network.addLayer(new BasicLayer(new ActivationTANH(),true,5));

   // Output layer
   network.addLayer(new BasicLayer(new ActivationTANH(),false,1));

   network.getStructure().finalizeStructure();
   network.reset();

   // train the neural network
   final ResilientPropagation train = new ResilientPropagation(network,
   trainingSet);

   int epoch = 1;

   do
    {
       train.iteration();
      System.out.println("Epoch #" + epoch + " Error:" + train.getError());
```

```
    epoch++;

    if (epoch >= 11000 && network.calculateError(trainingSet) >
    0.00225)
        {
         returnCode = 1;

         System.out.println("Try again");
         return returnCode;
        }
 } while(train.getError() > 0.0022);

// Save the network file
EncogDirectoryPersistence.saveObject(new File(networkFileName),
network);

System.out.println("Neural Network Results:");
double sumNormDifferencePerc = 0.00;
double averNormDifferencePerc = 0.00;
double maxNormDifferencePerc = 0.00;
int m = 0;
double xPointer = 0.00;

for(MLDataPair pair: trainingSet)
  {
      m++;
      xPointer++;

      final MLData output = network.compute(pair.getInput());

      MLData inputData = pair.getInput();
      MLData actualData = pair.getIdeal();
      MLData predictData = network.compute(inputData);

      // Calculate and print the results
      normInputXPointValue = inputData.getData(0);
      normTargetXPointValue = actualData.getData(0);
      normPredictXPointValue = predictData.getData(0);
```

```
denormInputXPointValue = ((minXPointDl - maxXPointDh)*normInpu
tXPointValue -
  Nh*minXPointDl + maxXPointDh *Nl)/(Nl - Nh);

denormTargetXPointValue =((minTargetValueDl -
maxTargetValueDh)* normTargetXPointValue -
  Nh*minTargetValueDl + maxTargetValueDh*Nl)/(Nl - Nh);
denormPredictXPointValue =((minTargetValueDl -
maxTargetValueDh)* normPredictXPointValue -
  Nh*minTargetValueDl + maxTargetValueDh*Nl)/(Nl - Nh);

valueDifference =
  Math.abs(((denormTargetXPointValue -
         denormPredictXPointValue)/
         denormTargetXPointValue)*100.00);

System.out.println ("RecordNumber = " + m +
"  denormTargetXPointValue = " +
  denormTargetXPointValue + "  denormPredictXPointValue = " +
  denormPredictXPointValue +
    "  valueDifference = " + valueDifference);

sumNormDifferencePerc = sumNormDifferencePerc +
valueDifference;

if (valueDifference > maxNormDifferencePerc)
  maxNormDifferencePerc = valueDifference;

xData.add(xPointer);
yData1.add(denormTargetXPointValue);
yData2.add(denormPredictXPointValue);

}   // End for pair loop

XYSeries series1 = Chart.addSeries("Actual data", xData, yData1);
XYSeries series2 = Chart.addSeries("Predict data", xData, yData2);

series1.setLineColor(XChartSeriesColors.BLUE);
series2.setMarkerColor(Color.ORANGE);
```

```java
      series1.setLineStyle(SeriesLines.SOLID);
      series2.setLineStyle(SeriesLines.SOLID);

      try
       {
         //Save the chart image
         BitmapEncoder.saveBitmapWithDPI(Chart, chartTrainFileName,
           BitmapFormat.JPG, 100);
         System.out.println ("Train Chart file has been saved") ;
       }
     catch (IOException ex)
      {
       ex.printStackTrace();
       System.exit(3);
      }

      // Finally, save this trained network
      EncogDirectoryPersistence.saveObject(new File(networkFileName),
      network);
      System.out.println ("Train Network has been saved") ;

      averNormDifferencePerc  = sumNormDifferencePerc/1000.00;

      System.out.println(" ");
      System.out.println("maxNormDifferencePerc = " +
      maxNormDifferencePerc + "  averNormDifferencePerc =
          " + averNormDifferencePerc);

      returnCode = 0.00;
      return returnCode;

   }    // End of the method


//==================================================
// This method load and test the trained network
//==================================================
```

```java
static public void loadAndTestNetwork()
 {
   System.out.println("Testing the networks results");

   List<Double> xData = new ArrayList<Double>();
   List<Double> yData1 = new ArrayList<Double>();
   List<Double> yData2 = new ArrayList<Double>();

   double targetToPredictPercent = 0;
   double maxGlobalResultDiff = 0.00;
   double averGlobalResultDiff = 0.00;
   double sumGlobalResultDiff = 0.00;
   double maxGlobalIndex = 0;
   double normInputXPointValueFromRecord = 0.00;
   double normTargetXPointValueFromRecord = 0.00;
   double normPredictXPointValueFromRecord = 0.00;

   BasicNetwork network;

   maxGlobalResultDiff = 0.00;
   averGlobalResultDiff = 0.00;
   sumGlobalResultDiff = 0.00;

   // Load the test dataset into mmemory
   MLDataSet testingSet =
       loadCSV2Memory(testFileName,numberOfInputNeurons,numberOfOutputNeu
       rons,true,
         CSVFormat.ENGLISH,false);

   // Load the saved trained network
   network =
     (BasicNetwork)EncogDirectoryPersistence.loadObject(new
     File(networkFileName));

   int i = - 1; // Index of the current record
   double xPoint = -0.00;
```

```java
for (MLDataPair pair:  testingSet)
{
    i++;
    xPoint = xPoint + 2.00;

    MLData inputData = pair.getInput();
    MLData actualData = pair.getIdeal();
    MLData predictData = network.compute(inputData);

    normInputXPointValueFromRecord = inputData.getData(0);
    normTargetXPointValueFromRecord = actualData.getData(0);
    normPredictXPointValueFromRecord = predictData.getData(0);

    // De-normalize them
    denormInputXPointValue = ((minXPointDl - maxXPointDh)*
        normInputXPointValueFromRecord - Nh*minXPointDl +
        maxXPointDh*Nl)/(Nl - Nh);

    denormTargetXPointValue = ((minTargetValueDl -
    maxTargetValueDh)*
        normTargetXPointValueFromRecord - Nh*minTargetValueDl +
        maxTargetValueDh*Nl)/(Nl - Nh);

    denormPredictXPointValue =((minTargetValueDl -
    maxTargetValueDh)*
        normPredictXPointValueFromRecord - Nh*minTargetValueDl +
        maxTargetValueDh*Nl)/(Nl - Nh);

    targetToPredictPercent = Math.abs((denormTargetXPointValue -
    denormPredictXPointValue)/
        denormTargetXPointValue*100);

    System.out.println("xPoint = " + xPoint
    + "   denormTargetXPointValue = " +
        denormTargetXPointValue + "   denormPredictXPointValue = " +
        denormPredictXPointValue +
            "     targetToPredictPercent = " + targetToPredictPercent);
```

```
   if (targetToPredictPercent > maxGlobalResultDiff)
      maxGlobalResultDiff = targetToPredictPercent;

   sumGlobalResultDiff = sumGlobalResultDiff +
   targetToPredictPercent;

   // Populate chart elements
   xData.add(xPoint);
   yData1.add(denormTargetXPointValue);
   yData2.add(denormPredictXPointValue);

 }  // End for pair loop

// Print the max and average results
System.out.println(" ");
averGlobalResultDiff = sumGlobalResultDiff/
intNumberOfRecordsInTestFile;

System.out.println("maxGlobalResultDiff = " + maxGlobalResultDiff +
"  i = " + maxGlobalIndex);
System.out.println("averGlobalResultDiff = " + averGlobalResultDiff);

// All testing batch files have been processed
XYSeries series1 = Chart.addSeries("Actual", xData, yData1);
XYSeries series2 = Chart.addSeries("Predicted", xData, yData2);

series1.setLineColor(XChartSeriesColors.BLUE);
series2.setMarkerColor(Color.ORANGE);
series1.setLineStyle(SeriesLines.SOLID);
series2.setLineStyle(SeriesLines.SOLID);

// Save the chart image
try
 {
    BitmapEncoder.saveBitmapWithDPI(Chart, chartTestFileName ,
    BitmapFormat.JPG, 100);
 }
```

```
     catch (Exception bt)
      {
        bt.printStackTrace();
      }

     System.out.println ("The Chart has been saved");
     System.out.println("End of testing for test records");

   } // End of the method


} // End of the class
```

Code Fragments for the Training Process

The training method is called in a loop until it successfully clears the error limit. We load the normalized training file and then create the network with one input layer (one neuron), seven hidden layers (each with five neurons), and the output layer (one neuron). Next, we train the network by looping over the epochs until the network error clears the error limit. At that point, we exit the loop. The network is trained, and we save it on disk (it will be used by the testing method). Listing 8-2 shows a fragment of the training method.

Listing 8-2. Fragment of the Code of the Training Method

```
// Load the training CSV file in memory
MLDataSet trainingSet =
loadCSV2Memory(trainFileName,numberOfInputNeurons,numberOfOutputNeurons,
     true,CSVFormat.ENGLISH,false);

// create a neural network
BasicNetwork network = new BasicNetwork();

// Input layer
network.addLayer(new BasicLayer(null,true,1));

// Hidden layer
network.addLayer(new BasicLayer(new ActivationTANH(),true,5));
network.addLayer(new BasicLayer(new ActivationTANH(),true,5));
network.addLayer(new BasicLayer(new ActivationTANH(),true,5));
```

```
network.addLayer(new BasicLayer(new ActivationTANH(),true,5));
network.addLayer(new BasicLayer(new ActivationTANH(),true,5));
network.addLayer(new BasicLayer(new ActivationTANH(),true,5));
network.addLayer(new BasicLayer(new ActivationTANH(),true,5));

// Output layer
network.addLayer(new BasicLayer(new ActivationTANH(),false,1));

network.getStructure().finalizeStructure();
network.reset();

// train the neural network
final ResilientPropagation train = new ResilientPropagation(network,
trainingSet);

int epoch = 1;

do
  {
    train.iteration();
    System.out.println("Epoch #" + epoch + " Error:" + train.getError());

    epoch++;

    if (epoch >= 11000 && network.calculateError(trainingSet) >
    0.00225)    // 0.0221    0.00008
      {
        returnCode = 1;
        System.out.println("Try again");
        return returnCode;
      }
  } while(train.getError() > 0.0022);

// Save the network file
EncogDirectoryPersistence.saveObject(new File(networkFileName),network);
```

Next we loop over the pair dataset and retrieve from the network the input, actual, and predicted values for each record. We then denormalize the retrieved values, put them in the log, and populate the chart data.

```java
int m = 0;
double xPointer = 0.00;

for(MLDataPair pair: trainingSet)
  {
      m++;
      xPointer++;

      final MLData output = network.compute(pair.getInput());

      MLData inputData = pair.getInput();
      MLData actualData = pair.getIdeal();
      MLData predictData = network.compute(inputData);

       // Calculate and print the results
       normInputXPointValue = inputData.getData(0);
       normTargetXPointValue = actualData.getData(0);
       normPredictXPointValue = predictData.getData(0);

       denormInputXPointValue = ((minXPointDl - maxXPointDh)*normInputX
       PointValue -
       Nh*minXPointDl + maxXPointDh *Nl)/(Nl - Nh);

       denormTargetXPointValue =((minTargetValueDl - maxTargetValueDh)*
        normTargetXPointValue -
           Nh*minTargetValueDl + maxTargetValueDh*Nl)/(Nl - Nh);
       denormPredictXPointValue =((minTargetValueDl - maxTargetValueDh)*
       normPredictXPointValue -
           Nh*minTargetValueDl + maxTargetValueDh*Nl)/(Nl - Nh);

      valueDifference =
        Math.abs(((denormTargetXPointValue -
          denormPredictXPointValue)/denormTargetXPointValue)*100.00);

      System.out.println ("RecordNumber = " + m +
      "   denormTargetXPointValue = " +
          denormTargetXPointValue + "  denormPredictXPointValue = " +
          denormPredictXPointValue +
              "   valueDifference = " + valueDifference);
```

```
      sumNormDifferencePerc = sumNormDifferencePerc + valueDifference;

      if (valueDifference > maxNormDifferencePerc)
      maxNormDifferencePerc = valueDifference;

      xData.add(xPointer);
      yData1.add(denormTargetXPointValue);
      yData2.add(denormPredictXPointValue);

   }   // End for pair loop
```

Finally, we calculate the average and maximum values of the results and save the chart file.

```
XYSeries series1 = Chart.addSeries("Actual data", xData, yData1);
XYSeries series2 = Chart.addSeries("Predict data", xData, yData2);

   series1.setLineColor(XChartSeriesColors.BLUE);
   series2.setMarkerColor(Color.ORANGE);
   series1.setLineStyle(SeriesLines.SOLID);
   series2.setLineStyle(SeriesLines.SOLID);

   try
    {
       //Save the chart image
       BitmapEncoder.saveBitmapWithDPI(Chart, chartTrainFileName,
       BitmapFormat.JPG, 100);
       System.out.println ("Train Chart file has been saved") ;
    }
   catch (IOException ex)
    {
       ex.printStackTrace();
       System.exit(3);
    }

   // Save this trained network
   EncogDirectoryPersistence.saveObject(new File(networkFileName),network);
   System.out.println ("Train Network has been saved") ;
```

```
averNormDifferencePerc  = sumNormDifferencePerc/1000.00;

System.out.println(" ");
System.out.println("maxNormDifferencePerc = " + maxNormDifferencePerc + "
  averNormDifferencePerc = " + averNormDifferencePerc);

returnCode = 0.00;
return returnCode;

} // End of the method
```

Unsatisfactory Training Results

Listing 8-3 shows the ending fragment of the training results.

Listing 8-3. Ending Fragment of the Training Results

```
RecordNumber =  983  TargetValue = 1036.19  PredictedValue =
930.03102  DiffPerc = 10.24513
RecordNumber =  984  TargetValue = 1095.63  PredictedValue =
915.36958  DiffPerc = 16.45267
RecordNumber =  985  TargetValue = 968.75   PredictedValue =
892.96942  DiffPerc = 7.822511
RecordNumber =  986  TargetValue = 896.24   PredictedValue =
863.64775  DiffPerc = 3.636554
RecordNumber =  987  TargetValue = 903.25   PredictedValue =
829.19287  DiffPerc = 8.198962
RecordNumber =  988  TargetValue = 825.88   PredictedValue =
791.96691  DiffPerc = 4.106298
RecordNumber =  989  TargetValue = 735.09   PredictedValue =
754.34279  DiffPerc = 2.619107
RecordNumber =  990  TargetValue = 797.87   PredictedValue =
718.23458  DiffPerc = 9.981002
RecordNumber =  991  TargetValue = 672.81   PredictedValue =
684.88576  DiffPerc = 1.794825
RecordNumber =  992  TargetValue = 619.14   PredictedValue =
654.90309  DiffPerc = 5.776254
```

```
RecordNumber =  993  TargetValue = 619.32   PredictedValue =
628.42044  DiffPerc = 1.469424
RecordNumber =  994  TargetValue = 590.47   PredictedValue =
605.28210  DiffPerc = 2.508528
RecordNumber =  995  TargetValue = 547.28   PredictedValue =
585.18808  DiffPerc = 6.926634
RecordNumber =  996  TargetValue = 514.62   PredictedValue =
567.78844  DiffPerc = 10.33159
RecordNumber =  997  TargetValue = 455.4    PredictedValue =
552.73603  DiffPerc = 21.37374
RecordNumber =  998  TargetValue = 470.43   PredictedValue =
539.71156  DiffPerc = 14.72728
RecordNumber =  999  TargetValue = 480.28   PredictedValue =
528.43269  DiffPerc = 10.02596
RecordNumber = 1000  TargetValue = 496.77   PredictedValue =
518.65485  DiffPerc = 4.405429

maxNormDifferencePerc = 97.69386964911284
averNormDifferencePerc = 7.232624870097155
```

This approximation is of a very low quality. Even with the network being well optimized, the average approximation error for all records is more than 8 percent, and the maximum approximation error (the worst approximated record) is more than 97 percent. Such function approximation is certainly not usable. Figure 8-3 shows the chart of the approximation results.

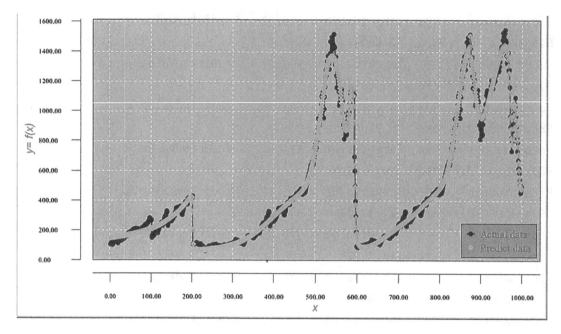

Figure 8-3. *Low-quality function approximation*

We knew that this approximation would not work and stated this at the beginning of the example. However, it was deliberately done to demonstrate the point. Now, we will show how this noncontinuous function can be successfully approximated using a neural network.

The problem with this function approximation is due to the function topology (sudden jumps or drops of the function values at certain points). We will break the input file in a series of one-record input files that we call *micro-batches*. By doing this, we eliminate the negative impact of the difficult function topology. After breaking the dataset, every record will stand isolated and not be linked to the previous or next function value. Breaking the input file into micro-batches creates 1,000 input files, which the network processes individually. We link each trained network with the record it represents. During the validation and testing processes, the logic finds the trained network that best matches the first field of the corresponding testing or validation record.

Approximating the Noncontinuous Function Using the Micro-Batch Method

Let's break the normalized training dataset into micro-batches. Each micro-batch dataset should contain the label record and one record from the original file to be processed. Table 8-3 shows how a micro-batch dataset looks.

Table 8-3. *Micro-Batch File*

xPoint	Function Value
-1	-0.938458442

We wrote a simple program to break the normalized training dataset into micro-batches. As a result of executing this program, we created 999 micro-batch datasets (numbered from 0 to 998). Figure 8-4 shows a fragment of the list of micro-batch datasets.

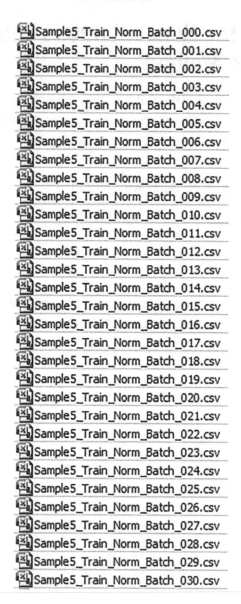

Figure 8-4. *Fragment of normalized training micro-batch datasets*

This set of micro-batch datasets is now our input for training the network.

Program Code for Micro-Batch Processing

Listing 8-4 shows the program code.

Listing 8-4. Program Code

```
// ================================================================
// Approximation of non-continuous function using the micro-batch method.
// The input is the normalized set of micro-batch files (each micro-batch
// includes a single day record).
// Each record consists of:
// - normDayValue
// - normTargetValue
//
// The number of inputLayer neurons is 12
// The number of outputLayer neurons is 1
//
// The difference of this program is that it independently trains many
// single-day networks. That allows training each daily network using the
// best value of weights/biases parameters, therefore achieving the best
// optimization results for each year.
//
// Each network is saved on disk and a map is created to link each saved
trained
// network with the corresponding training micro-batch file.
// ================================================================

package sample5_microbatches;

import java.io.BufferedReader;
import java.io.File;
import java.io.FileInputStream;
import java.io.PrintWriter;
import java.io.FileNotFoundException;
import java.io.FileReader;
import java.io.FileWriter;
import java.io.IOException;
```

```java
import java.io.InputStream;
import java.nio.file.*;
import java.util.Properties;
import java.time.YearMonth;
import java.awt.Color;
import java.awt.Font;
import java.io.BufferedReader;
import java.time.Month;
import java.time.ZoneId;
import java.util.ArrayList;
import java.util.Calendar;
import java.util.List;
import java.util.Locale;
import java.util.Properties;
import org.encog.Encog;
import org.encog.engine.network.activation.ActivationTANH;
import org.encog.engine.network.activation.ActivationReLU;
import org.encog.ml.data.MLData;
import org.encog.ml.data.MLDataPair;
import org.encog.ml.data.MLDataSet;
import org.encog.ml.data.buffer.MemoryDataLoader;
import org.encog.ml.data.buffer.codec.CSVDataCODEC;
import org.encog.ml.data.buffer.codec.DataSetCODEC;
import org.encog.neural.networks.BasicNetwork;
import org.encog.neural.networks.layers.BasicLayer;
import org.encog.neural.networks.training.propagation.
resilient.  ResilientPropagation;
import org.encog.persist.EncogDirectoryPersistence;
import org.encog.util.csv.CSVFormat;

import org.knowm.xchart.SwingWrapper;
import org.knowm.xchart.XYChart;
import org.knowm.xchart.XYChartBuilder;
import org.knowm.xchart.XYSeries;
import org.knowm.xchart.demo.charts.ExampleChart;
import org.knowm.xchart.style.Styler.LegendPosition;
```

```java
import org.knowm.xchart.style.colors.ChartColor;
import org.knowm.xchart.style.colors.XChartSeriesColors;
import org.knowm.xchart.style.lines.SeriesLines;
import org.knowm.xchart.style.markers.SeriesMarkers;
import org.knowm.xchart.BitmapEncoder;
import org.knowm.xchart.BitmapEncoder.BitmapFormat;
import org.knowm.xchart.QuickChart;
import org.knowm.xchart.SwingWrapper;

public class Sample5_Microbatches implements ExampleChart<XYChart>
{
   // Normalization parameters

   // Normalizing interval
   static double Nh =  1;
   static double Nl = -1;

   // inputFunctValueDiffPerc
  static double inputDayDh = 1000.00;
  static double inputDayDl = 1.00;

   // targetFunctValueDiffPerc
  static double targetFunctValueDiffPercDh = 1600.00;
  static double targetFunctValueDiffPercDl = 60.00;

   static String cvsSplitBy = ",";
   static Properties prop = null;

   static String strWorkingMode;
   static String strNumberOfBatchesToProcess;
   static String strTrainFileNameBase;
   static String strTestFileNameBase;
   static String strSaveTrainNetworkFileBase;
   static String strSaveTestNetworkFileBase;
   static String strValidateFileName;
   static String strTrainChartFileName;
   static String strTestChartFileName;
```

241

```java
static String strFunctValueTrainFile;
static String strFunctValueTestFile;
static int intDayNumber;
static double doubleDayNumber;
static int intWorkingMode;
static int numberOfTrainBatchesToProcess;
static int numberOfTestBatchesToProcess;
static int intNumberOfRecordsInTrainFile;
static int intNumberOfRecordsInTestFile;
static int intNumberOfRowsInBatches;
static int intInputNeuronNumber;
static int intOutputNeuronNumber;
static String strOutputFileName;
static String strSaveNetworkFileName;
static String strDaysTrainFileName;
static XYChart Chart;
static String iString;
static double inputFunctValueFromFile;
static double targetToPredictFunctValueDiff;
static int[] returnCodes  = new int[3];

static List<Double> xData = new ArrayList<Double>();
static List<Double> yData1 = new ArrayList<Double>();
static List<Double> yData2 = new ArrayList<Double>();

static double[] DaysyearDayTraining = new double[1200];
static String[] strTrainingFileNames = new String[1200];
static String[] strTestingFileNames = new String[1200];
static String[] strSaveTrainNetworkFileNames = new String[1200];
static double[] linkToSaveNetworkDayKeys = new double[1200];
static double[] linkToSaveNetworkTargetFunctValueKeys = new double[1200];
static double[] arrTrainFunctValues = new double[1200];
static double[] arrTestFunctValues = new double[1200];
```

```java
@Override
public XYChart getChart()
 {
   // Create Chart

   Chart = new XYChartBuilder().width(900).height(500).title(getClass().
     getSimpleName()).xAxisTitle("day").yAxisTitle("y=f(day)").build();

   // Customize Chart
   Chart.getStyler().setPlotBackgroundColor(ChartColor.
   getAWTColor(ChartColor.GREY));
   Chart.getStyler().setPlotGridLinesColor(new Color(255, 255, 255));
   Chart.getStyler().setChartBackgroundColor(Color.WHITE);
   Chart.getStyler().setLegendBackgroundColor(Color.PINK);
   Chart.getStyler().setChartFontColor(Color.MAGENTA);
   Chart.getStyler().setChartTitleBoxBackgroundColor(new Color(0, 222, 0));
   Chart.getStyler().setChartTitleBoxVisible(true);
   Chart.getStyler().setChartTitleBoxBorderColor(Color.BLACK);
   Chart.getStyler().setPlotGridLinesVisible(true);
   Chart.getStyler().setAxisTickPadding(20);
   Chart.getStyler().setAxisTickMarkLength(15);
   Chart.getStyler().setPlotMargin(20);
   Chart.getStyler().setChartTitleVisible(false);
   Chart.getStyler().setChartTitleFont(new Font(Font.MONOSPACED,
   Font.BOLD, 24));
   Chart.getStyler().setLegendFont(new Font(Font.SERIF, Font.PLAIN, 18));
   // Chart.getStyler().setLegendPosition(LegendPosition.InsideSE);
   Chart.getStyler().setLegendPosition(LegendPosition.OutsideE);
   Chart.getStyler().setLegendSeriesLineLength(12);
   Chart.getStyler().setAxisTitleFont(new Font(Font.SANS_SERIF,Font.
   ITALIC, 18));
   Chart.getStyler().setAxisTickLabelsFont(new Font(Font.SERIF,
   Font.PLAIN, 11));
   //Chart.getStyler().setDayPattern("yyyy-MM");
   Chart.getStyler().setDecimalPattern("#0.00");
```

```
// Config data

// Training mode
intWorkingMode = 0;

// Testing mode
// intWorkingMode = 1;

numberOfTrainBatchesToProcess = 1000;
numberOfTestBatchesToProcess = 999;
intNumberOfRowsInBatches = 1;
intInputNeuronNumber = 1;
intOutputNeuronNumber = 1;
strTrainFileNameBase = "C:/My_Neural_Network_Book/Temp_Files/Sample5_
Train_Norm_Batch_";
strTestFileNameBase = "C:/My_Neural_Network_Book/Temp_Files/Sample5_
Test_Norm_Batch_";
strSaveTrainNetworkFileBase =
   "C:/Book_Examples/Sample5_Save_Network_Batch_";
strTrainChartFileName =
   "C:/Book_Examples/Sample5_Chart_Train_File_Microbatch.jpg";
strTestChartFileName =
   "C:/Book_Examples/Sample5_Chart_Test_File_Microbatch.jpg";

// Generate training batch file names and the corresponding
// SaveNetwork file names

intDayNumber = -1;   // Day number for the chart

for (int i = 0; i < numberOfTrainBatchesToProcess; i++)
 {
   intDayNumber++;

   iString = Integer.toString(intDayNumber);

   if (intDayNumber >= 10 & intDayNumber < 100   )
    {
      strOutputFileName = strTrainFileNameBase + "0" + iString + ".csv";
      strSaveNetworkFileName = strSaveTrainNetworkFileBase + "0" +
```

```
      iString + ".csv";
  }
 else
  {
    if (intDayNumber < 10)
     {
       strOutputFileName = strTrainFileNameBase + "00" +
         iString + ".csv";
       strSaveNetworkFileName = strSaveTrainNetworkFileBase + "00" +
         iString + ".csv";
     }
    else
     {
       strOutputFileName = strTrainFileNameBase + iString +
         ".csv";

       strSaveNetworkFileName = strSaveTrainNetworkFileBase +
         iString + ".csv";
     }
  }

    strTrainingFileNames[intDayNumber] = strOutputFileName;
    strSaveTrainNetworkFileNames[intDayNumber] =
    strSaveNetworkFileName;

} // End the FOR loop

// Build the array linkToSaveNetworkFunctValueDiffKeys
String tempLine;
double tempNormFunctValueDiff = 0.00;
double tempNormFunctValueDiffPerc = 0.00;
double tempNormTargetFunctValueDiffPerc = 0.00;
String[] tempWorkFields;
try
 {
    intDayNumber = -1;  // Day number for the chart
```

```
    for (int m = 0; m < numberOfTrainBatchesToProcess; m++)
      {
          intDayNumber++;

          BufferedReader br3 = new BufferedReader(new
                  FileReader(strTrainingFileNames[intDayNumber]));
          tempLine = br3.readLine();

          // Skip the label record and zero batch record
          tempLine = br3.readLine();

          // Brake the line using comma as separator
          tempWorkFields = tempLine.split(cvsSplitBy);
          tempNormFunctValueDiffPerc = Double.parseDouble(tempWork
          Fields[0]);
          tempNormTargetFunctValueDiffPerc = Double.parseDouble(
          tempWorkFields[1]);
          linkToSaveNetworkDayKeys[intDayNumber] =
          tempNormFunctValueDiffPerc;
          linkToSaveNetworkTargetFunctValueKeys[intDayNumber] =
              tempNormTargetFunctValueDiffPerc;
  }   // End the FOR loop

  // Generate testing batche file names
  if(intWorkingMode == 1)
    {
      intDayNumber = -1;

      for (int i = 0; i < numberOfTestBatchesToProcess; i++)
        {
          intDayNumber++;
          iString = Integer.toString(intDayNumber);

          // Construct the testing batch names
          if (intDayNumber >= 10 & intDayNumber < 100  )
            {
              strOutputFileName = strTestFileNameBase + "0" +
                iString + ".csv";
            }
```

```
        else
         {
           if (intDayNumber < 10)
            {
              strOutputFileName = strTestFileNameBase + "00" +
                iString + ".csv";
            }
           else
            {
              strOutputFileName = strTestFileNameBase +
                iString + ".csv";
            }
          }

      strTestingFileNames[intDayNumber] = strOutputFileName;

    }  // End the FOR loop

    }   // End of IF

  }     // End for try
catch (IOException io1)
 {
   io1.printStackTrace();
   System.exit(1);
 }

// Load, train, and test Function Values file in memory
//loadTrainFunctValueFileInMemory();

if(intWorkingMode == 0)
   {
     // Train mode
     int paramErrorCode;
     int paramBatchNumber;
     int paramR;
     int paramDayNumber;
     int paramS;
```

```
        File file1 = new File(strTrainChartFileName);
        if(file1.exists())
            file1.delete();
       returnCodes[0] = 0;      // Clear the error Code
       returnCodes[1] = 0;      // Set the initial batch Number to 0;
       returnCodes[2] = 0;      // Day number;
      do
      {
        paramErrorCode = returnCodes[0];
        paramBatchNumber = returnCodes[1];
        paramDayNumber = returnCodes[2];
        returnCodes =  trainBatches(paramErrorCode,paramBatchNumber,
        paramDayNumber);
      } while (returnCodes[0] > 0);

    }    // End the train logic
    else
    {
      // Testing mode
      File file2 = new File(strTestChartFileName);

      if(file2.exists())
        file2.delete();

      loadAndTestNetwork();

      // End the test logic
    }

    Encog.getInstance().shutdown();
    //System.exit(0);
    return Chart;

  }  // End of method

// =========================================================
// Load CSV to memory.
// @return The loaded dataset.
// =========================================================
```

```java
public static MLDataSet loadCSV2Memory(String filename, int input, int
ideal, boolean headers, CSVFormat format, boolean significance)
  {
     DataSetCODEC codec = new CSVDataCODEC(new File(filename), format,
     headers, input, ideal,
         significance);
     MemoryDataLoader load = new MemoryDataLoader(codec);
     MLDataSet dataset = load.external2Memory();
     return dataset;
  }

// ===========================================================
//   The main method.
//   @param Command line arguments. No arguments are used.
// ===========================================================
public static void main(String[] args)
 {
  ExampleChart<XYChart> exampleChart = new Sample5_Microbatches();
   XYChart Chart = exampleChart.getChart();
   new SwingWrapper<XYChart>(Chart).displayChart();
 } // End of the main method

//===============================================================================
// This method trains batches as individual network1s
// saving them in separate trained datasets
//===============================================================================
static public int[] trainBatches(int paramErrorCode,
         int paramBatchNumber,int paramDayNumber)
  {
     int rBatchNumber;
     double targetToPredictFunctValueDiff = 0;
     double maxGlobalResultDiff = 0.00;
     double averGlobalResultDiff = 0.00;
     double sumGlobalResultDiff = 0.00;
     double normInputFunctValueDiffPercFromRecord = 0.00;
     double normTargetFunctValue1 = 0.00;
     double normPredictFunctValue1 = 0.00;
```

```
double denormInputDayFromRecord1;
double denormInputFunctValueDiffPercFromRecord;
double denormTargetFunctValue1 = 0.00;
double denormAverPredictFunctValue11 = 0.00;
BasicNetwork network1 = new BasicNetwork();

// Input layer
network1.addLayer(new BasicLayer(null,true,intInputNeuronNumber));

// Hidden layer.
network1.addLayer(new BasicLayer(new ActivationTANH(),true,7));
network1.addLayer(new BasicLayer(new ActivationTANH(),true,7));
network1.addLayer(new BasicLayer(new ActivationTANH(),true,7));
network1.addLayer(new BasicLayer(new ActivationTANH(),true,7));
network1.addLayer(new BasicLayer(new ActivationTANH(),true,7));
network1.addLayer(new BasicLayer(new ActivationTANH(),true,7));
network1.addLayer(new BasicLayer(new ActivationTANH(),true,7));

// Output layer
network1.addLayer(new BasicLayer(new ActivationTANH(),false,
intOutputNeuronNumber));

network1.getStructure().finalizeStructure();
network1.reset();

maxGlobalResultDiff = 0.00;
averGlobalResultDiff = 0.00;
sumGlobalResultDiff = 0.00;

// Loop over batches
intDayNumber = paramDayNumber;   // Day number for the chart

for (rBatchNumber = paramBatchNumber; rBatchNumber <
numberOfTrainBatchesToProcess;
    rBatchNumber++)
{
  intDayNumber++;
```

```
// Load the training file in memory
MLDataSet trainingSet =
    loadCSV2Memory(strTrainingFileNames[rBatchNumber],
    intInputNeuronNumber,
        intOutputNeuronNumber, true,CSVFormat.ENGLISH,false);
// train the neural network1
ResilientPropagation train = new ResilientPropagation(network1,
trainingSet);
int epoch = 1;
do
   {
     train.iteration();
     epoch++;

       for (MLDataPair pair11:  trainingSet)
       {
         MLData inputData1 = pair11.getInput();
         MLData actualData1 = pair11.getIdeal();
         MLData predictData1 = network1.compute(inputData1);

         // These values are Normalized as the whole input is
         normInputFunctValueDiffPercFromRecord = inputData1.
         getData(0);
         normTargetFunctValue1 = actualData1.getData(0);
         normPredictFunctValue1 = predictData1.getData(0);

         denormInputFunctValueDiffPercFromRecord =((inputDayDl -
             inputDayDh)*normInputFunctValueDiffPercFromRecord -
             Nh*inputDayDl +
                inputDayDh*Nl)/(Nl - Nh);
         denormTargetFunctValue1 = ((targetFunctValueDiffPercDl -
             targetFunctValueDiffPercDh)*normTargetFunctValue1 -
             Nh*targetFunctValueDiffPercDl +
                 targetFunctValueDiffPercDh*Nl)/(Nl - Nh);
         denormAverPredictFunctValue11 =((targetFunctValueDiffPercDl -
             targetFunctValueDiffPercDh)*normPredictFunctValue1 -
             Nh*targetFunctValueDiffPercDl +
```

```
                    targetFunctValueDiffPercDh*Nl)/(Nl - Nh);

        targetToPredictFunctValueDiff = (Math.abs(denormTarget
        FunctValue1 -
             denormAverPredictFunctValue11)/
             denormTargetFunctValue1)*100;
    }

   if (epoch >= 1000 && targetToPredictFunctValueDiff > 0.0000071)
   {
     returnCodes[0] = 1;
     returnCodes[1] = rBatchNumber;
     returnCodes[2] = intDayNumber-1;

     return returnCodes;
   }

 } while(targetToPredictFunctValueDiff > 0.000007);

// This batch is optimized

// Save the network1 for the current batch
EncogDirectoryPersistence.saveObject(new
    File(strSaveTrainNetworkFileNames[rBatchNumber]),network1);

// Get the results after the network1 optimization
int i = - 1;

for (MLDataPair pair1:  trainingSet)
 {
  i++;
  MLData inputData1 = pair1.getInput();
  MLData actualData1 = pair1.getIdeal();
  MLData predictData1 = network1.compute(inputData1);

  // These values are Normalized as the whole input is
  normInputFunctValueDiffPercFromRecord = inputData1.getData(0);
  normTargetFunctValue1 = actualData1.getData(0);
  normPredictFunctValue1 = predictData1.getData(0);
```

```
        // De-normalize the obtained values
        denormInputFunctValueDiffPercFromRecord =((inputDayDl -
          inputDayDh)*normInputFunctValueDiffPercFromRecord -
             Nh*inputDayDl + inputDayDh*Nl)/(Nl - Nh);

        denormTargetFunctValue1 = ((targetFunctValueDiffPercDl -
          targetFunctValueDiffPercDh)*normTargetFunctValue1 -
             Nh*targetFunctValueDiffPercDl +
targetFunctValueDiffPercDh*Nl)/(Nl - Nh);

        denormAverPredictFunctValue11 =((targetFunctValueDiffPercDl -
          targetFunctValueDiffPercDh)*normPredictFunctValue1 -
             Nh*targetFunctValueDiffPercDl +
             targetFunctValueDiffPercDh*Nl)/(Nl - Nh);

        //inputFunctValueFromFile = arrTrainFunctValues[rBatchNumber];

        targetToPredictFunctValueDiff = (Math.abs(denormTargetFunctValue1 -
          denormAverPredictFunctValue11)/denormTargetFunctValue1)*100;

          System.out.println("intDayNumber = " + intDayNumber +
          "  targetFunctionValue = " +
            denormTargetFunctValue1 + "  predictFunctionValue = " +
            denormAverPredictFunctValue11 +
               "  valurDiff = " + targetToPredictFunctValueDiff);

        if (targetToPredictFunctValueDiff > maxGlobalResultDiff)
          maxGlobalResultDiff =targetToPredictFunctValueDiff;

        sumGlobalResultDiff = sumGlobalResultDiff +targetToPredictFunct
        ValueDiff;

        // Populate chart elements
        doubleDayNumber = (double) rBatchNumber+1;
        xData.add(doubleDayNumber);
        yData1.add(denormTargetFunctValue1);
        yData2.add(denormAverPredictFunctValue11);

      }  // End for FunctValue pair1 loop

    }  // End of the loop over batches
```

```
sumGlobalResultDiff = sumGlobalResultDiff +targetToPredict
FunctValueDiff;
averGlobalResultDiff = sumGlobalResultDiff/
numberOfTrainBatchesToProcess;

// Print the max and average results

System.out.println(" ");
System.out.println(" ");
System.out.println("maxGlobalResultDiff = " + maxGlobalResultDiff);
System.out.println("averGlobalResultDiff = " + averGlobalResultDiff);

XYSeries series1 = Chart.addSeries("Actual", xData, yData1);
XYSeries series2 = Chart.addSeries("Predicted", xData, yData2);

series1.setLineColor(XChartSeriesColors.BLUE);
series2.setMarkerColor(Color.ORANGE);
series1.setLineStyle(SeriesLines.SOLID);
series2.setLineStyle(SeriesLines.SOLID);

// Save the chart image
try
  {
    BitmapEncoder.saveBitmapWithDPI(Chart, strTrainChartFileName,
    BitmapFormat.JPG, 100);
  }
  catch (Exception bt)
  {
    bt.printStackTrace();
  }

System.out.println ("The Chart has been saved");

returnCodes[0] = 0;
returnCodes[1] = 0;
returnCodes[2] = 0;
return returnCodes;

} // End of method
```

```java
//==========================================================================
// Load the previously saved trained network1 and tests it by
// processing the Test record
//==========================================================================
static public void loadAndTestNetwork()
 {
   System.out.println("Testing the network1s results");

   List<Double> xData = new ArrayList<Double>();
   List<Double> yData1 = new ArrayList<Double>();
   List<Double> yData2 = new ArrayList<Double>();

   double targetToPredictFunctValueDiff = 0;
   double maxGlobalResultDiff = 0.00;
   double averGlobalResultDiff = 0.00;
   double sumGlobalResultDiff = 0.00;
   double maxGlobalIndex = 0;
   double normInputDayFromRecord1 = 0.00;
   double normTargetFunctValue1 = 0.00;
   double normPredictFunctValue1 = 0.00;
   double denormInputDayFromRecord1 = 0.00;
   double denormTargetFunctValue1 = 0.00;
   double denormAverPredictFunctValue1 = 0.00;
   double normInputDayFromRecord2 = 0.00;
   double normTargetFunctValue2 = 0.00;
   double normPredictFunctValue2 = 0.00;
   double denormInputDayFromRecord2 = 0.00;
   double denormTargetFunctValue2 = 0.00;
   double denormAverPredictFunctValue2 = 0.00;
   double normInputDayFromTestRecord = 0.00;
   double denormInputDayFromTestRecord = 0.00;
   double denormAverPredictFunctValue = 0.00;
   double denormTargetFunctValueFromTestRecord = 0.00;
   String tempLine;
   String[] tempWorkFields;
   double dayKeyFromTestRecord = 0.00;
```

255

```
double targetFunctValueFromTestRecord = 0.00;
double r1 = 0.00;
double r2 = 0.00;
BufferedReader br4;
BasicNetwork network1;
BasicNetwork network2;
int k1 = 0;
int k3 = 0;

try
{
    // Process testing records
    maxGlobalResultDiff = 0.00;
    averGlobalResultDiff = 0.00;
    sumGlobalResultDiff = 0.00;

    for (k1 = 0; k1 < numberOfTestBatchesToProcess; k1++)
     {
        // Read the corresponding test micro-batch file.
        br4 = new BufferedReader(new FileReader(strTesting
        FileNames[k1]));
        tempLine = br4.readLine();

        // Skip the label record
        tempLine = br4.readLine();

        // Brake the line using comma as separator
        tempWorkFields = tempLine.split(cvsSplitBy);

        dayKeyFromTestRecord = Double.parseDouble(tempWorkFields[0]);
        targetFunctValueFromTestRecord = Double.parseDouble(
        tempWorkFields[1]);

        // De-normalize the dayKeyFromTestRecord
        denormInputDayFromTestRecord =
          ((inputDayDl - inputDayDh)*dayKeyFromTestRecord -
                Nh*inputDayDl + inputDayDh*Nl)/(Nl - Nh);
```

```
// De-normalize the targetFunctValueFromTestRecord
denormTargetFunctValueFromTestRecord =
((targetFunctValueDiffPercDl -
   targetFunctValueDiffPercDh)*targetFunctValueFromTestRecord -
     Nh*targetFunctValueDiffPercDl +
     targetFunctValueDiffPercDh*Nl)/(Nl - Nh);

// Load the corresponding training micro-batch dataset in memory
MLDataSet trainingSet1 =
     loadCSV2Memory(strTrainingFileNames[k1],intInputNeuron
     Number,intOutputNeuronNumber,
        true,CSVFormat.ENGLISH,false);
 network1 = (BasicNetwork)EncogDirectoryPersistence.
 loadObject(new File(strSaveTrainNetworkFileNames[k1]));

// Get the results after the network1 optimization
int iMax = 0;
int i = - 1; // Index of the array to get results

for (MLDataPair pair1:  trainingSet1)
 {
    i++;
    iMax = i+1;

    MLData inputData1 = pair1.getInput();
    MLData actualData1 = pair1.getIdeal();
    MLData predictData1 = network1.compute(inputData1);

    // These values are Normalized
    normInputDayFromRecord1 = inputData1.getData(0);
    normTargetFunctValue1 = actualData1.getData(0);
    normPredictFunctValue1 = predictData1.getData(0);

    // De-normalize the obtained values
    denormInputDayFromRecord1 =
      ((inputDayDl - inputDayDh)*normInputDayFromRecord1 -
        Nh*inputDayDl + inputDayDh*Nl)/(Nl - Nh);
```

```
                    denormTargetFunctValue1 = ((targetFunctValueDiffPercDl -
                      targetFunctValueDiffPercDh)*normTargetFunctValue1 -
                        Nh*targetFunctValueDiffPercDl +
                          targetFunctValueDiffPercDh*Nl)/(Nl - Nh);

                    denormAverPredictFunctValue1 =((targetFunctValueDiffPercDl -
                      targetFunctValueDiffPercDh)*normPredictFunctValue1 -
                        Nh*targetFunctValueDiffPercDl +
                            targetFunctValueDiffPercDh*Nl)/(Nl - Nh);

          }  // End for pair1

          // Now calculate everything again for the SaveNetwork (which
          // key is greater than dayKeyFromTestRecord value)in memory

      MLDataSet trainingSet2 =
        loadCSV2Memory(strTrainingFileNames[k1+1],intInputNeuronNumber,
          intOutputNeuronNumber,true,CSVFormat.ENGLISH,false);
      network2 =
          (BasicNetwork)EncogDirectoryPersistence.
            loadObject(new File(strSaveTrainNetworkFileNames[k1+1]));

        // Get the results after the network1 optimization
        iMax = 0;
        i = - 1;

        for (MLDataPair pair2:  trainingSet2)
        {
            i++;
            iMax = i+1;

            MLData inputData2 = pair2.getInput();
            MLData actualData2 = pair2.getIdeal();
            MLData predictData2 = network2.compute(inputData2);

            // These values are Normalized
            normInputDayFromRecord2 = inputData2.getData(0);
            normTargetFunctValue2 = actualData2.getData(0);
            normPredictFunctValue2 = predictData2.getData(0);
```

```
    // De-normalize the obtained values
    denormInputDayFromRecord2 =
      ((inputDayDl - inputDayDh)*normInputDayFromRecord2 -
        Nh*inputDayDl + inputDayDh*Nl)/(Nl - Nh);

    denormTargetFunctValue2 = ((targetFunctValueDiffPercDl -
      targetFunctValueDiffPercDh)*normTargetFunctValue2 -
        Nh*targetFunctValueDiffPercDl +
        targetFunctValueDiffPercDh*Nl)/(Nl - Nh);

    denormAverPredictFunctValue2 =((targetFunctValueDiffPercDl -
      targetFunctValueDiffPercDh)*normPredictFunctValue2 -
        Nh*targetFunctValueDiffPercDl +
          targetFunctValueDiffPercDh*Nl)/(Nl - Nh);
} // End for pair1 loop

// Get the average of the denormAverPredictFunctValue1 and
denormAverPredictFunctValue2
denormAverPredictFunctValue = (denormAverPredictFunctValue1 +
      denormAverPredictFunctValue2)/2;

targetToPredictFunctValueDiff =
  (Math.abs(denormTargetFunctValueFromTestRecord -
    denormAverPredictFunctValue)/denormTargetFunctValue
    FromTestRecord)*100;

  System.out.println("Record Number = " + k1 + "  DayNumber = " +
      denormInputDayFromTestRecord +
    "  denormTargetFunctValueFromTestRecord = " +
      denormTargetFunctValueFromTestRecord
      + "  denormAverPredictFunctValue = " +
          denormAverPredictFunctValue +
      "  valurDiff = " + targetToPredictFunctValueDiff);
  if (targetToPredictFunctValueDiff > maxGlobalResultDiff)
  {
    maxGlobalIndex = iMax;
    maxGlobalResultDiff =targetToPredictFunctValueDiff;
  }
```

```
            sumGlobalResultDiff = sumGlobalResultDiff +
              targetToPredictFunctValueDiff;

            // Populate chart elements

            xData.add(denormInputDayFromTestRecord);
            yData1.add(denormTargetFunctValueFromTestRecord);
            yData2.add(denormAverPredictFunctValue);

        }    // End of loop using k1

      // Print the max and average results

      System.out.println(" ");

      averGlobalResultDiff = sumGlobalResultDiff/
      numberOfTestBatchesToProcess;

      System.out.println("maxGlobalResultDiff = " + maxGlobalResultDiff +
        "  i = " + maxGlobalIndex);
      System.out.println("averGlobalResultDiff = " +
      averGlobalResultDiff);

    }      // End of TRY
   catch (IOException e1)
   {
        e1.printStackTrace();
   }

   // All testing batch files have been processed
   XYSeries series1 = Chart.addSeries("Actual", xData, yData1);
   XYSeries series2 = Chart.addSeries("Forecasted", xData, yData2);

   series1.setLineColor(XChartSeriesColors.BLUE);
   series2.setMarkerColor(Color.ORANGE);
   series1.setLineStyle(SeriesLines.SOLID);
   series2.setLineStyle(SeriesLines.SOLID);
```

```
    // Save the chart image
    try
     {
       BitmapEncoder.saveBitmapWithDPI(Chart, strTrainChartFileName,
         BitmapFormat.JPG, 100);
     }
    catch (Exception bt)
     {
       bt.printStackTrace();
     }

    System.out.println ("The Chart has been saved");
    System.out.println("End of testing for mini-batches training");

  } // End of the method


} // End of the  Encog class
```

The processing logic is quite different in this program. Let's start from the getChart() method. Apart from the usual statements needed by the XChart package, we generate here the names for the training micro-batches and save-network files. The generated filenames for micro-batches must match the micro-batch filenames being prepared on disk when we broke the normalized training file into micro-batches.

The names for saved-network files have a corresponding structure. These generated names will be used by the training method to save the trained networks corresponding to the micro-batches on disk. The generated names are saved in two arrays called strTrainingFileNames[] and strSaveTrainNetworkFileNames[].

Figure 8-5 shows a fragment of the generated saved network files.

```
Sample5_Save_Network_Batch_000.csv
Sample5_Save_Network_Batch_001.csv
Sample5_Save_Network_Batch_002.csv
Sample5_Save_Network_Batch_003.csv
Sample5_Save_Network_Batch_004.csv
Sample5_Save_Network_Batch_005.csv
Sample5_Save_Network_Batch_006.csv
Sample5_Save_Network_Batch_007.csv
Sample5_Save_Network_Batch_008.csv
Sample5_Save_Network_Batch_009.csv
Sample5_Save_Network_Batch_010.csv
Sample5_Save_Network_Batch_011.csv
Sample5_Save_Network_Batch_012.csv
Sample5_Save_Network_Batch_013.csv
Sample5_Save_Network_Batch_014.csv
Sample5_Save_Network_Batch_015.csv
Sample5_Save_Network_Batch_016.csv
Sample5_Save_Network_Batch_017.csv
Sample5_Save_Network_Batch_018.csv
Sample5_Save_Network_Batch_019.csv
Sample5_Save_Network_Batch_020.csv
Sample5_Save_Network_Batch_021.csv
```

Figure 8-5.   *Fragment of the generated saved network files*

Next, we generate and populate two arrays called linkToSaveNetworkDayKeys[] and linkToSaveNetworkTargetFunctValueKeys[]. For each consecutive day, we populate the linkToSaveNetworkDayKeys[] array with the Field 1 value from the training micro-batch records. We populate the linkToSaveNetworkTargetFunctValueKeys[] array with the names of the corresponding saved network file on disk. Therefore, those two arrays hold the link between the micro-batch dataset and the corresponding saved network dataset.

The program also generates the names of the testing micro-batch files, similar to the generated names for the training micro-batch files. When all this is done, we call the loadTrainFunctValueFileInMemory method that loads the training file values into memory.

Program Code for the getChart() Method

Listing 8-5 shows the program code for the getChart() method.

Listing 8-5. Code of the getChart Method

```
public XYChart getChart()
 {

  // Create the Chart

  Chart = new XYChartBuilder().width(900).height(500).title(getClass().
    getSimpleName()).xAxisTitle("day").yAxisTitle("y=f(day)").build();

  // Customize Chart
  Chart.getStyler().setPlotBackgroundColor(ChartColor.
  getAWTColor(ChartColor.GREY));
  Chart.getStyler().setPlotGridLinesColor(new Color(255, 255, 255));
  Chart.getStyler().setChartBackgroundColor(Color.WHITE);
  Chart.getStyler().setLegendBackgroundColor(Color.PINK);
  Chart.getStyler().setChartFontColor(Color.MAGENTA);
  Chart.getStyler().setChartTitleBoxBackgroundColor(new Color(0, 222, 0));
  Chart.getStyler().setChartTitleBoxVisible(true);
  Chart.getStyler().setChartTitleBoxBorderColor(Color.BLACK);
  Chart.getStyler().setPlotGridLinesVisible(true);
  Chart.getStyler().setAxisTickPadding(20);
  Chart.getStyler().setAxisTickMarkLength(15);
  Chart.getStyler().setPlotMargin(20);
  Chart.getStyler().setChartTitleVisible(false);
  Chart.getStyler().setChartTitleFont(new Font(Font.MONOSPACED,
  Font.BOLD, 24));
  Chart.getStyler().setLegendFont(new Font(Font.SERIF, Font.PLAIN, 18));
  // Chart.getStyler().setLegendPosition(LegendPosition.InsideSE);
  Chart.getStyler().setLegendPosition(LegendPosition.OutsideE);
  Chart.getStyler().setLegendSeriesLineLength(12);
  Chart.getStyler().setAxisTitleFont(new Font(Font.SANS_SERIF,Font.
  ITALIC, 18));
  Chart.getStyler().setAxisTickLabelsFont(new Font(Font.SERIF,
  Font.PLAIN, 11));
  //Chart.getStyler().setDayPattern("yyyy-MM");
  Chart.getStyler().setDecimalPattern("#0.00");
```

```
// Config data

// For training
//intWorkingMode = 0;

// For testing
intWorkingMode = 1;
// common config data

intNumberOfTrainBatchesToProcess = 1000;
intNumberOfTestBatchesToProcess = 1000;
intNumberOfRecordsInTestFile = 999;
intNumberOfRowsInBatches = 1;
intInputNeuronNumber = 1;
intOutputNeuronNumber = 1;
strTrainFileNameBase = "C:/Book_Examples/Sample5_Train_Norm_Batch_";
strTestFileNameBase = "C:/Book_Examples/Sample5_Test_Norm_Batch_";
strSaveTrainNetworkFileBase = "C:/Book_Examples/Sample5_Save_Network_
Batch_";
strTrainChartFileName = "C:/Book_Examples/Sample5_Chart_Train_File_
Microbatch.jpg";
strTestChartFileName = "C:/Book_Examples/Sample5_Chart_Test_File_
Microbatch.jpg";
strFunctValueTrainFile = "C:/Book_Examples/Sample5_Train_Real.csv";
strFunctValueTestFile = "C:/Book_Examples/Sample5_Test_Real.csv";

// Generate training micro-batch file names and the corresponding Save
Network file names

intDayNumber = -1;   // Day number for the chart

for (int i = 0; i < intNumberOfTrainBatchesToProcess; i++)
 {
   intDayNumber++;

   iString = Integer.toString(intDayNumber);
```

```
  if (intDayNumber >= 10 & intDayNumber < 100  )
  {
    strOutputFileName = strTrainFileNameBase + "0" + iString + ".csv";
    strSaveNetworkFileName = strSaveTrainNetworkFileBase + "0" +
    iString + ".csv";
  }
  else
  {
    if (intDayNumber < 10)
     {
       strOutputFileName = strTrainFileNameBase + "00" +
         iString + ".csv";
       strSaveNetworkFileName = strSaveTrainNetworkFileBase + "00" +
       iString + ".csv";
     }
    else
     {
       strOutputFileName = strTrainFileNameBase + iString + ".csv";

       strSaveNetworkFileName = strSaveTrainNetworkFileBase + iString
       + ".csv";
     }
  }

    strTrainingFileNames[intDayNumber] = strOutputFileName;
    strSaveTrainNetworkFileNames[intDayNumber] =
    strSaveNetworkFileName;

} // End the FOR loop

// Build the array linkToSaveNetworkFunctValueDiffKeys

String tempLine;
double tempNormFunctValueDiff = 0.00;
double tempNormFunctValueDiffPerc = 0.00;
double tempNormTargetFunctValueDiffPerc = 0.00;
```

```
    String[] tempWorkFields;

    try
     {
        intDayNumber = -1;  // Day number for the chart

        for (int m = 0; m < intNumberOfTrainBatchesToProcess; m++)
          {
            intDayNumber++;

            BufferedReader br3 = new BufferedReader(new
            FileReader(strTrainingFileNames[intDayNumber]));
            tempLine = br3.readLine();

            // Skip the label record and zero batch record
            tempLine = br3.readLine();

            // Brake the line using comma as separator
            tempWorkFields = tempLine.split(cvsSplitBy);

            tempNormFunctValueDiffPerc = Double.parseDouble(tempWork
            Fields[0]);
            tempNormTargetFunctValueDiffPerc = Double.parseDouble(
            tempWorkFields[1]);

            linkToSaveNetworkDayKeys[intDayNumber] =
            tempNormFunctValueDiffPerc;
            linkToSaveNetworkTargetFunctValueKeys[intDayNumber] =
                tempNormTargetFunctValueDiffPerc;

          }  // End the FOR loop

        // Generate testing micro-batch file names

        if(intWorkingMode == 1)
          {
            intDayNumber = -1;

            for (int i = 0; i < intNumberOfTestBatchesToProcess; i++)
              {
                intDayNumber++;
```

```java
            iString = Integer.toString(intDayNumber);

            // Construct the testing batch names
            if (intDayNumber >= 10 & intDayNumber < 100  )
             {
               strOutputFileName = strTestFileNameBase + "0" +
                 iString + ".csv";
             }
            else
             {
               if (intDayNumber < 10)
                {
                  strOutputFileName = strTestFileNameBase + "00" +
                    iString + ".csv";
                }
               else
                {
                  strOutputFileName = strTrainFileNameBase +
                    iString + ".csv";
                }
             }

          strTestingFileNames[intDayNumber] = strOutputFileName;

       }  // End the FOR loop

     }   // End of IF

  }      // End for try
catch (IOException io1)
 {
   io1.printStackTrace();
   System.exit(1);
 }

// Load, train, and test Function Values file in memory
loadTrainFunctValueFileInMemory();
```

When this part is done, the logic checks whether to run the training or testing method. When the workingMode field is 1, it calls the training method in a loop (the way we did it previously). However, because we now have many micro-batch training files (instead of the single dataset), we need to expand the errorCode array to hold one more value: the micro-batch number.

Code Fragment 1 of the Training Method

If after many iterations the network error is unable to clear the error limit, we exit the training method with a returnCode of 1. The control is returned to the logic inside the getChart() method that calls the training method in a loop. At that point, we need to return the parameters that the micro-batch method is being called with. Listing 8-6 shows code fragment 1 of the training method.

Listing 8-6. Code Fragment 1 of the Training Method

```
if(intWorkingMode == 0)
   {
      // Train batches and save the trained networks

      int paramErrorCode;
      int paramBatchNumber;
      int paramR;
      int paramDayNumber;
      int paramS;

      File file1 = new File(strTrainChartFileName);

      if(file1.exists())
        file1.delete();

    returnCodes[0] = 0;    // Clear the error Code
    returnCodes[1] = 0;    // Set the initial batch Number to 0;
    returnCodes[2] = 0;    // Set the initial day number to 0;

    do
      {
          paramErrorCode = returnCodes[0];
```

```
            paramBatchNumber = returnCodes[1];
            paramDayNumber = returnCodes[2];

            returnCodes =
            trainBatches(paramErrorCode,paramBatchNumber,paramDayNumber);
        } while (returnCodes[0] > 0);

    }   // End of the train logic
else
    {
        // Load and test the network logic

        File file2 = new File(strTestChartFileName);

        if(file2.exists())
         file2.delete();

        loadAndTestNetwork();

        // End of the test logic
    }

    Encog.getInstance().shutdown();
    return Chart;

}   // End of method
```

Code Fragment 2 of the Training Method

Here, most of the code should be familiar to you, except the logic involved in processing the micro-batches. First, we build the network. Next, we loop over the micro-batches (remember, there are many training micro-batch files instead of a single training dataset that we processed before). Inside the loop, we load the training micro-batch file in memory and then train the network using the current micro-batch file.

When the network is trained, we save it on disk, using the name from the linkToSaveNetworkDayKeys array that corresponds to the currently processed micro-batch file. Looping over the pair dataset, we retrieve the input, actual, and predicted values for each micro-batch, denormalize them, and print the results as the training log.

Within the network training loop, when after many iterations the network error is unable to clear the error limit, we set the returnCode to 1 and exit the training method. The control is returned to the logic that calls the training method in a loop. When we exit the training method, we now set three returnCode values: returnCode, micro-batch number, and day number. That helps the logic that calls the training method in a loop to stay within the same micro-batch and day of processing. We also populate the results for the chart elements. Finally, we add the chart data, calculate the average and maximum errors for all the micro-batches, print the results as the log file, and save the chart file. Listing 8-7 shows code fragment 2 of the training method.

Listing 8-7. Code Fragment 2 of the Training Method

```
// Build the network
BasicNetwork network = new BasicNetwork();

// Input layer
network.addLayer(new BasicLayer(null,true,intInputNeuronNumber));

// Hidden layer.
network.addLayer(new BasicLayer(new ActivationTANH(),true,5));
network.addLayer(new BasicLayer(new ActivationTANH(),true,5));
network.addLayer(new BasicLayer(new ActivationTANH(),true,5));
network.addLayer(new BasicLayer(new ActivationTANH(),true,5));
network.addLayer(new BasicLayer(new ActivationTANH(),true,5));
network.addLayer(new BasicLayer(new ActivationTANH(),true,5));
network.addLayer(new BasicLayer(new ActivationTANH(),true,5));

// Output layer
network.addLayer(new BasicLayer(new ActivationTANH(),false,
intOutputNeuronNumber));

network.getStructure().finalizeStructure();
network.reset();

maxGlobalResultDiff = 0.00;
averGlobalResultDiff = 0.00;
sumGlobalResultDiff = 0.00;
```

```
// Loop over micro-batches

intDayNumber = paramDayNumber;   // Day number for the chart

for (rBatchNumber = paramBatchNumber; rBatchNumber <
intNumberOfTrainBatchesToProcess; rBatchNumber++)
  {
      intDayNumber++;  // Day number for the chart

      // Load the training CVS file for the current batch in memory
      MLDataSet trainingSet =
          loadCSV2Memory(strTrainingFileNames[rBatchNumber],intInputNeuron
          Number,intOutputNeuronNumber
            ,true,CSVFormat.ENGLISH,false);

    // train the neural network
    ResilientPropagation train = new ResilientPropagation(network,
    trainingSet);

   int epoch = 1;
  double tempLastErrorPerc = 0.00;

  do
    {
        train.iteration();

      epoch++;

      for (MLDataPair pair1:  trainingSet)
        {
            MLData inputData = pair1.getInput();
            MLData actualData = pair1.getIdeal();
            MLData predictData = network.compute(inputData);

            // These values are Normalized as the whole input is
            normInputFunctValueDiffPercFromRecord = inputData.getData(0);

            normTargetFunctValue = actualData.getData(0);
            normPredictFunctValue = predictData.getData(0);
```

```
        denormInputFunctValueDiffPercFromRecord =
            ((inputDayDl - inputDayDh)*normInputFunctValueDiffPerc
            FromRecord - Nh*inputDayDl +
                    inputDayDh*Nl)/(Nl - Nh);

        denormTargetFunctValue =
            ((targetFunctValueDiffPercDl - targetFunctValueDiffPercDh)*
            normTargetFunctValue -
                Nh*targetFunctValueDiffPercDl +
                    targetFunctValueDiffPercDh*Nl)/(Nl - Nh);
        denormPredictFunctValue =
            ((targetFunctValueDiffPercDl - targetFunctValueDiffPercDh)*
            normPredictFunctValue -
                    Nh*targetFunctValueDiffPercDl +
                    targetFunctValueDiffPercDh*Nl)/(Nl - Nh);

        inputFunctValueFromFile = arrTrainFunctValues[rBatchNumber];

        targetToPredictFunctValueDiff = (Math.abs(denormTargetFunctValue -
                denormPredictFunctValue)/denormTargetFunctValue)*100;

    }

   if (epoch >= 500 &&targetToPredictFunctValueDiff > 0.0002)
      {
          returnCodes[0] = 1;
          returnCodes[1] = rBatchNumber;
          returnCodes[2] = intDayNumber-1;
          return returnCodes;
      }

  } while(targetToPredictFunctValueDiff >  0.0002);  // 0.00002

// Save the network for the current batch
EncogDirectoryPersistence.saveObject(new File(strSaveTrainNetwork
FileNames[rBatchNumber]),network);

// Get the results after the network optimization
int i = - 1;
```

```
for (MLDataPair pair:  trainingSet)
{
  i++;

  MLData inputData = pair.getInput();
  MLData actualData = pair.getIdeal();
  MLData predictData = network.compute(inputData);

  // These values are Normalized as the whole input is
  normInputFunctValueDiffPercFromRecord = inputData.getData(0);

  normTargetFunctValue = actualData.getData(0);
  normPredictFunctValue = predictData.getData(0);

  denormInputFunctValueDiffPercFromRecord =
     ((inputDayDl - inputDayDh)*normInputFunctValueDiffPercFrom
     Record - Nh*inputDayDl +
       inputDayDh*Nl)/(Nl - Nh);

  denormTargetFunctValue =
     ((targetFunctValueDiffPercDl - targetFunctValueDiffPercDh)*
      normTargetFunctValue -
        Nh*targetFunctValueDiffPercDl +
        targetFunctValueDiffPercDh*Nl)/(Nl - Nh);

  denormPredictFunctValue =
     ((targetFunctValueDiffPercDl - targetFunctValueDiffPercDh)*
      normPredictFunctValue -
        Nh*targetFunctValueDiffPercDl +
        targetFunctValueDiffPercDh*Nl)/(Nl - Nh);

   inputFunctValueFromFile = arrTrainFunctValues[rBatchNumber];

  targetToPredictFunctValueDiff =
         (Math.abs(denormTargetFunctValue - denormPredictFunctValue)/
         denormTargetFunctValue)*100;

  System.out.println("intDayNumber = " + intDayNumber
+ "  targetFunctionValue = " +
       denormTargetFunctValue +
```

```
            "  predictFunctionValue = " + denormPredictFunctValue +
              "  valurDiff = " +
            targetToPredictFunctValueDiff);

      if (targetToPredictFunctValueDiff > maxGlobalResultDiff)
        maxGlobalResultDiff =targetToPredictFunctValueDiff;

      sumGlobalResultDiff = sumGlobalResultDiff
      +targetToPredictFunctValueDiff;

      // Populate chart elements
      doubleDayNumber = (double) rBatchNumber+1;
      xData.add(doubleDayNumber);
      yData1.add(denormTargetFunctValue);
      yData2.add(denormPredictFunctValue);

    }  // End for the pair loop

  }  // End of the loop over batches

  sumGlobalResultDiff = sumGlobalResultDiff
  +targetToPredictFunctValueDiff;
  averGlobalResultDiff = sumGlobalResultDiff/
  intNumberOfTrainBatchesToProcess;

  // Print the max and average results

  System.out.println(" ");
  System.out.println(" ");
  System.out.println("maxGlobalResultDiff = " + maxGlobalResultDiff);
  System.out.println("averGlobalResultDiff = " + averGlobalResultDiff);

  XYSeries series1 = Chart.addSeries("Actual", xData, yData1);
  XYSeries series2 = Chart.addSeries("Predicted", xData, yData2);

  series1.setLineColor(XChartSeriesColors.BLUE);
  series2.setMarkerColor(Color.ORANGE);
  series1.setLineStyle(SeriesLines.SOLID);
  series2.setLineStyle(SeriesLines.SOLID);
```

```
// Save the chart image
try
  {
    BitmapEncoder.saveBitmapWithDPI(Chart, strTrainChartFileName,
    BitmapFormat.JPG, 100);
  }
  catch (Exception bt)
  {
      bt.printStackTrace();
  }

  System.out.println ("The Chart has been saved");

returnCodes[0] = 0;
returnCodes[1] = 0;
returnCodes[2] = 0;

return returnCodes;

} // End of method
```

Training Results for the Micro-Batch Method

Listing 8-8 shows the ending fragment of the training results.

Listing 8-8. Training Results

```
DayNumber =  989  TargeValue = 735.09  PredictedValue =
735.09005  DiffPercf = 6.99834E-6
DayNumber =  990  TargeValue = 797.87  PredictedValue =
797.86995  DiffPercf = 6.13569E-6
DayNumber =  991  TargeValue = 672.81  PredictedValue =
672.80996  DiffPercf = 5.94874E-6
DayNumber =  992  TargeValue = 619.14  PredictedValue =
619.14003  DiffPercf = 5.53621E-6
DayNumber =  993  TargeValue = 619.32  PredictedValue =
619.32004  DiffPercf = 5.65663E-6
```

```
DayNumber =  994  TargeValue = 590.47  PredictedValue =
590.47004  DiffPercf = 6.40373E-6
DayNumber =  995  TargeValue = 547.28  PredictedValue =
547.27996  DiffPercf = 6.49734E-6
DayNumber =  996  TargeValue = 514.62  PredictedValue =
514.62002  DiffPercf = 3.39624E-6
DayNumber =  997  TargeValue = 455.4   PredictedValue =
455.40000  DiffPercf = 2.73780E-7
DayNumber =  998  TargeValue = 470.43  PredictedValue =
470.42999  DiffPercf = 4.35234E-7
DayNumber =  999  TargeValue = 480.28  PredictedValue =
480.28002  DiffPercf = 3.52857E-6
DayNumber = 1000 TargeValue = 496.77  PredictedValue = 496.76999
DiffPercf = 9.81900E-7

maxGlobalResultDiff = 9.819000149262707E-7
averGlobalResultDiff = 1.9638000298525415E-9
```

Now, the training processing results are quite good, especially for the approximation of the noncontinuous function. The average error is 0.0000000019638000298525415, and the maximum error (the worst optimized record) is 0.0000009.819000149262707, so the chart looks great. Figure 8-6 shows the chart of the training processing results using micro-batches.

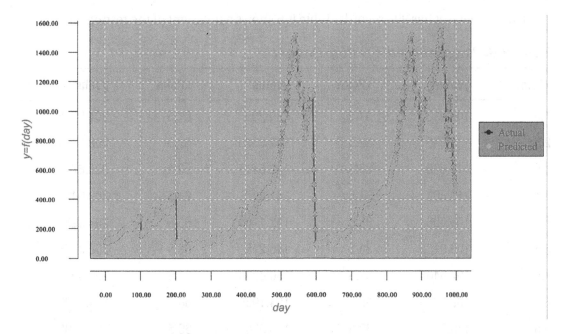

Figure 8-6. *Chart of training results using micro-batches*

For testing, we will build a file with values between the training points. For example, for two training records 1 and 2 we will calculate a new day as the average of the two training days. For the record's function value, we will calculate the average of the two training function values. This way, two consecutive training records will create a single test record with values averaging the training records. Table 8-4 shows how the test record looks.

Table 8-4. *Test Record*

1.5	108.918

It averages the two training records shown in Table 8-5.

Table 8-5. *Two Training Records*

1	107.387
2	110.449

The test dataset has 998 records. Table 8-6 shows a fragment of the testing dataset.

Table 8-6. *Fragment of the Testing Dataset*

xPoint	yValue	xPoint	yValue	xPoint	yValue
1.5	108.918	31.5	139.295	61.5	204.9745
2.5	113.696	32.5	142.3625	62.5	208.6195
3.5	117.806	33.5	142.6415	63.5	207.67
4.5	113.805	34.5	141.417	64.5	209.645
5.5	106.006	35.5	142.1185	65.5	208.525
6.5	106.6155	36.5	146.215	66.5	208.3475
7.5	107.5465	37.5	150.6395	67.5	203.801
8.5	109.5265	38.5	154.1935	68.5	194.6105
9.5	116.223	39.5	158.338	69.5	199.9695
10.5	118.1905	40.5	161.4155	70.5	207.9885
11.5	121.9095	41.5	161.851	71.5	206.2175
12.5	127.188	42.5	164.6005	72.5	199.209
13.5	130.667	43.5	165.935	73.5	193.6235
14.5	132.6525	44.5	165.726	74.5	199.5985
15.5	134.472	45.5	171.9045	75.5	206.252
16.5	135.4405	46.5	178.1175	76.5	208.113
17.5	133.292	47.5	182.7085	77.5	209.791
18.5	130.646	48.5	181.5475	78.5	213.623
19.5	125.5585	49.5	182.102	79.5	217.2275
20.5	117.5155	50.5	186.5895	80.5	216.961
21.5	119.236	51.5	187.8145	81.5	214.721
22.5	125.013	52.5	190.376	82.5	216.248
23.5	125.228	53.5	194.19	83.5	221.882
24.5	128.5005	54.5	194.545	84.5	225.885
25.5	133.9045	55.5	196.702	85.5	232.1255

(*continued*)

Table 8-6. (*continued*)

xPoint	yValue	xPoint	yValue	xPoint	yValue
26.5	138.7075	56.5	198.783	86.5	236.318
27.5	140.319	57.5	199.517	87.5	237.346
28.5	135.412	58.5	204.2805	88.5	239.8
29.5	133.6245	59.5	206.323	89.5	241.7605
30.5	137.074	60.5	202.6945	90.5	244.6855

Table 8-7 shows a fragment of the normalized testing dataset.

Table 8-7. *Fragment of the Normalized Testing Dataset*

xPoint	y	xPoint	y	xPoint	y
-0.9990	-0.9365	-0.9389	-0.8970	-0.8789	-0.8117
-0.9970	-0.9303	-0.9369	-0.8930	-0.8769	-0.8070
-0.9950	-0.9249	-0.9349	-0.8927	-0.8749	-0.8082
-0.9930	-0.9301	-0.9329	-0.8943	-0.8729	-0.8057
-0.9910	-0.9403	-0.9309	-0.8934	-0.8709	-0.8071
-0.9890	-0.9395	-0.9289	-0.8880	-0.8689	-0.8073
-0.9870	-0.9383	-0.9269	-0.8823	-0.8669	-0.8132
-0.9850	-0.9357	-0.9249	-0.8777	-0.8649	-0.8252
-0.9830	-0.9270	-0.9229	-0.8723	-0.8629	-0.8182
-0.9810	-0.9244	-0.9209	-0.8683	-0.8609	-0.8078
-0.9790	-0.9196	-0.9189	-0.8677	-0.8589	-0.8101
-0.9770	-0.9127	-0.9169	-0.8642	-0.8569	-0.8192
-0.9750	-0.9082	-0.9149	-0.8624	-0.8549	-0.8265
-0.9730	-0.9056	-0.9129	-0.8627	-0.8529	-0.8187
-0.9710	-0.9033	-0.9109	-0.8547	-0.8509	-0.8101

(*continued*)

Table 8-7. (*continued*)

xPoint	y	xPoint	y	xPoint	y
-0.9690	-0.9020	-0.9089	-0.8466	-0.8488	-0.8076
-0.9670	-0.9048	-0.9069	-0.8406	-0.8468	-0.8055
-0.9650	-0.9083	-0.9049	-0.8421	-0.8448	-0.8005
-0.9630	-0.9149	-0.9029	-0.8414	-0.8428	-0.7958
-0.9610	-0.9253	-0.9009	-0.8356	-0.8408	-0.7962
-0.9590	-0.9231	-0.8989	-0.8340	-0.8388	-0.7991
-0.9570	-0.9156	-0.8969	-0.8307	-0.8368	-0.7971
-0.9550	-0.9153	-0.8949	-0.8257	-0.8348	-0.7898
-0.9530	-0.9110	-0.8929	-0.8253	-0.8328	-0.7846
-0.9510	-0.9040	-0.8909	-0.8225	-0.8308	-0.7765
-0.9489	-0.8978	-0.8889	-0.8198	-0.8288	-0.7710
-0.9469	-0.8957	-0.8869	-0.8188	-0.8268	-0.7697
-0.9449	-0.9021	-0.8849	-0.8126	-0.8248	-0.7665
-0.9429	-0.9044	-0.8829	-0.8100	-0.8228	-0.7639
-0.9409	-0.8999	-0.8809	-0.8147	-0.8208	-0.7601

Similar to the normalized training dataset, we break the normalized testing dataset into micro-batches. Each micro-batch dataset should contain the label record and the record from the original file to be processed. As a result, we will get 998 micro-batch datasets (numbered from 0 to 997). Figure 8-7 shows a fragment of the list of normalized test micro-batch files.

Sample5_Test_Norm_Batch_000.csv
Sample5_Test_Norm_Batch_001.csv
Sample5_Test_Norm_Batch_002.csv
Sample5_Test_Norm_Batch_003.csv
Sample5_Test_Norm_Batch_004.csv
Sample5_Test_Norm_Batch_005.csv
Sample5_Test_Norm_Batch_006.csv
Sample5_Test_Norm_Batch_007.csv
Sample5_Test_Norm_Batch_008.csv
Sample5_Test_Norm_Batch_009.csv
Sample5_Test_Norm_Batch_010.csv
Sample5_Test_Norm_Batch_011.csv
Sample5_Test_Norm_Batch_012.csv
Sample5_Test_Norm_Batch_013.csv
Sample5_Test_Norm_Batch_014.csv
Sample5_Test_Norm_Batch_015.csv
Sample5_Test_Norm_Batch_016.csv
Sample5_Test_Norm_Batch_017.csv
Sample5_Test_Norm_Batch_018.csv
Sample5_Test_Norm_Batch_019.csv
Sample5_Test_Norm_Batch_020.csv
Sample5_Test_Norm_Batch_021.csv
Sample5_Test_Norm_Batch_022.csv
Sample5_Test_Norm_Batch_023.csv
Sample5_Test_Norm_Batch_024.csv
Sample5_Test_Norm_Batch_025.csv
Sample5_Test_Norm_Batch_026.csv
Sample5_Test_Norm_Batch_027.csv
Sample5_Test_Norm_Batch_028.csv
Sample5_Test_Norm_Batch_029.csv
Sample5_Test_Norm_Batch_030.csv
Sample5_Test_Norm_Batch_031.csv

Figure 8-7. *Fragment of the normalized micro-batch test dataset*

This set of files is now the input to the neural network testing process.

Testing the Processing Logic

Here, we loop over micro-batches. For each test micro-batch, we read its record, retrieve the record values, and denormalize them. Next, we load the micro-batch dataset for point 1 (which is the closest point to the testing record, but less than it) in memory. We also load the corresponding saved network file in memory. Looping over the pairs dataset, we retrieve the input, active, and predicted values for the micro-batch and denormalize them.

We also load the micro-batch dataset for point 2 (which is the closest point to the testing record, but greater than it) in memory, and we load the corresponding saved network file in memory. Looping over the pairs dataset, we retrieve the input, active, and predicted values for the micro-batch and denormalize them.

Next, we calculate the average predicted function values for point 1 and point 2. Finally, we calculate the error percent and print the results as the processing log. The rest is just the miscellaneous stuff. Listing 8-9 shows the program code for the testing method.

Listing 8-9. Code of the Testing Method

```
for (k1 = 0; k1 < intNumberOfRecordsInTestFile; k1++)
   {
            // Read the corresponding test micro-batch file.
            br4 = new BufferedReader(new FileReader(strTestingFileNames
            [k1]));
            tempLine = br4.readLine();

            // Skip the label record
            tempLine = br4.readLine();

            // Brake the line using comma as separator
            tempWorkFields = tempLine.split(cvsSplitBy);

            dayKeyFromRecord = Double.parseDouble(tempWorkFields[0]);
            targetFunctValueFromRecord = Double.parseDouble(tempWork
            Fields[1]);

            // Load the corresponding test micro-batch dataset in memory
            MLDataSet testingSet =
               loadCSV2Memory(strTestingFileNames[k1],intInputNeuronNumber,
               intOutputNeuronNumber,
                  true,CSVFormat.ENGLISH,false);

            // Load the corresponding save network for the currently
            processed micro-batch
            r1 = linkToSaveNetworkDayKeys[k1];
```

```
network =
  (BasicNetwork)EncogDirectoryPersistence.loadObject(new
    File(strSaveTrainNetworkFileNames[k1]));

// Get the results after the network optimization
int iMax = 0;
int i = - 1; // Index of the array to get results

for (MLDataPair pair:  testingSet)
 {
    i++;
    iMax = i+1;

    MLData inputData = pair.getInput();
    MLData actualData = pair.getIdeal();
    MLData predictData = network.compute(inputData);

    // These values are Normalized as the whole input is
    normInputDayFromRecord = inputData.getData(0);
    normTargetFunctValue = actualData.getData(0);
    normPredictFunctValue = predictData.getData(0);

    denormInputDayFromRecord =
      ((inputDayDl - inputDayDh)*normInputDayFromRecord -
        Nh*inputDayDl + inputDayDh*Nl)/(Nl - Nh);

    denormTargetFunctValue = ((targetFunctValueDiffPercDl -
      targetFunctValueDiffPercDh)*normTargetFunctValue -
        Nh*targetFunctValueDiffPercDl +
        targetFunctValueDiffPercDh*Nl)/(Nl - Nh);

    denormPredictFunctValue =((targetFunctValueDiffPercDl -
      targetFunctValueDiffPercDh)*normPredictFunctValue -
        Nh*targetFunctValueDiffPercDl +
          targetFunctValueDiffPercDh*Nl)/(Nl - Nh);

    targetToPredictFunctValueDiff =
      (Math.abs(denormTargetFunctValue -
        denormPredictFunctValue)/denormTargetFunctValue)*100;
```

```java
            System.out.println("DayNumber = " +
            denormInputDayFromRecord +
               "  targetFunctionValue = " + denormTargetFunctValue +
               "  predictFunctionValue = " + denormPredictFunctValue +
               "  valurDiff = " + targetToPredictFunctValueDiff);

            if (targetToPredictFunctValueDiff > maxGlobalResultDiff)
             {
               maxGlobalIndex = iMax;
               maxGlobalResultDiff =targetToPredictFunctValueDiff;
             }

            sumGlobalResultDiff = sumGlobalResultDiff +
               targetToPredictFunctValueDiff;

            // Populate chart elements

            xData.add(denormInputDayFromRecord);
            yData1.add(denormTargetFunctValue);
            yData2.add(denormPredictFunctValue);

          }  // End for pair loop

        }    // End of loop using k1

      // Print the max and average results

      System.out.println(" ");

      averGlobalResultDiff = sumGlobalResultDiff/
      intNumberOfRecordsInTestFile;

      System.out.println("maxErrorPerc = " + maxGlobalResultDiff);
      System.out.println("averErroPerc = " + averGlobalResultDiff);

    }
  catch (IOException e1)
   {
        e1.printStackTrace();
   }
```

```
 // All testing batch files have been processed
   XYSeries series1 = Chart.addSeries("Actual", xData, yData1);
   XYSeries series2 = Chart.addSeries("Forecasted", xData, yData2);

   series1.setLineColor(XChartSeriesColors.BLUE);
   series2.setMarkerColor(Color.ORANGE);
   series1.setLineStyle(SeriesLines.SOLID);
   series2.setLineStyle(SeriesLines.SOLID);

   // Save the chart image
   try
    {
      BitmapEncoder.saveBitmapWithDPI(Chart, strTrainChartFileName,
        BitmapFormat.JPG, 100);
    }
   catch (Exception bt)
    {
      bt.printStackTrace();
    }

   System.out.println ("The Chart has been saved");

   System.out.println("End of testing for mini-batches training");

 } // End of the method
```

Testing the Results for the Micro-Batch Method

Listing 8-10 shows the end fragment of the testing results.

Listing 8-10. End Fragment of the Testing Results

```
DayNumber = 986.5  TargetValue = 899.745  AverPredictedValue =
899.74503  DiffPerc = 3.47964E-6
DayNumber = 987.5  TargetValue = 864.565  AverPredictedValue =
864.56503  DiffPerc = 3.58910E-6
DayNumber = 988.5  TargetValue = 780.485  AverPredictedValue =
780.48505  DiffPerc = 6.14256E-6
```

```
DayNumber = 989.5  TargetValue = 766.48    AverPredictedValue =
766.48000  DiffPerc = 1.62870E-7
DayNumber = 990.5  TargetValue = 735.34    AverPredictedValue =
735.33996  DiffPerc = 6.05935E-6
DayNumber = 991.5  TargetValue = 645.975  AverPredictedValue =
645.97500  DiffPerc = 4.53557E-7
DayNumber = 992.5  TargetValue = 619.23    AverPredictedValue =
619.23003  DiffPerc = 5.59670E-6
DayNumber = 993.5  TargetValue = 604.895  AverPredictedValue =
604.89504  DiffPerc = 6.02795E-6
DayNumber = 994.5  TargetValue = 568.875  AverPredictedValue =
568.87500  DiffPerc = 2.02687E-7
DayNumber = 995.5  TargetValue = 530.95    AverPredictedValue =
530.94999  DiffPerc = 1.71056E-6
DayNumber = 996.5  TargetValue = 485.01    AverPredictedValue =
485.01001  DiffPerc = 1.92301E-6
DayNumber = 997.5  TargetValue = 462.915  AverPredictedValue =
462.91499  DiffPerc = 7.96248E-8
DayNumber = 998.5  TargetValue = 475.355  AverPredictedValue =
475.35501  DiffPerc = 1.57186E-6
DayNumber = 999.5  TargetValue = 488.525  AverPredictedValue =
488.52501  DiffPerc = 1.23894E-6

maxErrorPerc = 6.840306081962611E-6
averErrorPerc  = 2.349685401959033E-6
```

Now, the testing results are also pretty good, considering that the function is noncontinuous. The maxErrorPerc field, which is the worst error among all records, is less than 0.0000068 percent, and the averErrorPerc field is less than 0.0000023 percent. If the day of the current micro-batch test file is not in the middle of two saved network keys, calculate the values proportionally or use interpolation for that purpose.

Figure 8-8 shows the chart of the testing results. Both the actual and predicted charts practically overlap.

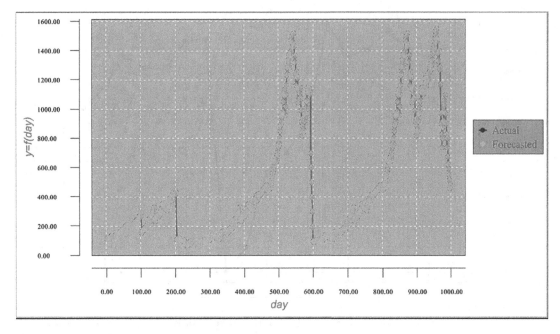

Figure 8-8. *Chart of the test results*

Digging Deeper

Neural network back-propagation is considered as a universal function approximation mechanism. However, there is a strict limitation for the types of functions neural networks are able to approximate: the functions must be continuous (universal approximation theorem).

Let's discuss what happens when the network attempts to approximate a noncontinuous function. To research this question, we use a small noncontinuous function that is given by its values at 20 points. These points surround the point of a rapidly changing function pattern. Figure 8-9 shows the chart.

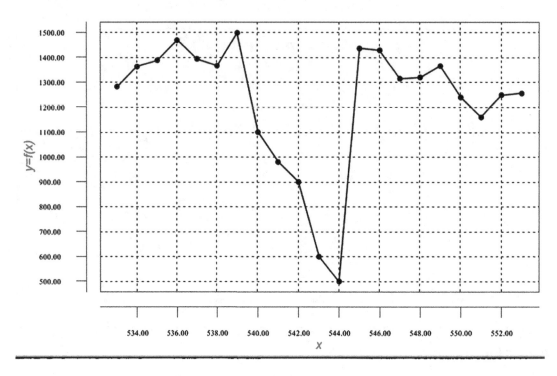

Figure 8-9. *Chart of the function with rapidly changing pattern*

Table 8-8 shows the function values at 20 points.

Table 8-8. *Function Values*

xPoint	Function Value
533	1282.71
534	1362.93
535	1388.91
536	1469.25
537	1394.46
538	1366.42
539	1498.58
540	1100
541	980
542	900
543	600
544	500
545	1436.51
546	1429.4
547	1314.95
548	1320.28
549	1366.01
550	1239.94
551	1160.33
552	1249.46
553	1255.82

This file is normalized before being processed. Figure 8-10 shows the network architecture used for approximating this function.

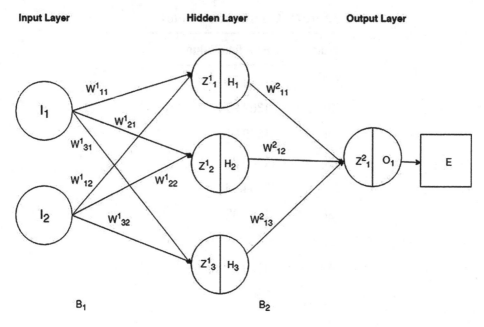

Figure 8-10. *Network architecture*

Executing the training process shows the following results:

- The maximum error percent (the maximum percent of the difference between the actual and predicted function values) is greater than 130.06 percent.

- The average error percent (the average percent of the difference between the actual and predicted function values) is greater than 16.25 percent.

Figure 8-11 shows the chart of the processing results.

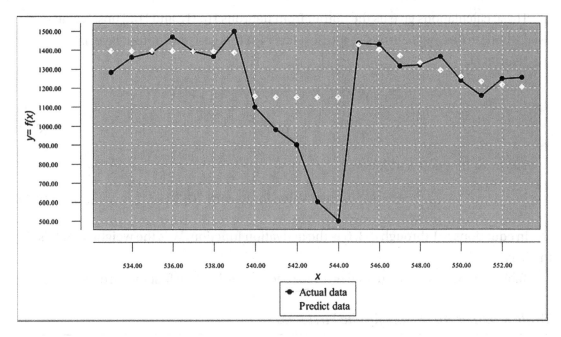

Figure 8-11. *Chart of the processing results*

Our goal is to understand what happens during this noncontinuous function approximation process that leads to such poor results. To research this, we will calculate the forward pass result (the error) for each record. The calculation for a forward pass is done using equations 8-1 through 8-5.

Neuron H_1

$$Z^1_1 = W^1_{11}*I_1 + B_1*1$$

$$H_1 = 6(Z^1_1) \tag{8-1}$$

Neuron H_2

$$Z^1_2 = W^1_{21}*I_1 + B_1*1$$

$$H_2 = 6(Z^1_2) \tag{8-2}$$

Neuron H_3

$$Z^1_3 = W^1_{31}*I_1 + B_1*1$$

$$H_3 = 6(Z^1_3) \tag{8-3}$$

These calculations give us the output from neurons H_1, H_2, and H_3. Those values are used when processing neurons in the next layer (in this case, the output layer).

Neuron O_1

$$Z^2_1 = W^2_{11}{}^*H_1 + W^2_{12}{}^*H_2 + W^2_{13}{}^*H_3 + B_2{}^*1$$

$$O_1 = 6(Z^2_1) \tag{8-4}$$

The error function is as follows:

$$E = 0.5{}^* \text{(Actual Value for Record - } O_1\text{)}^2 \tag{8-5}$$

In equations 8-1 through 8-3, 6 is the activation function, W is the weight, and B is the bias.

Table 8-9 shows the calculated error for each record for the first forward pass.

Table 8-9. *Records Errors for the First Pass*

Day	Function Value		
-0.76	-0.410177778		
-0.68	-0.053644444		
-0.6	0.061822222		
-0.52	0.418888889		
-0.44	0.086488889	**Max**	**0.202629155**
-0.36	-0.038133333	**Min**	**0.156038965**
-0.28	0.549244444		
-0.2	-1.222222222	**Difference Percent**	**29.86**
-0.12	-1.755555556		
-0.04	-2.111111111		
0.04	-3.444444444		
0.12	-3.888888889		
0.2	0.273377778		
0.28	0.241777778		

(continued)

Table 8-9. (*continued*)

Day	Function Value
0.36	-0.266888889
0.44	-0.2432
0.52	-0.039955556
0.6	-0.600266667
0.68	-0.954088889
0.76	-0.557955556
0.84	-0.529688889

The difference between the maximum and minimum error values for all records is very large and is about 30 percent. That's where the problem exists. When all records are processed, this point is the epoch. At that point, the network calculates the average error (for all processed errors in the epoch) and then processes the back-propagation step to redistribute the average error among all neurons in the output and hidden layers, adjusting their weights and bias values.

The calculated errors for all records depend on the initial (randomly assigned) weight/bias parameters set for this first pass. When the function consists of continuous (monotone) function values that are gradually changed in an orderly way, the errors calculated for each record based on the initial weight/bias values are close enough, and the average error is close to the error calculated for each record. However, when the function is noncontinuous, its pattern rapidly changes at some points. That leads to the situation when the randomly selected initial weight/bias values are not good for all records, leading to a wide difference between record errors.

Next, the back-propagation adjusts the initial weight/bias values of the neurons, but the problem continues to exist. Those adjusted values are not good for all records that belong to different function pattern (topologies).

Tip   The micro-batch method requires a larger volume of calculation than the conventional way of network processing, so it should be used only when the conventional method is unable to deliver good approximation results.

Summary

Neural network approximation of noncontinuous functions is a difficult task for neural networks. It is practically impossible to obtain a good-quality approximation for such functions. This chapter introduced the micro-batch method that is able to approximate any noncontinuous function with high-precision results. The next chapter shows how the micro-batch method substantially improves the approximation results for continuous functions with complex topology.

CHAPTER 9

Approximation of Continuous Functions with Complex Topology

This chapter shows that the micro-batch method substantially improves the approximation results of continuous functions with complex topology.

Example: Approximation of Continuous Functions with Complex Topology Using a Conventional Neural Network Process

Figure 9-1 shows one such function. The function has the formula $y = \sqrt{e^{-(\ )}}$, but let's pretend that the function formula is unknown and that the function is given to us by its values at certain points.

© Igor Livshin 2022
I. Livshin, *Artificial Neural Networks with Java*, https://doi.org/10.1007/978-1-4842-7368-5_9

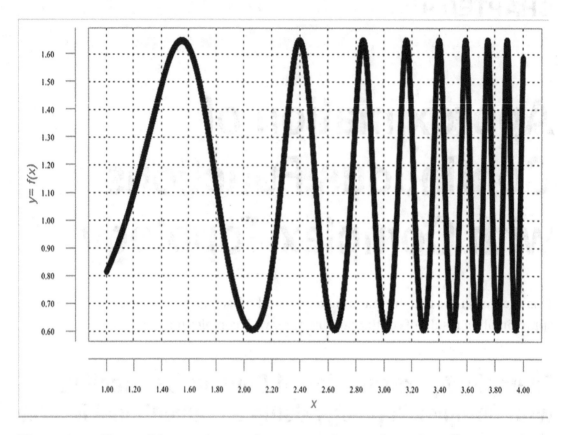

Figure 9-1. *Chart of the continuous function with complicated topology*

Again, we will make a first attempt to approximate this function using the conventional neural network process. Table 9-1 shows a fragment of the training dataset.

Table 9-1. *Fragment of the Training Dataset*

Point x	Function Value
1	0.81432914
1.0003	0.814632027
1.0006	0.814935228
1.0009	0.815238744
1.0012	0.815542575
1.0015	0.815846721
1.0018	0.816151183
1.0021	0.816455961
1.0024	0.816761055
1.0027	0.817066464
1.003	0.817372191
1.0033	0.817678233
1.0036	0.817984593
1.0039	0.818291269
1.0042	0.818598262

Table 9-2 shows a fragment of the testing dataset.

Table 9-2. *Fragment of the Testing Dataset*

Point x	Point y
1.000015	0.814344277
1.000315	0.814647179
1.000615	0.814950396
1.000915	0.815253928
1.001215	0.815557774
1.001515	0.815861937
1.001815	0.816166415
1.002115	0.816471208
1.002415	0.816776318
1.002715	0.817081743
1.003015	0.817387485
1.003315	0.817693544
1.003615	0.817999919
1.003915	0.818306611
1.004215	0.81861362

Both the training and testing datasets were normalized before processing.

Network Architecture for the Example

Figure 9-2 shows the network architecture for this example.

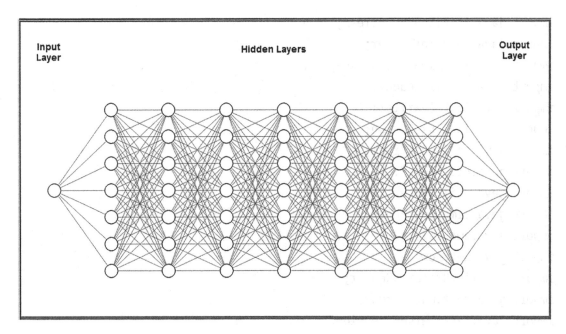

Figure 9-2. *Network architecture*

Program Code for the Example

Listing 9-1 shows the program code for this example.

Listing 9-1. Program Code

```
// =============================================================
// Approximation of the complex function using the conventional approach.
// The complex function values are given at 1000 points.
//
// The input file consists of records with two fields:
// Field1 - xPoint value
// Field2 - Function value at the xPoint
//
// The input file is normalized.
// =============================================================

package articleidi_complexformula_traditional;

import java.io.BufferedReader;
import java.io.File;
```

```java
import java.io.FileInputStream;
import java.io.PrintWriter;
import java.io.FileNotFoundException;
import java.io.FileReader;
import java.io.FileWriter;
import java.io.IOException;
import java.io.InputStream;
import java.nio.file.*;
import java.util.Properties;
import java.time.YearMonth;
import java.awt.Color;
import java.awt.Font;
import java.io.BufferedReader;
import java.text.DateFormat;
import java.text.ParseException;
import java.text.SimpleDateFormat;
import java.time.LocalDate;
import java.time.Month;
import java.time.ZoneId;
import java.util.ArrayList;
import java.util.Calendar;
import java.util.Date;
import java.util.List;
import java.util.Locale;
import java.util.Properties;

import org.encog.Encog;
import org.encog.engine.network.activation.ActivationTANH;
import org.encog.engine.network.activation.ActivationReLU;
import org.encog.ml.data.MLData;
import org.encog.ml.data.MLDataPair;
import org.encog.ml.data.MLDataSet;
import org.encog.ml.data.buffer.MemoryDataLoader;
import org.encog.ml.data.buffer.codec.CSVDataCODEC;
import org.encog.ml.data.buffer.codec.DataSetCODEC;
import org.encog.neural.networks.BasicNetwork;
```

```java
import org.encog.neural.networks.layers.BasicLayer;
import org.encog.neural.networks.training.propagation.resilient.
ResilientPropagation;
import org.encog.persist.EncogDirectoryPersistence;
import org.encog.util.csv.CSVFormat;

import org.knowm.xchart.SwingWrapper;
import org.knowm.xchart.XYChart;
import org.knowm.xchart.XYChartBuilder;
import org.knowm.xchart.XYSeries;
import org.knowm.xchart.demo.charts.ExampleChart;
import org.knowm.xchart.style.Styler.LegendPosition;
import org.knowm.xchart.style.colors.ChartColor;
import org.knowm.xchart.style.colors.XChartSeriesColors;
import org.knowm.xchart.style.lines.SeriesLines;
import org.knowm.xchart.style.markers.SeriesMarkers;
import org.knowm.xchart.BitmapEncoder;
import org.knowm.xchart.BitmapEncoder.BitmapFormat;
import org.knowm.xchart.QuickChart;
import org.knowm.xchart.SwingWrapper;

public class ArticleIDI_ComplexFormula_Traditional implements
ExampleChart<XYChart>
{
    // Interval to normalize
    static double Nh =   1;
    static double Nl = -1;

    // First column
    static double minXPointDl = 0.95;
    static double maxXPointDh = 4.05;

    // Second column - target data
    static double minTargetValueDl = 0.60;
    static double maxTargetValueDh = 1.65;

    static double doublePointNumber = 0.00;
    static int intPointNumber = 0;
```

```
static InputStream input = null;
static double[] arrPrices = new double[2500];
static double normInputXPointValue = 0.00;
static double normPredictXPointValue = 0.00;
static double normTargetXPointValue = 0.00;
static double normDifferencePerc = 0.00;
static double returnCode = 0.00;
static double denormInputXPointValue = 0.00;
static double denormPredictXPointValue = 0.00;
static double denormTargetXPointValue = 0.00;
static double valueDifference = 0.00;
static int numberOfInputNeurons;
static int numberOfOutputNeurons;
 static int numberOfRecordsInFile;
static String trainFileName;
static String priceFileName;
static String testFileName;
static String chartTrainFileName;
static String chartTestFileName;
static String networkFileName;
static int workingMode;
static String cvsSplitBy = ",";

static List<Double> xData = new ArrayList<Double>();
static List<Double> yData1 = new ArrayList<Double>();
static List<Double> yData2 = new ArrayList<Double>();

static XYChart Chart;

@Override
public XYChart getChart()
 {
  // Create Chart

  XYSeries series1 = Chart.addSeries("Actual data", xData, yData1);
     XYSeries series2 = Chart.addSeries("Predict data", xData, yData2);
```

```
series1.setLineColor(XChartSeriesColors.BLACK);
series2.setLineColor(XChartSeriesColors.YELLOW);

series1.setMarkerColor(Color.BLACK);
series2.setMarkerColor(Color.WHITE);
series1.setLineStyle(SeriesLines.SOLID);
series2.setLineStyle(SeriesLines.DASH_DASH);

try
   {
     // Configuration

     // Training mode
     //workingMode = 1;
     //numberOfRecordsInFile = 10001;
     //trainFileName = "C:/Article_To_Publish/IGI_Global/
     ComplexFormula_Calculate_Train_Norm.csv";
     //chartTrainFileName = "C:/Article_To_Publish/IGI_Global/
     ComplexFormula_Chart_Train_Results";

     // Testing mode
     workingMode = 2;
     numberOfRecordsInFile = 10001;
     testFileName = "C:/Article_To_Publish/IGI_Global/ComplexFormula_
     Calculate_Test_Norm.csv";
     chartTestFileName = "C:/Article_To_Publish/IGI_Global/
     ComplexFormula_Chart_Test_Results";

     // Common part of config data
     networkFileName = "C:/Article_To_Publish/IGI_Global/
     ComplexFormula_Saved_Network_File.csv";
     numberOfInputNeurons = 1;
     numberOfOutputNeurons = 1;

     // Check the working mode to run

     if(workingMode == 1)
      {
        // Training mode
```

```java
             File file1 = new File(chartTrainFileName);
             File file2 = new File(networkFileName);

             if(file1.exists())
                file1.delete();

             if(file2.exists())
                file2.delete();

             returnCode = 0;     // Clear the error Code

             do
              {
                returnCode = trainValidateSaveNetwork();
              } while (returnCode > 0);
            }
          else
            {
               // Test mode
               loadAndTestNetwork();
            }
        }
     catch (Throwable t)
       {
           t.printStackTrace();
          System.exit(1);
       }
     finally
       {
          Encog.getInstance().shutdown();
       }
    Encog.getInstance().shutdown();

    return Chart;

  } // End of the method
```

```java
// ==========================================================
// Load CSV to memory.
// @return The loaded dataset.
// ==========================================================
public static MLDataSet loadCSV2Memory(String filename, int input, int
ideal, boolean headers,
      CSVFormat format, boolean significance)
  {

    DataSetCODEC codec = new CSVDataCODEC(new File(filename), format,
    headers, input, ideal,
        significance);
    MemoryDataLoader load = new MemoryDataLoader(codec);
    MLDataSet dataset = load.external2Memory();
    return dataset;

  }

// ==========================================================
//  The main method.
//  @param Command line arguments. No arguments are used.
// ==========================================================
public static void main(String[] args)
 {
   ExampleChart<XYChart> exampleChart = new ArticleIDI_ComplexFormula_
   Traditional();
   XYChart Chart = exampleChart.getChart();
   new SwingWrapper<XYChart>(Chart).displayChart();
 } // End of the main method

//===================================================================
// This method trains, Validates, and saves the trained network file
//===================================================================
static public double trainValidateSaveNetwork()
 {
   // Load the training CSV file in memory
```

```
MLDataSet trainingSet =
  loadCSV2Memory(trainFileName,numberOfInputNeurons,
  numberOfOutputNeurons,
    true,CSVFormat.ENGLISH,false);

// create a neural network
BasicNetwork network = new BasicNetwork();

// Input layer
network.addLayer(new BasicLayer(null,true,1));

// Hidden layer
network.addLayer(new BasicLayer(new ActivationTANH(),true,7));
network.addLayer(new BasicLayer(new ActivationTANH(),true,7));
network.addLayer(new BasicLayer(new ActivationTANH(),true,7));
network.addLayer(new BasicLayer(new ActivationTANH(),true,7));
network.addLayer(new BasicLayer(new ActivationTANH(),true,7));
network.addLayer(new BasicLayer(new ActivationTANH(),true,7));
network.addLayer(new BasicLayer(new ActivationTANH(),true,7));

// Output layer
network.addLayer(new BasicLayer(new ActivationTANH(),false,1));

network.getStructure().finalizeStructure();
network.reset();

//Train the neural network
final ResilientPropagation train = new ResilientPropagation(network,
trainingSet);

int epoch = 1;

do
 {
    train.iteration();
    System.out.println("Epoch #" + epoch + " Error:" + train.
    getError());

  epoch++;
```

```java
   if (epoch >= 6000 && network.calculateError(trainingSet) > 0.101)
      {
       returnCode = 1;

       System.out.println("Try again");
       return returnCode;
      }
 } while(train.getError() > 0.10);

// Save the network file
EncogDirectoryPersistence.saveObject(new File(networkFileName),
network);

System.out.println("Neural Network Results:");

double sumNormDifferencePerc = 0.00;
double averNormDifferencePerc = 0.00;
double maxNormDifferencePerc = 0.00;

int m = 0;

double stepValue = 0.00031;
double startingPoint = 1.00;
double xPoint = startingPoint - stepValue;

for(MLDataPair pair: trainingSet)
  {
     m++;
     xPoint = xPoint + stepValue;

     if(m == 0)
      continue;

     final MLData output = network.compute(pair.getInput());

     MLData inputData = pair.getInput();
     MLData actualData = pair.getIdeal();
     MLData predictData = network.compute(inputData);
```

```java
            // Calculate and print the results
            normInputXPointValue = inputData.getData(0);
            normTargetXPointValue = actualData.getData(0);
            normPredictXPointValue = predictData.getData(0);

            denormInputXPointValue = ((minXPointDl - maxXPointDh)*
            normInputXPointValue -
              Nh*minXPointDl + maxXPointDh *Nl)/(Nl - Nh);

            denormTargetXPointValue =((minTargetValueDl - maxTarget
            ValueDh)*normTargetXPointValue -
              Nh*minTargetValueDl + maxTargetValueDh*Nl)/(Nl - Nh);

            denormPredictXPointValue =((minTargetValueDl -
            maxTargetValueDh)*normPredictXPointValue -
            Nh*minTargetValueDl + maxTargetValueDh*Nl)/(Nl - Nh);

            valueDifference =
              Math.abs(((denormTargetXPointValue -
                denormPredictXPointValue)/
                denormTargetXPointValue)*100.00);

            System.out.println ("xPoint = " + xPoint +
            "  denormTargetXPointValue = " +
              denormTargetXPointValue + "  denormPredictXPointValue = " +
              denormPredictXPointValue +
                "  valueDifference = " + valueDifference);

            sumNormDifferencePerc = sumNormDifferencePerc +
            valueDifference;

            if (valueDifference > maxNormDifferencePerc)
              maxNormDifferencePerc = valueDifference;

            xData.add(xPoint);
            yData1.add(denormTargetXPointValue);
            yData2.add(denormPredictXPointValue);

        }   // End for pair loop
```

```
XYSeries series1 = Chart.addSeries("Actual data", xData, yData1);
XYSeries series2 = Chart.addSeries("Predict data", xData, yData2);

series1.setLineColor(XChartSeriesColors.BLACK);
series2.setLineColor(XChartSeriesColors.YELLOW);

series1.setMarkerColor(Color.BLACK);
series2.setMarkerColor(Color.WHITE);
series1.setLineStyle(SeriesLines.SOLID);
series2.setLineStyle(SeriesLines.DASH_DASH);

try
  {
    //Save the chart image
    BitmapEncoder.saveBitmapWithDPI(Chart, chartTrainFileName,
      BitmapFormat.JPG, 100);
    System.out.println ("Train Chart file has been saved") ;
  }
catch (IOException ex)
 {
  ex.printStackTrace();
  System.exit(3);
 }

// Finally, save this trained network
EncogDirectoryPersistence.saveObject(new File(networkFileName),
network);
System.out.println ("Train Network has been saved");

averNormDifferencePerc  = sumNormDifferencePerc/
(numberOfRecordsInFile-1);

System.out.println(" ");
System.out.println("maxErrorDifferencePerc = " +
maxNormDifferencePerc + "
    averErrorDifferencePerc = " + averNormDifferencePerc);

returnCode = 0.00;
return returnCode;
```

```java
  }   // End of the method

//=====================================================
// This method load and test the trained network
//=====================================================
static public void loadAndTestNetwork()
 {
  System.out.println("Testing the networks results");

  List<Double> xData = new ArrayList<Double>();
  List<Double> yData1 = new ArrayList<Double>();
  List<Double> yData2 = new ArrayList<Double>();

  double targetToPredictPercent = 0;
  double maxGlobalResultDiff = 0.00;
  double averGlobalResultDiff = 0.00;
  double sumGlobalResultDiff = 0.00;
  double maxGlobalIndex = 0;
  double normInputXPointValueFromRecord = 0.00;
  double normTargetXPointValueFromRecord = 0.00;
  double normPredictXPointValueFromRecord = 0.00;

  BasicNetwork network;

  maxGlobalResultDiff = 0.00;
  averGlobalResultDiff = 0.00;
  sumGlobalResultDiff = 0.00;

  // Load the test dataset into memory
  MLDataSet testingSet =
  loadCSV2Memory(testFileName,numberOfInputNeurons,numberOfOutputNeurons,
  true,
    CSVFormat.ENGLISH,false);

  // Load the saved trained network
  network =
    (BasicNetwork)EncogDirectoryPersistence.loadObject(new
    File(networkFileName));
```

```
int i = - 1; // Index of the current record
double stepValue = 0.000298;
double startingPoint = 1.01;
double xPoint = startingPoint - stepValue;

for (MLDataPair pair:  testingSet)
 {
     i++;
     xPoint = xPoint + stepValue;

     MLData inputData = pair.getInput();
     MLData actualData = pair.getIdeal();
     MLData predictData = network.compute(inputData);

     // These values are Normalized as the whole input is
     normInputXPointValueFromRecord = inputData.getData(0);
     normTargetXPointValueFromRecord = actualData.getData(0);
     normPredictXPointValueFromRecord = predictData.getData(0);

     denormInputXPointValue = ((minXPointDl - maxXPointDh)*
       normInputXPointValueFromRecord - Nh*minXPointDl +
       maxXPointDh*Nl)/(Nl - Nh);
     denormTargetXPointValue = ((minTargetValueDl -
     maxTargetValueDh)*
       normTargetXPointValueFromRecord - Nh*minTargetValueDl +
       maxTargetValueDh*Nl)/(Nl - Nh);
     denormPredictXPointValue =((minTargetValueDl -
     maxTargetValueDh)*
       normPredictXPointValueFromRecord - Nh*minTargetValueDl +
       maxTargetValueDh*Nl)/(Nl - Nh);

     targetToPredictPercent = Math.abs((denormTargetXPointValue -
     denormPredictXPointValue)/
       denormTargetXPointValue*100);

     System.out.println("xPoint = " + xPoint
     + "  denormTargetXPointValue = " +
       denormTargetXPointValue + "  denormPredictXPointValue = " +
       denormPredictXPointValue +
```

```
            "     targetToPredictPercent = " + targetToPredictPercent);

       if (targetToPredictPercent > maxGlobalResultDiff)
          maxGlobalResultDiff = targetToPredictPercent;

       sumGlobalResultDiff = sumGlobalResultDiff +
       targetToPredictPercent;

       // Populate chart elements
       xData.add(xPoint);
       yData1.add(denormTargetXPointValue);
       yData2.add(denormPredictXPointValue);

   }  // End for pair loop

// Print the max and average results
System.out.println(" ");
averGlobalResultDiff = sumGlobalResultDiff/(numberOfRecordsInFile-1);

System.out.println("maxErrorPerc = " + maxGlobalResultDiff);
System.out.println("averErrorPerc = " + averGlobalResultDiff);

// All testing batch files have been processed
XYSeries series1 = Chart.addSeries("Actual", xData, yData1);
XYSeries series2 = Chart.addSeries("Predicted", xData, yData2);

series1.setLineColor(XChartSeriesColors.BLACK);
series2.setLineColor(XChartSeriesColors.YELLOW);

series1.setMarkerColor(Color.BLACK);
series2.setMarkerColor(Color.WHITE);
series1.setLineStyle(SeriesLines.SOLID);
series2.setLineStyle(SeriesLines.DASH_DASH);

// Save the chart image
try
 {
   BitmapEncoder.saveBitmapWithDPI(Chart, chartTestFileName ,
   BitmapFormat.JPG, 100);
 }
```

```
    catch (Exception bt)
     {
        bt.printStackTrace();
     }

    System.out.println ("The Chart has been saved");
    System.out.println("End of testing for test records");

  } // End of the method

} // End of the class
```

Training Processing Results for the Example

Listing 9-2 shows the end fragment of the conventional network processing results.

Listing 9-2. The End Fragment of the Conventional Training Results

```
xPoint = 4.08605  TargetValue = 1.24795  PredictedValue = 1.15899  DifPerc
= 7.12794
xPoint = 4.08636  TargetValue = 1.25699  PredictedValue = 1.16125  DifPerc
= 7.61624
xPoint = 4.08667  TargetValue = 1.26602  PredictedValue = 1.16346  DifPerc
= 8.10090
xPoint = 4.08698  TargetValue = 1.27504  PredictedValue = 1.16562  DifPerc
= 8.58150
xPoint = 4.08729  TargetValue = 1.28404  PredictedValue = 1.16773  DifPerc
= 9.05800
xPoint = 4.08760  TargetValue = 1.29303  PredictedValue = 1.16980  DifPerc
= 9.53011
xPoint = 4.08791  TargetValue = 1.30199  PredictedValue = 1.17183  DifPerc
= 9.99747
xPoint = 4.08822  TargetValue = 1.31093  PredictedValue = 1.17381  DifPerc
= 10.4599
xPoint = 4.08853  TargetValue = 1.31984  PredictedValue = 1.17575  DifPerc
= 10.9173
xPoint = 4.08884  TargetValue = 1.32871  PredictedValue = 1.17765  DifPerc
= 11.3694
```

xPoint = 4.08915   TargetValue = 1.33755   PredictedValue = 1.17951   DifPerc
= 11.8159

xPoint = 4.08946   TargetValue = 1.34635   PredictedValue = 1.18133   DifPerc
= 12.25680

xPoint = 4.08978   TargetValue = 1.35510   PredictedValue = 1.18311   DifPerc
= 12.69162

xPoint = 4.09008   TargetValue = 1.36380   PredictedValue = 1.18486   DifPerc
= 13.12047

xPoint = 4.09039   TargetValue = 1.37244   PredictedValue = 1.18657   DifPerc
= 13.54308

xPoint = 4.09070   TargetValue = 1.38103   PredictedValue = 1.18825   DifPerc
= 13.95931

xPoint = 4.09101   TargetValue = 1.38956   PredictedValue = 1.18999   DifPerc
= 14.36898

xPoint = 4.09132   TargetValue = 1.39802   PredictedValue = 1.19151   DifPerc
= 14.77197

xPoint = 4.09164   TargetValue = 1.40642   PredictedValue = 1.19309   DifPerc
= 15.16812

xPoint = 4.09194   TargetValue = 1.41473   PredictedValue = 1.19464   DifPerc
= 15.55732

xPoint = 4.09225   TargetValue = 1.42297   PredictedValue = 1.19616   DifPerc
= 15.93942

xPoint = 4.09256   TargetValue = 1.43113   PredictedValue = 1.19765   DifPerc
= 16.31432

xPoint = 4.09287   TargetValue = 1.43919   PredictedValue = 1.19911   DifPerc
= 16.68189

xPoint = 4.09318   TargetValue = 1.44717   PredictedValue = 1.20054   DifPerc
= 17.04203

xPoint = 4.09349   TargetValue = 1.45505   PredictedValue = 1.20195   DifPerc
= 17.39463

xPoint = 4.09380   TargetValue = 1.46283   PredictedValue = 1.20333   DifPerc
= 17.73960

xPoint = 4.09411   TargetValue = 1.47051   PredictedValue = 1.20469   DifPerc
= 18.07683

xPoint = 4.09442 TargetValue = 1.47808 PredictedValue = 1.20602 DifPerc
= 18.40624
xPoint = 4.09473 TargetValue = 1.48553 PredictedValue = 1.20732 DifPerc
= 18.72775
xPoint = 4.09504 TargetValue = 1.49287 PredictedValue = 1.20861 DifPerc
= 19.04127
xPoint = 4.09535 TargetValue = 1.50009 PredictedValue = 1.20987 DifPerc
= 19.34671
xPoint = 4.09566 TargetValue = 1.50718 PredictedValue = 1.21111 DifPerc
= 19.64402
xPoint = 4.09597 TargetValue = 1.51414 PredictedValue = 1.21232 DifPerc
= 19.93312
xPoint = 4.09628 TargetValue = 1.52097 PredictedValue = 1.21352 DifPerc
= 20.21393
xPoint = 4.09659 TargetValue = 1.52766 PredictedValue = 1.21469 DifPerc
= 20.48640
xPoint = 4.09690 TargetValue = 1.53420 PredictedValue = 1.21585 DifPerc
= 20.75045
xPoint = 4.09721 TargetValue = 1.54060 PredictedValue = 1.21699 DifPerc
= 21.00605
xPoint = 4.09752 TargetValue = 1.54686 PredictedValue = 1.21810 DifPerc
= 21.25312
xPoint = 4.09783 TargetValue = 1.55296 PredictedValue = 1.21920 DifPerc
= 21.49161
xPoint = 4.09814 TargetValue = 1.55890 PredictedValue = 1.22028 DifPerc
= 21.72147
xPoint = 4.09845 TargetValue = 1.56468 PredictedValue = 1.22135 DifPerc
= 21.94265
xPoint = 4.09876 TargetValue = 1.57030 PredictedValue = 1.22239 DifPerc
= 22.15511
xPoint = 4.09907 TargetValue = 1.57574 PredictedValue = 1.22342 DifPerc
= 22.35878
xPoint = 4.09938 TargetValue = 1.58101 PredictedValue = 1.22444 DifPerc
= 22.55363

xPoint = 4.09969   TargetValue = 1.58611   PredictedValue = 1.22544   DifPerc
= 22.73963

maxErrorPerc = 86.08183780343387
averErrorPerc = 10.116005438206885

With the conventional process, the approximation results are as follows:

- The maximum error percent is more than 86.08 percent.

- The average error percent is more than 10. 11 percent.

Figure 9-3 shows the chart of the training approximation results using conventional network processing.

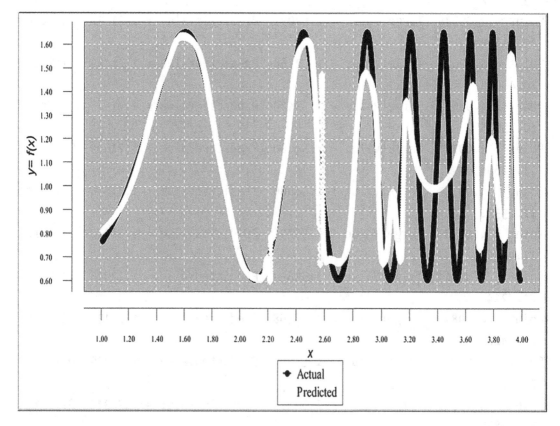

Figure 9-3. *Chart of the training approximation results using conventional network processing*

Obviously, such approximation is useless.

Approximation of Continuous Functions with Complex Topology Using the Micro-Batch Method

Now, we will approximate this function using the micro-batch method. Again, the normalized training dataset is broken into a set of training micro-batch files, and it is now the input to the training process. Listing 9-3 shows the ending fragment of the training processing results (using the macro-batch method) after execution.

Listing 9-3. Ending Fragment of the Training Processing Results (Using the Macro-Batch Method)

```
DayNumber = 9950  TargetValue = 1.19376  PredictedValue = 1.19376  DiffPerc
= 4.66352E-6
DayNumber = 9951  TargetValue = 1.20277  PredictedValue = 1.20277  DiffPerc
= 5.30417E-6
DayNumber = 9952  TargetValue = 1.21180  PredictedValue = 1.21180  DiffPerc
= 4.79291E-6
DayNumber = 9953  TargetValue = 1.22083  PredictedValue = 1.22083  DiffPerc
= 5.03070E-6
DayNumber = 9954  TargetValue = 1.22987  PredictedValue = 1.22987  DiffPerc
= 3.79647E-6
DayNumber = 9955  TargetValue = 1.23891  PredictedValue = 1.23891  DiffPerc
= 8.06431E-6
DayNumber = 9956  TargetValue = 1.24795  PredictedValue = 1.24795  DiffPerc
= 7.19851E-6
DayNumber = 9957  TargetValue = 1.25699  PredictedValue = 1.25699  DiffPerc
= 4.57148E-6
DayNumber = 9958  TargetValue = 1.26602  PredictedValue = 1.26602  DiffPerc
= 5.88300E-6
DayNumber = 9959  TargetValue = 1.27504  PredictedValue = 1.27504  DiffPerc
= 3.02448E-6
DayNumber = 9960  TargetValue = 1.28404  PredictedValue = 1.28404  DiffPerc
= 7.04155E-6
DayNumber = 9961  TargetValue = 1.29303  PredictedValue = 1.29303  DiffPerc
= 8.62206E-6
```

DayNumber = 9962   TargetValue = 1.30199   PredictedValue = 1.30199   DiffPerc
= 9.16473E-8
DayNumber = 9963   TargetValue = 1.31093   PredictedValue = 1.31093   DiffPerc
= 1.89459E-6
DayNumber = 9964   TargetValue = 1.31984   PredictedValue = 1.31984   DiffPerc
= 4.16695E-6
DayNumber = 9965   TargetValue = 1.32871   PredictedValue = 1.32871   DiffPerc
= 8.68118E-6
DayNumber = 9966   TargetValue = 1.33755   PredictedValue = 1.33755   DiffPerc
= 4.55866E-6
DayNumber = 9967   TargetValue = 1.34635   PredictedValue = 1.34635   DiffPerc
= 6.67697E-6
DayNumber = 9968   TargetValue = 1.35510   PredictedValue = 1.35510   DiffPerc
= 4.80264E-6
DayNumber = 9969   TargetValue = 1.36378   PredictedValue = 1.36380   DiffPerc
= 8.58688E-7
DayNumber = 9970   TargetValue = 1.37244   PredictedValue = 1.37245   DiffPerc
= 5.19317E-6
DayNumber = 9971   TargetValue = 1.38103   PredictedValue = 1.38104   DiffPerc
= 7.11052E-6
DayNumber = 9972   TargetValue = 1.38956   PredictedValue = 1.38956   DiffPerc
= 5.15382E-6
DayNumber = 9973   TargetValue = 1.39802   PredictedValue = 1.39802   DiffPerc
= 5.90734E-6
DayNumber = 9974   TargetValue = 1.40642   PredictedValue = 1.40642   DiffPerc
= 6.20744E-7
DayNumber = 9975   TargetValue = 1.41473   PredictedValue = 1.41473   DiffPerc
= 5.67234E-7
DayNumber = 9976   TargetValue = 1.42297   PredictedValue = 1.42297   DiffPerc
= 5.54862E-6
DayNumber = 9977   TargetValue = 1.43113   PredictedValue = 1.43113   DiffPerc
= 3.28318E-6
DayNumber = 9978   TargetValue = 1.43919   PredictedValue = 1.43919   DiffPerc
= 7.84136E-6

DayNumber = 9979 TargetValue = 1.44717 PredictedValue = 1.44717 DiffPerc
= 6.51767E-6

DayNumber = 9980 TargetValue = 1.45505 PredictedValue = 1.45505 DiffPerc
= 6.59220E-6

DayNumber = 9981 TargetValue = 1.46283 PredictedValue = 1.46283 DiffPerc
= 9.08060E-7

DayNumber = 9982 TargetValue = 1.47051 PredictedValue = 1.47051 DiffPerc
= 8.59549E-6

DayNumber = 9983 TargetValue = 1.47808 PredictedValue = 1.47808 DiffPerc
= 5.49575E-7

DayNumber = 9984 TargetValue = 1.48553 PredictedValue = 1.48553 DiffPerc
= 1.07879E-6

DayNumber = 9985 TargetValue = 1.49287 PredictedValue = 1.49287 DiffPerc
= 2.22734E-6

DayNumber = 9986 TargetValue = 1.50009 PredictedValue = 1.50009 DiffPerc
= 1.28405E-6

DayNumber = 9987 TargetValue = 1.50718 PredictedValue = 1.50718 DiffPerc
= 8.88272E-6

DayNumber = 9988 TargetValue = 1.51414 PredictedValue = 1.51414 DiffPerc
= 4.91930E-6

DayNumber = 9989 TargetValue = 1.52097 PredictedValue = 1.52097 DiffPerc
= 3.46714E-6

DayNumber = 9990 TargetValue = 1.52766 PredictedValue = 1.52766 DiffPerc
= 7.67496E-6

DayNumber = 9991 TargetValue = 1.53420 PredictedValue = 1.53420 DiffPerc
= 4.67918E-6

DayNumber = 9992 TargetValue = 1.54061 PredictedValue = 1.54061 DiffPerc
= 2.20484E-6

DayNumber = 9993 TargetValue = 1.54686 PredictedValue = 1.54686 DiffPerc
= 7.42466E-6

DayNumber = 9994 TargetValue = 1.55296 PredictedValue = 1.55296 DiffPerc
= 3.86183E-6

DayNumber = 9995 TargetValue = 1.55890 PredictedValue = 1.55890 DiffPerc
= 6.34568E-7

```
DayNumber = 9996   TargetValue = 1.56468   PredictedValue = 1.56468   DiffPerc
= 6.23860E-6
DayNumber = 9997   TargetValue = 1.57029   PredictedValue = 1.57029   DiffPerc
= 3.66380E-7
DayNumber = 9998   TargetValue = 1.57574   PredictedValue = 1.57574   DiffPerc
= 4.45560E-6
DayNumber = 9999   TargetValue = 1.58101   PredictedValue = 1.58101   DiffPerc
= 6.19952E-6
DayNumber = 10000   TargetValue = 1.5861   PredictedValue = 1.58611   DiffPerc
= 1.34336E-6

maxGlobalResultDiff = 1.3433567671366473E-6
averGlobalResultDiff = 2.686713534273295E-10
```

The training processing results (which use the micro-batch method) are as follows:

- The maximum error is less than 0.00000134 percent.

- The average error is less than 0.000000000269 percent.

Figure 9-4 shows the chart of the training approximation results (the micro-batch method was used). Both charts (actual values are shown in black, and predicted values are shown in white) practically overlap.

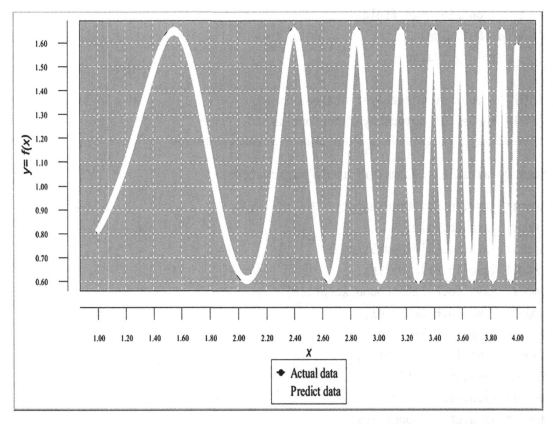

Figure 9-4. *Chart of the training approximation results (the micro-batch method was used)*

Like with the training dataset, the normalized testing dataset is broken into a set of micro-batch files that are now the input to the testing process.

Program Code for the Example Using the Micro-Batch Method

Listing 9-4 shows the program code for this example.

Listing 9-4. Program Code

```
// ======================================================
// Approximation of continuous function with complex topology
// using the micro-batch method. The input is the normalized set of
// micro-batch files. Each micro-batch includes a single day record
```

```java
// that contains two fields:
// - normDayValue
// - normTargetValue
//
// The number of inputLayer neurons is 1
// The number of outputLayer neurons is 1
// =====================================================

package articleigi_complexformula_microbatchest;

import java.io.BufferedReader;
import java.io.File;
import java.io.FileInputStream;
import java.io.PrintWriter;
import java.io.FileNotFoundException;
import java.io.FileReader;
import java.io.FileWriter;
import java.io.IOException;
import java.io.InputStream;
import java.nio.file.*;
import java.util.Properties;
import java.time.YearMonth;
import java.awt.Color;
import java.awt.Font;
import java.io.BufferedReader;
import java.text.DateFormat;
import java.text.ParseException;
import java.text.SimpleDateFormat;
import java.time.LocalDate;
import java.time.Month;
import java.time.ZoneId;
import java.util.ArrayList;
import java.util.Calendar;
import java.util.Date;
import java.util.List;
import java.util.Locale;
import java.util.Properties;
```

```java
import org.encog.Encog;
import org.encog.engine.network.activation.ActivationTANH;
import org.encog.engine.network.activation.ActivationReLU;
import org.encog.ml.data.MLData;
import org.encog.ml.data.MLDataPair;
import org.encog.ml.data.MLDataSet;
import org.encog.ml.data.buffer.MemoryDataLoader;
import org.encog.ml.data.buffer.codec.CSVDataCODEC;
import org.encog.ml.data.buffer.codec.DataSetCODEC;
import org.encog.neural.networks.BasicNetwork;
import org.encog.neural.networks.layers.BasicLayer;
import org.encog.neural.networks.training.propagation.resilient.
ResilientPropagation;
import org.encog.persist.EncogDirectoryPersistence;
import org.encog.util.csv.CSVFormat;

import org.knowm.xchart.SwingWrapper;
import org.knowm.xchart.XYChart;
import org.knowm.xchart.XYChartBuilder;
import org.knowm.xchart.XYSeries;
import org.knowm.xchart.demo.charts.ExampleChart;
import org.knowm.xchart.style.Styler.LegendPosition;
import org.knowm.xchart.style.colors.ChartColor;
import org.knowm.xchart.style.colors.XChartSeriesColors;
import org.knowm.xchart.style.lines.SeriesLines;
import org.knowm.xchart.style.markers.SeriesMarkers;
import org.knowm.xchart.BitmapEncoder;
import org.knowm.xchart.BitmapEncoder.BitmapFormat;
import org.knowm.xchart.QuickChart;
import org.knowm.xchart.SwingWrapper;

public class ArticleIGI_ComplexFormula_Microbatchest implements
ExampleChart<XYChart>
```

```
{
    // Normalization parameters

    // Normalizing interval
    static double Nh =  1;
    static double Nl = -1;

    // First 1
    static double minXPointDl = 0.95;
    static double maxXPointDh = 4.05;

    // Column 2
    static double minTargetValueDl = 0.60;
    static double maxTargetValueDh = 1.65;

    static String cvsSplitBy = ",";
    static Properties prop = null;

    static String strWorkingMode;
    static String strNumberOfBatchesToProcess;
    static String strTrainFileNameBase;
    static String strTestFileNameBase;
    static String strSaveTrainNetworkFileBase;
    static String strSaveTestNetworkFileBase;
    static String strValidateFileName;
    static String strTrainChartFileName;
    static String strTestChartFileName;
    static String strFunctValueTrainFile;
    static String strFunctValueTestFile;
    static int intDayNumber;
    static double doubleDayNumber;
    static int intWorkingMode;
    static int numberOfTrainBatchesToProcess;
    static int numberOfTestBatchesToProcess;
    static int intNumberOfRecordsInTrainFile;
    static int intNumberOfRecordsInTestFile;
    static int intNumberOfRowsInBatches;
    static int intInputNeuronNumber;
```

```java
static int intOutputNeuronNumber;
static String strOutputFileName;
static String strSaveNetworkFileName;
static String strDaysTrainFileName;
static XYChart Chart;
static String iString;
static double inputFunctValueFromFile;
static double targetToPredictFunctValueDiff;
static int[] returnCodes  = new int[3];

static List<Double> xData = new ArrayList<Double>();
static List<Double> yData1 = new ArrayList<Double>();
static List<Double> yData2 = new ArrayList<Double>();

static double[] DaysyearDayTraining = new double[10200];
static String[] strTrainingFileNames = new String[10200];
static String[] strTestingFileNames = new String[10200];
static String[] strSaveTrainNetworkFileNames = new String[10200];
static double[] linkToSaveNetworkDayKeys = new double[10200];
static double[] linkToSaveNetworkTargetFunctValueKeys = new
double[10200];
static double[] arrTrainFunctValues = new double[10200];
static double[] arrTestFunctValues = new double[10200];

@Override
public XYChart getChart()
 {
   // Create Chart

  Chart = new XYChartBuilder().width(900).height(500).title(getClass().
    getSimpleName()).xAxisTitle("day").yAxisTitle("y=f(day)").build();

  // Customize Chart
  Chart = new  XYChartBuilder().width(900).height(500).title(getClass().
          getSimpleName()).xAxisTitle("x").yAxisTitle("y= f(x)").
          build();
```

```
// Customize Chart
Chart.getStyler().setPlotBackgroundColor(ChartColor.
getAWTColor(ChartColor.GREY));
Chart.getStyler().setPlotGridLinesColor(new Color(255, 255, 255));

//Chart.getStyler().setPlotBackgroundColor(ChartColor.
getAWTColor(ChartColor.WHITE));
//Chart.getStyler().setPlotGridLinesColor(new Color(0, 0, 0));
Chart.getStyler().setChartBackgroundColor(Color.WHITE);
//Chart.getStyler().setLegendBackgroundColor(Color.PINK);
Chart.getStyler().setLegendBackgroundColor(Color.WHITE);
//Chart.getStyler().setChartFontColor(Color.MAGENTA);
Chart.getStyler().setChartFontColor(Color.BLACK);
Chart.getStyler().setChartTitleBoxBackgroundColor(new Color(0, 222, 0));
Chart.getStyler().setChartTitleBoxVisible(true);
Chart.getStyler().setChartTitleBoxBorderColor(Color.BLACK);
Chart.getStyler().setPlotGridLinesVisible(true);
Chart.getStyler().setAxisTickPadding(20);
Chart.getStyler().setAxisTickMarkLength(15);
Chart.getStyler().setPlotMargin(20);
Chart.getStyler().setChartTitleVisible(false);
Chart.getStyler().setChartTitleFont(new Font(Font.MONOSPACED, Font.
BOLD, 24));
Chart.getStyler().setLegendFont(new Font(Font.SERIF, Font.PLAIN, 18));
//Chart.getStyler().setLegendPosition(LegendPosition.InsideSE);
Chart.getStyler().setLegendPosition(LegendPosition.OutsideS);
Chart.getStyler().setLegendSeriesLineLength(12);
Chart.getStyler().setAxisTitleFont(new Font(Font.SANS_SERIF, Font.
ITALIC, 18));
Chart.getStyler().setAxisTickLabelsFont(new Font(Font.SERIF, Font.
PLAIN, 11));
Chart.getStyler().setDatePattern("yyyy-MM");
Chart.getStyler().setDecimalPattern("#0.00");
```

```
// Config data

// Training mode
intWorkingMode = 0;

// Testing mode
//intWorkingMode = 1;

numberOfTrainBatchesToProcess = 10000;
numberOfTestBatchesToProcess = 9999;
intNumberOfRowsInBatches = 1;
intInputNeuronNumber = 1;
intOutputNeuronNumber = 1;
strTrainFileNameBase = "C:/Article_To_Publish/IGI_Global/Work_Files_
ComplexFormula/ComplexFormula_Train_Norm_Batch_";
strTestFileNameBase = "C:/Article_To_Publish/IGI_Global/Work_Files_
ComplexFormula/ComplexFormula_Test_Norm_Batch_";
strSaveTrainNetworkFileBase =
  "C:/Article_To_Publish/IGI_Global/Work_Files_ComplexFormula/Save_
  Network_MicroBatch_";
strTrainChartFileName =
  "C:/Article_To_Publish/IGI_Global/Chart_Microbatch_Train_Results.jpg";
strTestChartFileName =
  "C:/Article_To_Publish/IGI_Global/Chart_Microbatch_Test_
  MicroBatch.jpg";

// Generate training batch file names and the corresponding
// SaveNetwork file names

intDayNumber = -1;   // Day number for the chart

for (int i = 0; i < numberOfTrainBatchesToProcess; i++)
 {
   intDayNumber++;

   iString = Integer.toString(intDayNumber);

   strOutputFileName = strTrainFileNameBase + iString + ".csv";

   strSaveNetworkFileName = strSaveTrainNetworkFileBase + iString + ".csv";
```

```
    strTrainingFileNames[intDayNumber] = strOutputFileName;
    strSaveTrainNetworkFileNames[intDayNumber] = strSaveNetworkFileName;

  }  // End the FOR loop

  // Build the array linkToSaveNetworkFunctValueDiffKeys
  String tempLine;
  double tempNormFunctValueDiff = 0.00;
  double tempNormFunctValueDiffPerc = 0.00;
  double tempNormTargetFunctValueDiffPerc = 0.00;

  String[] tempWorkFields;

  try
    {
      intDayNumber = -1;  // Day number for the chart

      for (int m = 0; m < numberOfTrainBatchesToProcess; m++)
        {
          intDayNumber++;

          BufferedReader br3 = new BufferedReader(new FileReader(strTr
          ainingFileNames[intDayNumber]));
          tempLine = br3.readLine();

          // Skip the label record and zero batch record
          tempLine = br3.readLine();

          // Brake the line using comma as separator
          tempWorkFields = tempLine.split(cvsSplitBy);

          tempNormFunctValueDiffPerc = Double.parseDouble(tempWork
          Fields[0]);
          tempNormTargetFunctValueDiffPerc = Double.parseDouble(
          tempWorkFields[1]);

          linkToSaveNetworkDayKeys[intDayNumber] =
          tempNormFunctValueDiffPerc;
          linkToSaveNetworkTargetFunctValueKeys[intDayNumber] =
              tempNormTargetFunctValueDiffPerc;
```

```
   }  // End the FOR loop

  // Generate testing batch file names

  if(intWorkingMode == 1)
   {
     intDayNumber = -1;

     for (int i = 0; i < numberOfTestBatchesToProcess; i++)
      {
        intDayNumber++;
        iString = Integer.toString(intDayNumber);

        // Construct the testing batch names
        strOutputFileName = strTestFileNameBase + iString + ".csv";
        strTestingFileNames[intDayNumber] = strOutputFileName;

      }  // End the FOR loop

   }   // End of IF

 }      // End for try
catch (IOException io1)
 {
   io1.printStackTrace();
   System.exit(1);
 }

// Load, train, and test Function Values file in memory
//loadTrainFunctValueFileInMemory();

// Test the mode
if(intWorkingMode == 0)
  {
    // Train mode

    int paramErrorCode;
    int paramBatchNumber;
    int paramR;
    int paramDayNumber;
```

```java
        int paramS;

        File file1 = new File(strTrainChartFileName);

        if(file1.exists())
          file1.delete();

        returnCodes[0] = 0;      // Clear the error Code
        returnCodes[1] = 0;      // Set the initial batch Number to 0;
        returnCodes[2] = 0;      // Day number;

      do
       {
         paramErrorCode = returnCodes[0];
         paramBatchNumber = returnCodes[1];
         paramDayNumber = returnCodes[2];

         returnCodes =
           trainBatches(paramErrorCode,paramBatchNumber,paramDayNumber);
       } while (returnCodes[0] > 0);

      }   // End the train logic
     else
      {
        // Testing mode

        File file2 = new File(strTestChartFileName);

        if(file2.exists())
          file2.delete();

        loadAndTestNetwork();

        // End the test logic
      }

     Encog.getInstance().shutdown();
     //System.exit(0);
     return Chart;

   }  // End of method
```

```java
// =========================================================
// Load CSV to memory.
// @return The loaded dataset.
// =========================================================
public static MLDataSet loadCSV2Memory(String filename, int input, int
ideal,
        boolean headers, CSVFormat format, boolean significance)
  {

    DataSetCODEC codec = new CSVDataCODEC(new File(filename), format,
    headers, input,
        ideal, significance);
    MemoryDataLoader load = new MemoryDataLoader(codec);
    MLDataSet dataset = load.external2Memory();
    return dataset;

  }

// =========================================================
//  The main method.
//  @param Command line arguments. No arguments are used.
// =========================================================
public static void main(String[] args)
 {

    ExampleChart<XYChart> exampleChart = new ArticleIGI_ComplexFormula_
    Microbatchest();
    XYChart Chart = exampleChart.getChart();
    new SwingWrapper<XYChart>(Chart).displayChart();
 } // End of the main method

//=========================================================
// This method trains batches as individual network1s
// saving them in separate trained datasets
//=========================================================
static public int[] trainBatches(int paramErrorCode,
                                  int paramBatchNumber,
                                  int paramDayNumber)
```

```
  {
    int rBatchNumber;
    double targetToPredictFunctValueDiff = 0;
    double maxGlobalResultDiff = 0.00;
    double averGlobalResultDiff = 0.00;
    double sumGlobalResultDiff = 0.00;

    double normInputFunctValueDiffPercFromRecord = 0.00;
    double normTargetFunctValue1 = 0.00;
    double normPredictFunctValue1 = 0.00;
    double denormInputDayFromRecord1;
    double denormInputFunctValueDiffPercFromRecord;
    double denormTargetFunctValue1 = 0.00;
    double denormAverPredictFunctValue11 = 0.00;

    BasicNetwork network1 = new BasicNetwork();

    // Input layer
    network1.addLayer(new BasicLayer(null,true,intInputNeuronNumber));

    // Hidden layer.
    network1.addLayer(new BasicLayer(new ActivationTANH(),true,7));
    network1.addLayer(new BasicLayer(new ActivationTANH(),true,7));
    network1.addLayer(new BasicLayer(new ActivationTANH(),true,7));
    network1.addLayer(new BasicLayer(new ActivationTANH(),true,7));
    network1.addLayer(new BasicLayer(new ActivationTANH(),true,7));
    network1.addLayer(new BasicLayer(new ActivationTANH(),true,7));
    network1.addLayer(new BasicLayer(new ActivationTANH(),true,7));

    // Output layer
    network1.addLayer(new BasicLayer(new ActivationTANH(),false,
    intOutputNeuronNumber));

    network1.getStructure().finalizeStructure();
    network1.reset();

    maxGlobalResultDiff = 0.00;
    averGlobalResultDiff = 0.00;
    sumGlobalResultDiff = 0.00;
```

```
// Loop over batches
intDayNumber = paramDayNumber;   // Day number for the chart

for (rBatchNumber = paramBatchNumber; rBatchNumber < numberOfTrain
BatchesToProcess;
      rBatchNumber++)
 {
   intDayNumber++;

  // Load the training file in memory
  MLDataSet trainingSet =
     loadCSV2Memory(strTrainingFileNames[rBatchNumber],intInput
     NeuronNumber,
        intOutputNeuronNumber,true,CSVFormat.ENGLISH,false);

  // train the neural network1
  ResilientPropagation train = new ResilientPropagation(network1,
  trainingSet);

  int epoch = 1;

  do
    {
      train.iteration();

      epoch++;

      for (MLDataPair pair11:  trainingSet)
       {
         MLData inputData1 = pair11.getInput();
         MLData actualData1 = pair11.getIdeal();
         MLData predictData1 = network1.compute(inputData1);

         // These values are Normalized as the whole input is
         normInputFunctValueDiffPercFromRecord = inputData1.
         getData(0);

         normTargetFunctValue1 = actualData1.getData(0);
         normPredictFunctValue1 = predictData1.getData(0);
```

```
            denormInputFunctValueDiffPercFromRecord =((minXPointDl -
              maxXPointDh)*normInputFunctValueDiffPercFromRecord -
              Nh*minXPointDl +
                maxXPointDh*Nl)/(Nl - Nh);

            denormTargetFunctValue1 = ((minTargetValueDl -
              maxTargetValueDh)*normTargetFunctValue1 -
              Nh*minTargetValueDl +
                maxTargetValueDh*Nl)/(Nl - Nh);

            denormAverPredictFunctValue11 =((minTargetValueDl -
              maxTargetValueDh)*normPredictFunctValue1 -
              Nh*minTargetValueDl +
                  maxTargetValueDh*Nl)/(Nl - Nh);

            //inputFunctValueFromFile = arrTrainFunctValues[rBatchNumber];

            targetToPredictFunctValueDiff = (Math.
            abs(denormTargetFunctValue1 -
                denormAverPredictFunctValue11)/
                denormTargetFunctValue1)*100;
        }

     if (epoch >= 1000 && targetToPredictFunctValueDiff > 0.0000091)
      {
        returnCodes[0] = 1;
        returnCodes[1] = rBatchNumber;
        returnCodes[2] = intDayNumber-1;

        return returnCodes;
      }

    } while(targetToPredictFunctValueDiff > 0.000009);

  // This batch is optimized

  // Save the network1 for the cur rend batch
  EncogDirectoryPersistence.saveObject(new
      File(strSaveTrainNetworkFileNames[rBatchNumber]),network1);
```

```java
// Get the results after the network1 optimization
int i = - 1;

for (MLDataPair pair1:  trainingSet)
 {
  i++;

  MLData inputData1 = pair1.getInput();
  MLData actualData1 = pair1.getIdeal();
  MLData predictData1 = network1.compute(inputData1);

  // These values are Normalized as the whole input is
  normInputFunctValueDiffPercFromRecord = inputData1.getData(0);
  normTargetFunctValue1 = actualData1.getData(0);
  normPredictFunctValue1 = predictData1.getData(0);

  // De-normalize the obtained values
  denormInputFunctValueDiffPercFromRecord =((minXPointDl -
    maxXPointDh)*normInputFunctValueDiffPercFromRecord -
       Nh*minXPointDl + maxXPointDh*Nl)/(Nl - Nh);

  denormTargetFunctValue1 = ((minTargetValueDl -
    maxTargetValueDh)*normTargetFunctValue1 -
       Nh*minTargetValueDl + maxTargetValueDh*Nl)/(Nl - Nh);

  denormAverPredictFunctValue11 =((minTargetValueDl -
    maxTargetValueDh)*normPredictFunctValue1 -
       Nh*minTargetValueDl + maxTargetValueDh*Nl)/(Nl - Nh);

  //inputFunctValueFromFile = arrTrainFunctValues[rBatchNumber];

  targetToPredictFunctValueDiff = (Math.abs(denormTargetFunctValue1 -
    denormAverPredictFunctValue11)/denormTargetFunctValue1)*100;

  System.out.println("intDayNumber = " + intDayNumber
  + "  targetFunctionValue = " +
      denormTargetFunctValue1 + "  predictFunctionValue = " +
         denormAverPredictFunctValue11 +
            "  valurDiff = " + targetToPredictFunctValueDiff);
```

```
    if (targetToPredictFunctValueDiff > maxGlobalResultDiff)
      maxGlobalResultDiff =targetToPredictFunctValueDiff;

    sumGlobalResultDiff = sumGlobalResultDiff
    +targetToPredictFunctValueDiff;

    // Populate chart elements
    //doubleDayNumber = (double) rBatchNumber+1;
    xData.add(denormInputFunctValueDiffPercFromRecord);
    yData1.add(denormTargetFunctValue1);
    yData2.add(denormAverPredictFunctValue11);

    }  // End for FunctValue pair1 loop

}  // End of the loop over batches

sumGlobalResultDiff = sumGlobalResultDiff
+targetToPredictFunctValueDiff;
averGlobalResultDiff = sumGlobalResultDiff/
numberOfTrainBatchesToProcess;

// Print the max and average results

System.out.println(" ");
System.out.println(" ");
System.out.println("maxGlobalResultDiff = " + maxGlobalResultDiff);
System.out.println("averGlobalResultDiff = " + averGlobalResultDiff);

XYSeries series1 = Chart.addSeries("Actual data", xData, yData1);
XYSeries series2 = Chart.addSeries("Predict data", xData, yData2);

series1.setLineColor(XChartSeriesColors.BLACK);
series2.setLineColor(XChartSeriesColors.YELLOW);

series1.setMarkerColor(Color.BLACK);
series2.setMarkerColor(Color.WHITE);
series1.setLineStyle(SeriesLines.SOLID);
series2.setLineStyle(SeriesLines.DASH_DASH);
```

```java
// Save the chart image
try
  {
    BitmapEncoder.saveBitmapWithDPI(Chart, strTrainChartFileName,
    BitmapFormat.JPG, 100);
  }
  catch (Exception bt)
  {
    bt.printStackTrace();
  }

System.out.println ("The Chart has been saved");

returnCodes[0] = 0;
returnCodes[1] = 0;
returnCodes[2] = 0;

return returnCodes;

} // End of method

//===================================================
// Load the previously saved trained network1 and tests it by
// processing the Test record
//===================================================

static public void loadAndTestNetwork()
 {
    System.out.println("Testing the network1s results");

    List<Double> xData = new ArrayList<Double>();
    List<Double> yData1 = new ArrayList<Double>();
    List<Double> yData2 = new ArrayList<Double>();

    double targetToPredictFunctValueDiff = 0;
    double maxGlobalResultDiff = 0.00;
    double averGlobalResultDiff = 0.00;
    double sumGlobalResultDiff = 0.00;
    double maxGlobalIndex = 0;
```

```
double normInputDayFromRecord1 = 0.00;
double normTargetFunctValue1 = 0.00;
double normPredictFunctValue1 = 0.00;
double denormInputDayFromRecord1 = 0.00;
double denormTargetFunctValue1 = 0.00;
double denormAverPredictFunctValue1 = 0.00;

double normInputDayFromRecord2 = 0.00;
double normTargetFunctValue2 = 0.00;
double normPredictFunctValue2 = 0.00;
double denormInputDayFromRecord2 = 0.00;
double denormTargetFunctValue2 = 0.00;
double denormAverPredictFunctValue2 = 0.00;

double normInputDayFromTestRecord = 0.00;
double denormInputDayFromTestRecord = 0.00;
double denormAverPredictFunctValue = 0.00;

double denormTargetFunctValueFromTestRecord = 0.00;

String tempLine;
String[] tempWorkFields;
double dayKeyFromTestRecord = 0.00;
double targetFunctValueFromTestRecord = 0.00;
double r1 = 0.00;
double r2 = 0.00;
BufferedReader br4;

BasicNetwork network1;
BasicNetwork network2;
int k1 = 0;
int k3 = 0;

try
 {
    // Process testing records
    maxGlobalResultDiff = 0.00;
    averGlobalResultDiff = 0.00;
```

```
sumGlobalResultDiff = 0.00;

for (k1 = 0; k1 < numberOfTestBatchesToProcess; k1++)
 {
    // if(k1 == 9998)
    //   k1 = k1;

    // Read the corresponding test micro-batch file.
    br4 = new BufferedReader(new FileReader(strTestingFileNames[k1]));
    tempLine = br4.readLine();

    // Skip the label record
    tempLine = br4.readLine();

    // Brake the line using comma as separator
    tempWorkFields = tempLine.split(cvsSplitBy);

    dayKeyFromTestRecord = Double.parseDouble(tempWorkFields[0]);
    targetFunctValueFromTestRecord = Double.parseDouble(tempWork
    Fields[1]);

    // De-normalize the dayKeyFromTestRecord
    denormInputDayFromTestRecord =
      ((minXPointDl - maxXPointDh)*dayKeyFromTestRecord -
           Nh*minXPointDl + maxXPointDh*Nl)/(Nl - Nh);

      // De-normalize the targetFunctValueFromTestRecord
    denormTargetFunctValueFromTestRecord = ((minTargetValueDl -
      maxTargetValueDh)*targetFunctValueFromTestRecord -
        Nh*minTargetValueDl + maxTargetValueDh*Nl)/(Nl - Nh);

    // Load the corresponding training micro-batch dataset in
    memory
    MLDataSet trainingSet1 = loadCSV2Memory(strTrainingFileNames[k1
    ],intInputNeuronNumber,
      intOutputNeuronNumber,true,CSVFormat.ENGLISH,false);

    //MLDataSet testingSet =
    //   loadCSV2Memory(strTestingFileNames[k1],intInputNeuronNumber,
    //       intOutputNeuronNumber,true,CSVFormat.ENGLISH,false);
```

```
network1 =
 (BasicNetwork)EncogDirectoryPersistence.
   loadObject(new File(strSaveTrainNetworkFileNames[k1]));

// Get the results after the network1 optimization
int iMax = 0;
int i = - 1; // Index of the array to get results

for (MLDataPair pair1:  trainingSet1)
 {
    i++;
    iMax = i+1;

    MLData inputData1 = pair1.getInput();
    MLData actualData1 = pair1.getIdeal();
    MLData predictData1 = network1.compute(inputData1);

    // These values are Normalized
    normInputDayFromRecord1 = inputData1.getData(0);
    normTargetFunctValue1 = actualData1.getData(0);
    normPredictFunctValue1 = predictData1.getData(0);

    // De-normalize the obtained values
    denormInputDayFromRecord1 =
      ((minXPointDl - maxXPointDh)*normInputDayFromRecord1 -
        Nh*minXPointDl + maxXPointDh*Nl)/(Nl - Nh);

    denormTargetFunctValue1 = ((minTargetValueDl -
      maxTargetValueDh)*normTargetFunctValue1 -
        Nh*minTargetValueDl +
        maxTargetValueDh*Nl)/(Nl - Nh);

    denormAverPredictFunctValue1 =((minTargetValueDl -
      maxTargetValueDh)*normPredictFunctValue1 -
        Nh*minTargetValueDl +
          maxTargetValueDh*Nl)/(Nl - Nh);

 }  // End for pair1
```

```
// ------------------------------------------------------------
// Now calculate everything again for the SaveNetwork (which
// key is greater than dayKeyFromTestRecord value)in memory
// ------------------------------------------------------------

MLDataSet trainingSet2 = loadCSV2Memory(strTrainingFileNames
[k1+1],intInputNeuronNumber,
   intOutputNeuronNumber,true,CSVFormat.ENGLISH,false);

network2 =
   (BasicNetwork)EncogDirectoryPersistence.
      loadObject(new File(strSaveTrainNetworkFileNames
      [k1+1]));

// Get the results after the network1 optimization
iMax = 0;
i = - 1; // Index of the array to get results

for (MLDataPair pair2:  trainingSet2)
{
   i++;
   iMax = i+1;

   MLData inputData2 = pair2.getInput();
   MLData actualData2 = pair2.getIdeal();
   MLData predictData2 = network2.compute(inputData2);

   // These values are Normalized
   normInputDayFromRecord2 = inputData2.getData(0);
   normTargetFunctValue2 = actualData2.getData(0);
   normPredictFunctValue2 = predictData2.getData(0);

   // De-normalize the obtained values
   denormInputDayFromRecord2 =
      ((minXPointDl - maxXPointDh)*normInputDayFromRecord2 -
         Nh*minXPointDl + maxXPointDh*Nl)/(Nl - Nh);

   denormTargetFunctValue2 = ((minTargetValueDl -
      maxTargetValueDh)*normTargetFunctValue2 -
```

```
                Nh*minTargetValueDl +
                  maxTargetValueDh*Nl)/(Nl - Nh);

          denormAverPredictFunctValue2 =((minTargetValueDl -
            maxTargetValueDh)*normPredictFunctValue2 -
              Nh*minTargetValueDl +
                maxTargetValueDh*Nl)/(Nl - Nh);
    }   // End for pair1 loop

    // Get the average of the denormAverPredictFunctValue1 and
    denormAverPredictFunctValue2
    denormAverPredictFunctValue = (denormAverPredictFunctValue1 +
        denormAverPredictFunctValue2)/2;

    targetToPredictFunctValueDiff =
      (Math.abs(denormTargetFunctValueFromTestRecord -
        denormAverPredictFunctValue)/
        denormTargetFunctValueFromTestRecord)*100;

     System.out.println("Record Number = " + k1 + "  DayNumber = " +
        denormInputDayFromTestRecord +
          "  denormTargetFunctValueFromTestRecord = " +
              denormTargetFunctValueFromTestRecord +
                "  denormAverPredictFunctValue = " +
                denormAverPredictFunctValue +
                  "  valurDiff = " +
                    targetToPredictFunctValueDiff);

    if (targetToPredictFunctValueDiff > maxGlobalResultDiff)
     {
       maxGlobalIndex = iMax;
       maxGlobalResultDiff =targetToPredictFunctValueDiff;
     }

    sumGlobalResultDiff = sumGlobalResultDiff +
      targetToPredictFunctValueDiff;
```

```
        // Populate chart elements

        xData.add(denormInputDayFromTestRecord);
        yData1.add(denormTargetFunctValueFromTestRecord);
        yData2.add(denormAverPredictFunctValue);

    }    // End of loop using k1

    // Print the max and average results

    System.out.println(" ");

    averGlobalResultDiff = sumGlobalResultDiff/
    numberOfTestBatchesToProcess;

    System.out.println("maxGlobalResultDiff = " + maxGlobalResultDiff +
        "  i = " + maxGlobalIndex);
    System.out.println("averGlobalResultDiff = " +
    averGlobalResultDiff);

}      // End of TRY
catch (IOException e1)
{
        e1.printStackTrace();
}

// All testing batch files have been processed
XYSeries series1 = Chart.addSeries("Actual data", xData, yData1);
XYSeries series2 = Chart.addSeries("Predict data", xData, yData2);

series1.setLineColor(XChartSeriesColors.BLACK);
series2.setLineColor(XChartSeriesColors.YELLOW);

series1.setMarkerColor(Color.BLACK);
series2.setMarkerColor(Color.WHITE);
series1.setLineStyle(SeriesLines.SOLID);
series2.setLineStyle(SeriesLines.DASH_DASH);
```

```
// Save the chart image
try
  {
     BitmapEncoder.saveBitmapWithDPI(Chart, strTrainChartFileName,
        BitmapFormat.JPG, 100);
  }
catch (Exception bt)
   {
     bt.printStackTrace();
   }

 System.out.println ("The Chart has been saved");
 System.out.println("End of testing for mini-batches training");

} // End of the method

} // End of the  Encog class
```

Listing 9-5 shows the ending fragment of the testing results after execution.

Listing 9-5. Ending Fragment of the Testing Processing Results

```
DayNumber = 3.98411  TargetValue = 1.17624  AverPredicedValue =
1.18028  DiffPerc = 0.34348
DayNumber = 3.98442  TargetValue = 1.18522  AverPredicedValue =
1.18927  DiffPerc = 0.34158
DayNumber = 3.98472  TargetValue = 1.19421  AverPredicedValue =
1.19827  DiffPerc = 0.33959
DayNumber = 3.98502  TargetValue = 1.20323  AverPredicedValue =
1.20729  DiffPerc = 0.33751
DayNumber = 3.98532  TargetValue = 1.21225  AverPredicedValue =
1.21631  DiffPerc = 0.33534
DayNumber = 3.98562  TargetValue = 1.22128  AverPredicedValue =
1.22535  DiffPerc = 0.33307
DayNumber = 3.98592  TargetValue = 1.23032  AverPredicedValue =
1.23439  DiffPerc = 0.33072
DayNumber = 3.98622  TargetValue = 1.23936  AverPredicedValue =
1.24343  DiffPerc = 0.32828
```

DayNumber = 3.98652 TargetValue = 1.24841 AverPredicedValue =
1.25247 DiffPerc = 0.32575
DayNumber = 3.98682 TargetValue = 1.25744 AverPredicedValue =
1.26151 DiffPerc = 0.32313
DayNumber = 3.98712 TargetValue = 1.26647 AverPredicedValue =
1.27053 DiffPerc = 0.32043
DayNumber = 3.98742 TargetValue = 1.27549 AverPredicedValue =
1.27954 DiffPerc = 0.31764
DayNumber = 3.98772 TargetValue = 1.28449 AverPredicedValue =
1.28854 DiffPerc = 0.31477
DayNumber = 3.98802 TargetValue = 1.29348 AverPredicedValue =
1.29751 DiffPerc = 0.31181
DayNumber = 3.98832 TargetValue = 1.30244 AverPredicedValue =
1.30646 DiffPerc = 0.30876
DayNumber = 3.98862 TargetValue = 1.31138 AverPredicedValue =
1.31538 DiffPerc = 0.30563
DayNumber = 3.98892 TargetValue = 1.32028 AverPredicedValue =
1.32428 DiffPerc = 0.30242
DayNumber = 3.98922 TargetValue = 1.32916 AverPredicedValue =
1.33313 DiffPerc = 0.29913
DayNumber = 3.98952 TargetValue = 1.33799 AverPredicedValue =
1.34195 DiffPerc = 0.29576
DayNumber = 3.98982 TargetValue = 1.34679 AverPredicedValue =
1.35072 DiffPerc = 0.29230
DayNumber = 3.99012 TargetValue = 1.35554 AverPredicedValue =
1.35945 DiffPerc = 0.28876
DayNumber = 3.99042 TargetValue = 1.36423 AverPredicedValue =
1.36812 DiffPerc = 0.28515
DayNumber = 3.99072 TargetValue = 1.37288 AverPredicedValue =
1.37674 DiffPerc = 0.28144
DayNumber = 3.99102 TargetValue = 1.38146 AverPredicedValue =
1.38530 DiffPerc = 0.27768
DayNumber = 3.99132 TargetValue = 1.38999 AverPredicedValue =
1.39379 DiffPerc = 0.27383

DayNumber = 3.99162 TargetValue = 1.39844 AverPredicedValue = 1.40222 DiffPerc = 0.26990

DayNumber = 3.99192 TargetValue = 1.40683 AverPredicedValue = 1.41057 DiffPerc = 0.26590

DayNumber = 3.99222 TargetValue = 1.41515 AverPredicedValue = 1.41885 DiffPerc = 0.26183

DayNumber = 3.99252 TargetValue = 1.42338 AverPredicedValue = 1.42705 DiffPerc = 0.25768

DayNumber = 3.99282 TargetValue = 1.43153 AverPredicedValue = 1.43516 DiffPerc = 0.25346

DayNumber = 3.99312 TargetValue = 1.43960 AverPredicedValue = 1.44318 DiffPerc = 0.24918

DayNumber = 3.99342 TargetValue = 1.44757 AverPredicedValue = 1.45111 DiffPerc = 0.24482

DayNumber = 3.99372 TargetValue = 1.45544 AverPredicedValue = 1.45894 DiffPerc = 0.24040

DayNumber = 3.99402 TargetValue = 1.46322 AverPredicedValue = 1.46667 DiffPerc = 0.23591

DayNumber = 3.99432 TargetValue = 1.47089 AverPredicedValue = 1.47429 DiffPerc = 0.23134

DayNumber = 3.99462 TargetValue = 1.47845 AverPredicedValue = 1.48180 DiffPerc = 0.22672

DayNumber = 3.99492 TargetValue = 1.48590 AverPredicedValue = 1.48920 DiffPerc = 0.22204

DayNumber = 3.99522 TargetValue = 1.49323 AverPredicedValue = 1.49648 DiffPerc = 0.21729

DayNumber = 3.99552 TargetValue = 1.50044 AverPredicedValue = 1.50363 DiffPerc = 0.21247

DayNumber = 3.99582 TargetValue = 1.50753 AverPredicedValue = 1.51066 DiffPerc = 0.20759

DayNumber = 3.99612 TargetValue = 1.51448 AverPredicedValue = 1.51755 DiffPerc = 0.20260

DayNumber = 3.99642 TargetValue = 1.52130 AverPredicedValue = 1.52431 DiffPerc = 0.19770

```
DayNumber = 3.99672  TargetValue = 1.52799  AverPredicedValue =
1.53093  DiffPerc = 0.19260
DayNumber = 3.99702  TargetValue = 1.53453  AverPredicedValue =
1.53740  DiffPerc = 0.18751
DayNumber = 3.99732  TargetValue = 1.54092  AverPredicedValue =
1.54373  DiffPerc = 0.18236
DayNumber = 3.99762  TargetValue = 1.54717  AverPredicedValue =
1.54991  DiffPerc = 0.17715
DayNumber = 3.99792  TargetValue = 1.55326  AverPredicedValue =
1.55593  DiffPerc = 0.17188
DayNumber = 3.99822  TargetValue = 1.55920  AverPredicedValue =
1.56179  DiffPerc = 0.16657
DayNumber = 3.99852  TargetValue = 1.56496  AverPredicedValue =
1.56749  DiffPerc = 0.16120
DayNumber = 3.99882  TargetValue = 1.57057  AverPredicedValue =
1.57302  DiffPerc = 0.15580
DayNumber = 3.99912  TargetValue = 1.57601  AverPredicedValue =
1.57838  DiffPerc = 0.15034
DayNumber = 3.99942  TargetValue = 1.58127  AverPredicedValue =
1.58356  DiffPerc = 0.14484

maxGlobalResultDiff = 0.3620154382225759
averGlobalResultDiff = 0.07501532301280595
```

The testing processing results (the micro-batch method was used) are as follows:

- The maximum error is about 0.36 percent.

- The average error is about 0.075 percent.

Figure 9-5 shows the chart of the testing processing results (the micro-batch method was used). Again, both charts (actual values are shown in black, and predicted values are shown in white) practically overlap.

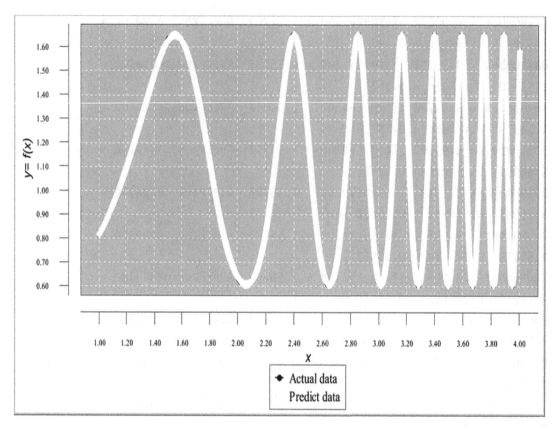

Figure 9-5. *Chart of the testing processing results (the micro-batch method was used)*

Example: Approximation of Spiral-like Functions

In this section, we will discuss a group of functions that are spiral-like. These functions have a common property. At some points, they have multiple function values for a single x point. A function in this group is notoriously difficult to approximate using neural networks. We will attempt to approximate the function shown in Figure 9-6.

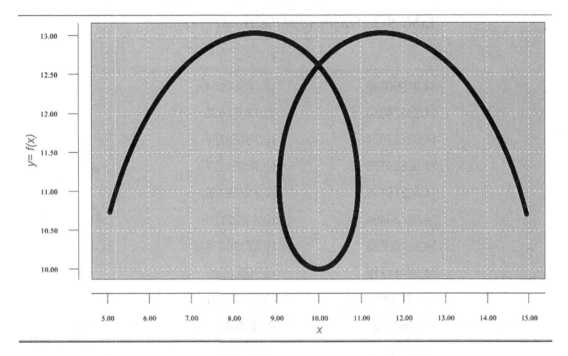

Figure 9-6. *Function with multiple values for some xPoints*

The function is described by two equations:

x(t) = 10 + 0.5*t*Cos(0.3*t).
y(t) = 10 + 0.5*t*Sin(0.3*t).

Here, t is an angle.

Plotting the values of x and y produces the chart shown in Figure 9-6. Again, we pretend that the function formula is unknown, and the function is given to us by its values at 1,000 points. As usual, we first try to approximate this function in a conventional way. Table 9-3 shows a fragment of the training dataset.

Table 9-3. *Fragment of the Training Dataset*

x	y
14.94996248	10.70560004
14.93574853	10.73381636
14.92137454	10.76188757
14.90684173	10.78981277
14.89215135	10.81759106
14.87730464	10.84522155
14.86230283	10.87270339
14.84714718	10.90003569
14.83183894	10.92721761
14.81637936	10.9542483
14.80076973	10.98112693
14.78501129	11.00785266
14.76910532	11.03442469
14.7530531	11.06084221
14.73685592	11.08710443
14.72051504	11.11321054
14.70403178	11.13915979
14.68740741	11.1649514
14.67064324	11.19058461
14.65374057	11.21605868
14.6367007	11.24137288
14.61952494	11.26652647
14.60221462	11.29151873
14.58477103	11.31634896

(*continued*)

Table 9-3. (*continued*)

x	y
14.56719551	11.34101647
14.54948938	11.36552056
14.53165396	11.38986056
14.51369059	11.41403579
14.49560061	11.43804562
14.47738534	11.46188937
14.45904613	11.48556643

The testing dataset is prepared for the points not used in training. Table 9-4 shows a fragment of the testing dataset.

Table 9-4. *Fragment of the Testing Dataset*

x	y
14.9499625	10.70560004
14.9357557	10.73380229
14.921389	10.76185957
14.9068637	10.78977099
14.8921809	10.81753565
14.8773419	10.84515266
14.8623481	10.87262116
14.8472005	10.89994029
14.8319005	10.92710918
14.8164493	10.954127
14.8008481	10.98099291

(*continued*)

Table 9-4. (*continued*)

x	y
14.7850984	11.00770609
14.7692012	11.03426572
14.7531579	11.060671
14.7369698	11.08692113
14.7206381	11.11301533
14.7041642	11.13895282
14.6875493	11.16473284
14.6707947	11.19035462
14.6539018	11.21581743
14.6368718	11.24112053
14.619706	11.26626319
14.6024058	11.29124469
14.5849724	11.31606434
14.5674072	11.34072143
14.5497115	11.36521527
14.5318866	11.38954519
14.5139339	11.41371053
14.4958547	11.43771062
14.4776503	11.46154483
14.4593221	11.48521251

Both training and testing datasets were normalized before processing.

Network Architecture for the Example

Figure 9-7 shows the network architecture.

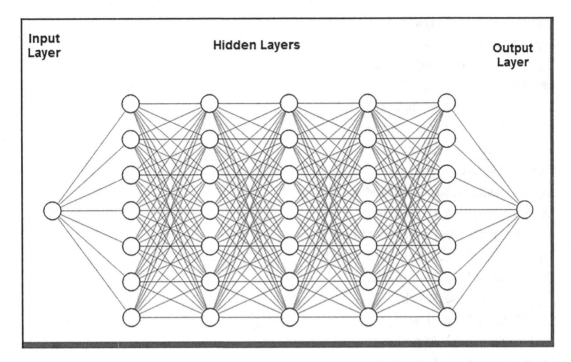

Figure 9-7. *Network architecture*

Program Code for Example

Listing 9-6 shows the program code of the approximation using the conventional process.

Listing 9-6. Program Code of the Conventional Approximation Process

```
// ====================================================
// Approximation spiral-like function using the conventional process.
// The input file is normalized.
// ====================================================
package sample8;

import java.io.BufferedReader;
import java.io.File;
import java.io.FileInputStream;
import java.io.PrintWriter;
import java.io.FileNotFoundException;
import java.io.FileReader;
```

```java
import java.io.FileWriter;
import java.io.IOException;
import java.io.InputStream;
import java.nio.file.*;
import java.util.Properties;
import java.time.YearMonth;
import java.awt.Color;
import java.awt.Font;
import java.io.BufferedReader;
import java.text.DateFormat;
import java.text.ParseException;
import java.text.SimpleDateFormat;
import java.time.LocalDate;
import java.time.Month;
import java.time.ZoneId;
import java.util.ArrayList;
import java.util.Calendar;
import java.util.Date;
import java.util.List;
import java.util.Locale;
import java.util.Properties;

import org.encog.Encog;
import org.encog.engine.network.activation.ActivationTANH;
import org.encog.engine.network.activation.ActivationReLU;
import org.encog.ml.data.MLData;
import org.encog.ml.data.MLDataPair;
import org.encog.ml.data.MLDataSet;
import org.encog.ml.data.buffer.MemoryDataLoader;
import org.encog.ml.data.buffer.codec.CSVDataCODEC;
import org.encog.ml.data.buffer.codec.DataSetCODEC;
import org.encog.neural.networks.BasicNetwork;
import org.encog.neural.networks.layers.BasicLayer;
import org.encog.neural.networks.training.propagation.resilient.
ResilientPropagation;
import org.encog.persist.EncogDirectoryPersistence;
```

```java
import org.encog.util.csv.CSVFormat;

import org.knowm.xchart.SwingWrapper;
import org.knowm.xchart.XYChart;
import org.knowm.xchart.XYChartBuilder;
import org.knowm.xchart.XYSeries;
import org.knowm.xchart.demo.charts.ExampleChart;
import org.knowm.xchart.style.Styler.LegendPosition;
import org.knowm.xchart.style.colors.ChartColor;
import org.knowm.xchart.style.colors.XChartSeriesColors;
import org.knowm.xchart.style.lines.SeriesLines;
import org.knowm.xchart.style.markers.SeriesMarkers;
import org.knowm.xchart.BitmapEncoder;
import org.knowm.xchart.BitmapEncoder.BitmapFormat;
import org.knowm.xchart.QuickChart;
import org.knowm.xchart.SwingWrapper;

public class Sample8 implements ExampleChart<XYChart>
{
    // Interval to normalize
    static double Nh =  1;
    static double Nl = -1;

    // First column
    static double minXPointDl = 1.00;
    static double maxXPointDh = 20.00;

    // Second column - target data
    static double minTargetValueDl = 1.00;
    static double maxTargetValueDh = 20.00;
    static double doublePointNumber = 0.00;
    static int intPointNumber = 0;
    static InputStream input = null;
    static double[] arrPrices = new double[2500];
    static double normInputXPointValue = 0.00;
    static double normPredictXPointValue = 0.00;
    static double normTargetXPointValue = 0.00;
```

```java
static double normDifferencePerc = 0.00;
static double returnCode = 0.00;
static double denormInputXPointValue = 0.00;
static double denormPredictXPointValue = 0.00;
static double denormTargetXPointValue = 0.00;
static double valueDifference = 0.00;
static int numberOfInputNeurons;
static int numberOfOutputNeurons;
static int intNumberOfRecordsInTestFile;
static String trainFileName;
static String priceFileName;
static String testFileName;
static String chartTrainFileName;
static String chartTestFileName;
static String networkFileName;
static int workingMode;
static String cvsSplitBy = ",";

static int numberOfInputRecords = 0;

static List<Double> xData = new ArrayList<Double>();
static List<Double> yData1 = new ArrayList<Double>();
static List<Double> yData2 = new ArrayList<Double>();

static XYChart Chart;

@Override
public XYChart getChart()
 {
  // Create Chart

  Chart = new  XYChartBuilder().width(900).height(500).title(getClass().
          getSimpleName()).xAxisTitle("x").yAxisTitle("y= f(x)").build();

  // Customize Chart
  Chart = new  XYChartBuilder().width(900).height(500).title(getClass().
          getSimpleName()).xAxisTitle("x").yAxisTitle("y= f(x)").
          build();
```

```java
// Customize Chart
Chart.getStyler().setPlotBackgroundColor(ChartColor.
getAWTColor(ChartColor.GREY));
Chart.getStyler().setPlotGridLinesColor(new Color(255, 255, 255));

//Chart.getStyler().setPlotBackgroundColor(ChartColor.
getAWTColor(ChartColor.WHITE));
//Chart.getStyler().setPlotGridLinesColor(new Color(0, 0, 0));
Chart.getStyler().setChartBackgroundColor(Color.WHITE);
//Chart.getStyler().setLegendBackgroundColor(Color.PINK);
Chart.getStyler().setLegendBackgroundColor(Color.WHITE);
//Chart.getStyler().setChartFontColor(Color.MAGENTA);
Chart.getStyler().setChartFontColor(Color.BLACK);
Chart.getStyler().setChartTitleBoxBackgroundColor(new Color(0, 222, 0));
Chart.getStyler().setChartTitleBoxVisible(true);
Chart.getStyler().setChartTitleBoxBorderColor(Color.BLACK);
Chart.getStyler().setPlotGridLinesVisible(true);
Chart.getStyler().setAxisTickPadding(20);
Chart.getStyler().setAxisTickMarkLength(15);
Chart.getStyler().setPlotMargin(20);
Chart.getStyler().setChartTitleVisible(false);
Chart.getStyler().setChartTitleFont(new Font(Font.MONOSPACED,
Font.BOLD, 24));
Chart.getStyler().setLegendFont(new Font(Font.SERIF, Font.PLAIN, 18));
//Chart.getStyler().setLegendPosition(LegendPosition.InsideSE);
Chart.getStyler().setLegendPosition(LegendPosition.OutsideS);
Chart.getStyler().setLegendSeriesLineLength(12);
Chart.getStyler().setAxisTitleFont(new Font(Font.SANS_SERIF,
Font.ITALIC, 18));
Chart.getStyler().setAxisTickLabelsFont(new Font(Font.SERIF,
Font.PLAIN, 11));
Chart.getStyler().setDatePattern("yyyy-MM");
Chart.getStyler().setDecimalPattern("#0.00");
```

```
try
  {
    // Configuration

    // Training mode
    workingMode = 1;
    numberOfInputRecords = 1001;
    trainFileName =
        C:/My_Neural_Network_Book/Book_Examples/Sample8_Calculate_
        Train_Norm.csv";
    chartTrainFileName =
      "C:/My_Neural_Network_Book/Book_Examples/
          Sample8_Chart_ComplexFormula_Spiral_Train_Results.csv";

    // Testing mode
    //workingMode = 2;
    //numberOfInputRecords = 1003;
    //intNumberOfRecordsInTestFile = 3;
    //testFileName = "C:/Book_Examples/Sample2_Norm.csv";
    //chartTestFileName = "XYLine_Test_Results_Chart";

    // Common part of config data
    networkFileName = "C:/My_Neural_Network_Book/Book_Examples/
          Sample8_Saved_Network_File.csv";

    numberOfInputNeurons = 1;
    numberOfOutputNeurons = 1;

    // Check the working mode to run

    if(workingMode == 1)
     {
       // Training mode
       File file1 = new File(chartTrainFileName);
       File file2 = new File(networkFileName);

       if(file1.exists())
         file1.delete();
```

```java
        if(file2.exists())
          file2.delete();

        returnCode = 0;      // Clear the error Code

        do
         {
           returnCode = trainValidateSaveNetwork();
         }  while (returnCode > 0);
      }
     else
      {
         // Test mode
         loadAndTestNetwork();
      }
   }
  catch (Throwable t)
   {
     t.printStackTrace();
     System.exit(1);
   }
  finally
   {
     Encog.getInstance().shutdown();
   }
Encog.getInstance().shutdown();

return Chart;

} // End of the method

// ==========================================================
// Load CSV to memory.
// @return The loaded dataset.
// ==========================================================
public static MLDataSet loadCSV2Memory(String filename, int input,
int ideal, boolean headers,
        CSVFormat format, boolean significance)
```

```
    {
        DataSetCODEC codec = new CSVDataCODEC(new File(filename), format,
        headers, input, ideal,
             significance);
        MemoryDataLoader load = new MemoryDataLoader(codec);
        MLDataSet dataset = load.external2Memory();
        return dataset;
    }

// ==========================================================
//  The main method.
//  @param Command line arguments. No arguments are used.
// ==========================================================
public static void main(String[] args)
 {
    ExampleChart<XYChart> exampleChart = new Sample8();
    XYChart Chart = exampleChart.getChart();
    new SwingWrapper<XYChart>(Chart).displayChart();
 } // End of the main method

//========================================================================
// This method trains, Validates, and saves the trained network file
//========================================================================
static public double trainValidateSaveNetwork()
 {
    // Load the training CSV file in memory
    MLDataSet trainingSet =
      loadCSV2Memory(trainFileName,numberOfInputNeurons,
      numberOfOutputNeurons,
        true,CSVFormat.ENGLISH,false);

    // create a neural network
    BasicNetwork network = new BasicNetwork();

    // Input layer
    network.addLayer(new BasicLayer(null,true,1));
```

```java
// Hidden layer
network.addLayer(new BasicLayer(new ActivationTANH(),true,10));
network.addLayer(new BasicLayer(new ActivationTANH(),true,10));
network.addLayer(new BasicLayer(new ActivationTANH(),true,10));
network.addLayer(new BasicLayer(new ActivationTANH(),true,10));
network.addLayer(new BasicLayer(new ActivationTANH(),true,10));
network.addLayer(new BasicLayer(new ActivationTANH(),true,10));
network.addLayer(new BasicLayer(new ActivationTANH(),true,10));

// Output layer
//network.addLayer(new BasicLayer(new ActivationLOG(),false,1));
network.addLayer(new BasicLayer(new ActivationTANH(),false,1));

network.getStructure().finalizeStructure();
network.reset();

// train the neural network
final ResilientPropagation train = new ResilientPropagation(network,
trainingSet);

int epoch = 1;

do
 {
    train.iteration();
    System.out.println("Epoch #" + epoch + " Error:" + train.
    getError());

  epoch++;

  if (epoch >= 11000 && network.calculateError(trainingSet) > 0.2251)
     {
       returnCode = 1;

       System.out.println("Try again");
       return returnCode;
     }
 } while(train.getError() > 0.225);
```

```java
// Save the network file
EncogDirectoryPersistence.saveObject(new File(networkFileName),
network);

System.out.println("Neural Network Results:");

double sumNormDifferencePerc = 0.00;
double averNormDifferencePerc = 0.00;
double maxNormDifferencePerc = 0.00;

int m = 0;
double xPointer = 0.00;

for(MLDataPair pair: trainingSet)
  {
      m++;
      xPointer++;

      //if(m == 0)
      // continue;

       final MLData output = network.compute(pair.getInput());

       MLData inputData = pair.getInput();
       MLData actualData = pair.getIdeal();
       MLData predictData = network.compute(inputData);

       // Calculate and print the results
       normInputXPointValue = inputData.getData(0);
       normTargetXPointValue = actualData.getData(0);
       normPredictXPointValue = predictData.getData(0);

       denormInputXPointValue = ((minXPointD1 - maxXPointDh)*
       normInputXPointValue -
          Nh*minXPointD1 + maxXPointDh *N1)/(N1 - Nh);

       denormTargetXPointValue =((minTargetValueD1 -
       maxTargetValueDh)* normTargetXPointValue -
          Nh*minTargetValueD1 + maxTargetValueDh*N1)/(N1 - Nh);
```

```java
        denormPredictXPointValue =((minTargetValueDl -
        maxTargetValueDh)* normPredictXPointValue -
          Nh*minTargetValueDl + maxTargetValueDh*Nl)/(Nl - Nh);

        valueDifference =
          Math.abs(((denormTargetXPointValue -
            denormPredictXPointValue)/
            denormTargetXPointValue)*100.00);

        System.out.println ("Day = " + denormInputXPointValue +
        "  denormTargetXPointValue = " +
          denormTargetXPointValue + "  denormPredictXPointValue = " +
          denormPredictXPointValue +
            "  valueDifference = " + valueDifference);
        //System.out.println("intPointNumber = " + intPointNumber);

        sumNormDifferencePerc = sumNormDifferencePerc +
        valueDifference;

        if (valueDifference > maxNormDifferencePerc)
          maxNormDifferencePerc = valueDifference;

        xData.add(denormInputXPointValue);
        yData1.add(denormTargetXPointValue);
        yData2.add(denormPredictXPointValue);

}    // End for pair loop

XYSeries series1 = Chart.addSeries("Actual data", xData, yData1);
XYSeries series2 = Chart.addSeries("Predict data", xData, yData2);

series1.setLineColor(XChartSeriesColors.BLACK);
series2.setLineColor(XChartSeriesColors.LIGHT_GREY);

series1.setMarkerColor(Color.BLACK);
series2.setMarkerColor(Color.WHITE);
series1.setLineStyle(SeriesLines.NONE);
series2.setLineStyle(SeriesLines.SOLID);
```

```
   try
    {
      //Save the chart image
      BitmapEncoder.saveBitmapWithDPI(Chart, chartTrainFileName,
        BitmapFormat.JPG, 100);
      System.out.println ("Train Chart file has been saved") ;
    }
  catch (IOException ex)
   {
    ex.printStackTrace();
    System.exit(3);
   }

   // Finally, save this trained network
   EncogDirectoryPersistence.saveObject(new File(networkFileName),
   network);
   System.out.println ("Train Network has been saved") ;

   averNormDifferencePerc  = sumNormDifferencePerc/
   numberOfInputRecords;

   System.out.println(" ");
   System.out.println("maxNormDifferencePerc = " +
   maxNormDifferencePerc + "
       averNormDifferencePerc = " + averNormDifferencePerc);

   returnCode = 0.00;
   return returnCode;

 }    // End of the method
//=================================================
// This method load and test the trained network
//=================================================
static public void loadAndTestNetwork()
 {
   System.out.println("Testing the networks results");

   List<Double> xData = new ArrayList<Double>();
```

```
List<Double> yData1 = new ArrayList<Double>();
List<Double> yData2 = new ArrayList<Double>();

double targetToPredictPercent = 0;
double maxGlobalResultDiff = 0.00;
double averGlobalResultDiff = 0.00;
double sumGlobalResultDiff = 0.00;
double maxGlobalIndex = 0;
double normInputXPointValueFromRecord = 0.00;
double normTargetXPointValueFromRecord = 0.00;
double normPredictXPointValueFromRecord = 0.00;

BasicNetwork network;

maxGlobalResultDiff = 0.00;
averGlobalResultDiff = 0.00;
sumGlobalResultDiff = 0.00;

// Load the test dataset into memory
MLDataSet testingSet =
loadCSV2Memory(testFileName,numberOfInputNeurons,numberOfOutputNeurons,
true,
   CSVFormat.ENGLISH,false);

// Load the saved trained network
network =
   (BasicNetwork)EncogDirectoryPersistence.loadObject(new
   File(networkFileName));

int i = - 1; // Index of the current record
double xPoint = -0.00;

for (MLDataPair pair:  testingSet)
 {
     i++;
     xPoint = xPoint + 2.00;

     MLData inputData = pair.getInput();
     MLData actualData = pair.getIdeal();
```

```java
MLData predictData = network.compute(inputData);

// These values are Normalized as the whole input is
normInputXPointValueFromRecord = inputData.getData(0);
normTargetXPointValueFromRecord = actualData.getData(0);
normPredictXPointValueFromRecord = predictData.getData(0);

denormInputXPointValue = ((minXPointDl - maxXPointDh)*
  normInputXPointValueFromRecord - Nh*minXPointDl +
  maxXPointDh*Nl)/(Nl - Nh);
denormTargetXPointValue = ((minTargetValueDl -
maxTargetValueDh)*
  normTargetXPointValueFromRecord - Nh*minTargetValueDl +
  maxTargetValueDh*Nl)/(Nl - Nh);
denormPredictXPointValue =((minTargetValueDl -
maxTargetValueDh)*
  normPredictXPointValueFromRecord - Nh*minTargetValueDl +
  maxTargetValueDh*Nl)/(Nl - Nh);

targetToPredictPercent = Math.abs((denormTargetXPointValue -
denormPredictXPointValue)/
  denormTargetXPointValue*100);

System.out.println("xPoint = " + xPoint
+ "   denormTargetXPointValue = " +
  denormTargetXPointValue + "   denormPredictXPointValue = " +
  denormPredictXPointValue + "
        targetToPredictPercent = " + targetToPredictPercent);

if (targetToPredictPercent > maxGlobalResultDiff)
   maxGlobalResultDiff = targetToPredictPercent;

sumGlobalResultDiff = sumGlobalResultDiff +
targetToPredictPercent;

// Populate chart elements
xData.add(xPoint);
yData1.add(denormTargetXPointValue);
yData2.add(denormPredictXPointValue);
```

```
  }  // End for pair loop

  // Print the max and average results
  System.out.println(" ");
  averGlobalResultDiff = sumGlobalResultDiff/numberOfInputRecords;

  System.out.println("maxGlobalResultDiff = " + maxGlobalResultDiff +
  "  i = " + maxGlobalIndex);
  System.out.println("averGlobalResultDiff = " + averGlobalResultDiff);

  // All testing batch files have been processed
  XYSeries series1 = Chart.addSeries("Actual", xData, yData1);
  XYSeries series2 = Chart.addSeries("Predicted", xData, yData2);

  series1.setLineColor(XChartSeriesColors.BLUE);
  series2.setMarkerColor(Color.ORANGE);
  series1.setLineStyle(SeriesLines.SOLID);
  series2.setLineStyle(SeriesLines.SOLID);

  // Save the chart image
  try
   {
     BitmapEncoder.saveBitmapWithDPI(Chart, chartTestFileName ,
     BitmapFormat.JPG, 100);
   }
  catch (Exception bt)
   {
     bt.printStackTrace();
   }

  System.out.println ("The Chart has been saved");
  System.out.println("End of testing for test records");

 } // End of the method

} // End of the class
```

The function was approximated using conventional network processing. Listing 9-7 shows the end fragment of the conventional processing results.

Listing 9-7. The End Fragment of the Conventional Training Results

```
Day = 5.57799  TargetValue = 11.53242  PredictedValue = 1.15068  DiffPerc =
90.02216
Day = 5.55941  TargetValue = 11.50907  PredictedValue = 1.15073  DiffPerc =
90.00153
Day = 5.54095  TargetValue = 11.48556  PredictedValue = 1.15077  DiffPerc =
89.98067
Day = 5.52261  TargetValue = 11.46188  PredictedValue = 1.15082  DiffPerc =
89.95958
Day = 5.50439  TargetValue = 11.43804  PredictedValue = 1.15086  DiffPerc =
89.93824
Day = 5.48630  TargetValue = 11.41403  PredictedValue = 1.15091  DiffPerc =
89.91667
Day = 5.46834  TargetValue = 11.38986  PredictedValue = 1.15096  DiffPerc =
89.89485
Day = 5.45051  TargetValue = 11.36552  PredictedValue = 1.15100  DiffPerc =
89.87280
Day = 5.43280  TargetValue = 11.34101  PredictedValue = 1.15105  DiffPerc =
89.85049
Day = 5.41522  TargetValue = 11.31634  PredictedValue = 1.15110  DiffPerc =
89.82794
Day = 5.39778  TargetValue = 11.29151  PredictedValue = 1.15115  DiffPerc =
89.80515
Day = 5.38047  TargetValue = 11.26652  PredictedValue = 1.15120  DiffPerc =
89.78210
Day = 5.36329  TargetValue = 11.24137  PredictedValue = 1.15125  DiffPerc =
89.75880
Day = 5.34625  TargetValue = 11.21605  PredictedValue = 1.15130  DiffPerc =
89.73525
Day = 5.32935  TargetValue = 11.19058  PredictedValue = 1.15134  DiffPerc =
89.71144
Day = 5.31259  TargetValue = 11.16495  PredictedValue = 1.15139  DiffPerc =
89.68737
Day = 5.29596  TargetValue = 11.13915  PredictedValue = 1.15144  DiffPerc =
89.66305
```

```
Day = 5.27948  TargetValue = 11.11321  PredictedValue = 1.15149  DiffPerc =
89.63846
Day = 5.26314  TargetValue = 11.08710  PredictedValue = 1.15154  DiffPerc =
89.61361
Day = 5.24694  TargetValue = 11.06084  PredictedValue = 1.15159  DiffPerc =
89.58850
Day = 5.23089  TargetValue = 11.03442  PredictedValue = 1.15165  DiffPerc =
89.56311
Day = 5.21498  TargetValue = 11.00785  PredictedValue = 1.15170  DiffPerc =
89.53746
Day = 5.19923  TargetValue = 10.98112  PredictedValue = 1.15175  DiffPerc =
89.51153
Day = 5.18362  TargetValue = 10.95424  PredictedValue = 1.15180  DiffPerc =
89.48534
Day = 5.16816  TargetValue = 10.92721  PredictedValue = 1.15185  DiffPerc =
89.45886
Day = 5.15285  TargetValue = 10.90003  PredictedValue = 1.15190  DiffPerc =
89.43211
Day = 5.13769  TargetValue = 10.87270  PredictedValue = 1.15195  DiffPerc =
89.40508
Day = 5.12269  TargetValue = 10.84522  PredictedValue = 1.15200  DiffPerc =
89.37776
Day = 5.10784  TargetValue = 10.81759  PredictedValue = 1.15205  DiffPerc =
89.35016
Day = 5.09315  TargetValue = 10.78981  PredictedValue = 1.15210  DiffPerc =
89.32228
Day = 5.07862  TargetValue = 10.76188  PredictedValue = 1.15215  DiffPerc =
89.29410

maxErrorPerc = 91.1677948809837
averErrorPerc = 90.04645291133258
```

With the conventional process, the approximation results are as follows:

- The maximum error percent is more than 91.16 percent.

- The average error percent is more than 90.0611 percent.

Figure 9-8 shows the chart of the training approximation results using conventional network processing.

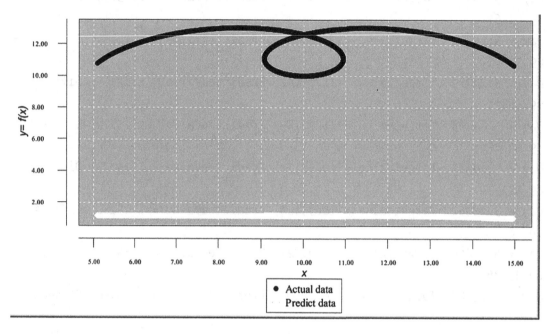

Figure 9-8. *Chart of the training approximation results using conventional network processing*

Obviously, such an approximation is completely useless.

Approximation of the Same Functions Using Micro-Batch Method

Now, let's approximate this function using the micro-batch method. Again, the normalized training dataset is broken into a set of training micro-batch files, and it is now the input to the training process.

Listing 9-8 shows the program code for the training method using the micro-batch process.

Listing 9-8. The Program Code for the Training Method Using the Micro-Batch Process

```
// =================================================================
// Approximation the spiral-like function using the micro-batch method.
// The input is the normalized set of micro-batch files (each micro-batch
// includes a single day record).
// Each record consists of:
// - normDayValue
// - normTargetValue
//
// The number of inputLayer neurons is 1
// The number of outputLayer neurons is 1
// Each network is saved on disk and a map is created to link each saved
trained
// network with the corresponding training micro-batch file.
// =================================================================

package sample8_microbatches;

import java.io.BufferedReader;
import java.io.File;
import java.io.FileInputStream;
import java.io.PrintWriter;
import java.io.FileNotFoundException;
import java.io.FileReader;
import java.io.FileWriter;
import java.io.IOException;
import java.io.InputStream;
import java.nio.file.*;
import java.util.Properties;
import java.time.YearMonth;
import java.awt.Color;
import java.awt.Font;
import java.io.BufferedReader;
import java.time.Month;
```

```java
import java.time.ZoneId;
import java.util.ArrayList;
import java.util.Calendar;
import java.util.List;
import java.util.Locale;
import java.util.Properties;
import org.encog.Encog;
import org.encog.engine.network.activation.ActivationTANH;
import org.encog.engine.network.activation.ActivationReLU;
import org.encog.ml.data.MLData;
import org.encog.ml.data.MLDataPair;
import org.encog.ml.data.MLDataSet;
import org.encog.ml.data.buffer.MemoryDataLoader;
import org.encog.ml.data.buffer.codec.CSVDataCODEC;
import org.encog.ml.data.buffer.codec.DataSetCODEC;
import org.encog.neural.networks.BasicNetwork;
import org.encog.neural.networks.layers.BasicLayer;
import org.encog.neural.networks.training.propagation.resilient.
   ResilientPropagation;
import org.encog.persist.EncogDirectoryPersistence;
import org.encog.util.csv.CSVFormat;

import org.knowm.xchart.SwingWrapper;
import org.knowm.xchart.XYChart;
import org.knowm.xchart.XYChartBuilder;
import org.knowm.xchart.XYSeries;
import org.knowm.xchart.demo.charts.ExampleChart;
import org.knowm.xchart.style.Styler.LegendPosition;
import org.knowm.xchart.style.colors.ChartColor;
import org.knowm.xchart.style.colors.XChartSeriesColors;
import org.knowm.xchart.style.lines.SeriesLines;
import org.knowm.xchart.style.markers.SeriesMarkers;
import org.knowm.xchart.BitmapEncoder;
import org.knowm.xchart.BitmapEncoder.BitmapFormat;
import org.knowm.xchart.QuickChart;
import org.knowm.xchart.SwingWrapper;
```

```java
public class Sample8_Microbatches implements ExampleChart<XYChart>
{
    // Normalization parameters

    // Normalizing interval
    static double Nh =  1;
    static double Nl = -1;

    // inputFunctValueDiffPerc
    static double inputDayDh = 20.00;
    static double inputDayDl = 1.00;

    // targetFunctValueDiffPerc
    static double targetFunctValueDiffPercDh = 20.00;
    static double targetFunctValueDiffPercDl = 1.00;

    static String cvsSplitBy = ",";
    static Properties prop = null;

    static String strWorkingMode;
    static String strNumberOfBatchesToProcess;
    static String strTrainFileNameBase;
    static String strTestFileNameBase;
    static String strSaveTrainNetworkFileBase;
    static String strSaveTestNetworkFileBase;
    static String strValidateFileName;
    static String strTrainChartFileName;
    static String strTestChartFileName;
    static String strFunctValueTrainFile;
    static String strFunctValueTestFile;
    static int intDayNumber;
    static double doubleDayNumber;
    static int intWorkingMode;
    static int numberOfTrainBatchesToProcess;
    static int numberOfTestBatchesToProcess;
    static int intNumberOfRecordsInTrainFile;
    static int intNumberOfRecordsInTestFile;
    static int intNumberOfRowsInBatches;
```

373

```java
    static int intInputNeuronNumber;
    static int intOutputNeuronNumber;
    static String strOutputFileName;
    static String strSaveNetworkFileName;
    static String strDaysTrainFileName;
    static XYChart Chart;
    static String iString;
    static double inputFunctValueFromFile;
    static double targetToPredictFunctValueDiff;
    static int[] returnCodes  = new int[3];

    static List<Double> xData = new ArrayList<Double>();
    static List<Double> yData1 = new ArrayList<Double>();
    static List<Double> yData2 = new ArrayList<Double>();

    static double[] DaysyearDayTraining = new double[1200];
    static String[] strTrainingFileNames = new String[1200];
    static String[] strTestingFileNames = new String[1200];
    static String[] strSaveTrainNetworkFileNames = new String[1200];
    static double[] linkToSaveNetworkDayKeys = new double[1200];
    static double[] linkToSaveNetworkTargetFunctValueKeys = new
double[1200];
    static double[] arrTrainFunctValues = new double[1200];
    static double[] arrTestFunctValues = new double[1200];

  @Override
  public XYChart getChart()
   {
     // Create Chart

    Chart = new XYChartBuilder().width(900).height(500).title(getClass().
      getSimpleName()).xAxisTitle("day").yAxisTitle("y=f(day)").build();

    // Customize Chart
    Chart.getStyler().setPlotBackgroundColor(ChartColor.
    getAWTColor(ChartColor.GREY));
    Chart.getStyler().setPlotGridLinesColor(new Color(255, 255, 255));
    Chart.getStyler().setChartBackgroundColor(Color.WHITE);
```

```
Chart.getStyler().setLegendBackgroundColor(Color.PINK);
Chart.getStyler().setChartFontColor(Color.MAGENTA);
Chart.getStyler().setChartTitleBoxBackgroundColor(new Color(0, 222, 0));
Chart.getStyler().setChartTitleBoxVisible(true);
Chart.getStyler().setChartTitleBoxBorderColor(Color.BLACK);
Chart.getStyler().setPlotGridLinesVisible(true);
Chart.getStyler().setAxisTickPadding(20);
Chart.getStyler().setAxisTickMarkLength(15);
Chart.getStyler().setPlotMargin(20);
Chart.getStyler().setChartTitleVisible(false);
Chart.getStyler().setChartTitleFont(new Font(Font.MONOSPACED,
Font.BOLD, 24));
Chart.getStyler().setLegendFont(new Font(Font.SERIF, Font.PLAIN, 18));
// Chart.getStyler().setLegendPosition(LegendPosition.InsideSE);
Chart.getStyler().setLegendPosition(LegendPosition.OutsideE);
Chart.getStyler().setLegendSeriesLineLength(12);
Chart.getStyler().setAxisTitleFont(new Font(Font.SANS_SERIF,
Font.ITALIC, 18));
Chart.getStyler().setAxisTickLabelsFont(new Font(Font.SERIF,
Font.PLAIN, 11));
//Chart.getStyler().setDayPattern("yyyy-MM");
Chart.getStyler().setDecimalPattern("#0.00");

// Config data

// Training mode
//intWorkingMode = 0;

// Testing mode
intWorkingMode = 1;

numberOfTrainBatchesToProcess = 1000;
numberOfTestBatchesToProcess = 999;
intNumberOfRowsInBatches = 1;
intInputNeuronNumber = 1;
intOutputNeuronNumber = 1;
strTrainFileNameBase =
```

```
 "C:/My_Neural_Network_Book/Book_Examples/Work_Files/Sample8_
 Microbatch_Train_";
strTestFileNameBase =
 "C:/My_Neural_Network_Book/Book_Examples/Work_Files/Sample8_
 Microbatch_Test_";
strSaveTrainNetworkFileBase =
 "C:/My_Neural_Network_Book/Book_Examples/Work_Files/Sample8_Save_
 Network_Batch_";
strTrainChartFileName = "C:/Book_Examples/Sample8_Chart_Train_File_
Microbatch.jpg";
strTestChartFileName = "C:/Book_Examples/Sample8_Chart_Test_File_
Microbatch.jpg";

// Generate training batche file names and the corresponding
// SaveNetwork file names

intDayNumber = -1;   // Day number for the chart

for (int i = 0; i < numberOfTrainBatchesToProcess; i++)
 {
   intDayNumber++;

   iString = Integer.toString(intDayNumber);

   if (intDayNumber >= 10 & intDayNumber < 100   )
    {
      strOutputFileName = strTrainFileNameBase + "0" + iString + ".csv";
      strSaveNetworkFileName = strSaveTrainNetworkFileBase + "0" +
        iString + ".csv";
    }
   else
    {
      if (intDayNumber < 10)
       {
         strOutputFileName = strTrainFileNameBase + "00" +
           iString + ".csv";
         strSaveNetworkFileName = strSaveTrainNetworkFileBase + "00" +
           iString + ".csv";
       }
```

```
    else
     {
        strOutputFileName = strTrainFileNameBase + iString +
          ".csv";

        strSaveNetworkFileName = strSaveTrainNetworkFileBase +
          iString + ".csv";
     }
   }

    strTrainingFileNames[intDayNumber] = strOutputFileName;
    strSaveTrainNetworkFileNames[intDayNumber] =
    strSaveNetworkFileName;

}  // End the FOR loop

// Build the array linkToSaveNetworkFunctValueDiffKeys
String tempLine;
double tempNormFunctValueDiff = 0.00;
double tempNormFunctValueDiffPerc = 0.00;
double tempNormTargetFunctValueDiffPerc = 0.00;

String[] tempWorkFields;

try
 {
    intDayNumber = -1;   // Day number for the chart

    for (int m = 0; m < numberOfTrainBatchesToProcess; m++)
      {
        intDayNumber++;

        BufferedReader br3 = new BufferedReader(new
          FileReader(strTrainingFileNames[intDayNumber]));

        tempLine = br3.readLine();

        // Skip the label record and zero batch record
        tempLine = br3.readLine();
```

```
              // Brake the line using comma as separator
              tempWorkFields = tempLine.split(cvsSplitBy);

              tempNormFunctValueDiffPerc = Double.parseDouble(tempWork
              Fields[0]);
              tempNormTargetFunctValueDiffPerc = Double.parseDouble(
              tempWorkFields[1]);

              linkToSaveNetworkDayKeys[intDayNumber] =
              tempNormFunctValueDiffPerc;

              linkToSaveNetworkTargetFunctValueKeys[intDayNumber] =
                  tempNormTargetFunctValueDiffPerc;

         }  // End the FOR loop

        // Generate testing batch file names

        if(intWorkingMode == 1)
         {
           intDayNumber = -1;

           for (int i = 0; i < numberOfTestBatchesToProcess; i++)
            {
              intDayNumber++;
              iString = Integer.toString(intDayNumber);

              // Construct the testing batch names
              if (intDayNumber >= 10 & intDayNumber < 100   )
               {
                 strOutputFileName = strTestFileNameBase + "0" +
                   iString + ".csv";
               }
              else
               {
                 if (intDayNumber < 10)
                  {
                    strOutputFileName = strTestFileNameBase + "00" +
                      iString + ".csv";
                  }
```

```
            else
              {
                strOutputFileName = strTestFileNameBase +
                  iString + ".csv";
              }
          }

      strTestingFileNames[intDayNumber] = strOutputFileName;

    }  // End the FOR loop

    }   // End of IF

  }     // End for try
catch (IOException io1)
  {
    io1.printStackTrace();
    System.exit(1);
  }

// Load, train, and test Function Values file in memory
//loadTrainFunctValueFileInMemory();

// Test the mode
if(intWorkingMode == 0)
  {
    // Train mode

    int paramErrorCode;
    int paramBatchNumber;
    int paramR;
    int paramDayNumber;
    int paramS;

    File file1 = new File(strTrainChartFileName);

    if(file1.exists())
      file1.delete();
```

```
      returnCodes[0] = 0;    // Clear the error Code
      returnCodes[1] = 0;    // Set the initial batch Number to 0;
      returnCodes[2] = 0;    // Day number;

    do
    {
      paramErrorCode = returnCodes[0];
      paramBatchNumber = returnCodes[1];
      paramDayNumber = returnCodes[2];

      returnCodes =
        trainBatches(paramErrorCode,paramBatchNumber,paramDayNumber);
    } while (returnCodes[0] > 0);

  }   // End the train logic
  else
  {
    // Testing mode

    File file2 = new File(strTestChartFileName);

    if(file2.exists())
      file2.delete();

    loadAndTestNetwork();

    // End the test logic
  }

  Encog.getInstance().shutdown();
  //System.exit(0);
  return Chart;

} // End of method

// =========================================================
// Load CSV to memory.
// @return The loaded dataset.
// =========================================================
```

```java
public static MLDataSet loadCSV2Memory(String filename, int input, int
ideal,
        boolean headers, CSVFormat format, boolean significance)
  {
     DataSetCODEC codec = new CSVDataCODEC(new File(filename), format,
     headers,
         input, ideal, significance);
     MemoryDataLoader load = new MemoryDataLoader(codec);
     MLDataSet dataset = load.external2Memory();
     return dataset;
  }

// ===========================================================
//  The main method.
//  @param Command line arguments. No arguments are used.
// ===========================================================
public static void main(String[] args)
 {

    ExampleChart<XYChart> exampleChart = new Sample8_Microbatches();
    XYChart Chart = exampleChart.getChart();
    new SwingWrapper<XYChart>(Chart).displayChart();
 } // End of the main method

//==========================================
// This method trains batches as individual network1s
// saving them in separate trained datasets
//==========================================
static public int[] trainBatches(int paramErrorCode,
                                  int paramBatchNumber,int paramDayNumber)
  {
     int rBatchNumber;
     double targetToPredictFunctValueDiff = 0;
     double maxGlobalResultDiff = 0.00;
     double averGlobalResultDiff = 0.00;
     double sumGlobalResultDiff = 0.00;
     double normInputFunctValueFromRecord = 0.00;
```

```
    double normTargetFunctValue1 = 0.00;
    double normPredictFunctValue1 = 0.00;
    double denormInputDayFromRecord;
    double denormInputFunctValueFromRecord = 0.00;
    double denormTargetFunctValue = 0.00;
    double denormPredictFunctValue1 = 0.00;

    BasicNetwork network1 = new BasicNetwork();

    // Input layer
    network1.addLayer(new BasicLayer(null,true,intInputNeuronNumber));

// Hidden layer.
network1.addLayer(new BasicLayer(new ActivationTANH(),true,7));
network1.addLayer(new BasicLayer(new ActivationTANH(),true,7));
network1.addLayer(new BasicLayer(new ActivationTANH(),true,7));
network1.addLayer(new BasicLayer(new ActivationTANH(),true,7));
network1.addLayer(new BasicLayer(new ActivationTANH(),true,7));

    // Output layer
    network1.addLayer(new BasicLayer(new ActivationTANH(),false,
    intOutputNeuronNumber));

    network1.getStructure().finalizeStructure();
    network1.reset();

    maxGlobalResultDiff = 0.00;
    averGlobalResultDiff = 0.00;
    sumGlobalResultDiff = 0.00;

    // Loop over batches
    intDayNumber = paramDayNumber;   // Day number for the chart

    for (rBatchNumber = paramBatchNumber; rBatchNumber <
    numberOfTrainBatchesToProcess;
        rBatchNumber++)
      {
        intDayNumber++;
```

```
//if(intDayNumber == 502)
// rBatchNumber = rBatchNumber;

// Load the training file in memory
MLDataSet trainingSet =
    loadCSV2Memory(strTrainingFileNames[rBatchNumber],
    intInputNeuronNumber,
        intOutputNeuronNumber,true,CSVFormat.ENGLISH,false);

// train the neural network1
ResilientPropagation train = new ResilientPropagation(network1,
trainingSet);

int epoch = 1;

do
  {
     train.iteration();

     epoch++;

     for (MLDataPair pair11:  trainingSet)
      {
        MLData inputData1 = pair11.getInput();
        MLData actualData1 = pair11.getIdeal();
        MLData predictData1 = network1.compute(inputData1);

        // These values are Normalized as the whole input is
        normInputFunctValueFromRecord = inputData1.getData(0);

        normTargetFunctValue1 = actualData1.getData(0);
        normPredictFunctValue1 = predictData1.getData(0);

        denormInputFunctValueFromRecord =((inputDayDl -
            inputDayDh)*normInputFunctValueFromRecord - Nh*inputDayDl +
                inputDayDh*Nl)/(Nl - Nh);
        denormTargetFunctValue = ((targetFunctValueDiffPercDl -
            targetFunctValueDiffPercDh)*normTargetFunctValue1 -
            Nh*targetFunctValueDiffPercDl +
                targetFunctValueDiffPercDh*Nl)/(Nl - Nh);
```

```
            denormPredictFunctValue1 =((targetFunctValueDiffPercDl -
              targetFunctValueDiffPercDh)*normPredictFunctValue1 -
              Nh*targetFunctValueDiffPercDl +
                  targetFunctValueDiffPercDh*Nl)/(Nl - Nh);

            //inputFunctValueFromFile = arrTrainFunctValues[rBatchNumber];

            targetToPredictFunctValueDiff = (Math.
            abs(denormTargetFunctValue -
                  denormPredictFunctValue1)/denormTargetFunctValue)*100;
         }

       if (epoch >= 1000 && Math.abs(targetToPredictFunctValueDiff) >
       0.0000091)
         {
           returnCodes[0] = 1;
           returnCodes[1] = rBatchNumber;
           returnCodes[2] = intDayNumber-1;

           return returnCodes;
         }

       //System.out.println("intDayNumber = " + intDayNumber);

     } while(Math.abs(targetToPredictFunctValueDiff) > 0.000009);

// This batch is optimized

// Save the network1 for the current batch
EncogDirectoryPersistence.saveObject(new
    File(strSaveTrainNetworkFileNames[rBatchNumber]),network1);

// Get the results after the network1 optimization
int i = - 1;

for (MLDataPair pair1:  trainingSet)
 {
   i++;

   MLData inputData1 = pair1.getInput();
   MLData actualData1 = pair1.getIdeal();
```

```
MLData predictData1 = network1.compute(inputData1);

// These values are Normalized as the whole input is
normInputFunctValueFromRecord = inputData1.getData(0);
normTargetFunctValue1 = actualData1.getData(0);
normPredictFunctValue1 = predictData1.getData(0);

// De-normalize the obtained values
denormInputFunctValueFromRecord =((inputDayDl -
   inputDayDh)*normInputFunctValueFromRecord -
      Nh*inputDayDl + inputDayDh*Nl)/(Nl - Nh);

denormTargetFunctValue = ((targetFunctValueDiffPercDl -
   targetFunctValueDiffPercDh)*normTargetFunctValue1 -
      Nh*targetFunctValueDiffPercDl +
      targetFunctValueDiffPercDh*Nl)/(Nl - Nh);

denormPredictFunctValue1 =((targetFunctValueDiffPercDl -
   targetFunctValueDiffPercDh)*normPredictFunctValue1 -
      Nh*targetFunctValueDiffPercDl +
      targetFunctValueDiffPercDh*Nl)/(Nl - Nh);

//inputFunctValueFromFile = arrTrainFunctValues[rBatchNumber];

targetToPredictFunctValueDiff = (Math.abs(denormTargetFunctValue -
      denormPredictFunctValue1)/denormTargetFunctValue)*100;

System.out.println("intDayNumber = " + intDayNumber
+ "  targetFunctionValue = " +
   denormTargetFunctValue + "  predictFunctionValue = " +
   denormPredictFunctValue1 +
      "  valurDiff = " + targetToPredictFunctValueDiff);

if (targetToPredictFunctValueDiff > maxGlobalResultDiff)
   maxGlobalResultDiff =targetToPredictFunctValueDiff;

sumGlobalResultDiff = sumGlobalResultDiff
+targetToPredictFunctValueDiff;
```

```java
      // Populate chart elements
      xData.add(denormInputFunctValueFromRecord);
      yData1.add(denormTargetFunctValue);
      yData2.add(denormPredictFunctValue1);

    }  // End for FunctValue pair1 loop

  }  // End of the loop over batches

  sumGlobalResultDiff = sumGlobalResultDiff
+targetToPredictFunctValueDiff;
  averGlobalResultDiff = sumGlobalResultDiff/
numberOfTrainBatchesToProcess;

  // Print the max and average results

  System.out.println(" ");
  System.out.println(" ");
  System.out.println("maxGlobalResultDiff = " + maxGlobalResultDiff);
  System.out.println("averGlobalResultDiff = " + averGlobalResultDiff);

  XYSeries series1 = Chart.addSeries("Actual", xData, yData1);
  XYSeries series2 = Chart.addSeries("Forecasted", xData, yData2);

  series1.setMarkerColor(Color.BLACK);
  series2.setMarkerColor(Color.WHITE);
  series1.setLineStyle(SeriesLines.SOLID);
  series2.setLineStyle(SeriesLines.SOLID);

  // Save the chart image
  try
    {
      BitmapEncoder.saveBitmapWithDPI(Chart, strTrainChartFileName,
      BitmapFormat.JPG, 100);
    }
   catch (Exception bt)
    {
      bt.printStackTrace();
    }
```

```java
    System.out.println ("The Chart has been saved");

    returnCodes[0] = 0;
    returnCodes[1] = 0;
    returnCodes[2] = 0;

    return returnCodes;

   } // End of method

//=========================================================
// Load the previously saved trained network1 and tests it by
// processing the Test record
//=========================================================

static public void loadAndTestNetwork()
 {
    System.out.println("Testing the network1s results");

    List<Double> xData = new ArrayList<Double>();
    List<Double> yData1 = new ArrayList<Double>();
    List<Double> yData2 = new ArrayList<Double>();

    double targetToPredictFunctValueDiff = 0;
    double maxGlobalResultDiff = 0.00;
    double averGlobalResultDiff = 0.00;
    double sumGlobalResultDiff = 0.00;
    double maxGlobalIndex = 0;

    double normInputDayFromRecord1 = 0.00;
    double normTargetFunctValue1 = 0.00;
    double normPredictFunctValue1 = 0.00;
    double denormInputDayFromRecord = 0.00;
    double denormTargetFunctValue = 0.00;
    double denormPredictFunctValue = 0.00;
    double normInputDayFromRecord2 = 0.00;
    double normTargetFunctValue2 = 0.00;
    double normPredictFunctValue2 = 0.00;
    double denormInputDayFromRecord2 = 0.00;
```

387

```
double denormTargetFunctValue2 = 0.00;
double denormPredictFunctValue2 = 0.00;
double normInputDayFromTestRecord = 0.00;
double denormInputDayFromTestRecord = 0.00;
double denormTargetFunctValueFromTestRecord = 0.00;

String tempLine;
String[] tempWorkFields;
double dayKeyFromTestRecord = 0.00;
double targetFunctValueFromTestRecord = 0.00;
double r1 = 0.00;
double r2 = 0.00;
BufferedReader br4;

BasicNetwork network1;
BasicNetwork network2;
int k1 = 0;
int k3 = 0;

try
 {
    // Process testing records
    maxGlobalResultDiff = 0.00;
    averGlobalResultDiff = 0.00;
    sumGlobalResultDiff = 0.00;

    for (k1 = 0; k1 < numberOfTestBatchesToProcess; k1++)
     {
        if(k1 == 100)
          k1 = k1;

        // Read the corresponding test micro-batch file.
        br4 = new BufferedReader(new FileReader(strTesting
        FileNames[k1]));
        tempLine = br4.readLine();

        // Skip the label record
        tempLine = br4.readLine();
```

```
// Brake the line using comma as separator
tempWorkFields = tempLine.split(cvsSplitBy);

dayKeyFromTestRecord = Double.parseDouble(tempWorkFields[0]);
targetFunctValueFromTestRecord = Double.parseDouble(tempWork
Fields[1]);

// De-normalize the dayKeyFromTestRecord
denormInputDayFromTestRecord =
  ((inputDayDl - inputDayDh)*dayKeyFromTestRecord -
        Nh*inputDayDl + inputDayDh*Nl)/(Nl - Nh);

  // De-normalize the targetFunctValueFromTestRecord
denormTargetFunctValueFromTestRecord =
((targetFunctValueDiffPercDl -
   targetFunctValueDiffPercDh)*targetFunctValueFromTestRecord -
     Nh*targetFunctValueDiffPercDl +
     targetFunctValueDiffPercDh*Nl)/(Nl - Nh);

// Load the corresponding training micro-batch dataset in memory
MLDataSet trainingSet1 = loadCSV2Memory(strTrainingFileNames[
k1],intInputNeuronNumber,
   intOutputNeuronNumber,true,CSVFormat.ENGLISH,false);

//MLDataSet testingSet =
//   loadCSV2Memory(strTestingFileNames[k1],intInputNeuronNumber,
//      intOutputNeuronNumber,true,CSVFormat.ENGLISH,false);

network1 =
 (BasicNetwork)EncogDirectoryPersistence.
   loadObject(new File(strSaveTrainNetworkFileNames[k1]));

// Get the results after the network1 optimization
int iMax = 0;
int i = - 1; // Index of the array to get results

for (MLDataPair pair1:  trainingSet1)
 {
   i++;
   iMax = i+1;
```

```
MLData inputData1 = pair1.getInput();
MLData actualData1 = pair1.getIdeal();
MLData predictData1 = network1.compute(inputData1);

// These values are Normalized as the whole input is
normInputDayFromRecord1 = inputData1.getData(0);
normTargetFunctValue1 = actualData1.getData(0);
normPredictFunctValue1 = predictData1.getData(0);

denormInputDayFromRecord =
   ((inputDayDl - inputDayDh)*normInputDayFromRecord1 -
      Nh*inputDayDl + inputDayDh*Nl)/(Nl - Nh);

denormTargetFunctValue = ((targetFunctValueDiffPercDl -
   targetFunctValueDiffPercDh)*normTargetFunctValue1 -
      Nh*targetFunctValueDiffPercDl +
      targetFunctValueDiffPercDh*Nl)/(Nl - Nh);

denormPredictFunctValue =((targetFunctValueDiffPercDl -
   targetFunctValueDiffPercDh)*normPredictFunctValue1 -
      Nh*targetFunctValueDiffPercDl +
         targetFunctValueDiffPercDh*Nl)/(Nl - Nh);

targetToPredictFunctValueDiff = (Math.
abs(denormTargetFunctValue -
   denormPredictFunctValue)/denormTargetFunctValue)*100;

System.out.println("Record Number = " + k1 + "
DayNumber = " +
      denormInputDayFromTestRecord +
  "  denormTargetFunctValueFromTestRecord = " +
      denormTargetFunctValueFromTestRecord +
         "  denormPredictFunctValue = " +
         denormPredictFunctValue +
            "  valurDiff = " +
               targetToPredictFunctValueDiff);
```

```java
      if (targetToPredictFunctValueDiff > maxGlobalResultDiff)
       {
         maxGlobalIndex = iMax;
         maxGlobalResultDiff =targetToPredictFunctValueDiff;
       }

      sumGlobalResultDiff = sumGlobalResultDiff +
        targetToPredictFunctValueDiff;

      // Populate chart elements

      xData.add(denormInputDayFromTestRecord);
      yData1.add(denormTargetFunctValueFromTestRecord);
      yData2.add(denormPredictFunctValue);

    }  // End for pair2 loop

  }   // End of loop using k1

// Print the max and average results

System.out.println(" ");

averGlobalResultDiff = sumGlobalResultDiff/
numberOfTestBatchesToProcess;

System.out.println("maxGlobalResultDiff = " + maxGlobalResultDiff +
  "  i = " + maxGlobalIndex);
System.out.println("averGlobalResultDiff = " +
averGlobalResultDiff);
}     // End of TRY
   catch (FileNotFoundException nf)
 {
     nf.printStackTrace();
 }
catch (IOException e1)
 {
     e1.printStackTrace();
 }
```

```
// All testing batch files have been processed
XYSeries series1 = Chart.addSeries("Actual", xData, yData1);
XYSeries series2 = Chart.addSeries("Forecasted", xData, yData2);

series1.setLineColor(XChartSeriesColors.BLACK);
series2.setLineColor(XChartSeriesColors.LIGHT_GREY);

series1.setMarkerColor(Color.BLACK);
series2.setMarkerColor(Color.WHITE);
series1.setLineStyle(SeriesLines.SOLID);
series2.setLineStyle(SeriesLines.SOLID);

// Save the chart image
try
 {
     BitmapEncoder.saveBitmapWithDPI(Chart, strTrainChartFileName,
       BitmapFormat.JPG, 100);
 }
catch (Exception bt)
 {
    bt.printStackTrace();
 }

System.out.println ("The Chart has been saved");
System.out.println("End of testing for mini-batches training");

} // End of the method


} // End of the  Encog class
```

Listing 9-9 shows the ending fragment of the training processing results (using the macro-batch method) after execution.

Listing 9-9. Ending Fragment of the Training Processing Results (Using the Macro-Batch Method)

```
DayNumber = 947  targetFunctionValue = 12.02166  predictFunctionValue =
12.02166 valurDiff = 5.44438E-6
DayNumber = 948  targetFunctionValue = 12.00232  predictFunctionValue =
12.00232 valurDiff = 3.83830E-6
DayNumber = 949  targetFunctionValue = 11.98281  predictFunctionValue =
11.98281 valurDiff = 2.08931E-6
DayNumber = 950  targetFunctionValue = 11.96312  predictFunctionValue =
11.96312 valurDiff = 6.72376E-6
DayNumber = 951  targetFunctionValue = 11.94325  predictFunctionValue =
11.94325 valurDiff = 4.16461E-7
DayNumber = 952  targetFunctionValue = 11.92320  predictFunctionValue =
11.92320 valurDiff = 1.27943E-6
DayNumber = 953  targetFunctionValue = 11.90298  predictFunctionValue =
11.90298 valurDiff = 8.38334E-6
DayNumber = 954  targetFunctionValue = 11.88258  predictFunctionValue =
11.88258 valurDiff = 5.87549E-6
DayNumber = 955  targetFunctionValue = 11.86200  predictFunctionValue =
11.86200 valurDiff = 4.55675E-6
DayNumber = 956  targetFunctionValue = 11.84124  predictFunctionValue =
11.84124 valurDiff = 6.53477E-6
DayNumber = 957  targetFunctionValue = 11.82031  predictFunctionValue =
11.82031 valurDiff = 2.55647E-6
DayNumber = 958  targetFunctionValue = 11.79920  predictFunctionValue =
11.79920 valurDiff = 8.20278E-6
DayNumber = 959  targetFunctionValue = 11.77792  predictFunctionValue =
11.77792 valurDiff = 4.94157E-7
DayNumber = 960  targetFunctionValue = 11.75647  predictFunctionValue =
11.75647 valurDiff = 1.48410E-6
DayNumber = 961  targetFunctionValue = 11.73483  predictFunctionValue =
11.73484 valurDiff = 3.67970E-6
DayNumber = 962  targetFunctionValue = 11.71303  predictFunctionValue =
11.71303 valurDiff = 6.83684E-6
```

```
DayNumber = 963  targetFunctionValue = 11.69105  predictFunctionValue =
11.69105 valurDiff = 4.30269E-6
DayNumber = 964  targetFunctionValue = 11.66890  predictFunctionValue =
11.66890 valurDiff = 1.69128E-6
DayNumber = 965  targetFunctionValue = 11.64658  predictFunctionValue =
11.64658 valurDiff = 7.90340E-6
DayNumber = 966  targetFunctionValue = 11.62409  predictFunctionValue =
11.62409 valurDiff = 8.19566E-6
DayNumber = 967  targetFunctionValue = 11.60142  predictFunctionValue =
11.60143 valurDiff = 4.52810E-6
DayNumber = 968  targetFunctionValue = 11.57859  predictFunctionValue =
11.57859 valurDiff = 6.21339E-6
DayNumber = 969  targetFunctionValue = 11.55559  predictFunctionValue =
11.55559 valurDiff = 7.36500E-6
DayNumber = 970  targetFunctionValue = 11.53241  predictFunctionValue =
11.53241 valurDiff = 3.67611E-6
DayNumber = 971  targetFunctionValue = 11.50907  predictFunctionValue =
11.50907 valurDiff = 2.04084E-6
DayNumber = 972  targetFunctionValue = 11.48556  predictFunctionValue =
11.48556 valurDiff = 3.10021E-6
DayNumber = 973  targetFunctionValue = 11.46188  predictFunctionValue =
11.46188 valurDiff = 1.04282E-6
DayNumber = 974  targetFunctionValue = 11.43804  predictFunctionValue =
11.43804 valurDiff = 6.05919E-7
DayNumber = 975  targetFunctionValue = 11.41403  predictFunctionValue =
11.41403 valurDiff = 7.53612E-6
DayNumber = 976  targetFunctionValue = 11.38986  predictFunctionValue =
11.38986 valurDiff = 5.25148E-6
DayNumber = 977  targetFunctionValue = 11.36552  predictFunctionValue =
11.36551 valurDiff = 6.09695E-6
DayNumber = 978  targetFunctionValue = 11.34101  predictFunctionValue =
11.34101 valurDiff = 6.10243E-6
DayNumber = 979  targetFunctionValue = 11.31634  predictFunctionValue =
11.31634 valurDiff = 1.14757E-6
DayNumber = 980  targetFunctionValue = 11.29151  predictFunctionValue =
11.29151 valurDiff = 6.88624E-6
```

DayNumber = 981 targetFunctionValue = 11.26652 predictFunctionValue =
11.26652 valurDiff = 1.22488E-6
DayNumber = 982 targetFunctionValue = 11.24137 predictFunctionValue =
11.24137 valurDiff = 7.90076E-6
DayNumber = 983 targetFunctionValue = 11.21605 predictFunctionValue =
11.21605 valurDiff = 6.28815E-6
DayNumber = 984 targetFunctionValue = 11.19058 predictFunctionValue =
11.19058 valurDiff = 6.75453E-7
DayNumber = 985 targetFunctionValue = 11.16495 predictFunctionValue =
11.16495 valurDiff = 7.05756E-6
DayNumber = 986 targetFunctionValue = 11.13915 predictFunctionValue =
11.13915 valurDiff = 4.99135E-6
DayNumber = 987 targetFunctionValue = 11.11321 predictFunctionValue =
11.11321 valurDiff = 8.69072E-6
DayNumber = 988 targetFunctionValue = 11.08710 predictFunctionValue =
11.08710 valurDiff = 7.41462E-6
DayNumber = 989 targetFunctionValue = 11.06084 predictFunctionValue =
11.06084 valurDiff = 1.54419E-6
DayNumber = 990 targetFunctionValue = 11.03442 predictFunctionValue =
11.03442 valurDiff = 4.10382E-6
DayNumber = 991 targetFunctionValue = 11.00785 predictFunctionValue =
11.00785 valurDiff = 1.71356E-6
DayNumber = 992 targetFunctionValue = 10.98112 predictFunctionValue =
10.98112 valurDiff = 5.21117E-6
DayNumber = 993 targetFunctionValue = 10.95424 predictFunctionValue =
10.95424 valurDiff = 4.91220E-7
DayNumber = 994 targetFunctionValue = 10.92721 predictFunctionValue =
10.92721 valurDiff = 7.11803E-7
DayNumber = 995 targetFunctionValue = 10.90003 predictFunctionValue =
10.90003 valurDiff = 8.30447E-6
DayNumber = 996 targetFunctionValue = 10.87270 predictFunctionValue =
10.87270 valurDiff = 6.86302E-6
DayNumber = 997 targetFunctionValue = 10.84522 predictFunctionValue =
10.84522 valurDiff = 6.56004E-6
DayNumber = 998 targetFunctionValue = 10.81759 predictFunctionValue =
10.81759 valurDiff = 6.24024E-6

```
DayNumber = 999  targetFunctionValue = 10.78981  predictFunctionValue =
10.78981 valurDiff = 8.63897E-6
DayNumber = 1000  targetFunctionValue = 10.76181 predictFunctionValue =
10.76188 valurDiff = 7.69201E-6

maxErrorPerc = 1.482606020077711E-6
averErrorPerc = 2.965212040155422E-9
```

The training processing results (that used the micro-batch method) are as follows:

- The maximum error is less than 0.00000148 percent.

- The average error is less than 0.00000000269 percent.

Figure 9-9 shows the chart of the training approximation results (the micro-batch method was used). The charts (actual values are shown in black, and predicted values are shown in white) practically overlap.

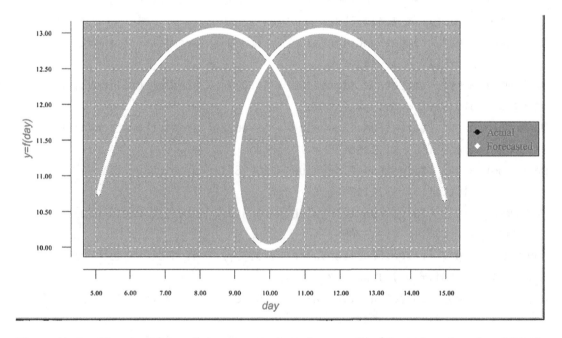

Figure 9-9. *Chart of the training approximation results (the micro-batch method was used)*

Like with the normalized training dataset, the normalized testing dataset is broken into a set of micro-batch files that are now the input to the testing process.

Listing 9-10 shows the ending fragment of the testing results after execution.

Listing 9-10. Ending Fragment of the Testing Results

```
DayNumber = 6.00372 TargettValue = 11.99207  PredictedValue =
12.00232  DiffPerc = 3.84430E-6
DayNumber = 5.98287 TargettValue = 11.97248  PredictedValue =
11.98281  DiffPerc = 2.09221E-6
DayNumber = 5.96212 TargettValue = 11.95270  PredictedValue =
11.96312  DiffPerc = 6.72750E-6
DayNumber = 5.94146 TargettValue = 11.93275  PredictedValue =
11.94325  DiffPerc = 4.20992E-7
DayNumber = 5.92089 TargettValue = 11.91262  PredictedValue =
11.92320  DiffPerc = 1.27514E-6
DayNumber = 5.90042 TargettValue = 11.89231  PredictedValue =
11.90298  DiffPerc = 8.38833E-6
DayNumber = 5.88004 TargettValue = 11.87183  PredictedValue =
11.88258  DiffPerc = 5.88660E-6
DayNumber = 5.85977 TargettValue = 11.85116  PredictedValue =
11.86200  DiffPerc = 4.55256E-6
DayNumber = 5.83959 TargettValue = 11.83033  PredictedValue =
11.84124  DiffPerc = 6.53740E-6
DayNumber = 5.81952 TargettValue = 11.80932  PredictedValue =
11.82031  DiffPerc = 2.55227E-6
DayNumber = 5.79955 TargettValue = 11.78813  PredictedValue =
11.79920  DiffPerc = 8.20570E-6
DayNumber = 5.77968 TargettValue = 11.76676  PredictedValue =
11.77792  DiffPerc = 4.91208E-7
DayNumber = 5.75992 TargettValue = 11.74523  PredictedValue =
11.75647  DiffPerc = 1.48133E-6
DayNumber = 5.74026 TargettValue = 11.72352  PredictedValue =
11.73484  DiffPerc = 3.68852E-6
DayNumber = 5.72071 TargettValue = 11.70163  PredictedValue =
11.71303  DiffPerc = 6.82806E-6
DayNumber = 5.70128 TargettValue = 11.67958  PredictedValue =
11.69105  DiffPerc = 4.31230E-6
```

DayNumber = 5.68195 TargettValue = 11.65735 PredictedValue =
11.66890 DiffPerc = 1.70449E-6
DayNumber = 5.66274 TargettValue = 11.63495 PredictedValue =
11.64658 DiffPerc = 7.91193E-6
DayNumber = 5.64364 TargettValue = 11.61238 PredictedValue =
11.62409 DiffPerc = 8.20057E-6
DayNumber = 5.62465 TargettValue = 11.58964 PredictedValue =
11.60143 DiffPerc = 4.52651E-6
DayNumber = 5.60578 TargettValue = 11.56673 PredictedValue =
11.57859 DiffPerc = 6.20537E-6
DayNumber = 5.58703 TargettValue = 11.54365 PredictedValue =
11.55559 DiffPerc = 7.37190E-6
DayNumber = 5.56840 TargettValue = 11.52040 PredictedValue =
11.53241 DiffPerc = 3.68228E-6
DayNumber = 5.54989 TargettValue = 11.49698 PredictedValue =
11.50907 DiffPerc = 2.05114E-6
DayNumber = 5.53150 TargettValue = 11.47340 PredictedValue =
11.48556 DiffPerc = 3.10919E-6
DayNumber = 5.51323 TargettValue = 11.44965 PredictedValue =
11.46188 DiffPerc = 1.03517E-6
DayNumber = 5.49509 TargettValue = 11.42573 PredictedValue =
11.43804 DiffPerc = 6.10184E-7
DayNumber = 5.47707 TargettValue = 11.40165 PredictedValue =
11.41403 DiffPerc = 7.53367E-6
DayNumber = 5.45918 TargettValue = 11.37740 PredictedValue =
11.38986 DiffPerc = 5.25199E-6
DayNumber = 5.44142 TargettValue = 11.35299 PredictedValue =
11.36551 DiffPerc = 6.09026E-6
DayNumber = 5.42379 TargettValue = 11.32841 PredictedValue =
11.34101 DiffPerc = 6.09049E-6
DayNumber = 5.40629 TargettValue = 11.30368 PredictedValue =
11.31634 DiffPerc = 1.13713E-6
DayNumber = 5.38893 TargettValue = 11.27878 PredictedValue =
11.29151 DiffPerc = 6.88165E-6
DayNumber = 5.37169 TargettValue = 11.25371 PredictedValue =
11.26652 DiffPerc = 1.22300E-6

DayNumber = 5.35460 TargettValue = 11.22849 PredictedValue =
11.24137 DiffPerc = 7.89661E-6
DayNumber = 5.33763 TargettValue = 11.20311 PredictedValue =
11.21605 DiffPerc = 6.30025E-6
DayNumber = 5.32081 TargettValue = 11.17756 PredictedValue =
11.19058 DiffPerc = 6.76200E-7
DayNumber = 5.30412 TargettValue = 11.15186 PredictedValue =
11.16495 DiffPerc = 7.04606E-6
DayNumber = 5.28758 TargettValue = 11.12601 PredictedValue =
11.13915 DiffPerc = 4.98925E-6
DayNumber = 5.27118 TargettValue = 11.09999 PredictedValue =
11.11321 DiffPerc = 8.69060E-6
DayNumber = 5.25492 TargettValue = 11.07382 PredictedValue =
11.08710 DiffPerc = 7.41171E-6
DayNumber = 5.23880 TargettValue = 11.04749 PredictedValue =
11.06084 DiffPerc = 1.54138E-6
DayNumber = 5.22283 TargettValue = 11.02101 PredictedValue =
11.03442 DiffPerc = 4.09728E-6
DayNumber = 5.20701 TargettValue = 10.99437 PredictedValue =
11.00785 DiffPerc = 1.71899E-6
DayNumber = 5.19133 TargettValue = 10.96758 PredictedValue =
10.98112 DiffPerc = 5.21087E-6
DayNumber = 5.17581 TargettValue = 10.94064 PredictedValue =
10.95424 DiffPerc = 4.97273E-7
DayNumber = 5.16043 TargettValue = 10.91355 PredictedValue =
10.92721 DiffPerc = 7.21563E-7
DayNumber = 5.14521 TargettValue = 10.88630 PredictedValue =
10.90003 DiffPerc = 8.29551E-6
DayNumber = 5.13013 TargettValue = 10.85891 PredictedValue =
10.87270 DiffPerc = 6.86988E-6
DayNumber = 5.11522 TargettValue = 10.83136 PredictedValue =
10.84522 DiffPerc = 6.55538E-6
DayNumber = 5.10046 TargettValue = 10.80367 PredictedValue =
10.81759 DiffPerc = 6.24113E-6
DayNumber = 5.08585 TargettValue = 10.77584 PredictedValue =
10.78981 DiffPerc = 8.64007E-6

```
maxErrorPerc = 9.002677165459051E-6
averErrorPerc = 4.567068981414947E-6
```

The testing processing results (the micro-batch method was used) are as follows:

- The maximum error is less than 0.00000900 percent.

- The average error is less than 0.00000457 percent.

Figure 9-10 shows the chart of the testing results (the micro-batch method was used). Again, both charts (actual values are shown in black, and predicted values are shown in white) practically overlap.

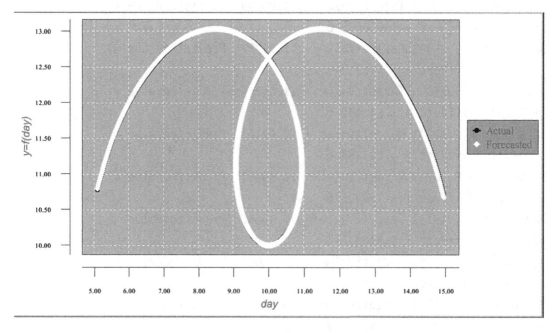

Figure 9-10. *Chart of the testing results (the micro-batch method was used)*

Summary

Neural networks have a problem approximating continuous functions with complex topology. It is difficult to obtain a good-quality approximation for such functions. This chapter showed that the micro-batch method is able to approximate such functions with high-precision results. In the next chapter, we will show how to use neural networks for the classification of objects.

CHAPTER 10

Using Neural Networks for the Classification of Objects

In this chapter, we use neural networks for the classification of objects. *Classification* is the task of recognizing various objects and determining the class that those objects belong to. As with many areas of artificial intelligence, classification is easily done by humans, while being quite difficult for computers.

Example: Classification of Records

Listing 10-1 shows five books, and each book belongs to a different area of human knowledge: medical, programming, engineering, electrical, and music. We are also given the three most frequently used words in each of the five books.

We have many records to be classified by the program we will develop here. Each record includes three words. If all three words in a record belong to a certain book, then the program should determine that the record belongs to that book. If a record has a mixture of words that don't belong to any of the five books, then the program should classify the record as belonging to an unknown book.

This example looks quite simple; the problem seems like it does not need a neural network and could be solved by using regular programming logic. But when the volume of books and records becomes very large, when there is a large number of unpredictable combinations of words included in each record, and when only a certain small number of words from one book is sufficient for a record to belong to a certain book, then only artificial intelligence can handle such a task.

© Igor Livshin 2022
I. Livshin, *Artificial Neural Networks with Java*, https://doi.org/10.1007/978-1-4842-7368-5_10

Listing 10-1. List of Five Books with Three Most Frequent Words

Book 1. Medical.
 surgery, blood, prescription,

Book 2. Programming.
file, java, debugging

Book3. Engineering.
combustion, screw, machine

Book 4. Electrical.
volt, solenoid, diode

Book 5. Music.
adagio, hymn, opera,

Extra words. We will use the following words in this list to include them
in the test dataset:
customer, wind, grass, paper, calculator, flower, printer, desk, photo,
map, pen, floor.

To simplify the processing, we assign numbers to all the words and use those
numbers instead of words when building the training and testing datasets. Table 10-1
shows the words–numbers cross-reference.

Table 10-1. *Words–Numbers Cross-Reference*

Word	Assigned Number
Surgery	1
Blood	2
Prescription	3
File	4
Java	5
Debugging	6
Combustion	7

(*continued*)

Table 10-1. (*continued*)

Word	Assigned Number
screw	8
machine	9
Volt	10
solenoid,	11
diode	12
adagio	13
hymn	14
opera	15
customer	16
wind	17
grass	18
paper	19
calculator	20
flower	21
printer	22
desk	23
photo	24
map	25
pen	26
floor	27

Training Dataset

Each record in the training dataset consists of three fields that hold words from the list of the most frequently used words in our books; also included in the record are five target fields. The five target fields indicate the book the record belongs to. This information is used for training the network. For example, the combination 1, 0, 0, 0, 0 means book #1, the combination 0, 1, 0, 0, 0 means book #2, and so on. Also, for each book, we need to build six records in the training dataset instead of one. They include all the possible permutations of words in a record. We use italics to highlight the portion of the records that holds the word–numbers. Table 10-2 shows all possible permutations of words in all records.

Table 10-2. *Permutations of Words in All Records*

Records for Book 1

1	*2*	*3*	1	0	0	0	0
1	*3*	*2*	1	0	0	0	0
2	*1*	*3*	1	0	0	0	0
2	*3*	*1*	1	0	0	0	0
3	*1*	*2*	1	0	0	0	0
3	*2*	*1*	1	0	0	0	0

Records for Book 2

4	*5*	*6*	0	1	0	0	0
4	*6*	*5*	0	1	0	0	0
5	*4*	*6*	0	1	0	0	0
5	*6*	*4*	0	1	0	0	0
6	*4*	*5*	0	1	0	0	0
6	*5*	*4*	0	1	0	0	0

Records for Book 3

7	*8*	*9*	0	0	1	0	0
7	*9*	*8*	0	0	1	0	0
8	*7*	*9*	0	0	1	0	0
8	*9*	*7*	0	0	1	0	0
9	*7*	*8*	0	0	1	0	0
9	*8*	*7*	0	0	1	0	0

(*continued*)

Table 10-2. *(continued)*

Records for Book 4

10	*11*	*12*	0	0	0	1	0
10	*12*	*11*	0	0	0	1	0
11	*10*	*12*	0	0	0	1	0
11	*12*	*10*	0	0	0	1	0
12	*10*	*11*	0	0	0	1	0
12	*11*	*10*	0	0	0	1	0

Records for Book 5

13	*14*	*15*	0	0	0	0	1
13	*15*	*14*	0	0	0	0	1
14	*13*	*15*	0	0	0	0	1
14	*15*	*13*	0	0	0	0	1
15	*13*	*14*	0	0	0	0	1
15	*14*	*13*	0	0	0	0	1

Putting it all together, Table 10-3 shows the training dataset.

Table 10-3. *Training Dataset*

Word1	Word2	Word3	Target1	Target2	Target3	Target4	Target5
1	2	3	1	0	0	0	0
1	3	2	1	0	0	0	0
2	1	3	1	0	0	0	0
2	3	1	1	0	0	0	0
3	1	2	1	0	0	0	0
3	2	1	1	0	0	0	0

(continued)

Table 10-3. (*continued*)

Word1	Word2	Word3	Target1	Target2	Target3	Target4	Target5
4	5	6	0	1	0	0	0
4	6	5	0	1	0	0	0
5	4	6	0	1	0	0	0
5	6	4	0	1	0	0	0
6	4	5	0	1	0	0	0
6	5	4	0	1	0	0	0
7	8	9	0	0	1	0	0
7	9	8	0	0	1	0	0
8	7	9	0	0	1	0	0
8	9	7	0	0	1	0	0
9	7	8	0	0	1	0	0
9	8	7	0	0	1	0	0
10	11	12	0	0	0	1	0
10	12	11	0	0	0	1	0
11	10	12	0	0	0	1	0
11	12	10	0	0	0	1	0
12	10	11	0	0	0	1	0
12	11	10	0	0	0	1	0
13	14	15	0	0	0	0	1
13	15	14	0	0	0	0	1
14	13	15	0	0	0	0	1
14	15	13	0	0	0	0	1
15	13	14	0	0	0	0	1
15	14	13	0	0	0	0	1

Network Architecture

The network has an input layer with three input neurons, six hidden layers with seven neurons each, and an output layer with five neurons, as shown in Figure 10-1.

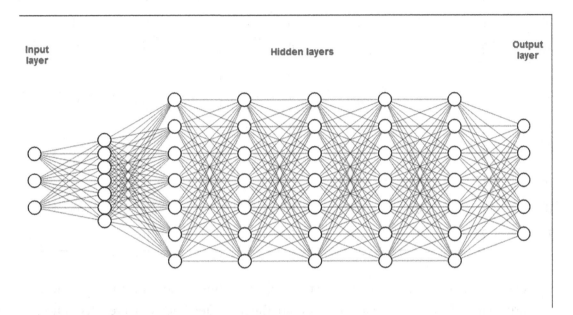

Figure 10-1. *Network architecture*

Testing Dataset

The testing dataset consists of records with randomly included words/numbers. These records don't belong to any single book, regardless that some of them include one or two words from the most frequently used list. Table 10-4 shows the testing dataset.

Table 10-4. *Testing Dataset*

Word1	Word2	Word3	Target 1	Target 2	Target 3	Target 4	Target 5
1	2	16	0	0	0	0	0
4	17	5	0	0	0	0	0
8	9	18	0	0	0	0	0
19	10	11	0	0	0	0	0
15	20	13	0	0	0	0	0

(*continued*)

Table 10-4. (*continued*)

Word1	Word2	Word3	Target 1	Target 2	Target 3	Target 4	Target 5
27	1	26	0	0	0	0	0
14	23	22	0	0	0	0	0
21	20	18	0	0	0	0	0
25	23	24	0	0	0	0	0
11	9	6	0	0	0	0	0
3	5	8	0	0	0	0	0
6	10	15	0	0	0	0	0
16	17	18	0	0	0	0	0
19	1	8	0	0	0	0	0
27	23	17	0	0	0	0	0

Actually, there is no need to include the target columns in the testing file; however, they are included for convenience (to compare the predicted and actual results). Those columns are not used for processing. As usual, we need to normalize the training and testing datasets on the interval [-1, 1]. Because this example features multiple neurons in the input and output layers, we will show here the normalization source code.

Program Code for Data Normalization

Listing 10-2 shows the program code for the normalization of the training and testing datasets.

Listing 10-2. Program Code for Data Normalization

```
// ================================================================
// This program normalizes all columns of the input CSV dataset putting the
// result in the output CSV file.
// ================================================================
```

```java
package sample5_norm;

import java.io.BufferedReader;
import java.io.BufferedWriter;
import java.io.PrintWriter;
import java.io.FileNotFoundException;
import java.io.FileReader;
import java.io.FileWriter;
import java.io.IOException;
import java.nio.file.*;

public class Sample5_Norm
{
   // Interval to normalize
   static double Nh =  1;
   static double Nl = -1;

   // First column
   static double minXPointDl = 1.00;
   static double maxXPointDh = 1000.00;

   // Second column - target data
   static double minTargetValueDl = 60.00;
   static double maxTargetValueDh = 1600.00;

   public static double normalize(double value, double Dh, double Dl)
    {
      double normalizedValue = (value - Dl)*(Nh - Nl)/(Dh - Dl) + Nl;

      return normalizedValue;
    }

   public static void main(String[] args)
    {
       // Normalize train file
       String inputFileName = "C:/Book_Examples/Sample5_Train_Real.csv";
       String outputNormFileName = "C:/Book_Examples/Sample5_Train_Norm.csv";

       // Normalize test file
```

```java
//String inputFileName = "C:/Book_Examples/Sample5_Test_Real.csv";
//String outputNormFileName = "C:/Book_Examples/Sample5_Test_Norm.csv";

BufferedReader br = null;
PrintWriter out = null;

String line = "";
String cvsSplitBy = ",";

double inputXPointValue;
double targetXPointValue;

double normInputXPointValue;
double normTargetXPointValue;

String strNormInputXPointValue;
String strNormTargetXPointValue;

String fullLine;

int i = -1;

try
 {
  Files.deleteIfExists(Paths.get(outputNormFileName));

  br = new BufferedReader(new FileReader(inputFileName));
  out = new
   PrintWriter(new BufferedWriter(new FileWriter(outputNormFileName)));

  while ((line = br.readLine()) != null)
   {
      i++;

      if(i == 0)
       {
         // Write the label line
         out.println(line);
       }
      else
       {
```

```java
      // Brake the line using comma as separator
      String[] workFields = line.split(cvsSplitBy);

      inputXPointValue = Double.parseDouble(workFields[0]);
      targetXPointValue = Double.parseDouble( workFields[1]);

      // Normalize these fields
      normInputXPointValue =
         normalize(inputXPointValue, maxXPointDh, minXPointDl);
      normTargetXPointValue =
      normalize(targetXPointValue, maxTargetValueDh, minTargetValueDl);

      // Convert normalized fields to string, so they can be inserted
      //into the output CSV file
      strNormInputXPointValue = Double.toString(normInputXPointValue);
      strNormTargetXPointValue = Double.toString(normTargetXPointValue);

      // Concatenate these fields into a string line with
      //coma separator
      fullLine  =
         strNormInputXPointValue + "," + strNormTargetXPointValue;

      // Put fullLine into the output file
      out.println(fullLine);

   } // End of IF Else

  }     // end of while

 } // end of TRY
catch (FileNotFoundException e)
 {
    e.printStackTrace();
    System.exit(1);
 }
catch (IOException io)
 {
    io.printStackTrace();
 }
```

```
        finally
         {
            if (br != null)
              {
                  try
                   {
                      br.close();
                      out.close();
                   }
                  catch (IOException e)
                   {
                      e.printStackTrace();
                   }
              }
         }

}
```

Table 10-5 shows the normalized training dataset.

Table 10-5. *Normalized Training Dataset*

Word 1	Word 2	Word 3	Target 1	Target 2	Target 3	Target 4	Target 5
-1	-0.966101695	-0.93220339	1	-1	-1	-1	-1
-1	-0.93220339	-0.966101695	1	-1	-1	-1	-1
-0.966101695	-1	-0.93220339	1	-1	-1	-1	-1
-0.966101695	-0.93220339	-1	1	-1	-1	-1	-1
-0.93220339	-1	-0.966101695	1	-1	-1	-1	-1
-0.93220339	-0.966101695	-1	1	-1	-1	-1	-1
-0.898305085	-0.86440678	-0.830508475	-1	1	-1	-1	-1

(*continued*)

Table 10-5. (*continued*)

Word 1	Word 2	Word 3	Target 1	Target 2	Target 3	Target 4	Target 5
-0.898305085	-0.830508475	-0.86440678	-1	1	-1	-1	-1
-0.86440678	-0.898305085	-0.830508475	-1	1	-1	-1	-1
-0.86440678	-0.830508475	-0.898305085	-1	1	-1	-1	-1
-0.830508475	-0.898305085	-0.86440678	-1	1	-1	-1	-1
-0.830508475	-0.86440678	-0.898305085	-1	1	-1	-1	-1
-0.796610169	-0.762711864	-0.728813559	-1	-1	1	-1	-1
-0.796610169	-0.728813559	-0.762711864	-1	-1	1	-1	-1
-0.762711864	-0.796610169	-0.728813559	-1	-1	1	-1	-1
-0.762711864	-0.728813559	-0.796610169	-1	-1	1	-1	-1
-0.728813559	-0.796610169	-0.762711864	-1	-1	1	-1	-1
-0.728813559	-0.762711864	-0.796610169	-1	-1	1	-1	-1
-0.694915254	-0.661016949	-0.627118644	-1	-1	-1	1	-1
-0.694915254	-0.627118644	-0.661016949	-1	-1	-1	1	-1
-0.661016949	-0.694915254	-0.627118644	-1	-1	-1	1	-1
-0.661016949	-0.627118644	-0.694915254	-1	-1	-1	1	-1
-0.627118644	-0.694915254	-0.661016949	-1	-1	-1	1	-1
-0.627118644	-0.661016949	-0.694915254	-1	-1	-1	1	-1
-0.593220339	-0.559322034	-0.525423729	-1	-1	-1	-1	1
-0.593220339	-0.525423729	-0.559322034	-1	-1	-1	-1	1
-0.559322034	-0.593220339	-0.525423729	-1	-1	-1	-1	1
-0.559322034	-0.525423729	-0.593220339	-1	-1	-1	-1	1
-0.525423729	-0.593220339	-0.559322034	-1	-1	-1	-1	1
-0.525423729	-0.559322034	-0.593220339	-1	-1	-1	-1	1

Table 10-6 shows the normalized testing dataset.

Table 10-6. *Normalized Testing Dataset*

Word1	Word2	Word3	Target 1	Target 2	Target 3	Target 4	Target 5
-1	-0.966101695	-0.491525424	-1	-1	-1	-1	-1
-0.898305085	-0.457627119	-0.86440678	-1	-1	-1	-1	-1
-0.762711864	-0.728813559	-0.423728814	-1	-1	-1	-1	-1
-0.389830508	-0.694915254	-0.661016949	-1	-1	-1	-1	-1
-0.525423729	-0.355932203	-0.593220339	-1	-1	-1	-1	-1
-0.118644068	-1	0.152542373	-1	-1	-1	-1	-1
-0.559322034	-0.254237288	-0.288135593	-1	-1	-1	-1	-1
-0.322033898	-0.355932203	-0.423728814	-1	-1	-1	-1	-1
-0.186440678	-0.254237288	-0.220338983	-1	-1	-1	-1	-1
-0.661016949	-0.728813559	-0.830508475	-1	-1	-1	-1	-1
-0.93220339	-0.86440678	-0.762711864	-1	-1	-1	-1	-1
-0.830508475	-0.69491525	-0.525423729	-1	-1	-1	-1	-1
-0.491525424	-0.45762711	-0.423728814	-1	-1	-1	-1	-1
-0.389830508	-1	-0.762711864	-1	-1	-1	-1	-1
-0.118644068	-0.25423728	-0.457627119	-1	-1	-1	-1	-1

Program Code for Classification

Listing 10-3 shows the classification program code.

Listing 10-3. Classification Program Code

```
// =========================================================================
// Example of using neural network for classification of objects.
// The normalized training/testing files consists of records of the following
// format: 3 input fields (word numbers) and 5 target fields (indicate the book
// the record belongs to).
```

```java
// ===========================================================================

package sample6;

import java.io.BufferedReader;
import java.io.File;
import java.io.FileInputStream;
import java.io.PrintWriter;
import java.io.FileNotFoundException;
import java.io.FileReader;
import java.io.FileWriter;
import java.io.IOException;
import java.io.InputStream;
import java.nio.file.*;
import java.util.Properties;
import java.time.YearMonth;
import java.awt.Color;
import java.awt.Font;
import java.io.BufferedReader;
import java.text.DateFormat;
import java.text.ParseException;
import java.text.SimpleDateFormat;
import java.time.LocalDate;
import java.time.Month;
import java.time.ZoneId;
import java.util.ArrayList;
import java.util.Calendar;
import java.util.Date;
import java.util.List;
import java.util.Locale;
import java.util.Properties;

import org.encog.Encog;
import org.encog.engine.network.activation.ActivationTANH;
import org.encog.engine.network.activation.ActivationReLU;
import org.encog.ml.data.MLData;
import org.encog.ml.data.MLDataPair;
```

```java
import org.encog.ml.data.MLDataSet;
import org.encog.ml.data.buffer.MemoryDataLoader;
import org.encog.ml.data.buffer.codec.CSVDataCODEC;
import org.encog.ml.data.buffer.codec.DataSetCODEC;
import org.encog.neural.networks.BasicNetwork;
import org.encog.neural.networks.layers.BasicLayer;
import org.encog.neural.networks.training.propagation.resilient.
ResilientPropagation;
import org.encog.persist.EncogDirectoryPersistence;
import org.encog.util.csv.CSVFormat;

import org.knowm.xchart.SwingWrapper;
import org.knowm.xchart.XYChart;
import org.knowm.xchart.XYChartBuilder;
import org.knowm.xchart.XYSeries;
import org.knowm.xchart.demo.charts.ExampleChart;
import org.knowm.xchart.style.Styler.LegendPosition;
import org.knowm.xchart.style.colors.ChartColor;
import org.knowm.xchart.style.colors.XChartSeriesColors;
import org.knowm.xchart.style.lines.SeriesLines;
import org.knowm.xchart.style.markers.SeriesMarkers;
import org.knowm.xchart.BitmapEncoder;
import org.knowm.xchart.BitmapEncoder.BitmapFormat;
import org.knowm.xchart.QuickChart;
import org.knowm.xchart.SwingWrapper;

public class Sample6 implements ExampleChart<XYChart>
{
    // Interval to normalize data
    static double Nh;
    static double Nl;

    // Normalization parameters for workBook number
    static double minWordNumberDl;
    static double maxWordNumberDh;

    // Normalization parameters for target values
```

```
static double minTargetValueDl;
static double maxTargetValueDh;

static double doublePointNumber = 0.00;
static int intPointNumber = 0;
static InputStream input = null;
static double[] arrPrices = new double[2500];
static double normInputWordNumber_01 = 0.00;
static double normInputWordNumber_02 = 0.00;
static double normInputWordNumber_03 = 0.00;
static double denormInputWordNumber_01 = 0.00;
static double denormInputWordNumber_02 = 0.00;
static double denormInputWordNumber_03 = 0.00;
static double normTargetBookNumber_01 = 0.00;
static double normTargetBookNumber_02 = 0.00;
static double normTargetBookNumber_03 = 0.00;
static double normTargetBookNumber_04 = 0.00;
static double normTargetBookNumber_05 = 0.00;
static double normPredictBookNumber_01 = 0.00;
static double normPredictBookNumber_02 = 0.00;
static double normPredictBookNumber_03 = 0.00;
static double normPredictBookNumber_04 = 0.00;
static double normPredictBookNumber_05 = 0.00;
static double denormTargetBookNumber_01 = 0.00;
static double denormTargetBookNumber_02 = 0.00;
static double denormTargetBookNumber_03 = 0.00;
static double denormTargetBookNumber_04 = 0.00;
static double denormTargetBookNumber_05 = 0.00;
static double denormPredictBookNumber_01 = 0.00;
static double denormPredictBookNumber_02 = 0.00;
static double denormPredictBookNumber_03 = 0.00;
static double denormPredictBookNumber_04 = 0.00;
static double denormPredictBookNumber_05 = 0.00;
static double normDifferencePerc = 0.00;
static double denormPredictXPointValue_01 = 0.00;
static double denormPredictXPointValue_02 = 0.00;
```

```java
static double denormPredictXPointValue_03 = 0.00;
static double denormPredictXPointValue_04 = 0.00;
static double denormPredictXPointValue_05 = 0.00;
static double valueDifference = 0.00;
static int numberOfInputNeurons;
static int numberOfOutputNeurons;
static int intNumberOfRecordsInTestFile;
static String trainFileName;
static String priceFileName;
static String testFileName;
static String chartTrainFileName;
static String chartTestFileName;
static String networkFileName;
static int workingMode;
static String cvsSplitBy = ",";
static int returnCode;

static List<Double> xData = new ArrayList<Double>();
static List<Double> yData1 = new ArrayList<Double>();
static List<Double> yData2 = new ArrayList<Double>();

static XYChart Chart;

@Override
public XYChart getChart()
 {

  // Create Chart
  Chart = new  XYChartBuilder().width(900).height(500).title(getClass().
          getSimpleName()).xAxisTitle("x").yAxisTitle("y= f(x)").build();

  // Customize Chart
  Chart.getStyler().setPlotBackgroundColor(ChartColor.
  getAWTColor(ChartColor.GREY));
  Chart.getStyler().setPlotGridLinesColor(new Color(255, 255, 255));
  Chart.getStyler().setChartBackgroundColor(Color.WHITE);
  Chart.getStyler().setLegendBackgroundColor(Color.PINK);
  Chart.getStyler().setChartFontColor(Color.MAGENTA);
```

```
Chart.getStyler().setChartTitleBoxBackgroundColor(new Color(0, 222, 0));
Chart.getStyler().setChartTitleBoxVisible(true);
Chart.getStyler().setChartTitleBoxBorderColor(Color.BLACK);
Chart.getStyler().setPlotGridLinesVisible(true);
Chart.getStyler().setAxisTickPadding(20);
Chart.getStyler().setAxisTickMarkLength(15);
Chart.getStyler().setPlotMargin(20);
Chart.getStyler().setChartTitleVisible(false);
Chart.getStyler().setChartTitleFont(new Font(Font.MONOSPACED, Font.
BOLD, 24));
Chart.getStyler().setLegendFont(new Font(Font.SERIF, Font.PLAIN, 18));
Chart.getStyler().setLegendPosition(LegendPosition.InsideSE);
Chart.getStyler().setLegendSeriesLineLength(12);
Chart.getStyler().setAxisTitleFont(new Font(Font.SANS_SERIF, Font.ITALIC, 18));
Chart.getStyler().setAxisTickLabelsFont(new Font(Font.SERIF, Font.PLAIN, 11));
Chart.getStyler().setDatePattern("yyyy-MM");
Chart.getStyler().setDecimalPattern("#0.00");

// Interval to normalize data
Nh = 1;
Nl = -1;

// Normalization parameters for workBook number
double minWordNumberDl = 1.00;
double maxWordNumberDh = 60.00;

// Normalization parameters for target values
minTargetValueDl = 0.00;
maxTargetValueDh = 1.00;

// Configuration (comment and uncomment the appropriate configuration)

// For training the network
workingMode = 1;
intNumberOfRecordsInTestFile = 31;
trainFileName = "C:/My_Neural_Network_Book/Book_Examples/Sample6_Norm_
Train_File.csv";

// For testing the trained network at non-trained points
```

```java
//workingMode = 2;
//intNumberOfRecordsInTestFile = 16;
//testFileName = "C:/My_Neural_Network_Book/Book_Examples/Sample6_Norm_
Test_File.csv";

networkFileName =
  "C:/My_Neural_Network_Book/Book_Examples/Sample6_Saved_Network_File.csv";
numberOfInputNeurons = 3;
numberOfOutputNeurons = 5;

// Check the working mode to run
if(workingMode == 1)
 {
  // Training mode
  File file1 = new File(chartTrainFileName);
  File file2 = new File(networkFileName);

  if(file1.exists())
    file1.delete();

  if(file2.exists())
    file2.delete();

  returnCode = 0;    // Clear the return code variable

  do
   {
     returnCode = trainValidateSaveNetwork();
   } while (returnCode > 0);
 }   // End the training mode
else
 {
   // Test mode
   loadAndTestNetwork();
 }

 Encog.getInstance().shutdown();
```

```java
    return Chart;

}  // End of the method

// ==========================================================
// Load CSV to memory.
// @return The loaded dataset.
// ==========================================================
public static MLDataSet loadCSV2Memory(String filename, int input, int ideal,
   boolean headers, CSVFormat format, boolean significance)
   {
      DataSetCODEC codec = new CSVDataCODEC(new File(filename), format,
        headers, input, ideal, significance);
      MemoryDataLoader load = new MemoryDataLoader(codec);
      MLDataSet dataset = load.external2Memory();
      return dataset;
   }

// ==========================================================
//  The main method.
//  @param Command line arguments. No arguments are used.
// ==========================================================
public static void main(String[] args)
 {
    ExampleChart<XYChart> exampleChart = new Sample6();
    XYChart Chart = exampleChart.getChart();
    new SwingWrapper<XYChart>(Chart).displayChart();
 } // End of the main method

//=================================================================
// This method trains, validates, and saves the trained network file on disk
//=================================================================
static public int trainValidateSaveNetwork()
 {
    // Load the training CSV file in memory
    MLDataSet trainingSet =
```

```
    loadCSV2Memory(trainFileName,numberOfInputNeurons,
    numberOfOutputNeurons,
      true,CSVFormat.ENGLISH,false);

// create a neural network
BasicNetwork network = new BasicNetwork();

// Input layer
network.addLayer(new BasicLayer(null,true,3));

// Hidden layer
network.addLayer(new BasicLayer(new ActivationTANH(),true,7));
network.addLayer(new BasicLayer(new ActivationTANH(),true,7));
network.addLayer(new BasicLayer(new ActivationTANH(),true,7));
network.addLayer(new BasicLayer(new ActivationTANH(),true,7));
network.addLayer(new BasicLayer(new ActivationTANH(),true,7));
network.addLayer(new BasicLayer(new ActivationTANH(),true,7));

// Output layer
network.addLayer(new BasicLayer(new ActivationTANH(),false,5));

network.getStructure().finalizeStructure();
network.reset();

// train the neural network
final ResilientPropagation train = new ResilientPropagation(network,
trainingSet);

int epoch = 1;

do
 {
    train.iteration();
    System.out.println("Epoch #" + epoch + " Error:" + train.getError());

    epoch++;

    if (epoch >= 1000 && network.calculateError(trainingSet) >
    0.0000000000000012)
        {
```

```
          returnCode = 1;

          System.out.println("Try again");
          return returnCode;
        }

    //} while(train.getError() > 0.02);
  } while (network.calculateError(trainingSet) > 0.0000000000000011);

// Save the network file
EncogDirectoryPersistence.saveObject(new File(networkFileName),network);

System.out.println("Neural Network Results:");

int m = 0;

for(MLDataPair pair: trainingSet)
  {
        m++;

        final MLData output = network.compute(pair.getInput());

        MLData inputData = pair.getInput();
        MLData actualData = pair.getIdeal();
        MLData predictData = network.compute(inputData);

        // Calculate and print the results

        normInputWordNumber_01 = inputData.getData(0);
        normInputWordNumber_02 = inputData.getData(1);
        normInputWordNumber_03 = inputData.getData(2);

        normTargetBookNumber_01 = actualData.getData(0);
        normTargetBookNumber_02 = actualData.getData(1);
        normTargetBookNumber_03 = actualData.getData(2);
        normTargetBookNumber_04 = actualData.getData(3);
        normTargetBookNumber_05 = actualData.getData(4);

        normPredictBookNumber_01 = predictData.getData(0);
        normPredictBookNumber_02 = predictData.getData(1);
        normPredictBookNumber_03 = predictData.getData(2);
```

```
normPredictBookNumber_04 = predictData.getData(3);
normPredictBookNumber_05 = predictData.getData(4);

// De-normalize the results
denormInputWordNumber_01 = ((minWordNumberDl -
  maxWordNumberDh)*normInputWordNumber_01 - Nh*minWordNumberDl +
    maxWordNumberDh *Nl)/(Nl - Nh);

denormInputWordNumber_02 = ((minWordNumberDl -
  maxWordNumberDh)*normInputWordNumber_02 - Nh*minWordNumberDl +
    maxWordNumberDh *Nl)/(Nl - Nh);

denormInputWordNumber_03 = ((minWordNumberDl -
  maxWordNumberDh)*normInputWordNumber_03 - Nh*minWordNumberDl +
    maxWordNumberDh *Nl)/(Nl - Nh);

denormTargetBookNumber_01 = ((minTargetValueDl -
maxTargetValueDh)*
  normTargetBookNumber_01 - Nh*minTargetValueDl +
    maxTargetValueDh*Nl)/(Nl - Nh);

denormTargetBookNumber_02 = ((minTargetValueDl -
maxTargetValueDh)*
  normTargetBookNumber_02 - Nh*minTargetValueDl +
    maxTargetValueDh*Nl)/(Nl - Nh);

denormTargetBookNumber_03 = ((minTargetValueDl -
maxTargetValueDh)*
  normTargetBookNumber_03 - Nh*minTargetValueDl +
    maxTargetValueDh*Nl)/(Nl - Nh);

denormTargetBookNumber_04 = ((minTargetValueDl - maxTargetValueDh)*
  normTargetBookNumber_04 - Nh*minTargetValueDl +
    maxTargetValueDh*Nl)/(Nl - Nh);

denormTargetBookNumber_05 = ((minTargetValueDl - maxTargetValueDh)*
  normTargetBookNumber_05 - Nh*minTargetValueDl +
    maxTargetValueDh*Nl)/(Nl - Nh);

denormPredictBookNumber_01 =((minTargetValueDl - maxTargetValueDh)*
```

```
         normPredictBookNumber_01 - Nh*minTargetValueDl +
           maxTargetValueDh*Nl)/(Nl - Nh);

    denormPredictBookNumber_02 =((minTargetValueDl - maxTargetValueDh)*
         normPredictBookNumber_02- Nh*minTargetValueDl +
           maxTargetValueDh*Nl)/(Nl - Nh);

    denormPredictBookNumber_03 =((minTargetValueDl - maxTargetValueDh)*
         normPredictBookNumber_03 - Nh*minTargetValueDl +
           maxTargetValueDh*Nl)/(Nl - Nh);

     denormPredictBookNumber_04 =((minTargetValueDl -
    maxTargetValueDh)*
         normPredictBookNumber_04 - Nh*minTargetValueDl +
           maxTargetValueDh*Nl)/(Nl - Nh);

    denormPredictBookNumber_05 =((minTargetValueDl - maxTargetValueDh)*
         normPredictBookNumber_05 - Nh*minTargetValueDl +
           maxTargetValueDh*Nl)/(Nl - Nh);

     System.out.println ("RecordNumber = " + m);

     System.out.println ("denormTargetBookNumber_01 = " +
     denormTargetBookNumber_01 +
          "   denormPredictBookNumber_01 = " +
           denormPredictBookNumber_01);

     System.out.println ("denormTargetBookNumber_02 = " +
     denormTargetBookNumber_02 +
          "   denormPredictBookNumber_02 = " +
           denormPredictBookNumber_02);

     System.out.println ("denormTargetBookNumber_03 = " +
     denormTargetBookNumber_03 +
          "   denormPredictBookNumber_03 = " +
           denormPredictBookNumber_03);

     System.out.println ("denormTargetBookNumber_04 = " +
     denormTargetBookNumber_04 +
```

```
                   "   denormPredictBookNumber_04 = " +
                   denormPredictBookNumber_04);

            System.out.println ("denormTargetBookNumber_05 = " +
            denormTargetBookNumber_05 +
                   "   denormPredictBookNumber_05 = " +
                   denormPredictBookNumber_05);

        //System.out.println (" ");

        // Print the classification results
        if(Math.abs(denormPredictBookNumber_01) > 0.85)
          if(Math.abs(denormPredictBookNumber_01) > 0.85  &
             Math.abs(denormPredictBookNumber_02) < 0.2   &
             Math.abs(denormPredictBookNumber_03) < 0.2   &
             Math.abs(denormPredictBookNumber_04) < 0.2   &
             Math.abs(denormPredictBookNumber_05) < 0.2)
              {
                System.out.println ("Record 1 belongs to book 1");
                System.out.println (" ");
              }
          else
           {
             System.out.println ("Wrong results for record 1");
             System.out.println (" ");
           }

        if(Math.abs(denormPredictBookNumber_02) > 0.85)
         if(Math.abs(denormPredictBookNumber_01) < 0.2  &
            Math.abs(denormPredictBookNumber_02) > 0.85 &
            Math.abs(denormPredictBookNumber_03) < 0.2  &
            Math.abs(denormPredictBookNumber_04) < 0.2  &
            Math.abs(denormPredictBookNumber_05) < 0.2)
             {
               System.out.println ("Record 2 belongs to book 2");
               System.out.println (" ");
             }
```

```
      else
        {
          System.out.println ("Wrong results for record 2");
          System.out.println (" ");
        }

  if(Math.abs(denormPredictBookNumber_03) > 0.85)
   if(Math.abs(denormPredictBookNumber_01) < 0.2 &
      Math.abs(denormPredictBookNumber_02) < 0.2  &
      Math.abs(denormPredictBookNumber_03) > 0.85 &
      Math.abs(denormPredictBookNumber_04) < 0.2  &
      Math.abs(denormPredictBookNumber_05) < 0.2)
        {
          System.out.println ("Record 3 belongs to book 3");
          System.out.println (" ");
        }
    else
      {
        System.out.println ("Wrong results for record 3");
        System.out.println (" ");
      }

  if(Math.abs(denormPredictBookNumber_04) > 0.85)
   if(Math.abs(denormPredictBookNumber_01) < 0.2  &
      Math.abs(denormPredictBookNumber_02) < 0.2  &
      Math.abs(denormPredictBookNumber_03) < 0.2  &
      Math.abs(denormPredictBookNumber_04) > 0.85 &
      Math.abs(denormPredictBookNumber_05) < 0.2)
        {
          System.out.println ("Record 4 belongs to book 4");
          System.out.println (" ");
        }
    else
      {
        System.out.println ("Wrong results for record 4");
        System.out.println (" ");
      }
```

```
            if(Math.abs(denormPredictBookNumber_05) > 0.85)
             if(Math.abs(denormPredictBookNumber_01) < 0.2  &
                Math.abs(denormPredictBookNumber_02) < 0.2  &
                Math.abs(denormPredictBookNumber_03) < 0.2  &
                Math.abs(denormPredictBookNumber_04) < 0.2 &
                Math.abs(denormPredictBookNumber_05) > 0.85)
                 {
                    System.out.println ("Record 5 belongs to book 5");
                    System.out.println (" ");
                 }
             else
              {
                 System.out.println ("Wrong results for record 5");
                 System.out.println (" ");
              }

      }   // End for pair loop

      returnCode = 0;
      return returnCode;

   }   // End of the method


//========================================================================
// Load and test the trained network at non-trainable points
//========================================================================
static public void loadAndTestNetwork()
 {
   System.out.println("Testing the networks results");

   List<Double> xData = new ArrayList<Double>();
   List<Double> yData1 = new ArrayList<Double>();
   List<Double> yData2 = new ArrayList<Double>();

   double targetToPredictPercent = 0;
   double maxGlobalResultDiff = 0.00;
   double averGlobalResultDiff = 0.00;
```

```
double sumGlobalResultDiff = 0.00;
double normInputWordNumberFromRecord = 0.00;
double normTargetBookNumberFromRecord = 0.00;
double normPredictXPointValueFromRecord = 0.00;
BasicNetwork network;
maxGlobalResultDiff = 0.00;
averGlobalResultDiff = 0.00;
sumGlobalResultDiff = 0.00;

// Load the test dataset into memory
MLDataSet testingSet =
loadCSV2Memory(testFileName,numberOfInputNeurons,numberOfOutputNeurons,
  true,CSVFormat.ENGLISH,false);

// Load the saved trained network
network =
 (BasicNetwork)EncogDirectoryPersistence.loadObject(new
 File(networkFileName));

int i = 0;

for (MLDataPair pair:  testingSet)
 {
     i++;

     MLData inputData = pair.getInput();
     MLData actualData = pair.getIdeal();
     MLData predictData = network.compute(inputData);

     // These values are Normalized as the whole input is
     normInputWordNumberFromRecord = inputData.getData(0);
     normTargetBookNumberFromRecord = actualData.getData(0);
     normPredictXPointValueFromRecord = predictData.getData(0);

     denormInputWordNumber_01 = ((minWordNumberDl -
         maxWordNumberDh)*normInputWordNumber_01 - Nh*minWordNumberDl +
             maxWordNumberDh *Nl)/(Nl - Nh);

        denormInputWordNumber_02 = ((minWordNumberDl -
```

```
          maxWordNumberDh)*normInputWordNumber_02 - Nh*minWordNumberDl +
              maxWordNumberDh *Nl)/(Nl - Nh);

        denormInputWordNumber_03 = ((minWordNumberDl -
          maxWordNumberDh)*normInputWordNumber_03 - Nh*minWordNumberDl +
              maxWordNumberDh *Nl)/(Nl - Nh);

    denormTargetBookNumber_01 = ((minTargetValueDl - maxTargetValueDh)*
          normTargetBookNumber_01 - Nh*minTargetValueDl +
            maxTargetValueDh*Nl)/(Nl - Nh);

      denormTargetBookNumber_02 = ((minTargetValueDl - maxTargetValueDh)*
          normTargetBookNumber_02 - Nh*minTargetValueDl +
            maxTargetValueDh*Nl)/(Nl - Nh);

      denormTargetBookNumber_03 = ((minTargetValueDl - maxTargetValueDh)*
          normTargetBookNumber_03 - Nh*minTargetValueDl +
            maxTargetValueDh*Nl)/(Nl - Nh);

      denormTargetBookNumber_04 = ((minTargetValueDl - maxTargetValueDh)*
          normTargetBookNumber_04 - Nh*minTargetValueDl +
            maxTargetValueDh*Nl)/(Nl - Nh);

      denormTargetBookNumber_05 = ((minTargetValueDl - maxTargetValueDh)*
          normTargetBookNumber_05 - Nh*minTargetValueDl +
            maxTargetValueDh*Nl)/(Nl - Nh);

      denormPredictBookNumber_01 =((minTargetValueDl - maxTargetValueDh)*
          normPredictBookNumber_01 - Nh*minTargetValueDl +
            maxTargetValueDh*Nl)/(Nl - Nh);

      denormPredictBookNumber_02 =((minTargetValueDl - maxTargetValueDh)*
          normPredictBookNumber_02- Nh*minTargetValueDl +
            maxTargetValueDh*Nl)/(Nl - Nh);

      denormPredictBookNumber_03 =((minTargetValueDl - maxTargetValueDh)*
          normPredictBookNumber_03 - Nh*minTargetValueDl +
            maxTargetValueDh*Nl)/(Nl - Nh);
```

```
denormPredictBookNumber_04 =((minTargetValueDl -
maxTargetValueDh)*
  normPredictBookNumber_04 - Nh*minTargetValueDl +
    maxTargetValueDh*Nl)/(Nl - Nh);

denormPredictBookNumber_05 =((minTargetValueDl -
maxTargetValueDh)*
  normPredictBookNumber_05 - Nh*minTargetValueDl +
    maxTargetValueDh*Nl)/(Nl - Nh);

System.out.println ("RecordNumber = " + i);

System.out.println ("denormTargetBookNumber_01 = " +
denormTargetBookNumber_01 +
    "  denormPredictBookNumber_01 = " +
    denormPredictBookNumber_01);

System.out.println ("denormTargetBookNumber_02 = " +
denormTargetBookNumber_02 +
    "  denormPredictBookNumber_02 = " +
    denormPredictBookNumber_02);

System.out.println ("denormTargetBookNumber_03 = " +
denormTargetBookNumber_03 +
    "  denormPredictBookNumber_03 = " +
    denormPredictBookNumber_03);

System.out.println ("denormTargetBookNumber_04 = " +
denormTargetBookNumber_04 +
    "  denormPredictBookNumber_04 = " +
    denormPredictBookNumber_04);

System.out.println ("denormTargetBookNumber_05 = " +
denormTargetBookNumber_05 +
    "  denormPredictBookNumber_05 = " +
    denormPredictBookNumber_05);

//System.out.println (" ");
```

```
if(Math.abs(denormPredictBookNumber_01) > 0.85  &
  Math.abs(denormPredictBookNumber_02) < 0.2    &
  Math.abs(denormPredictBookNumber_03) < 0.2    &
  Math.abs(denormPredictBookNumber_04) < 0.2    &
  Math.abs(denormPredictBookNumber_05) < 0.2
  ||
  Math.abs(denormPredictBookNumber_01) < 0.2  &
     Math.abs(denormPredictBookNumber_02) > 0.85 &
     Math.abs(denormPredictBookNumber_03) < 0.2   &
     Math.abs(denormPredictBookNumber_04) < 0.2   &
     Math.abs(denormPredictBookNumber_05) < 0.2
  |
 Math.abs(denormPredictBookNumber_01) < 0.2  &
     Math.abs(denormPredictBookNumber_02) > 0.85 &
     Math.abs(denormPredictBookNumber_03) < 0.2   &
     Math.abs(denormPredictBookNumber_04) < 0.2   &
     Math.abs(denormPredictBookNumber_05) < 0.2
||
  Math.abs(denormPredictBookNumber_01) < 0.2 &
     Math.abs(denormPredictBookNumber_02) < 0.2   &
     Math.abs(denormPredictBookNumber_03) > 0.85 &
     Math.abs(denormPredictBookNumber_04) < 0.2   &
     Math.abs(denormPredictBookNumber_05) < 0.2
     ||
 Math.abs(denormPredictBookNumber_01) < 0.2   &
     Math.abs(denormPredictBookNumber_02) < 0.2   &
     Math.abs(denormPredictBookNumber_03) < 0.2   &
     Math.abs(denormPredictBookNumber_04) > 0.85 &
     Math.abs(denormPredictBookNumber_05) < 0.2
     ||
 Math.abs(denormPredictBookNumber_01) < 0.2   &
     Math.abs(denormPredictBookNumber_02) < 0.2   &
     Math.abs(denormPredictBookNumber_03) < 0.2   &
     Math.abs(denormPredictBookNumber_04) < 0.2 &
     Math.abs(denormPredictBookNumber_05) > 0.85)
```

```
            {
                System.out.println ("Record belong to some book");
                System.out.println (" ");
            }
        else
            {
                System.out.println ("Unknown book");
                System.out.println (" ");
            }

        }  // End for pair loop

    }  // End of the method

}  // End of the class
```

The code fragment of the training method is shown in Listing 10-4.

Listing 10-4. Code Fragment of the Training Method

```
static public int trainValidateSaveNetwork()
  {
      // Load the training CSV file in memory
      MLDataSet trainingSet =
        loadCSV2Memory(trainFileName,numberOfInputNeurons,
        numberOfOutputNeurons,
          true,CSVFormat.ENGLISH,false);

      // create a neural network
      BasicNetwork network = new BasicNetwork();

      // Input layer
      network.addLayer(new BasicLayer(null,true,3));

      // Hidden layer
      network.addLayer(new BasicLayer(new ActivationTANH(),true,7));
      network.addLayer(new BasicLayer(new ActivationTANH(),true,7));
      network.addLayer(new BasicLayer(new ActivationTANH(),true,7));
      network.addLayer(new BasicLayer(new ActivationTANH(),true,7));
```

```java
network.addLayer(new BasicLayer(new ActivationTANH(),true,7));
network.addLayer(new BasicLayer(new ActivationTANH(),true,7));

// Output layer
network.addLayer(new BasicLayer(new ActivationTANH(),false,5));

network.getStructure().finalizeStructure();
network.reset();

//Train the neural network
final ResilientPropagation train = new ResilientPropagation(network,
trainingSet);

int epoch = 1;

do
 {
     train.iteration();
    System.out.println("Epoch #" + epoch + " Error:" + train.getError());

   epoch++;

   if (epoch >= 1000 && network.calculateError(trainingSet) >
   0.0000000000000012)
      {
        returnCode = 1;
        System.out.println("Try again");
        return returnCode;
      }

} while (network.calculateError(trainingSet) > 0.0000000000000011);

// Save the network file
EncogDirectoryPersistence.saveObject(new File(networkFileName),network);

System.out.println("Neural Network Results:");

double sumNormDifferencePerc = 0.00;
double averNormDifferencePerc = 0.00;
double maxNormDifferencePerc = 0.00;
```

```
int m = 0;

for(MLDataPair pair: trainingSet)
  {
       m++;

       final MLData output = network.compute(pair.getInput());

       MLData inputData = pair.getInput();
       MLData actualData = pair.getIdeal();
       MLData predictData = network.compute(inputData);

       // Calculate and print the results

       normInputWordNumber_01 = inputData.getData(0);
       normInputWordNumber_02 = inputData.getData(1);
       normInputWordNumber_03 = inputData.getData(2);

       normTargetBookNumber_01 = actualData.getData(0);
       normTargetBookNumber_02 = actualData.getData(1);
       normTargetBookNumber_03 = actualData.getData(2);
       normTargetBookNumber_04 = actualData.getData(3);
       normTargetBookNumber_05 = actualData.getData(4);

       normPredictBookNumber_01 = predictData.getData(0);
       normPredictBookNumber_02 = predictData.getData(1);
       normPredictBookNumber_03 = predictData.getData(2);
       normPredictBookNumber_04 = predictData.getData(3);
       normPredictBookNumber_05 = predictData.getData(4);

       denormInputWordNumber_01 = ((minWordNumberDl -
         maxWordNumberDh)*normInputWordNumber_01 - Nh*minWordNumberDl +
           maxWordNumberDh *Nl)/(Nl - Nh);

       denormInputWordNumber_02 = ((minWordNumberDl -
         maxWordNumberDh)*normInputWordNumber_02 - Nh*minWordNumberDl +
           maxWordNumberDh *Nl)/(Nl - Nh);

       denormInputWordNumber_03 = ((minWordNumberDl -
         maxWordNumberDh)*normInputWordNumber_03 - Nh*minWordNumberDl +
```

```
            maxWordNumberDh *Nl)/(Nl - Nh);

    denormTargetBookNumber_01 = ((minTargetValueDl - maxTargetValueDh)*
      normTargetBookNumber_01 - Nh*minTargetValueDl +
        maxTargetValueDh*Nl)/(Nl - Nh);

    denormTargetBookNumber_02 = ((minTargetValueDl - maxTargetValueDh)*
      normTargetBookNumber_02 - Nh*minTargetValueDl +
        maxTargetValueDh*Nl)/(Nl - Nh);

    denormTargetBookNumber_03 = ((minTargetValueDl - maxTargetValueDh)*
      normTargetBookNumber_03 - Nh*minTargetValueDl +
        maxTargetValueDh*Nl)/(Nl - Nh);

    denormTargetBookNumber_04 = ((minTargetValueDl - maxTargetValueDh)*
      normTargetBookNumber_04 - Nh*minTargetValueDl +
        maxTargetValueDh*Nl)/(Nl - Nh);

    denormTargetBookNumber_05 = ((minTargetValueDl - maxTargetValueDh)*
      normTargetBookNumber_05 - Nh*minTargetValueDl +
        maxTargetValueDh*Nl)/(Nl - Nh);

    denormPredictBookNumber_01 =((minTargetValueDl - maxTargetValueDh)*
      normPredictBookNumber_01 - Nh*minTargetValueDl +
        maxTargetValueDh*Nl)/(Nl - Nh);

    denormPredictBookNumber_02 =((minTargetValueDl - maxTargetValueDh)*
      normPredictBookNumber_02- Nh*minTargetValueDl +
        maxTargetValueDh*Nl)/(Nl - Nh);

    denormPredictBookNumber_03 =((minTargetValueDl - maxTargetValueDh)*
      normPredictBookNumber_03 - Nh*minTargetValueDl +
        maxTargetValueDh*Nl)/(Nl - Nh);

    denormPredictBookNumber_04 =((minTargetValueDl - maxTargetValueDh)*
      normPredictBookNumber_04 - Nh*minTargetValueDl +
        maxTargetValueDh*Nl)/(Nl - Nh);

    denormPredictBookNumber_05 =((minTargetValueDl - maxTargetValueDh)*
      normPredictBookNumber_05 - Nh*minTargetValueDl +
```

```
      maxTargetValueDh*Nl)/(Nl - Nh);

System.out.println ("RecordNumber = " + m);


System.out.println ("denormTargetBookNumber_01 = " +
denormTargetBookNumber_01 +
     "   denormPredictBookNumber_01 = " +
       denormPredictBookNumber_01);

System.out.println ("denormTargetBookNumber_02 = " +
denormTargetBookNumber_02 +
     "   denormPredictBookNumber_02 = " +
       denormPredictBookNumber_02);

System.out.println ("denormTargetBookNumber_03 = " +
denormTargetBookNumber_03 +
     "   denormPredictBookNumber_03 = " +
       denormPredictBookNumber_03);

System.out.println ("denormTargetBookNumber_04 = " +
denormTargetBookNumber_04 +
     "   denormPredictBookNumber_04 = " +
       denormPredictBookNumber_04);

System.out.println ("denormTargetBookNumber_05 = " +
denormTargetBookNumber_05 +
     "   denormPredictBookNumber_05 = " +
       denormPredictBookNumber_05);

//System.out.println (" ");

// Print the classification results in the log
if(Math.abs(denormPredictBookNumber_01) > 0.85)
  if(Math.abs(denormPredictBookNumber_01) > 0.85  &
     Math.abs(denormPredictBookNumber_02) < 0.2    &
     Math.abs(denormPredictBookNumber_03) < 0.2    &
     Math.abs(denormPredictBookNumber_04) < 0.2    &
     Math.abs(denormPredictBookNumber_05) < 0.2)
     {
```

```
              System.out.println ("Record 1 belongs to book 1");
              System.out.println (" ");
          }
      else
       {
         System.out.println ("Wrong results for record 1");
         System.out.println (" ");
       }

    if(Math.abs(denormPredictBookNumber_02) > 0.85)
     if(Math.abs(denormPredictBookNumber_01) < 0.2  &
        Math.abs(denormPredictBookNumber_02) > 0.85 &
        Math.abs(denormPredictBookNumber_03) < 0.2  &
        Math.abs(denormPredictBookNumber_04) < 0.2  &
        Math.abs(denormPredictBookNumber_05) < 0.2)
         {
           System.out.println ("Record 2 belongs to book 2");
           System.out.println (" ");
         }
      else
       {
         System.out.println ("Wrong results for record 2");
         System.out.println (" ");
       }

    if(Math.abs(denormPredictBookNumber_03) > 0.85)
     if(Math.abs(denormPredictBookNumber_01) < 0.2 &
        Math.abs(denormPredictBookNumber_02) < 0.2  &
        Math.abs(denormPredictBookNumber_03) > 0.85 &
        Math.abs(denormPredictBookNumber_04) < 0.2  &
        Math.abs(denormPredictBookNumber_05) < 0.2)
         {
           System.out.println ("Record 3 belongs to book 3");
           System.out.println (" ");
         }
```

```
else
 {
   System.out.println ("Wrong results for record 3");
   System.out.println (" ");
 }

if(Math.abs(denormPredictBookNumber_04) > 0.85)
 if(Math.abs(denormPredictBookNumber_01) < 0.2  &
    Math.abs(denormPredictBookNumber_02) < 0.2  &
    Math.abs(denormPredictBookNumber_03) < 0.2  &
    Math.abs(denormPredictBookNumber_04) > 0.85 &
    Math.abs(denormPredictBookNumber_05) < 0.2)
     {
       System.out.println ("Record 4 belongs to book 4");
       System.out.println (" ");
     }
 else
  {
    System.out.println ("Wrong results for record 4");
    System.out.println (" ");
  }

if(Math.abs(denormPredictBookNumber_05) > 0.85)
 if(Math.abs(denormPredictBookNumber_01) < 0.2  &
    Math.abs(denormPredictBookNumber_02) < 0.2  &
    Math.abs(denormPredictBookNumber_03) < 0.2  &
    Math.abs(denormPredictBookNumber_04) < 0.2 &
    Math.abs(denormPredictBookNumber_05) > 0.85)
     {
       System.out.println ("Record 5 belongs to book 5");
       System.out.println (" ");
     }
```

```
            else
            {
               System.out.println ("Wrong results for record 5");
               System.out.println (" ");
            }

      }   // End for pair loop

      returnCode = 0;
      return returnCode;

   }   // End of the method
```

Listing 10-5 shows the code fragment of the testing method.

Here, we load the test dataset and the previously saved trained network in memory. Next, we loop over the pair dataset and retrieve for each record three input book numbers and five target book numbers. We denormalize the obtained values and then check whether the record belongs to one of our five books.

Listing 10-5. Code Fragment of the Testing Method

```
// Load the test dataset into memory
MLDataSet testingSet =
    loadCSV2Memory(testFileName,numberOfInputNeurons,
    numberOfOutputNeurons,
       true,CSVFormat.ENGLISH,false);

// Load the saved trained network
network =
    (BasicNetwork)EncogDirectoryPersistence.loadObject(new
File(networkFileName));

 int i = 0;

for (MLDataPair pair:  testingSet)
    {
          i++;

          MLData inputData = pair.getInput();
```

```
MLData actualData = pair.getIdeal();
MLData predictData = network.compute(inputData);

// These values are Normalized as the whole input is
normInputWordNumberFromRecord = inputData.getData(0);
normTargetBookNumberFromRecord = actualData.getData(0);
normPredictXPointValueFromRecord = predictData.getData(0);

denormInputWordNumber_01 = ((minWordNumberDl -
    maxWordNumberDh)*normInputWordNumber_01 - Nh*minWordNumberDl +
        maxWordNumberDh *Nl)/(Nl - Nh);

    denormInputWordNumber_02 = ((minWordNumberDl -
    maxWordNumberDh)*normInputWordNumber_02 - Nh*minWordNumberDl +
        maxWordNumberDh *Nl)/(Nl - Nh);

    denormInputWordNumber_03 = ((minWordNumberDl -
    maxWordNumberDh)*normInputWordNumber_03 - Nh*minWordNumberDl +
        maxWordNumberDh *Nl)/(Nl - Nh);

denormTargetBookNumber_01 = ((minTargetValueDl - maxTargetValueDh)*
    normTargetBookNumber_01 - Nh*minTargetValueDl +
        maxTargetValueDh*Nl)/(Nl - Nh);

    denormTargetBookNumber_02 = ((minTargetValueDl - maxTargetValueDh)*
    normTargetBookNumber_02 - Nh*minTargetValueDl +
        maxTargetValueDh*Nl)/(Nl - Nh);

    denormTargetBookNumber_03 = ((minTargetValueDl - maxTargetValueDh)*
    normTargetBookNumber_03 - Nh*minTargetValueDl +
        maxTargetValueDh*Nl)/(Nl - Nh);

    denormTargetBookNumber_04 = ((minTargetValueDl - maxTargetValueDh)*
    normTargetBookNumber_04 - Nh*minTargetValueDl +
        maxTargetValueDh*Nl)/(Nl - Nh);

    denormTargetBookNumber_05 = ((minTargetValueDl - maxTargetValueDh)*
    normTargetBookNumber_05 - Nh*minTargetValueDl +
        maxTargetValueDh*Nl)/(Nl - Nh);
```

```
    denormPredictBookNumber_01 =((minTargetValueDl - maxTargetValueDh)*
      normPredictBookNumber_01 - Nh*minTargetValueDl +
        maxTargetValueDh*Nl)/(Nl - Nh);

    denormPredictBookNumber_02 =((minTargetValueDl - maxTargetValueDh)*
      normPredictBookNumber_02- Nh*minTargetValueDl +
        maxTargetValueDh*Nl)/(Nl - Nh);

    denormPredictBookNumber_03 =((minTargetValueDl - maxTargetValueDh)*
      normPredictBookNumber_03 - Nh*minTargetValueDl +
        maxTargetValueDh*Nl)/(Nl - Nh);

    denormPredictBookNumber_04 =((minTargetValueDl - maxTargetValueDh)*
      normPredictBookNumber_04 - Nh*minTargetValueDl +
        maxTargetValueDh*Nl)/(Nl - Nh);

    denormPredictBookNumber_05 =((minTargetValueDl - maxTargetValueDh)*
      normPredictBookNumber_05 - Nh*minTargetValueDl +
        maxTargetValueDh*Nl)/(Nl - Nh);

  System.out.println ("RecordNumber = " + i);

  System.out.println ("denormTargetBookNumber_01 = " +
  denormTargetBookNumber_01 +
        "   denormPredictBookNumber_01 = " +
          denormPredictBookNumber_01);

  System.out.println ("denormTargetBookNumber_02 = " +
  denormTargetBookNumber_02 +
        "   denormPredictBookNumber_02 = " +
          denormPredictBookNumber_02);

  System.out.println ("denormTargetBookNumber_03 = " +
  denormTargetBookNumber_03 +
        "   denormPredictBookNumber_03 = " +
          denormPredictBookNumber_03);

  System.out.println ("denormTargetBookNumber_04 = " +
  denormTargetBookNumber_04 +
```

```
        "   denormPredictBookNumber_04 = " +
            denormPredictBookNumber_04);

   System.out.println ("denormTargetBookNumber_05 = " +
   denormTargetBookNumber_05 +
        "   denormPredictBookNumber_05 = " +
            denormPredictBookNumber_05);

//System.out.println (" ");

if(Math.abs(denormPredictBookNumber_01) > 0.85  &
  Math.abs(denormPredictBookNumber_02) < 0.2    &
  Math.abs(denormPredictBookNumber_03) < 0.2    &
  Math.abs(denormPredictBookNumber_04) < 0.2    &
  Math.abs(denormPredictBookNumber_05) < 0.2
  |
  Math.abs(denormPredictBookNumber_01) < 0.2  &
     Math.abs(denormPredictBookNumber_02) > 0.85 &
     Math.abs(denormPredictBookNumber_03) < 0.2  &
     Math.abs(denormPredictBookNumber_04) < 0.2  &
     Math.abs(denormPredictBookNumber_05) < 0.2

  |
  Math.abs(denormPredictBookNumber_01) < 0.2  &
     Math.abs(denormPredictBookNumber_02) > 0.85 &
     Math.abs(denormPredictBookNumber_03) < 0.2  &
     Math.abs(denormPredictBookNumber_04) < 0.2  &
     Math.abs(denormPredictBookNumber_05) < 0.2
  |
  Math.abs(denormPredictBookNumber_01) < 0.2 &
     Math.abs(denormPredictBookNumber_02) < 0.2  &
     Math.abs(denormPredictBookNumber_03) > 0.85 &
     Math.abs(denormPredictBookNumber_04) < 0.2  &
     Math.abs(denormPredictBookNumber_05) < 0.2
  |
  Math.abs(denormPredictBookNumber_01) < 0.2  &
     Math.abs(denormPredictBookNumber_02) < 0.2  &
```

```
                Math.abs(denormPredictBookNumber_03) < 0.2  &
                Math.abs(denormPredictBookNumber_04) > 0.85 &
                Math.abs(denormPredictBookNumber_05) < 0.2
            |
        Math.abs(denormPredictBookNumber_01) < 0.2  &
                Math.abs(denormPredictBookNumber_02) < 0.2  &
                Math.abs(denormPredictBookNumber_03) < 0.2  &
                Math.abs(denormPredictBookNumber_04) < 0.2 &
                Math.abs(denormPredictBookNumber_05) > 0.85)
                {
                    System.out.println ("Record belong to some book");
                    System.out.println (" ");
                }
        else
         {
                System.out.println ("Unknown book");
                System.out.println (" ");
         }

    }  // End for pair loop


} // End of the method
```

Training Results

Listing 10-6 shows the training/validation results.

Listing 10-6. Training/Validation Results

```
RecordNumber = 1
denormTargetBookNumber_01 = 1.0    denormPredictBookNumber_01 = 1.0
denormTargetBookNumber_02 = -0.0   denormPredictBookNumber_02 =
3.6221384780432686E-9
denormTargetBookNumber_03 = -0.0   denormPredictBookNumber_03 = -0.0
denormTargetBookNumber_04 = -0.0   denormPredictBookNumber_04 =
1.3178162894256218E-8
```

denormTargetBookNumber_05 = -0.0 denormPredictBookNumber_05 =
2.220446049250313E-16
    Record 1 belongs to book 1

RecordNumber = 2
denormTargetBookNumber_01 = 1.0 denormPredictBookNumber_01 = 1.0
denormTargetBookNumber_02 = -0.0 denormPredictBookNumber_02 =
3.6687665128098956E-9
denormTargetBookNumber_03 = -0.0 denormPredictBookNumber_03 = -0.0
denormTargetBookNumber_04 = -0.0 denormPredictBookNumber_04 =
1.0430401597982808E-8
denormTargetBookNumber_05 = -0.0 denormPredictBookNumber_05 =
2.220446049250313E-16
    Record 1 belongs to book 1

RecordNumber = 3
denormTargetBookNumber_01 = 1.0 denormPredictBookNumber_01 = 1.0
denormTargetBookNumber_02 = -0.0 denormPredictBookNumber_02 =
4.35402175424926E-9
denormTargetBookNumber_03 = -0.0 denormPredictBookNumber_03 = -0.0
denormTargetBookNumber_04 = -0.0 denormPredictBookNumber_04 =
9.684705759571699E-9
denormTargetBookNumber_05 = -0.0 denormPredictBookNumber_05 =
2.220446049250313E-16
    Record 1 belongs to book 1

RecordNumber = 4
denormTargetBookNumber_01 = 1.0 denormPredictBookNumber_01 = 1.0
denormTargetBookNumber_02 = -0.0 denormPredictBookNumber_02 =
6.477930192261283E-9
denormTargetBookNumber_03 = -0.0 denormPredictBookNumber_03 = -0.0
denormTargetBookNumber_04 = -0.0 denormPredictBookNumber_04 =
4.863816960298806E-9
denormTargetBookNumber_05 = -0.0 denormPredictBookNumber_05 =
2.220446049250313E-16
    Record 1 belongs to book 1

```
RecordNumber = 5
denormTargetBookNumber_01 = 1.0      denormPredictBookNumber_01 = 1.0
denormTargetBookNumber_02 = -0.0     denormPredictBookNumber_02 =
1.7098276960947345E-8
denormTargetBookNumber_03 = -0.0     denormPredictBookNumber_03 = -0.0
denormTargetBookNumber_04 = -0.0     denormPredictBookNumber_04 =
4.196660130517671E-9
denormTargetBookNumber_05 = -0.0     denormPredictBookNumber_05 =
2.220446049250313E-16
     Record 1 belongs to book 1

RecordNumber = 6
denormTargetBookNumber_01 = 1.0      denormPredictBookNumber_01 = 1.0
denormTargetBookNumber_02 = -0.0     denormPredictBookNumber_02 =
9.261896322110275E-8
denormTargetBookNumber_03 = -0.0     denormPredictBookNumber_03 = -0.0
denormTargetBookNumber_04 = -0.0     denormPredictBookNumber_04 =
2.6307949707593536E-9
denormTargetBookNumber_05 = -0.0     denormPredictBookNumber_05 =
2.7755575615628914E-16
     Record 1 belongs to book 1

RecordNumber = 7
denormTargetBookNumber_01 = -0.0     denormPredictBookNumber_01 =
5.686340287525127E-12
denormTargetBookNumber_02 = 1.0      denormPredictBookNumber_02 =
0.9999999586267019
denormTargetBookNumber_03 = -0.0     denormPredictBookNumber_03 = -0.0
denormTargetBookNumber_04 = -0.0     denormPredictBookNumber_04 =
1.1329661653292078E-9
denormTargetBookNumber_05 = -0.0     denormPredictBookNumber_05 =
9.43689570931383E-16
     Record 2 belongs to book 2

RecordNumber = 8
denormTargetBookNumber_01 = -0.0     denormPredictBookNumber_01 = -0.0
```

denormTargetBookNumber_02 = 1.0   denormPredictBookNumber_02 =
0.9999999999998506
denormTargetBookNumber_03 = -0.0 denormPredictBookNumber_03 = -0.0
denormTargetBookNumber_04 = -0.0 denormPredictBookNumber_04 =
1.091398971198032E-9
denormTargetBookNumber_05 = -0.0 denormPredictBookNumber_05 =
2.6645352591003757E-15
    Record 2 belongs to book 2

RecordNumber = 9
denormTargetBookNumber_01 = -0.0 denormPredictBookNumber_01 = -0.0
denormTargetBookNumber_02 = 1.0   denormPredictBookNumber_02 =
0.9999999999999962
denormTargetBookNumber_03 = -0.0 denormPredictBookNumber_03 = -0.0
denormTargetBookNumber_04 = -0.0 denormPredictBookNumber_04 =
1.0686406759496947E-9
denormTargetBookNumber_05 = -0.0 denormPredictBookNumber_05 =
3.7192471324942744E-15
    Record 2 belongs to book 2

RecordNumber = 10
denormTargetBookNumber_01 = -0.0 denormPredictBookNumber_01 = -0.0
denormTargetBookNumber_02 = 1.0   denormPredictBookNumber_02 =
0.9999999999999798
denormTargetBookNumber_03 = -0.0 denormPredictBookNumber_03 =
2.2352120154778277E-12
denormTargetBookNumber_04 = -0.0 denormPredictBookNumber_04 =
7.627692921730045E-10
denormTargetBookNumber_05 = -0.0 denormPredictBookNumber_05 =
1.9817480989559044E-14
    Record 2 belongs to book 2

RecordNumber = 11
denormTargetBookNumber_01 = -0.0 denormPredictBookNumber_01 = -0.0
denormTargetBookNumber_02 = 1.0   denormPredictBookNumber_02 =
0.9999999999999603

denormTargetBookNumber_03 = -0.0   denormPredictBookNumber_03 =
1.2451872866137137E-11
denormTargetBookNumber_04 = -0.0   denormPredictBookNumber_04 =
7.404629132068408E-10
denormTargetBookNumber_05 = -0.0   denormPredictBookNumber_05 =
2.298161660974074E-14
    Record 2 belongs to book 2

RecordNumber = 12
denormTargetBookNumber_01 = -0.0   denormPredictBookNumber_01 = -0.0
denormTargetBookNumber_02 = 1.0   denormPredictBookNumber_02 =
0.9999999999856213
denormTargetBookNumber_03 = -0.0   denormPredictBookNumber_03 =
7.48775297876314E-8
denormTargetBookNumber_04 = -0.0   denormPredictBookNumber_04 =
6.947271091739537E-10
denormTargetBookNumber_05 = -0.0   denormPredictBookNumber_05 =
4.801714581503802E-14
    Record 2 belongs to book 2

RecordNumber = 13
denormTargetBookNumber_01 = -0.0   denormPredictBookNumber_01 = -0.0
denormTargetBookNumber_02 = -0.0   denormPredictBookNumber_02 =
7.471272545078733E-9
denormTargetBookNumber_03 = 1.0   denormPredictBookNumber_03 =
0.9999999419988991
denormTargetBookNumber_04 = -0.0   denormPredictBookNumber_04 =
2.5249974888730264E-9
denormTargetBookNumber_05 = -0.0   denormPredictBookNumber_05 =
2.027711332175386E-12
    Record 3 belongs to book 3

RecordNumber = 14
denormTargetBookNumber_01 = -0.0   denormPredictBookNumber_01 = -0.0
denormTargetBookNumber_02 = -0.0   denormPredictBookNumber_02 =
2.295386103412511E-13

denormTargetBookNumber_03 = 1.0   denormPredictBookNumber_03 =
0.9999999999379154
denormTargetBookNumber_04 = -0.0   denormPredictBookNumber_04 =
4.873732140087128E-9
denormTargetBookNumber_05 = -0.0   denormPredictBookNumber_05 =
4.987454893523591E-12
Record 3 belongs to book 3

RecordNumber = 15
denormTargetBookNumber_01 = -0.0   denormPredictBookNumber_01 = -0.0
denormTargetBookNumber_02 = -0.0   denormPredictBookNumber_02 =
2.692845946228317E-13
denormTargetBookNumber_03 = 1.0   denormPredictBookNumber_03 =
0.9999999998630087
denormTargetBookNumber_04 = -0.0   denormPredictBookNumber_04 =
4.701179112664988E-9
denormTargetBookNumber_05 = -0.0   denormPredictBookNumber_05 =
4.707678691318051E-12
      Record 3 belongs to book 3

RecordNumber = 16
denormTargetBookNumber_01 = -0.0   denormPredictBookNumber_01 = -0.0
denormTargetBookNumber_02 = -0.0   denormPredictBookNumber_02 = -0.0
denormTargetBookNumber_03 = 1.0   denormPredictBookNumber_03 =
0.9999999999999996
denormTargetBookNumber_04 = -0.0   denormPredictBookNumber_04 =
2.0469307360215794E-8
denormTargetBookNumber_05 = -0.0   denormPredictBookNumber_05 =
2.843247859374287E-11
      Record 3 belongs to book 3

RecordNumber = 17
denormTargetBookNumber_01 = -0.0   denormPredictBookNumber_01 = -0.0
denormTargetBookNumber_02 = -0.0   denormPredictBookNumber_02 = -0.0
denormTargetBookNumber_03 = 1.0   denormPredictBookNumber_03 =
0.9999999999999987
denormTargetBookNumber_04 = -0.0   denormPredictBookNumber_04 =
1.977055869017974E-8

denormTargetBookNumber_05 = -0.0   denormPredictBookNumber_05 =
2.68162714256448E-11
    Record 3 belongs to book 3

RecordNumber = 18
denormTargetBookNumber_01 = -0.0   denormPredictBookNumber_01 = -0.0
denormTargetBookNumber_02 = -0.0   denormPredictBookNumber_02 = -0.0
denormTargetBookNumber_03 = 1.0   denormPredictBookNumber_03 =
0.9999999885142061
denormTargetBookNumber_04 = -0.0   denormPredictBookNumber_04 =
2.6820915488556807E-8
denormTargetBookNumber_05 = -0.0   denormPredictBookNumber_05 =
7.056188966458876E-12
    Record 3 belongs to book 3

RecordNumber = 19
denormTargetBookNumber_01 = -0.0   denormPredictBookNumber_01 = -0.0
denormTargetBookNumber_02 = -0.0   denormPredictBookNumber_02 = -0.0
denormTargetBookNumber_03 = -0.0   denormPredictBookNumber_03 =
2.983344798979104E-8
denormTargetBookNumber_04 = 1.0   denormPredictBookNumber_04 =
0.9999999789933758
denormTargetBookNumber_05 = -0.0   denormPredictBookNumber_05 =
1.7987472622493783E-10
    Record 4 belongs to book 4

RecordNumber = 20
denormTargetBookNumber_01 = -0.0   denormPredictBookNumber_01 = -0.0
denormTargetBookNumber_02 = -0.0   denormPredictBookNumber_02 = -0.0
denormTargetBookNumber_03 = -0.0   denormPredictBookNumber_03 =
1.0003242317813132E-7
denormTargetBookNumber_04 = 1.0   denormPredictBookNumber_04 =
0.9999999812213116
denormTargetBookNumber_05 = -0.0   denormPredictBookNumber_05 =
2.2566659652056842E-10
    Record 4 belongs to book 4

```
RecordNumber = 21
denormTargetBookNumber_01 = -0.0    denormPredictBookNumber_01 = -0.0
denormTargetBookNumber_02 = -0.0    denormPredictBookNumber_02 = -0.0
denormTargetBookNumber_03 = -0.0    denormPredictBookNumber_03 =
1.4262971415046621E-8
denormTargetBookNumber_04 = 1.0     denormPredictBookNumber_04 =
0.9999999812440078
denormTargetBookNumber_05 = -0.0    denormPredictBookNumber_05 =
2.079504346497174E-10
    Record 4 belongs to book 4

RecordNumber = 22
denormTargetBookNumber_01 = -0.0    denormPredictBookNumber_01 = -0.0
denormTargetBookNumber_02 = -0.0    denormPredictBookNumber_02 = -0.0
denormTargetBookNumber_03 = -0.0    denormPredictBookNumber_03 =
5.790115659154438E-8
denormTargetBookNumber_04 = 1.0     denormPredictBookNumber_04 =
0.9999999845075942
denormTargetBookNumber_05 = -0.0    denormPredictBookNumber_05 =
2.9504404475133583E-10
    Record 4 belongs to book 4

RecordNumber = 23
denormTargetBookNumber_01 = -0.0    denormPredictBookNumber_01 = -0.0
denormTargetBookNumber_02 = -0.0    denormPredictBookNumber_02 = -0.0
denormTargetBookNumber_03 = -0.0    denormPredictBookNumber_03 =
6.890162551620449E-9
denormTargetBookNumber_04 = 1.0     denormPredictBookNumber_04 =
0.999999984526581
denormTargetBookNumber_05 = -0.0    denormPredictBookNumber_05 =
2.6966767707747863E-10
    Record 4 belongs to book 4

RecordNumber = 24
denormTargetBookNumber_01 = -0.0    denormPredictBookNumber_01 = -0.0
denormTargetBookNumber_02 = -0.0    denormPredictBookNumber_02 = -0.0
```

451

denormTargetBookNumber_03 = -0.0   denormPredictBookNumber_03 =
9.975842318876715E-9
denormTargetBookNumber_04 = 1.0   denormPredictBookNumber_04 =
0.9999999856956441
denormTargetBookNumber_05 = -0.0   denormPredictBookNumber_05 =
3.077177401777931E-10
    Record 4 belongs to book 4

RecordNumber = 25
denormTargetBookNumber_01 = -0.0   denormPredictBookNumber_01 = -0.0
denormTargetBookNumber_02 = -0.0   denormPredictBookNumber_02 = -0.0
denormTargetBookNumber_03 = -0.0   denormPredictBookNumber_03 =
3.569367024169878E-14
denormTargetBookNumber_04 = -0.0   denormPredictBookNumber_04 =
1.8838704707313525E-8
denormTargetBookNumber_05 = 1.0   denormPredictBookNumber_05 =
0.9999999996959972
    Record 5 belongs to book 5

RecordNumber = 26
denormTargetBookNumber_01 = -0.0   denormPredictBookNumber_01 = -0.0
denormTargetBookNumber_02 = -0.0   denormPredictBookNumber_02 = -0.0
denormTargetBookNumber_03 = -0.0   denormPredictBookNumber_03 =
4.929390229335695E-14
denormTargetBookNumber_04 = -0.0   denormPredictBookNumber_04 =
1.943621164013365E-8
denormTargetBookNumber_05 = 1.0   denormPredictBookNumber_05 =
0.9999999997119369
    Record 5 belongs to book 5

RecordNumber = 27
denormTargetBookNumber_01 = -0.0   denormPredictBookNumber_01 = -0.0
denormTargetBookNumber_02 = -0.0   denormPredictBookNumber_02 = -0.0
denormTargetBookNumber_03 = -0.0   denormPredictBookNumber_03 =
1.532107773982716E-14
denormTargetBookNumber_04 = -0.0   denormPredictBookNumber_04 =
1.926626319592728E-8

```
denormTargetBookNumber_05 = 1.0   denormPredictBookNumber_05 =
0.9999999996935514
    Record 5 belongs to book 5

RecordNumber = 28
denormTargetBookNumber_01 = -0.0  denormPredictBookNumber_01 = -0.0
denormTargetBookNumber_02 = -0.0  denormPredictBookNumber_02 = -0.0
denormTargetBookNumber_03 = -0.0  denormPredictBookNumber_03 =
3.2862601528904634E-14
denormTargetBookNumber_04 = -0.0  denormPredictBookNumber_04 =
2.034116280968945E-8
denormTargetBookNumber_05 = 1.0   denormPredictBookNumber_05 =
0.9999999997226772
    Record 5 belongs to book 5

RecordNumber = 29
denormTargetBookNumber_01 = -0.0  denormPredictBookNumber_01 = -0.0
denormTargetBookNumber_02 = -0.0  denormPredictBookNumber_02 = -0.0
denormTargetBookNumber_03 = -0.0  denormPredictBookNumber_03 =
1.27675647831893E-14
denormTargetBookNumber_04 = -0.0  denormPredictBookNumber_04 =
2.014738198496957E-8
denormTargetBookNumber_05 = 1.0   denormPredictBookNumber_05 =
0.9999999997076233
    Record 5 belongs to book 5

RecordNumber = 30
denormTargetBookNumber_01 = -0.0  denormPredictBookNumber_01 = -0.0
denormTargetBookNumber_02 = -0.0  denormPredictBookNumber_02 = -0.0
denormTargetBookNumber_03 = -0.0  denormPredictBookNumber_03 =
2.0039525594484076E-14
denormTargetBookNumber_04 = -0.0  denormPredictBookNumber_04 =
2.0630209485172912E-8
denormTargetBookNumber_05 = 1.0  denormPredictBookNumber_05 =
0.9999999997212032
    Record 5 belongs to book 5
```

As shown in the log, the program correctly identified the book number that each record belongs to for all processed records.

Testing Results

Listing 10-7 shows the testing results.

Listing 10-7. Testing Results

```
RecordNumber = 1
   Unknown book

RecordNumber = 2
   Unknown book

RecordNumber = 3
   Unknown book

RecordNumber = 4
   Unknown book

RecordNumber = 5
   Unknown book

RecordNumber = 6
   Unknown book

RecordNumber = 7
   Unknown book

RecordNumber = 8
   Unknown book

RecordNumber = 9
   Unknown book

RecordNumber = 10
   Unknown book

RecordNumber = 11
   Unknown book
```

```
RecordNumber = 12
   Unknown book

RecordNumber = 13
   Unknown book

RecordNumber = 14
   Unknown book

RecordNumber = 15
   Unknown book
```

The testing process correctly classified the objects by determining that all processed records don't belong to any of our books.

Summary

The chapter explained how to use neural networks for the classification of objects. Specifically, the example in this chapter showed how a neural network was able to determine the book to which each testing record belongs. In the next chapter, we will learn the importance of selecting the correct processing model.

CHAPTER 11

The Importance of Selecting the Correct Model

The example discussed in this chapter will end up showing a negative result. However, we frequently learn a lot from our mistakes.

Example: Predicting Next Month's Stock Market Price

In this example, we will try to predict next month's price of the SPY exchange-traded fund (ETF), which is the exchange that mimics the S&P 500 stock market index. Someone's rational for developing such a project could sound somewhat like this:

> *"Yes, we know that the market prices are random, jumping daily up and down reacting to news. However, we use the monthly prices, which are more stable. In addition, the market experienced the conditions similar to the current situation many times in the past, and people (in general) should react approximately the same to similar conditions. By knowing how the market reacted in the past to the conditions similar to today's market, we should be able to closely predict the market behavior for the next month."*

We will use the ten-year historic monthly prices for the SPY ETF and will attempt to predict next month's price. Of course, using the historical SPY data of a longer duration should positively contribute to the accuracy of prediction; however, this is an example, and it should be reasonable small. The input dataset contains data for ten years (120 months), from January 2000 until January 2009, and we want to predict the SPY price at the end of February 2009. Table 11-1 shows the historical monthly SPY prices for that period.

© Igor Livshin 2022
I. Livshin, *Artificial Neural Networks with Java*, https://doi.org/10.1007/978-1-4842-7368-5_11

Table 11-1. *Historical Monthly SPY ETF Prices*

Date	Price	Date	Price
200001	1394.46	200501	1181.27
200002	1366.42	200502	1203.6
200003	1498.58	200503	1180.59
200004	1452.43	200504	1156.85
200005	1420.6	200505	1191.5
200006	1454.6	200506	1191.33
200007	1430.83	200507	1234.18
200008	1517.68	200508	1220.33
200009	1436.51	200509	1228.81
200010	1429.4	200510	1207.01
200011	1314.95	200511	1249.48
200012	1320.28	200512	1248.29
200101	1366.01	200601	1280.08
200102	1239.94	200602	1280.66
200103	1160.33	200603	1294.87
200104	1249.46	200604	1310.61
200105	1255.82	200605	1270.09
200106	1224.38	200606	1270.2
200107	1211.23	200607	1276.66
200108	1133.58	200608	1303.82
200109	1040.94	200609	1335.85
200110	1059.78	200610	1377.94
200111	1139.45	200611	1400.63
200112	1148.08	200612	1418.3
200201	1130.2	200701	1438.24
200202	1106.73	200702	1406.82

(*continued*)

Table 11-1. (*continued*)

Date	Price	Date	Price
200203	1147.39	200703	1420.86
200204	1076.92	200704	1482.37
200205	1067.14	200705	1530.62
200206	989.82	200706	1503.35
200207	911.62	200707	1455.27
200208	916.07	200708	1473.99
200209	815.28	200709	1526.75
200210	885.76	200710	1549.38
200211	936.31	200711	1481.14
200212	879.82	200712	1468.36
200301	855.7	200801	1378.55
200302	841.15	200802	1330.63
200303	848.18	200803	1322.7
200304	916.92	200804	1385.59
200305	963.59	200805	1400.38
200306	974.5	200806	1280
200307	990.31	200807	1267.38
200308	1008.01	200808	1282.83
200309	995.97	200809	1166.36
200310	1050.71	200810	968.75
200311	1058.2	200811	896.24
200312	1111.92	200812	903.25
200401	1131.13	200901	825.88
200402	1144.94	200902	735.09
200403	1126.21	200903	797.87

(*continued*)

Table 11-1. (*continued*)

Date	Price	Date	Price
200404	1107.3	200904	872.81
200405	1120.68	200905	919.14
200406	1140.84	200906	919.32
200407	1101.72	200907	987.48
200408	1104.24	200908	1020.62
200409	1114.58	200909	1057.08
200410	1130.2	200910	1036.19
200411	1173.82	200911	1095.63
200412	1211.92	200912	1115.1

Figure 11-1 shows the chart of the historical monthly SPY prices.

Figure 11-1. *SPY monthly chart for the interval January 2000 to January 2009*

Notice that the input dataset includes the market prices during two market crashes, so the network should be able to learn the market behavior during those crashes. We already learned from the previous examples that to make predictions outside the training range, we need to transform the original data to a format that will allow us to do this. As part of this transformation, we create the price differences dataset with records that include two fields.

– *Field 1*: Percent difference between the current and previous month prices

– *Field 2*: Percent difference between the next and current month prices

Table 11-2 shows the transformed price differences dataset.

Table 11-2. *Price Differences Dataset*

Field 1	Field 2		
priceDiffPerc	targetPriceDiffPerc	Date	InputPrice
-5.090352221	-2.010814222	200001	1394.46
-2.010814222	9.671989579	200002	1366.42
9.671989579	-3.079582004	200003	1498.58
-3.079582004	-2.191499762	200004	1452.43
-2.191499762	2.39335492	200005	1420.6
2.39335492	-1.63412622	200006	1454.6
-1.63412622	6.069903483	200007	1430.83
6.069903483	-5.348294766	200008	1517.68
-5.348294766	-0.494949565	200009	1436.51
-0.494949565	-8.006856024	200010	1429.4
-8.006856024	0.405338606	200011	1314.95
0.405338606	3.463659224	200012	1320.28
3.463659224	-9.229068601	200101	1366.01
-9.229068601	-6.420471958	200102	1239.94

(*continued*)

Table 11-2. *(continued)*

Field 1	Field 2		
priceDiffPerc	targetPriceDiffPerc	Date	InputPrice
-6.420471958	7.681435454	200103	1160.33
7.681435454	0.509019897	200104	1249.46
0.509019897	-2.503543501	200105	1255.82
-2.503543501	-1.07401297	200106	1224.38
-1.07401297	-6.410838569	200107	1211.23
-6.410838569	-8.172338962	200108	1133.58
-8.172338962	1.809902588	200109	1040.94
1.809902588	7.517597992	200110	1059.78
7.517597992	0.757382948	200111	1139.45
0.757382948	-1.557382761	200112	1148.08
-1.557382761	-2.076623606	200201	1130.2
-2.076623606	3.673886133	200202	1106.73
3.673886133	-6.141765224	200203	1147.39
-6.141765224	-0.908145452	200204	1076.92
-0.908145452	-7.245534794	200205	1067.14
-7.245534794	-7.90042634	200206	989.82
-7.90042634	0.488141989	200207	911.62
0.488141989	-11.00243431	200208	916.07
-11.00243431	8.64488274	200209	815.28
8.64488274	5.706963512	200210	885.76
5.706963512	-6.033258216	200211	936.31
-6.033258216	-2.741469846	200212	879.82
-2.741469846	-1.700362276	200301	855.7
-1.700362276	0.835760566	200302	841.15
0.835760566	8.104411799	200303	848.18

(continued)

Table 11-2. *(continued)*

Field 1	Field 2		
priceDiffPerc	targetPriceDiffPerc	Date	InputPrice
8.104411799	5.089866073	200304	916.92
5.089866073	1.132224286	200305	963.59
1.132224286	1.622370446	200306	974.5
1.622370446	1.787319122	200307	990.31
1.787319122	-1.194432595	200308	1008.01
-1.194432595	5.496149482	200309	995.97
5.496149482	0.71285131	200310	1050.71
0.71285131	5.076545077	200311	1058.2
5.076545077	1.727642276	200312	1111.92
1.727642276	1.220902991	200401	1131.13
1.220902991	-1.635893584	200402	1144.94
-1.635893584	-1.679082942	200403	1126.21
-1.679082942	1.208344622	200404	1107.3
1.208344622	1.798907806	200405	1120.68
1.798907806	-3.429052277	200406	1140.84
-3.429052277	0.228733253	200407	1101.72
0.228733253	0.93639064	200408	1104.24
0.93639064	1.401424752	200409	1114.58
1.401424752	3.859493895	200410	1130.2
3.859493895	3.245812816	200411	1173.82
3.245812816	-2.529044821	200412	1211.92
-2.529044821	1.890338365	200501	1181.27
1.890338365	-1.911764706	200502	1203.6
-1.911764706	-2.010858977	200503	1180.59
-2.010858977	2.99520249	200504	1156.85

(continued)

Table 11-2. *(continued)*

Field 1	Field 2		
priceDiffPerc	targetPriceDiffPerc	Date	InputPrice
2.99520249	-0.01426773	200505	1191.5
-0.01426773	3.59682036	200506	1191.33
3.59682036	-1.122202596	200507	1234.18
-1.122202596	0.694894004	200508	1220.33
0.694894004	-1.774074104	200509	1228.81
-1.774074104	3.518612108	200510	1207.01
3.518612108	-0.09523962	200511	1249.48
-0.09523962	2.546683864	200512	1248.29
2.546683864	0.045309668	200601	1280.08
0.045309668	1.109584121	200602	1280.66
1.109584121	1.215566041	200603	1294.87
1.215566041	-3.091690129	200604	1310.61
-3.091690129	0.008660804	200605	1270.09
0.008660804	0.508581326	200606	1270.2
0.508581326	2.127426253	200607	1276.66
2.127426253	2.456627449	200608	1303.82
2.456627449	3.15080286	200609	1335.85
3.15080286	1.646660958	200610	1377.94
1.646660958	1.261575148	200611	1400.63
1.261575148	1.405908482	200612	1418.3
1.405908482	-2.184614529	200701	1438.24
-2.184614529	0.997995479	200702	1406.82
0.997995479	4.329068311	200703	1420.86
4.329068311	3.25492286	200704	1482.37

(continued)

Table 11-2. *(continued)*

Field 1	Field 2		
priceDiffPerc	targetPriceDiffPerc	Date	InputPrice
3.25492286	-1.781630973	200705	1530.62
-1.781630973	-3.198190707	200706	1503.35
-3.198190707	1.286359232	200707	1455.27
1.286359232	3.579400132	200708	1473.99
3.579400132	1.482233503	200709	1526.75
1.482233503	-4.404342382	200710	1549.38
-4.404342382	-0.862848887	200711	1481.14
-0.862848887	-6.11634749	200712	1468.36
-6.11634749	-3.476116209	200801	1378.55
-3.476116209	-0.595958305	200802	1330.63
-0.595958305	4.754668481	200803	1322.7
4.754668481	1.067415325	200804	1385.59
1.067415325	-8.596238164	200805	1400.38
-8.596238164	-0.9859375	200806	1280
-0.9859375	1.219050324	200807	1267.38
1.219050324	-9.079145327	200808	1282.83
-9.079145327	-16.94245344	200809	1166.36
-16.94245344	-7.484903226	200810	968.75
-7.484903226	0.782156565	200811	896.24
0.782156565	-8.565734846	200812	903.25
-8.565734846	-10.99312249	200901	825.88
-10.99312249	8.540450829	200902	735.09
8.540450829	9.392507551	200903	797.87
9.392507551	5.308142666	200904	872.81
5.308142666	0.019583524	200905	919.14

(continued)

465

Table 11-2. *(continued)*

Field 1	Field 2		
priceDiffPerc	targetPriceDiffPerc	Date	InputPrice
0.019583524	7.414175695	200906	919.32
7.414175695	3.356017337	200907	987.48
3.356017337	3.572338383	200908	1020.62
3.572338383	-1.976198585	200909	1057.08
-1.976198585	5.736399695	200910	1036.19
5.736399695	1.777059774	200911	1095.63
1.777059774	-3.69742624	200912	1115.1

Columns 3 and 4 are included to facilitate the calculation of columns 1 and 2, but they are ignored during processing. As always, we normalize this dataset on the interval [-1, 1]. Table 11-3 shows the normalized dataset.

Table 11-3. *Normalized Price Differences Dataset*

priceDiffPerc	targetPriceDiffPerc	Date	inputPrice
-0.006023481	0.199279052	200001	1394.46
0.199279052	0.978132639	200002	1366.42
0.978132639	0.128027866	200003	1498.58
0.128027866	0.187233349	200004	1452.43
0.187233349	0.492890328	200005	1420.6
0.492890328	0.224391585	200006	1454.6
0.224391585	0.737993566	200007	1430.83
0.737993566	-0.023219651	200008	1517.68
-0.023219651	0.300336696	200009	1436.51
0.300336696	-0.200457068	200010	1429.4
-0.200457068	0.360355907	200011	1314.95

(continued)

Table 11-3. (*continued*)

priceDiffPerc	targetPriceDiffPerc	Date	inputPrice
0.360355907	0.564243948	200012	1320.28
0.564243948	-0.281937907	200101	1366.01
-0.281937907	-0.094698131	200102	1239.94
-0.094698131	0.84542903	200103	1160.33
0.84542903	0.367267993	200104	1249.46
0.367267993	0.166430433	200105	1255.82
0.166430433	0.261732469	200106	1224.38
0.261732469	-0.094055905	200107	1211.23
-0.094055905	-0.211489264	200108	1133.58
-0.211489264	0.453993506	200109	1040.94
0.453993506	0.834506533	200110	1059.78
0.834506533	0.38382553	200111	1139.45
0.38382553	0.229507816	200112	1148.08
0.229507816	0.19489176	200201	1130.2
0.19489176	0.578259076	200202	1106.73
0.578259076	-0.076117682	200203	1147.39
-0.076117682	0.272790303	200204	1076.92
0.272790303	-0.14970232	200205	1067.14
-0.14970232	-0.193361756	200206	989.82
-0.193361756	0.365876133	200207	911.62
0.365876133	-0.400162287	200208	916.07
-0.400162287	0.909658849	200209	815.28
0.909658849	0.713797567	200210	885.76
0.713797567	-0.068883881	200211	936.31
-0.068883881	0.150568677	200212	879.82

(*continued*)

Table 11-3. (*continued*)

priceDiffPerc	targetPriceDiffPerc	Date	inputPrice
0.150568677	0.219975848	200301	855.7
0.219975848	0.389050704	200302	841.15
0.389050704	0.873627453	200303	848.18
0.873627453	0.672657738	200304	916.92
0.672657738	0.408814952	200305	963.59
0.408814952	0.441491363	200306	974.5
0.441491363	0.452487941	200307	990.31
0.452487941	0.253704494	200308	1008.01
0.253704494	0.699743299	200309	995.97
0.699743299	0.380856754	200310	1050.71
0.380856754	0.671769672	200311	1058.2
0.671769672	0.448509485	200312	1111.92
0.448509485	0.414726866	200401	1131.13
0.414726866	0.224273761	200402	1144.94
0.224273761	0.221394471	200403	1126.21
0.221394471	0.413889641	200404	1107.3
0.413889641	0.45326052	200405	1120.68
0.45326052	0.104729848	200406	1140.84
0.104729848	0.348582217	200407	1101.72
0.348582217	0.395759376	200408	1104.24
0.395759376	0.42676165	200409	1114.58
0.42676165	0.590632926	200410	1130.2
0.590632926	0.549720854	200411	1173.82
0.549720854	0.164730345	200412	1211.92
0.164730345	0.459355891	200501	1181.27

(*continued*)

Table 11-3. (*continued*)

priceDiffPerc	targetPriceDiffPerc	Date	inputPrice
0.459355891	0.205882353	200502	1203.6
0.205882353	0.199276068	200503	1180.59
0.199276068	0.533013499	200504	1156.85
0.533013499	0.332382151	200505	1191.5
0.332382151	0.573121357	200506	1191.33
0.573121357	0.258519827	200507	1234.18
0.258519827	0.3796596	200508	1220.33
0.3796596	0.215061726	200509	1228.81
0.215061726	0.567907474	200510	1207.01
0.567907474	0.326984025	200511	1249.48
0.326984025	0.503112258	200512	1248.29
0.503112258	0.336353978	200601	1280.08
0.336353978	0.407305608	200602	1280.66
0.407305608	0.414371069	200603	1294.87
0.414371069	0.127220658	200604	1310.61
0.127220658	0.33391072	200605	1270.09
0.33391072	0.367238755	200606	1270.2
0.367238755	0.47516175	200607	1276.66
0.47516175	0.497108497	200608	1303.82
0.497108497	0.543386857	200609	1335.85
0.543386857	0.443110731	200610	1377.94
0.443110731	0.417438343	200611	1400.63
0.417438343	0.427060565	200612	1418.3
0.427060565	0.187692365	200701	1438.24
0.187692365	0.399866365	200702	1406.82

(*continued*)

Table 11-3. (*continued*)

priceDiffPerc	targetPriceDiffPerc	Date	inputPrice
0.399866365	0.621937887	200703	1420.86
0.621937887	0.550328191	200704	1482.37
0.550328191	0.214557935	200705	1530.62
0.214557935	0.12012062	200706	1503.35
0.12012062	0.419090615	200707	1455.27
0.419090615	0.571960009	200708	1473.99
0.571960009	0.4321489	200709	1526.75
0.4321489	0.039710508	200710	1549.38
0.039710508	0.275810074	200711	1481.14
0.275810074	-0.074423166	200712	1468.36
-0.074423166	0.101592253	200801	1378.55
0.101592253	0.29360278	200802	1330.63
0.29360278	0.650311232	200803	1322.7
0.650311232	0.404494355	200804	1385.59
0.404494355	-0.239749211	200805	1400.38
-0.239749211	0.267604167	200806	1280
0.267604167	0.414603355	200807	1267.38
0.414603355	-0.271943022	200808	1282.83
-0.271943022	-0.796163563	200809	1166.36
-0.796163563	-0.165660215	200810	968.75
-0.165660215	0.385477104	200811	896.24
0.385477104	-0.237715656	200812	903.25
-0.237715656	-0.399541499	200901	825.88
-0.399541499	0.902696722	200902	735.09
0.902696722	0.959500503	200903	797.87

(*continued*)

Table 11-3. (*continued*)

priceDiffPerc	targetPriceDiffPerc	Date	inputPrice
0.959500503	0.687209511	200904	872.81
0.687209511	0.334638902	200905	919.14
0.334638902	0.827611713	200906	919.32
0.827611713	0.557067822	200907	987.48
0.557067822	0.571489226	200908	1020.62
0.571489226	0.201586761	200909	1057.08
0.201586761	0.71575998	200910	1036.19
0.71575998	0.451803985	200911	1095.63
0.451803985	0.086838251	200912	1115.1

Again, ignore columns 3 and 4. They are used here for our convention of preparing this dataset, but they are not processed.

Including the Function Topology in the Dataset

Next, we want to include information about the function topology in the dataset, because it allows matching not only a single Field1 value but the set of 12 Field1 values (which means matching one year of data). To do this, we build the training file with the sliding window records. Each sliding window record consists of 12 `inputPriceDiffPerc` fields from 12 original records plus the `targetPriceDiffPerc` field from the next original record (the record that follows the original record 12). Listing 11-1 shows the resulting dataset.

Listing 11-1. *Training Dataset That Consists of Sliding Window Records*

Sliding Windows

0.723	0.724	0.623	0.854	-0.050	0.688	0.103	0.631	0.438	0.401	0.803	0.666	0.208
0.724	0.623	0.854	-0.050	0.688	0.103	0.631	0.438	0.401	0.803	0.666	0.394	0.596
0.623	0.854	-0.050	0.688	0.103	0.631	0.438	0.401	0.803	0.666	0.394	0.208	0.256
0.854	-0.050	0.688	0.103	0.631	0.438	0.401	0.803	0.666	0.394	0.208	0.596	-0.639
-0.050	0.688	0.103	0.631	0.438	0.401	0.803	0.666	0.394	0.208	0.596	0.256	0.749
0.688	0.103	0.631	0.438	0.401	0.803	0.666	0.394	0.208	0.596	0.256	-0.639	0.869
0.103	0.631	0.438	0.401	0.803	0.666	0.394	0.208	0.596	0.256	-0.639	0.749	0.728
0.631	0.438	0.401	0.803	0.666	0.394	0.208	0.596	0.256	-0.639	0.749	0.869	0.709
0.438	0.401	0.803	0.666	0.394	0.208	0.596	0.256	-0.639	0.749	0.869	0.728	0.607
0.401	0.803	0.666	0.394	0.208	0.596	0.256	-0.639	0.749	0.869	0.728	0.709	0.118
0.803	0.666	0.394	0.208	0.596	0.256	-0.639	0.749	0.869	0.728	0.709	0.607	0.592
0.666	0.394	0.208	0.596	0.256	-0.639	0.749	0.869	0.728	0.709	0.607	0.118	0.586
0.394	0.208	0.596	0.256	-0.639	0.749	0.869	0.728	0.709	0.607	0.118	0.592	0.167
0.208	0.596	0.256	-0.639	0.749	0.869	0.728	0.709	0.607	0.118	0.592	0.586	0.696
0.596	0.256	-0.639	0.749	0.869	0.728	0.709	0.607	0.118	0.592	0.586	0.167	0.120
0.256	-0.639	0.749	0.869	0.728	0.709	0.607	0.118	0.592	0.586	0.167	0.696	0.292
-0.639	0.749	0.869	0.728	0.709	0.607	0.118	0.592	0.586	0.167	0.696	0.120	0.143
0.749	0.869	0.728	0.709	0.607	0.118	0.592	0.586	0.167	0.696	0.120	0.292	0.750

0.869	0.728	0.709	0.607	0.118	0.592	0.586	0.167	0.696	0.120	0.292	0.143	0.460
0.728	0.709	0.607	0.118	0.592	0.586	0.167	0.696	0.120	0.292	0.143	0.750	0.719
0.709	0.607	0.118	0.592	0.586	0.167	0.696	0.120	0.292	0.143	0.750	0.460	-0.006
0.607	0.118	0.592	0.586	0.167	0.696	0.120	0.292	0.143	0.750	0.460	0.719	0.199
0.118	0.592	0.586	0.167	0.696	0.120	0.292	0.143	0.750	0.460	0.719	-0.006	0.978
0.592	0.586	0.167	0.696	0.120	0.292	0.143	0.750	0.460	0.719	-0.006	0.199	0.128
0.586	0.167	0.696	0.120	0.292	0.143	0.750	0.460	0.719	-0.006	0.199	0.978	0.187
0.167	0.696	0.120	0.292	0.143	0.750	0.460	0.719	-0.006	0.199	0.978	0.128	0.493
0.696	0.120	0.292	0.143	0.750	0.460	0.719	-0.006	0.199	0.978	0.128	0.187	0.224
0.120	0.292	0.143	0.750	0.460	0.719	-0.006	0.199	0.978	0.128	0.187	0.493	0.738
0.292	0.143	0.750	0.460	0.719	-0.006	0.199	0.978	0.128	0.187	0.493	0.224	-0.023
0.143	0.750	0.460	0.719	-0.006	0.199	0.978	0.128	0.187	0.493	0.224	0.738	0.300
0.750	0.460	0.719	-0.006	0.199	0.978	0.128	0.187	0.493	0.224	0.738	-0.023	-0.200
0.460	0.719	-0.006	0.199	0.978	0.128	0.187	0.493	0.224	0.738	-0.023	0.300	0.360
0.719	-0.006	0.199	0.978	0.128	0.187	0.493	0.224	0.738	-0.023	0.300	-0.200	0.564
-0.006	0.199	0.978	0.128	0.187	0.493	0.224	0.738	-0.023	0.300	-0.200	0.360	-0.282
0.199	0.978	0.128	0.187	0.493	0.224	0.738	-0.023	0.300	-0.200	0.360	0.564	-0.095
0.978	0.128	0.187	0.493	0.224	0.738	-0.023	0.300	-0.200	0.360	0.564	-0.282	0.845
0.128	0.187	0.493	0.224	0.738	-0.023	0.300	-0.200	0.360	0.564	-0.282	-0.095	0.367

(continued)

Listing 11-1. (*continued*)

Sliding Windows

0.187	0.493	0.224	0.738	-0.023	0.300	-0.200	0.360	0.564	-0.282	-0.095	0.845	0.367	0.166
0.493	0.224	0.738	-0.023	0.300	-0.200	0.360	0.564	-0.282	-0.095	0.845	0.367	0.166	0.262
0.224	0.738	-0.023	0.300	-0.200	0.360	0.564	-0.282	-0.095	0.845	0.367	0.166	0.262	-0.094
0.738	-0.023	0.300	-0.200	0.360	0.564	-0.282	-0.095	0.845	0.367	0.166	0.262	-0.094	-0.211
-0.023	0.300	-0.200	0.360	0.564	-0.282	-0.095	0.845	0.367	0.166	0.262	-0.094	-0.211	0.454
0.300	-0.200	0.360	0.564	-0.282	-0.095	0.845	0.367	0.166	0.262	-0.094	-0.211	0.454	0.835
-0.200	0.360	0.564	-0.282	-0.095	0.845	0.367	0.166	0.262	-0.094	-0.211	0.454	0.835	0.384
0.360	0.564	-0.282	-0.095	0.845	0.367	0.166	0.262	-0.094	-0.211	0.454	0.835	0.384	0.230
0.564	-0.282	-0.095	0.845	0.367	0.166	0.262	-0.094	-0.211	0.454	0.835	0.384	0.230	0.195
-0.282	-0.095	0.845	0.367	0.166	0.262	-0.094	-0.211	0.454	0.835	0.384	0.230	0.195	0.578
-0.095	0.845	0.367	0.166	0.262	-0.094	-0.211	0.454	0.835	0.384	0.230	0.195	0.578	-0.076
0.845	0.367	0.166	0.262	-0.094	-0.211	0.454	0.835	0.384	0.230	0.195	0.578	-0.076	0.273
0.367	0.166	0.262	-0.094	-0.211	0.454	0.835	0.384	0.230	0.195	0.578	-0.076	0.273	-0.150
0.166	0.262	-0.094	-0.211	0.454	0.835	0.384	0.230	0.195	0.578	-0.076	0.273	-0.150	-0.193
0.262	-0.094	-0.211	0.454	0.835	0.384	0.230	0.195	0.578	-0.076	0.273	-0.150	-0.193	0.366
-0.094	-0.211	0.454	0.835	0.384	0.230	0.195	0.578	-0.076	0.273	-0.150	-0.193	0.366	-0.400
-0.211	0.454	0.835	0.384	0.230	0.195	0.578	-0.076	0.273	-0.150	-0.193	0.366	-0.400	0.910
0.454	0.835	0.384	0.230	0.195	0.578	-0.076	0.273	-0.150	-0.193	0.366	-0.400	0.910	0.714

0.835	0.384	0.230	0.195	0.578	-0.076	0.273	-0.150	-0.193	0.366	-0.400	0.910	0.714	-0.069
0.384	0.230	0.195	0.578	-0.076	0.273	-0.150	-0.193	0.366	-0.400	0.910	0.714	-0.069	0.151
0.230	0.195	0.578	-0.076	0.273	-0.150	-0.193	0.366	-0.400	0.910	0.714	-0.069	0.151	0.220
0.195	0.578	-0.076	0.273	-0.150	-0.193	0.366	-0.400	0.910	0.714	-0.069	0.151	0.220	0.389
0.578	-0.076	0.273	-0.150	-0.193	0.366	-0.400	0.910	0.714	-0.069	0.151	0.220	0.389	0.874
-0.076	0.273	-0.150	-0.193	0.366	-0.400	0.910	0.714	-0.069	0.151	0.220	0.389	0.874	0.673
0.273	-0.150	-0.193	0.366	-0.400	0.910	0.714	-0.069	0.151	0.220	0.389	0.874	0.673	0.409
-0.150	-0.193	0.366	-0.400	0.910	0.714	-0.069	0.151	0.220	0.389	0.874	0.673	0.409	0.441
-0.193	0.366	-0.400	0.910	0.714	-0.069	0.151	0.220	0.389	0.874	0.673	0.409	0.441	0.452
0.366	-0.400	0.910	0.714	-0.069	0.151	0.220	0.389	0.874	0.673	0.409	0.441	0.452	0.254
-0.400	0.910	0.714	-0.069	0.151	0.220	0.389	0.874	0.673	0.409	0.441	0.452	0.254	0.700
0.910	0.714	-0.069	0.151	0.220	0.389	0.874	0.673	0.409	0.441	0.452	0.254	0.700	0.381
0.714	-0.069	0.151	0.220	0.389	0.874	0.673	0.409	0.441	0.452	0.254	0.700	0.381	0.672
-0.069	0.151	0.220	0.389	0.874	0.673	0.409	0.441	0.452	0.254	0.700	0.381	0.672	0.449
0.151	0.220	0.389	0.874	0.673	0.409	0.441	0.452	0.254	0.700	0.381	0.672	0.449	0.415
0.220	0.389	0.874	0.673	0.409	0.441	0.452	0.254	0.700	0.381	0.672	0.449	0.415	0.224
0.389	0.874	0.673	0.409	0.441	0.452	0.254	0.700	0.381	0.672	0.449	0.415	0.224	0.221
0.874	0.673	0.409	0.441	0.452	0.254	0.700	0.381	0.672	0.449	0.415	0.224	0.221	0.414
0.673	0.409	0.441	0.452	0.254	0.700	0.381	0.672	0.449	0.415	0.224	0.221	0.414	0.453

(continued)

Listing 11-1. (continued)

Sliding Windows

0.409	0.441	0.452	0.254	0.700	0.381	0.672	0.449	0.415	0.224	0.221	0.414	0.453	0.105
0.441	0.452	0.254	0.700	0.381	0.672	0.449	0.415	0.224	0.221	0.414	0.453	0.105	0.349
0.452	0.254	0.700	0.381	0.672	0.449	0.415	0.224	0.221	0.414	0.453	0.105	0.349	0.396
0.254	0.700	0.381	0.672	0.449	0.415	0.224	0.221	0.414	0.453	0.105	0.349	0.396	0.427
0.700	0.381	0.672	0.449	0.415	0.224	0.221	0.414	0.453	0.105	0.349	0.396	0.427	0.591
0.381	0.672	0.449	0.415	0.224	0.221	0.414	0.453	0.105	0.349	0.396	0.427	0.591	0.550
0.672	0.449	0.415	0.224	0.221	0.414	0.453	0.105	0.349	0.396	0.427	0.591	0.550	0.165
0.449	0.415	0.224	0.221	0.414	0.453	0.105	0.349	0.396	0.427	0.591	0.550	0.165	0.459
0.415	0.224	0.221	0.414	0.453	0.105	0.349	0.396	0.427	0.591	0.550	0.165	0.459	0.206
0.224	0.221	0.414	0.453	0.105	0.349	0.396	0.427	0.591	0.550	0.165	0.459	0.206	0.199
0.221	0.414	0.453	0.105	0.349	0.396	0.427	0.591	0.550	0.165	0.459	0.206	0.199	0.533
0.414	0.453	0.105	0.349	0.396	0.427	0.591	0.550	0.165	0.459	0.206	0.199	0.533	0.332
0.453	0.105	0.349	0.396	0.427	0.591	0.550	0.165	0.459	0.206	0.199	0.533	0.332	0.573
0.105	0.349	0.396	0.427	0.591	0.550	0.165	0.459	0.206	0.199	0.533	0.332	0.573	0.259
0.349	0.396	0.427	0.591	0.550	0.165	0.459	0.206	0.199	0.533	0.332	0.573	0.259	0.380
0.396	0.427	0.591	0.550	0.165	0.459	0.206	0.199	0.533	0.332	0.573	0.259	0.380	0.215
0.427	0.591	0.550	0.165	0.459	0.206	0.199	0.533	0.332	0.573	0.259	0.380	0.215	0.568
0.591	0.550	0.165	0.459	0.206	0.199	0.533	0.332	0.573	0.259	0.380	0.215	0.568	0.327
0.550	0.165	0.459	0.206	0.199	0.533	0.332	0.573	0.259	0.380	0.215	0.568	0.327	0.503

0.165	0.459	0.206	0.199	0.533	0.332	0.573	0.259	0.380	0.215	0.568	0.327	0.503	0.336
0.459	0.206	0.199	0.533	0.332	0.573	0.259	0.380	0.215	0.568	0.327	0.503	0.336	0.407
0.206	0.199	0.533	0.332	0.573	0.259	0.380	0.215	0.568	0.327	0.503	0.336	0.407	0.414
0.199	0.533	0.332	0.573	0.259	0.380	0.215	0.568	0.327	0.503	0.336	0.407	0.414	0.127
0.533	0.332	0.573	0.259	0.380	0.215	0.568	0.327	0.503	0.336	0.407	0.414	0.127	0.334
0.332	0.573	0.259	0.380	0.215	0.568	0.327	0.503	0.336	0.407	0.414	0.127	0.334	0.367
0.573	0.259	0.380	0.215	0.568	0.327	0.503	0.336	0.407	0.414	0.127	0.334	0.367	0.475
0.259	0.380	0.215	0.568	0.327	0.503	0.336	0.407	0.414	0.127	0.334	0.367	0.475	0.497
0.380	0.215	0.568	0.327	0.503	0.336	0.407	0.414	0.127	0.334	0.367	0.475	0.497	0.543
0.215	0.568	0.327	0.503	0.336	0.407	0.414	0.127	0.334	0.367	0.475	0.497	0.543	0.443
0.568	0.327	0.503	0.336	0.407	0.414	0.127	0.334	0.367	0.475	0.497	0.543	0.443	0.417
0.327	0.503	0.336	0.407	0.414	0.127	0.334	0.367	0.475	0.497	0.543	0.443	0.417	0.427
0.503	0.336	0.407	0.414	0.127	0.334	0.367	0.475	0.497	0.543	0.443	0.417	0.427	0.188
0.336	0.407	0.414	0.127	0.334	0.367	0.475	0.497	0.543	0.443	0.417	0.427	0.188	0.400
0.407	0.414	0.127	0.334	0.367	0.475	0.497	0.543	0.443	0.417	0.427	0.188	0.400	0.622
0.414	0.127	0.334	0.367	0.475	0.497	0.543	0.443	0.417	0.427	0.188	0.400	0.622	0.550
0.127	0.334	0.367	0.475	0.497	0.543	0.443	0.417	0.427	0.188	0.400	0.622	0.550	0.215
0.334	0.367	0.475	0.497	0.543	0.443	0.417	0.427	0.188	0.400	0.622	0.550	0.215	0.120
0.367	0.475	0.497	0.543	0.443	0.417	0.427	0.188	0.400	0.622	0.550	0.215	0.120	0.419

(continued)

Listing 11-1. *(continued)*

				Sliding Windows								
0.475	0.497	0.543	0.443	0.417	0.427	0.188	0.400	0.622	0.550	0.215	0.120	0.572
0.497	0.543	0.443	0.417	0.427	0.188	0.400	0.622	0.550	0.215	0.120	0.419	0.432
0.543	0.443	0.417	0.427	0.188	0.400	0.622	0.550	0.215	0.120	0.419	0.572	0.040
0.443	0.417	0.427	0.188	0.400	0.622	0.550	0.215	0.120	0.419	0.572	0.432	0.276
0.417	0.427	0.188	0.400	0.622	0.550	0.215	0.120	0.419	0.572	0.432	0.040	-0.074
0.427	0.188	0.400	0.622	0.550	0.215	0.120	0.419	0.572	0.432	0.040	0.276	0.102
0.188	0.400	0.622	0.550	0.215	0.120	0.419	0.572	0.432	0.040	0.276	-0.074	0.294
0.400	0.622	0.550	0.215	0.120	0.419	0.572	0.432	0.040	0.276	-0.074	0.102	0.650

Because the function is noncontinuous, we break this dataset into micro-batches (single month records).

Building Micro-Batch Files

Listing 11-2 shows the program code that builds micro-batch files from the normalized sliding window dataset.

Listing 11-2. Program Code That Builds the Micro-Batch File

```
// =============================================================
// Build micro-batch files from the normalized sliding windows file.
// Each micro-batch dataset should consists of 12 inputPriceDiffPerc fields
// taken from 12 records in the original file plus a single
targetPriceDiffPerc
// value taken from the next month record. Each micro-batch includes the label
// record.
// =============================================================

package sample7_build_microbatches;

import java.io.BufferedReader;
import java.io.BufferedWriter;
import java.io.File;
import java.io.FileInputStream;
import java.io.PrintWriter;
import java.io.FileNotFoundException;
import java.io.FileReader;
import java.io.FileWriter;
import java.io.IOException;
import java.io.InputStream;
import java.nio.file.*;
import java.util.Properties;
```

```java
public class Sample7_Build_MicroBatches
 {

    // Config for Training
    static int numberOfRowsInInputFile = 121;
    static int numberOfRowsInBatch = 13;
    static String  strInputFileName =
      "C:/My_Neural_Network_Book/Book_Examples/Sample7_SlidWindows_Train.csv";
    static String  strOutputFileNameBase =
      "C:/My_Neural_Network_Book/Temp_Files/Sample7_Microbatches_Train_Batch_";

    // Config for Testing
    //static int numberOfRowsInInputFile = 122;
    //static int numberOfRowsInBatch = 13;
    //static String  strInputFileName =
    //     "C:/My_Neural_Network_Book/Book_Examples/Sample7_SlidWindows_
           Test.csv";
    //static String  strOutputFileNameBase =
    //     "C:/My_Neural_Network_Book/Temp_Files/Sample7_Microbatches_Test_Batch_";

    static InputStream input = null;

    // ====================================================================
    // Main method
    // ====================================================================
    public static void main(String[] args)
     {
        BufferedReader br;
        PrintWriter out;
        String cvsSplitBy = ",";
        String line = "";
        String lineLabel = "";
        String[] strOutputFileNames = new String[1070];
        String iString;
        String strOutputFileName;
        String[] strArrLine = new String[1086];

        int i;
```

```java
int r;

// Read the original data and brake it into batches

try
 {
   // Delete all output file if they exist

   for (i = 0; i < numberOfRowsInInputFile; i++)
    {
      iString = Integer.toString(i);

      if(i < 10)
         strOutputFileName = strOutputFileNameBase + "00" + iString
         + ".csv";
      else
         if (i >= 10 && i < 100)
            strOutputFileName = strOutputFileNameBase + "0" +
            iString + ".csv";
          else
            strOutputFileName = strOutputFileNameBase + iString + ".csv";

      Files.deleteIfExists(Paths.get(strOutputFileName));
    }

   i = -1;    // Input line number
   r = -2;    // index to write in the memory
   br = new BufferedReader(new FileReader(strInputFileName));

   // Load all input recoeds into memory
   while ((line = br.readLine()) != null)
    {
      i++;
      r++;
      if (i == 0)
       {
         // Save the label line
         lineLabel = line;
       }
```

```java
        else
         {
            // Save the data in memory
            strArrLine[r] = line;
         }

      }  // End of WHILE

   br.close();

   // Build batches
   br = new BufferedReader(new FileReader(strInputFileName));

  for (i = 0; i < numberOfRowsInInputFile - 1; i++)
    {
      iString = Integer.toString(i);

      // Construct the mini-batch
       if(i < 10)
          strOutputFileName = strOutputFileNameBase + "00" + iString
          + ".csv";
      else
         if (i >= 10 && i < 100)
            strOutputFileName = strOutputFileNameBase + "0" +
            iString + ".csv";
          else
           strOutputFileName = strOutputFileNameBase + iString + ".csv";

      out = new PrintWriter(new BufferedWriter(new FileWriter
      (strOutputFileName)));

      // write the header line as it is
      out.println(lineLabel);
      out.println(strArrLine[i]);

      out.close();

    }  // End of FOR i loop

  }  // End of TRY
```

```
    catch (IOException io)
    {
        io.printStackTrace();
    }

  }  // End of the Main method

}  // End of the class
```

This program breaks the sliding windows dataset into micro-batch files. Figure 11-2 shows a fragment of the list of micro-batch files.

Figure 11-2. *Fragment of the list of micro-batch files*

Listing 11-3 shows how each micro-batch dataset looks when it is opened.

Listing 11-3. Sample of the Micro-Batch File

Sliding window micro-batch record

```
-0.006023481 0.199279052 0.978132639 0.128027866 0.187233349 0.492890328
0.224391585 0.737993566 -0.023219651 0.300336696 -0.200457068 0.360355907
-0.281937907
```

Micro-batch files are the training files to be processed by the network.

Network Architecture

Figure 11-3 shows the network architecture for this example. The network has 12 input neurons, seven hidden layers (each has 25 neurons), and the single output-layer neuron.

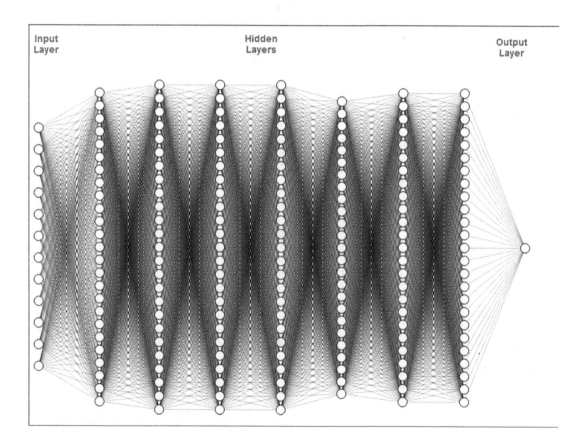

Figure 11-3. *Network architecture*

Now we are ready to build the network processing program.

Program Code

Listing 11-4 shows the program code.

Listing 11-4. Code of the Neural Network Processing Program

```
// =================================================================
// Approximate the SPY prices function using the micro-batch method.
// Each micro-batch file includes the label record and the data record.
// The data record contains 12 inputPriceDiffPerc fields plus one
// targetPriceDiffPerc field.
//
// The number of inputLayer neurons is 12
// The number of outputLayer neurons is 1
// =================================================================

package saple7;

import java.io.BufferedReader;
import java.io.File;
import java.io.FileInputStream;
import java.io.PrintWriter;
import java.io.FileNotFoundException;
import java.io.FileReader;
import java.io.FileWriter;
import java.io.IOException;
import java.io.InputStream;
import java.nio.file.*;
import java.util.Properties;
import java.time.YearMonth;
import java.awt.Color;
import java.awt.Font;
import java.io.BufferedReader;
import java.io.BufferedWriter;
```

```java
import java.text.DateFormat;
import java.text.ParseException;
import java.text.SimpleDateFormat;
import java.time.LocalDate;
import java.time.Month;
import java.time.ZoneId;
import java.util.ArrayList;
import java.util.Calendar;
import java.util.Date;
import java.util.List;
import java.util.Locale;
import java.util.Properties;
import org.encog.Encog;
import org.encog.engine.network.activation.ActivationTANH;
import org.encog.engine.network.activation.ActivationReLU;
import org.encog.ml.data.MLData;
import org.encog.ml.data.MLDataPair;
import org.encog.ml.data.MLDataSet;
import org.encog.ml.data.buffer.MemoryDataLoader;
import org.encog.ml.data.buffer.codec.CSVDataCODEC;
import org.encog.ml.data.buffer.codec.DataSetCODEC;
import org.encog.neural.networks.BasicNetwork;
import org.encog.neural.networks.layers.BasicLayer;
import org.encog.neural.networks.training.propagation.resilient.
ResilientPropagation;
import org.encog.persist.EncogDirectoryPersistence;
import org.encog.util.csv.CSVFormat;

import org.knowm.xchart.SwingWrapper;
import org.knowm.xchart.XYChart;
import org.knowm.xchart.XYChartBuilder;
import org.knowm.xchart.XYSeries;
import org.knowm.xchart.demo.charts.ExampleChart;
import org.knowm.xchart.style.Styler.LegendPosition;
import org.knowm.xchart.style.colors.ChartColor;
import org.knowm.xchart.style.colors.XChartSeriesColors;
```

```java
import org.knowm.xchart.style.lines.SeriesLines;
import org.knowm.xchart.style.markers.SeriesMarkers;
import org.knowm.xchart.BitmapEncoder;
import org.knowm.xchart.BitmapEncoder.BitmapFormat;
import org.knowm.xchart.QuickChart;
import org.knowm.xchart.SwingWrapper;

public class Saple7 implements ExampleChart<XYChart>
{
    // Normalization parameters

    // Normalizing interval
    static double Nh =  1;
    static double Nl = -1;

    // inputPriceDiffPerc
    static double inputPriceDiffPercDh = 10.00;
    static double inputPriceDiffPercDl = -20.00;

    // targetPriceDiffPerc
    static double targetPriceDiffPercDh = 10.00;
    static double targetPriceDiffPercDl = -20.00;

    static String cvsSplitBy = ",";
    static Properties prop = null;
    static Date workDate = null;
    static int paramErrorCode = 0;
    static int paramBatchNumber = 0;
    static int paramDayNumber = 0;
    static String strWorkingMode;
    static String strNumberOfBatchesToProcess;
    static String strNumberOfRowsInInputFile;
    static String strNumberOfRowsInBatches;
    static String strIputNeuronNumber;
    static String strOutputNeuronNumber;
    static String strNumberOfRecordsInTestFile;
    static String strInputFileNameBase;
    static String strTestFileNameBase;
```

```
static String strSaveNetworkFileNameBase;
static String strTrainFileName;
static String strValidateFileName;
static String strChartFileName;
static String strDatesTrainFileName;
static String strPricesFileName;
static int intWorkingMode;
static int intNumberOfBatchesToProcess;
static int intNumberOfRowsInBatches;
static int intInputNeuronNumber;
static int intOutputNeuronNumber;
static String strOutputFileName;
static String strSaveNetworkFileName;
static String strNumberOfMonths;
static String strYearMonth;
static XYChart Chart;
static String iString;
static double inputPriceFromFile;

//static List<Date> xData = new ArrayList<Date>();
static List<Double> xData = new ArrayList<Double>();
static List<Double> yData1 = new ArrayList<Double>();
static List<Double> yData2 = new ArrayList<Double>();

// These arrays is where the two Date files are loaded
static Date[] yearDateTraining = new Date[150];
static String[] strTrainingFileNames = new String[150];
static String[] strTestingFileNames = new String[150];
static String[] strSaveNetworkFileNames = new String[150];

static BufferedReader br3;

static double recordNormInputPriceDiffPerc_00 = 0.00;
static double recordNormInputPriceDiffPerc_01 = 0.00;
static double recordNormInputPriceDiffPerc_02 = 0.00;
static double recordNormInputPriceDiffPerc_03 = 0.00;
static double recordNormInputPriceDiffPerc_04 = 0.00;
```

```
static double recordNormInputPriceDiffPerc_05 = 0.00;
static double recordNormInputPriceDiffPerc_06 = 0.00;
static double recordNormInputPriceDiffPerc_07 = 0.00;
static double recordNormInputPriceDiffPerc_08 = 0.00;
static double recordNormInputPriceDiffPerc_09 = 0.00;
static double recordNormInputPriceDiffPerc_10 = 0.00;
static double recordNormInputPriceDiffPerc_11 = 0.00;

static double recordNormTargetPriceDiffPerc = 0.00;
static double tempMonth = 0.00;
static int intNumberOfSavedNetworks = 0;

static double[] linkToSaveInputPriceDiffPerc_00 = new double[150];
static double[] linkToSaveInputPriceDiffPerc_01 = new double[150];
static double[] linkToSaveInputPriceDiffPerc_02 = new double[150];
static double[] linkToSaveInputPriceDiffPerc_03 = new double[150];
static double[] linkToSaveInputPriceDiffPerc_04 = new double[150];
static double[] linkToSaveInputPriceDiffPerc_05 = new double[150];
static double[] linkToSaveInputPriceDiffPerc_06 = new double[150];
static double[] linkToSaveInputPriceDiffPerc_07 = new double[150];
static double[] linkToSaveInputPriceDiffPerc_08 = new double[150];
static double[] linkToSaveInputPriceDiffPerc_09 = new double[150];
static double[] linkToSaveInputPriceDiffPerc_10 = new double[150];
static double[] linkToSaveInputPriceDiffPerc_11 = new double[150];

static int[] returnCodes  = new int[3];
static int intDayNumber = 0;
static File file2 = null;
static double[] linkToSaveTargetPriceDiffPerc = new double[150];
static double[] arrPrices = new double[150];

@Override
public XYChart getChart()
 {

  // Create Chart
```

```
Chart = new XYChartBuilder().width(900).height(500).title(getClass().
getSimpleName()).xAxisTitle("Month").yAxisTitle("Price").build();

// Customize Chart
Chart.getStyler().setPlotBackgroundColor(ChartColor.
getAWTColor(ChartColor.GREY));
Chart.getStyler().setPlotGridLinesColor(new Color(255, 255, 255));
Chart.getStyler().setChartBackgroundColor(Color.WHITE);
Chart.getStyler().setLegendBackgroundColor(Color.PINK);
Chart.getStyler().setChartFontColor(Color.MAGENTA);
Chart.getStyler().setChartTitleBoxBackgroundColor(new Color(0, 222, 0));
Chart.getStyler().setChartTitleBoxVisible(true);
Chart.getStyler().setChartTitleBoxBorderColor(Color.BLACK);
Chart.getStyler().setPlotGridLinesVisible(true);
Chart.getStyler().setAxisTickPadding(20);
Chart.getStyler().setAxisTickMarkLength(15);
Chart.getStyler().setPlotMargin(20);
Chart.getStyler().setChartTitleVisible(false);
Chart.getStyler().setChartTitleFont(new Font(Font.MONOSPACED, Font.
BOLD, 24));
Chart.getStyler().setLegendFont(new Font(Font.SERIF, Font.PLAIN, 18));
// Chart.getStyler().setLegendPosition(LegendPosition.InsideSE);
Chart.getStyler().setLegendPosition(LegendPosition.OutsideE);
Chart.getStyler().setLegendSeriesLineLength(12);
Chart.getStyler().setAxisTitleFont(new Font(Font.SANS_SERIF, Font.
ITALIC, 18));
Chart.getStyler().setAxisTickLabelsFont(new Font(Font.SERIF, Font.
PLAIN, 11));
Chart.getStyler().setDatePattern("yyyy-MM");
Chart.getStyler().setDecimalPattern("#0.00");

// Training configuration
intWorkingMode = 0;
intNumberOfBatchesToProcess = 120;
strInputFileNameBase =
 "C:/My_Neural_Network_Book/Temp_Files/Sample7_Microbatches_Train_Batch_";
```

```
strSaveNetworkFileNameBase =
 "C:/My_Neural_Network_Book/Temp_Files/Sample7_Save_Network_Batch_";
strChartFileName = "C:/My_Neural_Network_Book/Temp_Files/Sample7
_XYLineChart_Train.jpg";
strDatesTrainFileName =
    "C:/My_Neural_Network_Book/Book_Examples/Sample7_Dates_Real
    _SP500_3000.csv";
strPricesFileName =
    "C:/My_Neural_Network_Book/Book_Examples/Sample7_InputPrice_SP500
    _200001_200901.csv";

// Testing configuration
//intWorkingMode = 1;
//intNumberOfBatchesToProcess = 121;
//intNumberOfSavedNetworks = 120;
//strInputFileNameBase =
 "C:/My_Neural_Network_Book/Temp_Files/Sample7_Microbatches_Test_Batch_";
//strSaveNetworkFileNameBase =
    "C:/My_Neural_Network_Book/Temp_Files/Sample7_Save_Network_Batch_";
//strChartFileName =
    "C:/My_Neural_Network_Book/Book_Examples/Sample7_XYLineChart_Test.jpg";
//strDatesTrainFileName =
    "C:/My_Neural_Network_Book/Book_Examples/Sample7_Dates_Real
    _SP500_3000.csv";
//strPricesFileName =
    "C:/My_Neural_Network_Book/Book_Examples/Sample7_InputPrice_SP500
    _200001_200901.csv";

// Common configuration
intNumberOfRowsInBatches = 1;
intInputNeuronNumber = 12;
intOutputNeuronNumber = 1;

// Generate training batch file names and the corresponding SaveNetwork
file names and
// save them arrays
for (int i = 0; i < intNumberOfBatchesToProcess; i++)
```

```java
  {
    iString = Integer.toString(i);

    // Construct the training batch names
    if (i < 10)
     {
       strOutputFileName = strInputFileNameBase + "00" + iString + ".csv";
       strSaveNetworkFileName = strSaveNetworkFileNameBase + "00" +
       iString + ".csv";
     }
    else
     {
       if(i >=10 && i < 100)
        {
         strOutputFileName = strInputFileNameBase + "0" + iString + ".csv";
         strSaveNetworkFileName = strSaveNetworkFileNameBase + "0" +
         iString + ".csv";
        }
       else
        {
          strOutputFileName = strInputFileNameBase + iString + ".csv";
          strSaveNetworkFileName = strSaveNetworkFileNameBase + iString
          + ".csv";
        }

     }

  strSaveNetworkFileNames[i] = strSaveNetworkFileName;

  if(intWorkingMode == 0)
   {
     strTrainingFileNames[i] = strOutputFileName;

     File file1 = new File(strSaveNetworkFileNames[i]);

     if(file1.exists())
         file1.delete();
   }
```

```
  else
   strTestingFileNames[i] = strOutputFileName;

}  // End the FOR loop

 // Build the array linkToSaveInputPriceDiffPerc_01
 String tempLine = null;
 String[] tempWorkFields = null;

 recordNormInputPriceDiffPerc_00 = 0.00;
 recordNormInputPriceDiffPerc_01 = 0.00;
 recordNormInputPriceDiffPerc_02 = 0.00;
 recordNormInputPriceDiffPerc_03 = 0.00;
 recordNormInputPriceDiffPerc_04 = 0.00;
 recordNormInputPriceDiffPerc_05 = 0.00;
 recordNormInputPriceDiffPerc_06 = 0.00;
 recordNormInputPriceDiffPerc_07 = 0.00;
 recordNormInputPriceDiffPerc_08 = 0.00;
 recordNormInputPriceDiffPerc_09 = 0.00;
 recordNormInputPriceDiffPerc_10 = 0.00;
 recordNormInputPriceDiffPerc_11 = 0.00;

 double recordNormTargetPriceDiffPerc = 0.00;

 try
  {
     for (int m = 0; m < intNumberOfBatchesToProcess; m++)
       {
           if(intWorkingMode == 0)
             br3 = new BufferedReader(new FileReader(strTrainingFileNam
             es[m]));

           if(intWorkingMode == 1)
            br3 = new BufferedReader(new FileReader(strTestingFileNames[m]));

           // Skip the label record
           tempLine = br3.readLine();
           tempLine = br3.readLine();
```

```
// Brake the line using comma as separator
tempWorkFields = tempLine.split(cvsSplitBy);

recordNormInputPriceDiffPerc_00 = Double.parseDouble(temp
WorkFields[0]);
recordNormInputPriceDiffPerc_01 = Double.parseDouble(temp
WorkFields[1]);
recordNormInputPriceDiffPerc_02 = Double.parseDouble(temp
WorkFields[2]);
recordNormInputPriceDiffPerc_03 = Double.parseDouble(temp
WorkFields[3]);
recordNormInputPriceDiffPerc_04 = Double.parseDouble(temp
WorkFields[4]);
recordNormInputPriceDiffPerc_05 = Double.parseDouble(temp
WorkFields[5]);
recordNormInputPriceDiffPerc_06 = Double.parseDouble(temp
WorkFields[6]);
recordNormInputPriceDiffPerc_07 = Double.parseDouble(temp
WorkFields[7]);
recordNormInputPriceDiffPerc_08 = Double.parseDouble(temp
WorkFields[8]);
recordNormInputPriceDiffPerc_09 = Double.parseDouble(temp
WorkFields[9]);
recordNormInputPriceDiffPerc_10 = Double.parseDouble(temp
WorkFields[10]);
recordNormInputPriceDiffPerc_11 = Double.parseDouble(temp
WorkFields[11]);

recordNormTargetPriceDiffPerc = Double.parseDouble(tempWork
Fields[12]);

linkToSaveInputPriceDiffPerc_00[m] =
recordNormInputPriceDiffPerc_00;
linkToSaveInputPriceDiffPerc_01[m] =
recordNormInputPriceDiffPerc_01;
linkToSaveInputPriceDiffPerc_02[m] =
recordNormInputPriceDiffPerc_02;
```

```
        linkToSaveInputPriceDiffPerc_03[m] =
        recordNormInputPriceDiffPerc_03;
        linkToSaveInputPriceDiffPerc_04[m] =
        recordNormInputPriceDiffPerc_04;
        linkToSaveInputPriceDiffPerc_05[m] =
        recordNormInputPriceDiffPerc_05;
        linkToSaveInputPriceDiffPerc_06[m] =
        recordNormInputPriceDiffPerc_06;
        linkToSaveInputPriceDiffPerc_07[m] =
        recordNormInputPriceDiffPerc_07;
        linkToSaveInputPriceDiffPerc_08[m] =
        recordNormInputPriceDiffPerc_08;
        linkToSaveInputPriceDiffPerc_09[m] =
        recordNormInputPriceDiffPerc_09;
        linkToSaveInputPriceDiffPerc_10[m] =
        recordNormInputPriceDiffPerc_10;
        linkToSaveInputPriceDiffPerc_11[m] =
        recordNormInputPriceDiffPerc_11;

        linkToSaveTargetPriceDiffPerc[m] =
        recordNormTargetPriceDiffPerc;

    }  // End the FOR loop

// Load dates into memory
loadDatesInMemory();

// Load Prices into memory
loadPriceFileInMemory();

file2 = new File(strChartFileName);

if(file2.exists())
   file2.delete();

// Test the working mode
if(intWorkingMode == 0)
   {
```

```
          // Train batches and save the trained networks
          int  paramBatchNumber;

          returnCodes[0] = 0;      // Clear the error Code
          returnCodes[1] = 0;      // Set the initial batch Number to 1;
          returnCodes[2] = 0;      // Set the initial day number;

          do
           {
              paramErrorCode = returnCodes[0];
              paramBatchNumber = returnCodes[1];
              paramDayNumber = returnCodes[2];

               returnCodes =
                trainBatches(paramErrorCode,paramBatchNumber,paramDayNumber);
             } while (returnCodes[0] > 0);

      }   // End the train logic
    else
     {
       if(intWorkingMode == 1)
         {
            // Load and test the network logic
            loadAndTestNetwork();
         }

      } // End of ELSE

  }      // End of Try
  catch (Exception e1)
   {
     e1.printStackTrace();
   }

  Encog.getInstance().shutdown();

  return Chart;

  } // End of method
```

```
// ==========================================================
// Load CSV to memory.
// @return The loaded dataset.
// ==========================================================
public static MLDataSet loadCSV2Memory(String filename, int input, int ideal,
   boolean headers, CSVFormat format, boolean significance)
   {
      DataSetCODEC codec = new CSVDataCODEC(new File(filename), format,
      headers, input, ideal,
         significance);
      MemoryDataLoader load = new MemoryDataLoader(codec);
      MLDataSet dataset = load.external2Memory();
      return dataset;
   }


// ==========================================================
//  The main method.
//  @param Command line arguments. No arguments are used.
// ==========================================================
public static void main(String[] args)
 {
   ExampleChart<XYChart> exampleChart = new Saple7();
   XYChart Chart = exampleChart.getChart();
   new SwingWrapper<XYChart>(Chart).displayChart();
 } // End of the main method


//=====================================================================
// Mode 0. Train batches as individual networks, saving them in separate
files on disk.
//=====================================================================
static public int[] trainBatches(int paramErrorCode,int
paramBatchNumber,
      int paramDayNumber)
  {
    int rBatchNumber;

    double realDenormTargetToPredictPricePerc = 0;
```

```
double maxGlobalResultDiff = 0.00;
double averGlobalResultDiff = 0.00;
double sumGlobalResultDiff = 0.00;
double normTargetPriceDiffPerc = 0.00;
double normPredictPriceDiffPerc = 0.00;
double normInputPriceDiffPercFromRecord = 0.00;
double denormTargetPriceDiffPerc;
double denormPredictPriceDiffPerc;
double denormInputPriceDiffPercFromRecord;
double workNormInputPrice;
Date tempDate;
double trainError;
double realDenormPredictPrice;
double realDenormTargetPrice;

// Build the network
BasicNetwork network = new BasicNetwork();

// Input layer
network.addLayer(new BasicLayer(null,true,intInputNeuronNumber));

// Hidden layer.
network.addLayer(new BasicLayer(new ActivationTANH(),true,25));
network.addLayer(new BasicLayer(new ActivationTANH(),true,25));
network.addLayer(new BasicLayer(new ActivationTANH(),true,25));
network.addLayer(new BasicLayer(new ActivationTANH(),true,25));
network.addLayer(new BasicLayer(new ActivationTANH(),true,25));
network.addLayer(new BasicLayer(new ActivationTANH(),true,25));
network.addLayer(new BasicLayer(new ActivationTANH(),true,25));

// Output layer
network.addLayer(new BasicLayer(new ActivationTANH(),false,intOutputN
euronNumber));

network.getStructure().finalizeStructure();
network.reset();

// Loop over batches
```

```
intDayNumber = paramDayNumber;   // Day number for the chart

for (rBatchNumber = paramBatchNumber; rBatchNumber <
intNumberOfBatchesToProcess;
        rBatchNumber++)
 {
   intDayNumber++;

   //if(rBatchNumber == 201)
   // rBatchNumber = rBatchNumber;

   // Load the training CVS file for the current batch in memory
   MLDataSet trainingSet = loadCSV2Memory(strTrainingFileNames[rBatchN
   umber],
     intInputNeuronNumber,intOutputNeuronNumber,true,CSVFormat.
     ENGLISH,false);

   // train the neural network
   ResilientPropagation train = new ResilientPropagation(network,
   trainingSet);

   int epoch = 1;
   double tempLastErrorPerc = 0.00;

   do
     {
       train.iteration();

       epoch++;

       for (MLDataPair pair1:  trainingSet)
        {
          MLData inputData = pair1.getInput();
          MLData actualData = pair1.getIdeal();
          MLData predictData = network.compute(inputData);

          // These values are normalized
          normTargetPriceDiffPerc = actualData.getData(0);
          normPredictPriceDiffPerc = predictData.getData(0);
```

```
            // De-normalize these values
            denormTargetPriceDiffPerc = ((targetPriceDiffPercDl -
            targetPriceDiffPercDh)*
               normTargetPriceDiffPerc - Nh*targetPriceDiffPercDl +
               targetPriceDiffPercDh*Nl)/(Nl - Nh);

            denormPredictPriceDiffPerc =((targetPriceDiffPercDl -
            targetPriceDiffPercDh)*
               normPredictPriceDiffPerc - Nh*targetPriceDiffPercDl +
               targetPriceDiffPercDh*Nl)/(Nl - Nh);

            inputPriceFromFile = arrPrices[rBatchNumber+12];

           realDenormTargetPrice = inputPriceFromFile + inputPriceFromFile*
               denormTargetPriceDiffPerc/100;

           realDenormPredictPrice = inputPriceFromFile + inputPriceFromFile*
               denormPredictPriceDiffPerc/100;

           realDenormTargetToPredictPricePerc = (Math.
           abs(realDenormTargetPrice -
                realDenormPredictPrice)/realDenormTargetPrice)*100;
         }

      if (epoch >= 500 && realDenormTargetToPredictPricePerc > 0.00091)
         {
         returnCodes[0] = 1;
         returnCodes[1] = rBatchNumber;
         returnCodes[2] = intDayNumber-1;

         //System.out.println("Try again");
         return returnCodes;
         }

         //System.out.println(realDenormTargetToPredictPricePerc);
      } while(realDenormTargetToPredictPricePerc >  0.0009);

   // This batch is optimized

   // Save the network for the current batch
```

```
EncogDirectoryPersistence.saveObject(new
      File(strSaveNetworkFileNames[rBatchNumber]),network);

  // Print the trained neural network results for the batch
  //System.out.println("Trained Neural Network Results");

  // Get the results after the network optimization
  int i = - 1; // Index of the array to get results

 maxGlobalResultDiff = 0.00;
 averGlobalResultDiff = 0.00;
 sumGlobalResultDiff = 0.00;

//if (rBatchNumber == 857)
//    i = i;

// Validation
for (MLDataPair pair:  trainingSet)
  {
    i++;

    MLData inputData = pair.getInput();
    MLData actualData = pair.getIdeal();
    MLData predictData = network.compute(inputData);

    // These values are Normalized as the whole input is
    normTargetPriceDiffPerc = actualData.getData(0);
    normPredictPriceDiffPerc = predictData.getData(0);
    //normInputPriceDiffPercFromRecord[i] = inputData.getData(0);
    normInputPriceDiffPercFromRecord = inputData.getData(0);

    // De-normalize this data to show the real result value
    denormTargetPriceDiffPerc = ((targetPriceDiffPercDl -
    targetPriceDiffPercDh)*
      normTargetPriceDiffPerc - Nh*targetPriceDiffPercDl +
      targetPriceDiffPercDh*Nl)/(Nl - Nh);

    denormPredictPriceDiffPerc =((targetPriceDiffPercDl -
    targetPriceDiffPercDh)*
```

```
      normPredictPriceDiffPerc - Nh*targetPriceDiffPercDl +
      targetPriceDiffPercDh*Nl)/(Nl - Nh);

  denormInputPriceDiffPercFromRecord = ((inputPriceDiffPercDl -
  inputPriceDiffPercDh)*
      normInputPriceDiffPercFromRecord - Nh*inputPriceDiffPercDl +
      inputPriceDiffPercDh*Nl)/(Nl - Nh);

  // Get the price of the 12th element of the row
  inputPriceFromFile = arrPrices[rBatchNumber+12];

  // Convert denormPredictPriceDiffPerc and denormTargetPriceDiffPerc
  // to real de-normalized prices

  realDenormTargetPrice = inputPriceFromFile +
      inputPriceFromFile*(denormTargetPriceDiffPerc/100);
  realDenormPredictPrice = inputPriceFromFile +
      inputPriceFromFile*(denormPredictPriceDiffPerc/100);
  realDenormTargetToPredictPricePerc = (Math.
  abs(realDenormTargetPrice -
      realDenormPredictPrice)/realDenormTargetPrice)*100;

  System.out.println("Month = " + (rBatchNumber+1) + "  targetPrice =
  " + realDenormTargetPrice +
      "  predictPrice = " + realDenormPredictPrice + "  diff = " +
      realDenormTargetToPredictPricePerc);

   if (realDenormTargetToPredictPricePerc > maxGlobalResultDiff)
     {
       maxGlobalResultDiff = realDenormTargetToPredictPricePerc;
     }

  sumGlobalResultDiff = sumGlobalResultDiff +
  realDenormTargetToPredictPricePerc;

  // Populate chart elements
  tempDate = yearDateTraining[rBatchNumber+14];
  //xData.add(tempDate);
  tempMonth = (double) rBatchNumber+14;
```

```
  xData.add(tempMonth);
  yData1.add(realDenormTargetPrice);
  yData2.add(realDenormPredictPrice);

  }  // End for Price pair loop

}  // End of the loop over batches

XYSeries series1 = Chart.addSeries("Actual price", xData, yData1);
XYSeries series2 = Chart.addSeries("Predicted price", xData, yData2);

series1.setLineColor(XChartSeriesColors.BLUE);
series2.setMarkerColor(Color.ORANGE);
series1.setLineStyle(SeriesLines.SOLID);
series2.setLineStyle(SeriesLines.SOLID);

 // Print the max and average results

 averGlobalResultDiff = sumGlobalResultDiff/
 intNumberOfBatchesToProcess;

 System.out.println(" ");
 System.out.println("maxGlobalResultDiff = " + maxGlobalResultDiff);
 System.out.println("averGlobalResultDiff = " + averGlobalResultDiff);
 System.out.println(" ");

 // Save the chart image
 try
  {
    BitmapEncoder.saveBitmapWithDPI(Chart, strChartFileName,
    BitmapFormat.JPG, 100);
  }
 catch (Exception bt)
  {
    bt.printStackTrace();
  }

 System.out.println ("Chart and Network have been saved");
 System.out.println("End of validating batches for training");
```

```
    returnCodes[0] = 0;
    returnCodes[1] = 0;
    returnCodes[2] = 0;

    return returnCodes;
  }  // End of method

//=======================================================================
// Mode 1. Load the previously saved trained network and process test
mini-batches
//=======================================================================

static public void loadAndTestNetwork()
  {
    System.out.println("Testing the networks results");

    List<Double> xData = new ArrayList<Double>();
    List<Double> yData1 = new ArrayList<Double>();
    List<Double> yData2 = new ArrayList<Double>();

    double realDenormTargetToPredictPricePerc = 0;
    double maxGlobalResultDiff = 0.00;
    double averGlobalResultDiff = 0.00;
    double sumGlobalResultDiff = 0.00;
    double maxGlobalIndex = 0;

    recordNormInputPriceDiffPerc_00 = 0.00;
    recordNormInputPriceDiffPerc_01 = 0.00;
    recordNormInputPriceDiffPerc_02 = 0.00;
    recordNormInputPriceDiffPerc_03 = 0.00;
    recordNormInputPriceDiffPerc_04 = 0.00;
    recordNormInputPriceDiffPerc_05 = 0.00;
    recordNormInputPriceDiffPerc_06 = 0.00;
    recordNormInputPriceDiffPerc_07 = 0.00;
    recordNormInputPriceDiffPerc_08 = 0.00;
    recordNormInputPriceDiffPerc_09 = 0.00;
    recordNormInputPriceDiffPerc_10 = 0.00;
    recordNormInputPriceDiffPerc_11 = 0.00;
```

```java
double recordNormTargetPriceDiffPerc = 0.00;
double normTargetPriceDiffPerc;
double normPredictPriceDiffPerc;
double normInputPriceDiffPercFromRecord;
double denormTargetPriceDiffPerc;
double denormPredictPriceDiffPerc;
double denormInputPriceDiffPercFromRecord;
double realDenormTargetPrice = 0.00;
double realDenormPredictPrice = 0.00;
double minVectorValue = 0.00;
String tempLine;
String[] tempWorkFields;
int tempMinIndex = 0;
double rTempPriceDiffPerc = 0.00;
double rTempKey = 0.00;
double vectorForNetworkRecord = 0.00;
double r_00 = 0.00;
double r_01 = 0.00;
double r_02 = 0.00;
double r_03 = 0.00;
double r_04 = 0.00;
double r_05 = 0.00;
double r_06 = 0.00;
double r_07 = 0.00;
double r_08 = 0.00;
double r_09 = 0.00;
double r_10 = 0.00;
double r_11 = 0.00;
double vectorDiff;
double r1 = 0.00;
double r2 = 0.00;
double vectorForRecord = 0.00;
int k1 = 0;
int k3 = 0;

BufferedReader br4;
```

```
    BasicNetwork network;

    try
     {
        maxGlobalResultDiff = 0.00;
        averGlobalResultDiff = 0.00;
        sumGlobalResultDiff = 0.00;

        for (k1 = 0; k1 < intNumberOfBatchesToProcess; k1++)
         {
            br4 = new BufferedReader(new FileReader(strTestingFileNames[k1]));
            tempLine = br4.readLine();

            // Skip the label record
            tempLine = br4.readLine();

            // Brake the line using comma as separator
            tempWorkFields = tempLine.split(cvsSplitBy);

            recordNormInputPriceDiffPerc_00 = Double.parseDouble(tempWork
            Fields[0]);
            recordNormInputPriceDiffPerc_01 = Double.parseDouble(tempWork
            Fields[1]);
            recordNormInputPriceDiffPerc_02 = Double.parseDouble(tempWork
            Fields[2]);
            recordNormInputPriceDiffPerc_03 = Double.parseDouble(tempWork
            Fields[3]);
            recordNormInputPriceDiffPerc_04 = Double.parseDouble(tempWork
            Fields[4]);
            recordNormInputPriceDiffPerc_05 = Double.parseDouble(tempWork
            Fields[5]);
            recordNormInputPriceDiffPerc_06 = Double.parseDouble(tempWork
            Fields[6]);
            recordNormInputPriceDiffPerc_07 = Double.parseDouble(tempWork
            Fields[7]);
            recordNormInputPriceDiffPerc_08 = Double.parseDouble(tempWork
            Fields[8]);
```

```
recordNormInputPriceDiffPerc_09 = Double.parseDouble(tempWork
Fields[9]);
recordNormInputPriceDiffPerc_10 = Double.parseDouble(tempWork
Fields[10]);
recordNormInputPriceDiffPerc_11 = Double.parseDouble(tempWork
Fields[11]);

recordNormTargetPriceDiffPerc = Double.parseDouble(tempWork
Fields[12]);

if(k1 < 120)
 {
   // Load the network for the current record
   network =
     (BasicNetwork)EncogDirectoryPersistence.loadObject(new
        File(strSaveNetworkFileNames[k1]));

 // Load the training file record
 MLDataSet testingSet =

 loadCSV2Memory(strTestingFileNames[k1],intInputNeuronNumber,
    intOutputNeuronNumber,true,CSVFormat.ENGLISH,false);

// Get the results from the loaded previously saved networks
 int i = - 1;

 for (MLDataPair pair:  testingSet)
  {
     i++;

     MLData inputData = pair.getInput();
     MLData actualData = pair.getIdeal();
     MLData predictData = network.compute(inputData);

     // These values are Normalized as the whole input is
     normTargetPriceDiffPerc = actualData.getData(0);
     normPredictPriceDiffPerc = predictData.getData(0);
     normInputPriceDiffPercFromRecord = inputData.getData(11);

     // De-normalize this data
```

```
              denormTargetPriceDiffPerc = ((targetPriceDiffPercDl -
                 targetPriceDiffPercDh)*normTargetPriceDiffPerc
                    - Nh*targetPriceDiffPercDl +
                    targetPriceDiffPercDh*Nl)/(Nl - Nh);
              denormPredictPriceDiffPerc =((targetPriceDiffPercDl -
              targetPriceDiffPercDh)*
                    normPredictPriceDiffPerc - Nh*targetPriceDiffPercDl +
                    targetPriceDiffPercDh*Nl)/(Nl - Nh);

              denormInputPriceDiffPercFromRecord =
              ((inputPriceDiffPercDl -
                    inputPriceDiffPercDh)*normInputPriceDiffPercFromReco
                    rd - Nh*inputPriceDiffPercDl +
                    inputPriceDiffPercDh*Nl)/(Nl - Nh);

              inputPriceFromFile = arrPrices[k1+12];

              // Convert denormPredictPriceDiffPerc and
              denormTargetPriceDiffPerc to a real
              // de-normalize price
              realDenormTargetPrice = inputPriceFromFile +
                    inputPriceFromFile*(denormTargetPriceDiffPerc/100);
              realDenormPredictPrice = inputPriceFromFile +
                    inputPriceFromFile*(denormPredictPriceDiffPerc/100);

              realDenormTargetToPredictPricePerc = (Math.abs
              (realDenormTargetPrice -
                    realDenormPredictPrice)/realDenormTargetPrice)*100;

              System.out.println("Month = " + (k1+1) +  "  targetPrice =
              " + realDenormTargetPrice +
                 "  predictPrice = " + realDenormPredictPrice +
                 "  diff = " +
                        realDenormTargetToPredictPricePerc);
         }  // End for pair loop

       } // End for IF
```

```
else
{

  vectorForRecord = Math.sqrt(
    Math.pow(recordNormInputPriceDiffPerc_00,2) +
    Math.pow(recordNormInputPriceDiffPerc_01,2) +
    Math.pow(recordNormInputPriceDiffPerc_02,2) +
    Math.pow(recordNormInputPriceDiffPerc_03,2) +
    Math.pow(recordNormInputPriceDiffPerc_04,2) +
    Math.pow(recordNormInputPriceDiffPerc_05,2) +
    Math.pow(recordNormInputPriceDiffPerc_06,2) +
    Math.pow(recordNormInputPriceDiffPerc_07,2) +
    Math.pow(recordNormInputPriceDiffPerc_08,2) +
    Math.pow(recordNormInputPriceDiffPerc_09,2) +
    Math.pow(recordNormInputPriceDiffPerc_10,2) +
    Math.pow(recordNormInputPriceDiffPerc_11,2));

  // Look for the network of previous days that closely matches
  // the value of vectorForRecord

  minVectorValue = 999.99;

  for (k3 = 0; k3 < intNumberOfSavedNetworks; k3++)
    {
      r_00 = linkToSaveInputPriceDiffPerc_00[k3];
      r_01 = linkToSaveInputPriceDiffPerc_01[k3];
      r_02 = linkToSaveInputPriceDiffPerc_02[k3];
      r_03 = linkToSaveInputPriceDiffPerc_03[k3];
      r_04 = linkToSaveInputPriceDiffPerc_04[k3];
      r_05 = linkToSaveInputPriceDiffPerc_05[k3];
      r_06 = linkToSaveInputPriceDiffPerc_06[k3];
      r_07 = linkToSaveInputPriceDiffPerc_07[k3];
      r_08 = linkToSaveInputPriceDiffPerc_08[k3];
      r_09 = linkToSaveInputPriceDiffPerc_09[k3];
      r_10 = linkToSaveInputPriceDiffPerc_10[k3];
      r_11 = linkToSaveInputPriceDiffPerc_11[k3];

      r2 = linkToSaveTargetPriceDiffPerc[k3];
```

```
                    vectorForNetworkRecord = Math.sqrt(
                    Math.pow(r_00,2) +
                    Math.pow(r_01,2) +
                    Math.pow(r_02,2) +
                    Math.pow(r_03,2) +
                    Math.pow(r_04,2) +
                    Math.pow(r_05,2) +
                    Math.pow(r_06,2) +
                    Math.pow(r_07,2) +
                    Math.pow(r_08,2) +
                    Math.pow(r_09,2) +
                    Math.pow(r_10,2) +
                    Math.pow(r_11,2));

                    vectorDiff = Math.abs(vectorForRecord -
                    vectorForNetworkRecord);

                    if(vectorDiff < minVectorValue)
                      {
                        minVectorValue = vectorDiff;

                        // Save this network record attributes
                        rTempKey = r_00;
                        rTempPriceDiffPerc = r2;
                        tempMinIndex = k3;
                      }

         }  // End  FOR k3 loop

network =
(BasicNetwork)EncogDirectoryPersistence.loadObject(new
      File(strSaveNetworkFileNames[tempMinIndex]));

  // Now, tempMinIndex points to the corresponding saved network
  // Load this network
  MLDataSet testingSet =
    loadCSV2Memory(strTestingFileNames[k1],intInputNeuronNumber,
      intOutputNeuronNumber,true,CSVFormat.ENGLISH,false);
```

```
// Get the results from the reviously saved and  now loaded network
int i = - 1;

for (MLDataPair pair:  testingSet)
 {
    i++;

    MLData inputData = pair.getInput();
    MLData actualData = pair.getIdeal();
    MLData predictData = network.compute(inputData);

    // These values are Normalized as the whole input is
    normTargetPriceDiffPerc = actualData.getData(0);
    normPredictPriceDiffPerc = predictData.getData(0);
    normInputPriceDiffPercFromRecord = inputData.getData(11);

// Renormalize this data to show the real result value
    denormTargetPriceDiffPerc = ((targetPriceDiffPercDl -
    targetPriceDiffPercDh)*
      normTargetPriceDiffPerc - Nh*targetPriceDiffPercDl +
      targetPriceDiffPercDh*Nl)/(Nl - Nh);

    denormPredictPriceDiffPerc =((targetPriceDiffPercDl -
    targetPriceDiffPercDh)*
      normPredictPriceDiffPerc - Nh*targetPriceDiffPercDl +
      targetPriceDiffPercDh*Nl)/(Nl - Nh);

    denormInputPriceDiffPercFromRecord =
    ((inputPriceDiffPercDl - inputPriceDiffPercDh)*
      normInputPriceDiffPercFromRecord - Nh*inputPrice
      DiffPercDl + inputPriceDiffPercDh*Nl)/(Nl -
          Nh);

    inputPriceFromFile = arrPrices[k1+12];

    // Convert denormPredictPriceDiffPerc and
      denormTargetPriceDiffPerc to a real
    // demoralize prices
    realDenormTargetPrice = inputPriceFromFile +
```

```
                    inputPriceFromFile*(denormTargetPriceDiffPerc/100);

          realDenormPredictPrice = inputPriceFromFile +
             inputPriceFromFile*(denormPredictPriceDiffPerc/100);

          realDenormTargetToPredictPricePerc = (Math.
          abs(realDenormTargetPrice -
             realDenormPredictPrice)/realDenormTargetPrice)*100;

          System.out.println("Month = " + (k1+1) +  "  targetPrice =
          " + realDenormTargetPrice +
            "  predictPrice = " + realDenormPredictPrice + "   diff = " +
                  realDenormTargetToPredictPricePerc);

        if (realDenormTargetToPredictPricePerc > maxGlobalResultDiff)
          {
             maxGlobalResultDiff = realDenormTargetToPredictPricePerc;
          }

          sumGlobalResultDiff = sumGlobalResultDiff +
          realDenormTargetToPredictPricePerc;

      } // End of IF

    }  // End for pair loop

    // Populate chart elements

    tempMonth = (double) k1+14;
    xData.add(tempMonth);
    yData1.add(realDenormTargetPrice);
    yData2.add(realDenormPredictPrice);

  }   // End of loop K1

// Print the max and average results

System.out.println(" ");
System.out.println(" ");
System.out.println("Results of processing testing batches");
```

```
  averGlobalResultDiff = sumGlobalResultDiff/intNumberOfBatchesToProcess;

  System.out.println("maxGlobalResultDiff = " + maxGlobalResultDiff +
  "   i = " + maxGlobalIndex);
  System.out.println("averGlobalResultDiff = " + averGlobalResultDiff);
  System.out.println(" ");
  System.out.println(" ");

}      // End of TRY
catch (IOException e1)
{
      e1.printStackTrace();
}

// All testing batch files have been processed
  XYSeries series1 = Chart.addSeries("Actual Price", xData, yData1);
  XYSeries series2 = Chart.addSeries("Forecasted Price", xData, yData2);

  series1.setLineColor(XChartSeriesColors.BLUE);
  series2.setMarkerColor(Color.ORANGE);
  series1.setLineStyle(SeriesLines.SOLID);
  series2.setLineStyle(SeriesLines.SOLID);

  // Save the chart image
  try
   {
     BitmapEncoder.saveBitmapWithDPI(Chart, strChartFileName,
     BitmapFormat.JPG, 100);
   }
  catch (Exception bt)
   {
     bt.printStackTrace();
   }

  System.out.println ("The Chart has been saved");
  System.out.println("End of testing for mini-batches training");

} // End of the method
```

```java
//================================================================
// Load training dates file in memory
//================================================================
public static void loadDatesInMemory()
 {
    BufferedReader br1 = null;

    DateFormat sdf = new SimpleDateFormat("yyyy-MM");

    Date dateTemporateDate = null;
    String strTempKeyorateDate;
    int intTemporateDate;

    String line = "";
    String cvsSplitBy = ",";

     try
       {
         br1 = new BufferedReader(new FileReader(strDatesTrainFileName));

         int i = -1;
         int r = -2;

         while ((line = br1.readLine()) != null)
          {
            i++;
            r++;

           // Skip the header line
           if(i > 0)
             {
               // Brake the line using comma as separator
               String[] workFields = line.split(cvsSplitBy);

               strTempKeyorateDate = workFields[0];
               intTemporateDate = Integer.parseInt(strTempKeyorateDate);

               try
                 {
```

```
                dateTemporateDate = convertIntegerToDate(intTemporateDate);
              }
          catch (ParseException e)
            {
              e.printStackTrace();
              System.exit(1);
            }

            yearDateTraining[r] = dateTemporateDate;
          }

      }  // end of the while loop

       br1.close();

     }
   catch (IOException ex)
     {
       ex.printStackTrace();
       System.err.println("Error opening files = " + ex);
       System.exit(1);
     }

  }


//================================================================
// Convert the month date as integer to the Date variable
//================================================================
public static Date convertIntegerToDate(int denormInputDateI) throws
ParseException
  {

      int numberOfYears = denormInputDateI/12;
      int numberOfMonths = denormInputDateI - numberOfYears*12;

      if (numberOfMonths == 0)
       {
          numberOfYears = numberOfYears - 1;
          numberOfMonths = 12;
       }
```

```java
    String strNumberOfYears = Integer.toString(numberOfYears);

    if(numberOfMonths < 10)
      {
        strNumberOfMonths = Integer.toString(numberOfMonths);
        strNumberOfMonths = "0" + strNumberOfMonths;
      }
    else
      {
        strNumberOfMonths = Integer.toString(numberOfMonths);
      }

    //strYearMonth = "01-" + strNumberOfMonths + "-" + strNumberOfYears
    + "T09:00:00.000Z";
    strYearMonth = strNumberOfYears + "-" + strNumberOfMonths;

    DateFormat sdf = new SimpleDateFormat("yyyy-MM");

    try
      {
       workDate = sdf.parse(strYearMonth);
      }
    catch (ParseException e)
      {
        e.printStackTrace();
      }

   return workDate;

} // End of method

//========================================================
// Convert the month date as integer to the string strDate variable
//========================================================
public static String convertIntegerToString(int denormInputDateI)
 {
    int numberOfYears = denormInputDateI/12;
    int numberOfMonths = denormInputDateI - numberOfYears*12;
```

516

```java
    if (numberOfMonths == 0)
     {
       numberOfYears = numberOfYears - 1;
       numberOfMonths = 12;
     }

    String strNumberOfYears = Integer.toString(numberOfYears);

    if(numberOfMonths < 10)
      {
        strNumberOfMonths = Integer.toString(numberOfMonths);
        strNumberOfMonths = "0" + strNumberOfMonths;
      }
    else
      {
        strNumberOfMonths = Integer.toString(numberOfMonths);
      }

     strYearMonth = strNumberOfYears + "-" + strNumberOfMonths;

   return strYearMonth;

}   // End of method

//================================================================
// Load Prices file in memory
//================================================================
public static void loadPriceFileInMemory()
 {
    BufferedReader br1 = null;

    String line = "";
    String cvsSplitBy = ",";
    String strTempKeyPrice = "";
    double tempPrice = 0.00;

     try
       {
         br1 = new BufferedReader(new FileReader(strPricesFileName));
```

```
        int i = -1;
        int r = -2;

        while ((line = br1.readLine()) != null)
         {
           i++;
           r++;

           // Skip the header line
           if(i > 0)
            {
              // Brake the line using comma as separator
              String[] workFields = line.split(cvsSplitBy);

              strTempKeyPrice = workFields[0];
              tempPrice = Double.parseDouble(strTempKeyPrice);
              arrPrices[r] = tempPrice;

            }
         } // end of the while loop

         br1.close();

      }
     catch (IOException ex)
      {
          ex.printStackTrace();
          System.err.println("Error opening files = " + ex);
          System.exit(1);
      }

   }

} // End of the Encog class
```

Training Process

For the most part, the training method logic is similar to what was used in the preceding examples, so it does not need any explanation, with the exception of one part that needs to be discussed here.

Sometimes, we deal with functions of very small values, so the calculated errors are even smaller. There are situations when the network errors reach the microscopic values with 14 or more zeros after the dot, for example: 0.000000000000025. When you get such errors, you start questioning the accuracy of the calculation. In this code, we included the example of handling such situations.

Instead of simply calling the `train.getError()` method to determine the network error, we use the pair dataset to retrieve the input, actual, and predicted function values from the network for each epoch, denormalize those values, and calculate the error percent difference between the calculated and actual values. We exit from the pair loop with the `returnCode` 0 when this difference becomes less than the error limit, as shown in Listing 11-5.

Listing 11-5. Checking the Error Using the Actual Function Values

```
int epoch = 1;
double tempLastErrorPerc = 0.00;

 do
     {
         train.iteration();

         epoch++;

     for (MLDataPair pair1:  trainingSet)
        {
             MLData inputData = pair1.getInput();
             MLData actualData = pair1.getIdeal();
              MLData predictData = network.compute(inputData);

             // These values are Normalized as the whole input is
             normTargetPriceDiffPerc = actualData.getData(0);
             normPredictPriceDiffPerc = predictData.getData(0);
```

```
                denormTargetPriceDiffPerc = ((targetPriceDiffPercDl -
                    targetPriceDiffPercDh)*normTargetPriceDiffPerc -
                        Nh*targetPriceDiffPercDl +
                        targetPriceDiffPercDh*Nl)/(Nl - Nh);

                denormPredictPriceDiffPerc =((targetPriceDiffPercDl -
                        targetPriceDiffPercDh)*normPredictPriceDiffPerc -
                        Nh*targetPriceDiffPercDl +
                        targetPriceDiffPercDh*Nl)/(Nl - Nh);

                inputPriceFromFile = arrPrices[rBatchNumber+12];

                realDenormTargetPrice = inputPriceFromFile +
                    inputPriceFromFile*denormTargetPriceDiffPerc/100;

                realDenormPredictPrice = inputPriceFromFile +
                    inputPriceFromFile*denormPredictPriceDiffPerc/100;

                realDenormTargetToPredictPricePerc = (Math.
                abs(realDenormTargetPrice -
                    realDenormPredictPrice)/realDenormTargetPrice)*100;
            }

        if (epoch >= 500 && realDenormTargetToPredictPricePerc > 0.00091)
            {
                returnCodes[0] = 1;
                returnCodes[1] = rBatchNumber;
                returnCodes[2] = intDayNumber-1;

                return returnCodes;
            }

    } while(realDenormTargetToPredictPricePerc >  0.0009);
```

Training Results

Listing 11-6 shows the training results.

Listing 11-6. Training Results

```
Month =  1   targetPrice = 1239.94000   predictPrice = 1239.93074   diff = 7.46675E-4
Month =  2   targetPrice = 1160.33000   predictPrice = 1160.32905   diff = 8.14930E-5
Month =  3   targetPrice = 1249.46000   predictPrice = 1249.44897   diff = 8.82808E-4
Month =  4   targetPrice = 1255.82000   predictPrice = 1255.81679   diff = 2.55914E-4
Month =  5   targetPrice = 1224.38000   predictPrice = 1224.37483   diff = 4.21901E-4
Month =  6   targetPrice = 1211.23000   predictPrice = 1211.23758   diff = 6.25530E-4
Month =  7   targetPrice = 1133.58000   predictPrice = 1133.59013   diff = 8.94046E-4
Month =  8   targetPrice = 1040.94000   predictPrice = 1040.94164   diff = 1.57184E-4
Month =  9   targetPrice = 1059.78000   predictPrice = 1059.78951   diff = 8.97819E-4
Month = 10   targetPrice = 1139.45000   predictPrice = 1139.45977   diff = 8.51147E-4
Month = 11   targetPrice = 1148.08000   predictPrice = 1148.07912   diff = 7.66679E-5
Month = 12   targetPrice = 1130.20000   predictPrice = 1130.20593   diff = 5.24564E-4
Month = 13   targetPrice = 1106.73000   predictPrice = 1106.72654   diff = 3.12787E-4
Month = 14   targetPrice = 1147.39000   predictPrice = 1147.39283   diff = 2.46409E-4
Month = 15   targetPrice = 1076.92000   predictPrice = 1076.92461   diff = 4.28291E-4
Month = 16   targetPrice = 1067.14000   predictPrice = 1067.14948   diff = 8.88156E-4
Month = 17   targetPrice = 989.819999   predictPrice = 989.811316   diff = 8.77328E-4
Month = 18   targetPrice = 911.620000   predictPrice = 911.625389   diff = 5.91142E-4
Month = 19   targetPrice = 916.070000   predictPrice = 916.071216   diff = 1.32725E-4
Month = 20   targetPrice = 815.280000   predictPrice = 815.286704   diff = 8.22304E-4
Month = 21   targetPrice = 885.760000   predictPrice = 885.767730   diff = 8.72729E-4
Month = 22   targetPrice = 936.310000   predictPrice = 936.307290   diff = 2.89468E-4
Month = 23   targetPrice = 879.820000   predictPrice = 879.812595   diff = 8.41647E-4
Month = 24   targetPrice = 855.700000   predictPrice = 855.700307   diff = 3.58321E-5
Month = 25   targetPrice = 841.150000   predictPrice = 841.157407   diff = 8.80559E-4
Month = 26   targetPrice = 848.180000   predictPrice = 848.177279   diff = 3.22296E-4
Month = 27   targetPrice = 916.920000   predictPrice = 916.914394   diff = 6.11352E-4
Month = 28   targetPrice = 963.590000   predictPrice = 963.591678   diff = 1.74172E-4
Month = 29   targetPrice = 974.500000   predictPrice = 974.505665   diff = 5.81287E-4
Month = 30   targetPrice = 990.310000   predictPrice = 990.302895   diff = 7.17406E-4
```

```
Month = 31   targetPrice = 1008.01000   predictPrice = 1008.00861   diff = 1.37856E-4
Month = 32   targetPrice = 995.970000   predictPrice = 995.961734   diff = 8.29902E-4
Month = 33   targetPrice = 1050.71000   predictPrice = 1050.70954   diff = 4.42062E-5
Month = 34   targetPrice = 1058.20000   predictPrice = 1058.19690   diff = 2.93192E-4
Month = 35   targetPrice = 1111.92000   predictPrice = 1111.91406   diff = 5.34581E-4
Month = 36   targetPrice = 1131.13000   predictPrice = 1131.12351   diff = 5.73549E-4
Month = 37   targetPrice = 1144.94000   predictPrice = 1144.94240   diff = 2.09638E-4
Month = 38   targetPrice = 1126.21000   predictPrice = 1126.21747   diff = 6.63273E-4
Month = 39   targetPrice = 1107.30000   predictPrice = 1107.30139   diff = 1.25932E-4
Month = 40   targetPrice = 1120.68000   predictPrice = 1120.67926   diff = 6.62989E-5
Month = 41   targetPrice = 1140.84000   predictPrice = 1140.83145   diff = 7.49212E-4
Month = 42   targetPrice = 1101.72000   predictPrice = 1101.72597   diff = 5.42328E-4
Month = 43   targetPrice = 1104.24000   predictPrice = 1104.23914   diff = 7.77377E-5
Month = 44   targetPrice = 1114.58000   predictPrice = 1114.58307   diff = 2.75127E-4
Month = 45   targetPrice = 1130.20000   predictPrice = 1130.19238   diff = 6.74391E-4
Month = 46   targetPrice = 1173.82000   predictPrice = 1173.82891   diff = 7.58801E-4
Month = 47   targetPrice = 1211.92000   predictPrice = 1211.92000   diff = 4.97593E-7
Month = 48   targetPrice = 1181.27000   predictPrice = 1181.27454   diff = 3.84576E-4
Month = 49   targetPrice = 1203.60000   predictPrice = 1203.60934   diff = 7.75922E-4
Month = 50   targetPrice = 1180.59000   predictPrice = 1180.60006   diff = 8.51986E-4
Month = 51   targetPrice = 1156.85000   predictPrice = 1156.85795   diff = 6.87168E-4
Month = 52   targetPrice = 1191.50000   predictPrice = 1191.50082   diff = 6.89121E-5
Month = 53   targetPrice = 1191.32000   predictPrice = 1191.32780   diff = 1.84938E-4
Month = 54   targetPrice = 1234.18000   predictPrice = 1234.18141   diff = 1.14272E-4
Month = 55   targetPrice = 1220.33000   predictPrice = 1220.33276   diff = 2.26146E-4
Month = 56   targetPrice = 1228.81000   predictPrice = 1228.80612   diff = 3.15986E-4
Month = 57   targetPrice = 1207.01000   predictPrice = 1207.00419   diff = 4.81617E-4
Month = 58   targetPrice = 1249.48000   predictPrice = 1249.48941   diff = 7.52722E-4
Month = 59   targetPrice = 1248.29000   predictPrice = 1248.28153   diff = 6.78199E-4
Month = 60   targetPrice = 1280.08000   predictPrice = 1280.07984   diff = 1.22483E-5
Month = 61   targetPrice = 1280.66000   predictPrice = 1280.66951   diff = 7.42312E-4
Month = 62   targetPrice = 1294.87000   predictPrice = 1294.86026   diff = 7.51869E-4
Month = 63   targetPrice = 1310.61000   predictPrice = 1310.60544   diff = 3.48001E-4
Month = 64   targetPrice = 1270.09000   predictPrice = 1270.08691   diff = 2.43538E-4
Month = 65   targetPrice = 1270.20000   predictPrice = 1270.19896   diff = 8.21560E-5
```

Month = 66 targetPrice = 1276.66000 predictPrice = 1276.66042 diff = 3.26854E-5
Month = 67 targetPrice = 1303.82000 predictPrice = 1303.82874 diff = 6.70418E-4
Month = 68 targetPrice = 1335.85000 predictPrice = 1335.84632 diff = 2.75638E-4
Month = 69 targetPrice = 1377.94000 predictPrice = 1377.94691 diff = 5.01556E-4
Month = 70 targetPrice = 1400.63000 predictPrice = 1400.63379 diff = 2.70408E-4
Month = 71 targetPrice = 1418.30000 predictPrice = 1418.31183 diff = 8.34099E-4
Month = 72 targetPrice = 1438.24000 predictPrice = 1438.24710 diff = 4.93547E-4
Month = 73 targetPrice = 1406.82000 predictPrice = 1406.81500 diff = 3.56083E-4
Month = 74 targetPrice = 1420.86000 predictPrice = 1420.86304 diff = 2.13861E-4
Month = 75 targetPrice = 1482.37000 predictPrice = 1482.37807 diff = 5.44135E-4
Month = 76 targetPrice = 1530.62000 predictPrice = 1530.60780 diff = 7.96965E-4
Month = 77 targetPrice = 1503.35000 predictPrice = 1503.35969 diff = 6.44500E-4
Month = 78 targetPrice = 1455.27000 predictPrice = 1455.25870 diff = 7.77012E-4
Month = 79 targetPrice = 1473.99000 predictPrice = 1474.00301 diff = 8.82764E-4
Month = 80 targetPrice = 1526.75000 predictPrice = 1526.74507 diff = 3.23149E-4
Month = 81 targetPrice = 1549.38000 predictPrice = 1549.38480 diff = 3.10035E-4
Month = 82 targetPrice = 1481.14000 predictPrice = 1481.14819 diff = 5.52989E-4
Month = 83 targetPrice = 1468.36000 predictPrice = 1468.34730 diff = 8.64876E-4
Month = 84 targetPrice = 1378.55000 predictPrice = 1378.53761 diff = 8.98605E-4
Month = 85 targetPrice = 1330.63000 predictPrice = 1330.64177 diff = 8.84310E-4
Month = 86 targetPrice = 1322.70000 predictPrice = 1322.71089 diff = 8.23113E-4
Month = 87 targetPrice = 1385.59000 predictPrice = 1385.58259 diff = 5.34831E-4
Month = 88 targetPrice = 1400.38000 predictPrice = 1400.36749 diff = 8.93019E-4
Month = 89 targetPrice = 1279.99999 predictPrice = 1279.98926 diff = 8.38844E-4
Month = 90 targetPrice = 1267.38   predictPrice = 1267.39112 diff = 8.77235E-4
Month = 91 targetPrice = 1282.83000 predictPrice = 1282.82564 diff = 3.40160E-4
Month = 92 targetPrice = 1166.36000 predictPrice = 1166.35838 diff = 1.38537E-4
Month = 93 targetPrice = 968.750000 predictPrice = 968.756639 diff = 6.85325E-4
Month = 94 targetPrice = 896.24000   predictPrice = 896.236238 diff = 4.19700E-4
Month = 95 targetPrice = 903.250006 predictPrice = 903.250891 diff = 9.86647E-5
Month = 96 targetPrice = 825.880000 predictPrice = 825.877467 diff = 3.06702E-4
Month = 97 targetPrice = 735.090000 predictPrice = 735.089888 diff = 1.51705E-5
Month = 98 targetPrice = 797.870000 predictPrice = 797.864377 diff = 7.04777E-4
Month = 99 targetPrice = 872.810000 predictPrice = 872.817137 diff = 8.17698E-4
Month = 100 targetPrice = 919.14000   predictPrice = 919.144707 diff = 5.12104E-4

```
Month = 101 targetPrice = 919.32000    predictPrice = 919.311948    diff = 8.75905E-4
Month = 102 targetPrice = 987.48000    predictPrice = 987.485732    diff = 5.80499E-4
Month = 103 targetPrice = 1020.6200    predictPrice = 1020.62163    diff = 1.60605E-4
Month = 104 targetPrice = 1057.0800    predictPrice = 1057.07122    diff = 8.30374E-4
Month = 105 targetPrice = 1036.1900    predictPrice = 1036.18940    diff = 5.79388E-5
Month = 106 targetPrice = 1095.6300    predictPrice = 1095.63936    diff = 8.54512E-4
Month = 107 targetPrice = 1115.1000    predictPrice = 1115.09792    diff = 1.86440E-4
Month = 108 targetPrice = 1073.8700    predictPrice = 1073.87962    diff = 8.95733E-4
Month = 109 targetPrice = 1104.4900    predictPrice = 1104.48105    diff = 8.10355E-4
Month = 110 targetPrice = 1169.4300    predictPrice = 1169.42384    diff = 5.26459E-4
Month = 111 targetPrice = 1186.6900    predictPrice = 1186.68972    diff = 2.39657E-5
Month = 112 targetPrice = 1089.4100    predictPrice = 1089.40111    diff = 8.16044E-4
Month = 113 targetPrice = 1030.7100    predictPrice = 1030.71574    diff = 5.57237E-4
Month = 114 targetPrice = 1101.6000    predictPrice = 1101.59105    diff = 8.12503E-4
Month = 115 targetPrice = 1049.3300    predictPrice = 1049.32154    diff = 8.06520E-4
Month = 116 targetPrice = 1141.2000    predictPrice = 1141.20704    diff = 6.1701E-4
Month = 117 targetPrice = 1183.2600    predictPrice = 1183.27030    diff = 8.705E-4
Month = 118 targetPrice = 1180.5500    predictPrice = 1180.54438    diff = 4.763E-4
Month = 119 targetPrice = 1257.6400    predictPrice = 1257.63292    diff = 5.628E-4
Month = 120 targetPrice = 1286.1200    predictPrice = 1286.11021    diff = 7.608E-4

maxErrorPerc = 7.607871107092592E-4
averErrorPerc = 6.339892589243827E-6
```

The log shows that due to the use of the micro-batch method, the approximation results for this noncontinuous function are pretty good.

maxErrorDifferencePerc is less than 0.000761 percent, and averErrorDifferencePerc is less than 0.00000634 percent.

Figure 11-4 shows the chart of the training/validating results.

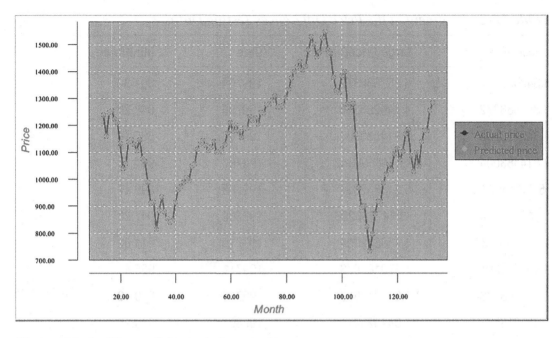

Figure 11-4. *Chart of the training results*

Testing Dataset

The testing dataset has the same format as the training dataset. As mentioned at the beginning of this example, our goal is to predict the market price for the next month, based on the ten-year historical data. Therefore, the testing dataset is the same as the training dataset, but it should include at the end one extra micro-batch record that will be used for the next month's price prediction (outside of the network training range). Table 11-4 shows a fragment of the price differences testing dataset.

Table 11-4. *Fragment of the Price Differences Testing Dataset*

priceDiffPerc	targetPriceDiffPerc	Date	inputPrice
5.840553677	5.857688372	199704	801.34
5.857688372	4.345263356	199705	848.28
4.345263356	7.814583004	199706	885.14
7.814583004	-5.746560342	199707	954.31
-5.746560342	5.315352374	199708	899.47
5.315352374	-3.447766236	199709	947.28
-3.447766236	4.458682294	199710	914.62
4.458682294	1.573163073	199711	955.4
1.573163073	1.015013963	199712	970.43
1.015013963	7.04492594	199801	980.28
7.04492594	4.994568014	199802	1049.34
4.994568014	0.907646925	199803	1101.75
0.907646925	-1.882617495	199804	1111.75
-1.882617495	3.943822079	199805	1090.82
3.943822079	-1.161539547	199806	1133.84
-1.161539547	-14.57967109	199807	1120.67
-14.57967109	6.239553736	199808	957.28
6.239553736	8.029419573	199809	1017.01
8.029419573	5.91260342	199810	1098.67
5.91260342	5.63753083	199811	1163.63
5.63753083	4.10094124	199812	1229.23
4.10094124	-3.228251696	199901	1279.64
-3.228251696	3.879418249	199902	1238.33
3.879418249	3.79439819	199903	1286.37
3.79439819	-2.497041597	199904	1335.18

(continued)

Table 11-4. (*continued*)

priceDiffPerc	targetPriceDiffPerc	Date	inputPrice
-2.497041597	5.443833344	199905	1301.84
5.443833344	-3.204609859	199906	1372.71
-3.204609859	-0.625413932	199907	1328.72
-0.625413932	-2.855173772	199908	1320.41
-2.855173772	6.253946722	199909	1282.71

Table 11-5 shows a fragment of the normalized testing dataset.

Table 11-5. *Fragment of the Normalized Testing Dataset*

priceDiffPerc	targetPriceDiffPerc	Date	inputPrice
0.722703578	0.723845891	199704	801.34
0.723845891	0.623017557	199705	848.28
0.623017557	0.854305534	199706	885.14
0.854305534	-0.049770689	199707	954.31
-0.049770689	0.687690158	199708	899.47
0.687690158	0.103482251	199709	947.28
0.103482251	0.63057882	199710	914.62
0.63057882	0.438210872	199711	955.4
0.438210872	0.401000931	199712	970.43
0.401000931	0.802995063	199801	980.28
0.802995063	0.666304534	199802	1049.34
0.666304534	0.393843128	199803	1101.75
0.393843128	0.2078255	199804	1111.75
0.2078255	0.596254805	199805	1090.82
0.596254805	0.255897364	199806	1133.84

(*continued*)

Table 11-5. (*continued*)

priceDiffPerc	targetPriceDiffPerc	Date	inputPrice
0.255897364	-0.638644739	199807	1120.67
-0.638644739	0.749303582	199808	957.28
0.749303582	0.868627972	199809	1017.01
0.868627972	0.727506895	199810	1098.67
0.727506895	0.709168722	199811	1163.63
0.709168722	0.606729416	199812	1229.23
0.606729416	0.118116554	199901	1279.64
0.118116554	0.591961217	199902	1238.33
0.591961217	0.586293213	199903	1286.37
0.586293213	0.166863894	199904	1335.18
0.166863894	0.696255556	199905	1301.84
0.696255556	0.119692676	199906	1372.71
0.119692676	0.291639071	199907	1328.72
0.291639071	0.142988415	199908	1320.41
0.142988415	0.750263115	199909	1282.71

Finally, Table 11-6 shows the sliding window testing dataset. This is the dataset used to test the trained network.

Table 11-6. Fragment of the Sliding Window Testing Dataset

Sliding Windows													
0.723	0.724	0.623	0.854	-0.050	0.688	0.103	0.631	0.438	0.401	0.803	0.666	0.394	0.208
0.724	0.623	0.854	-0.050	0.688	0.103	0.631	0.438	0.401	0.803	0.666	0.394	0.208	0.596
0.623	0.854	-0.050	0.688	0.103	0.631	0.438	0.401	0.803	0.666	0.394	0.208	0.596	0.256
0.854	-0.050	0.688	0.103	0.631	0.438	0.401	0.803	0.666	0.394	0.208	0.596	0.256	-0.639
-0.050	0.688	0.103	0.631	0.438	0.401	0.803	0.666	0.394	0.208	0.596	0.256	-0.639	0.749
0.688	0.103	0.631	0.438	0.401	0.803	0.666	0.394	0.208	0.596	0.256	-0.639	0.749	0.869
0.103	0.631	0.438	0.401	0.803	0.666	0.394	0.208	0.596	0.256	-0.639	0.749	0.869	0.728
0.631	0.438	0.401	0.803	0.666	0.394	0.208	0.596	0.256	-0.639	0.749	0.869	0.728	0.709
0.438	0.401	0.803	0.666	0.394	0.208	0.596	0.256	-0.639	0.749	0.869	0.728	0.709	0.607
0.401	0.803	0.666	0.394	0.208	0.596	0.256	-0.639	0.749	0.869	0.728	0.709	0.607	0.118
0.803	0.666	0.394	0.208	0.596	0.256	-0.639	0.749	0.869	0.728	0.709	0.607	0.118	0.592
0.666	0.394	0.208	0.596	0.256	-0.639	0.749	0.869	0.728	0.709	0.607	0.118	0.592	0.586
0.394	0.208	0.596	0.256	-0.639	0.749	0.869	0.728	0.709	0.607	0.118	0.592	0.586	0.167
0.208	0.596	0.256	-0.639	0.749	0.869	0.728	0.709	0.607	0.118	0.592	0.586	0.167	0.696
0.596	0.256	-0.639	0.749	0.869	0.728	0.709	0.607	0.118	0.592	0.586	0.167	0.696	0.120
0.256	-0.639	0.749	0.869	0.728	0.709	0.607	0.118	0.592	0.586	0.167	0.696	0.120	0.292
-0.639	0.749	0.869	0.728	0.709	0.607	0.118	0.592	0.586	0.167	0.696	0.120	0.292	0.143

(continued)

529

Table 11-6. (*continued*)

Sliding Windows												
0.749	0.869	0.728	0.709	0.607	0.118	0.592	0.586	0.167	0.696	0.120	0.292	0.750
0.869	0.728	0.709	0.607	0.118	0.592	0.586	0.167	0.696	0.120	0.292	0.143	0.460
0.728	0.709	0.607	0.118	0.592	0.586	0.167	0.696	0.120	0.292	0.143	0.750	0.719
0.709	0.607	0.118	0.592	0.586	0.167	0.696	0.120	0.292	0.143	0.750	0.460	-0.006
0.607	0.118	0.592	0.586	0.167	0.696	0.120	0.292	0.143	0.750	0.460	0.719	0.199
0.118	0.592	0.586	0.167	0.696	0.120	0.292	0.143	0.750	0.460	0.719	-0.006	0.978
0.592	0.586	0.167	0.696	0.120	0.292	0.143	0.750	0.460	0.719	-0.006	0.199	0.128
0.586	0.167	0.696	0.120	0.292	0.143	0.750	0.460	0.719	-0.006	0.199	0.978	0.187
0.167	0.696	0.120	0.292	0.143	0.750	0.460	0.719	-0.006	0.199	0.978	0.128	0.493
0.696	0.120	0.292	0.143	0.750	0.460	0.719	-0.006	0.199	0.978	0.128	0.187	0.224
0.120	0.292	0.143	0.750	0.460	0.719	-0.006	0.199	0.978	0.128	0.187	0.493	0.738
0.292	0.143	0.750	0.460	0.719	-0.006	0.199	0.978	0.128	0.187	0.493	0.224	-0.023
0.143	0.750	0.460	0.719	-0.006	0.199	0.978	0.128	0.187	0.493	0.224	0.738	0.300
0.750	0.460	0.719	-0.006	0.199	0.978	0.128	0.187	0.493	0.224	0.738	-0.023	-0.200
0.460	0.719	-0.006	0.199	0.978	0.128	0.187	0.493	0.224	0.738	-0.023	0.300	0.360
0.719	-0.006	0.199	0.978	0.128	0.187	0.493	0.224	0.738	-0.023	0.300	-0.200	0.564

-0.282	0.360	-0.200	0.300	-0.023	0.738	0.224	0.493	0.187	0.128	0.978	0.199	-0.006
-0.095	0.564	0.360	-0.200	0.300	-0.023	0.738	0.224	0.493	0.187	0.128	0.978	0.199
0.845	-0.282	0.564	0.360	-0.200	0.300	-0.023	0.738	0.224	0.493	0.187	0.128	0.978
0.367	-0.095	-0.282	0.564	0.360	-0.200	0.300	-0.023	0.738	0.224	0.493	0.187	0.128
0.166	0.845	-0.095	-0.282	0.564	0.360	-0.200	0.300	-0.023	0.738	0.224	0.493	0.187
0.262	0.367	0.845	-0.095	-0.282	0.564	0.360	-0.200	0.300	-0.023	0.738	0.224	0.493
-0.094	0.166	0.367	0.845	-0.095	-0.282	0.564	0.360	-0.200	0.300	-0.023	0.738	0.224
-0.211	0.262	0.166	0.367	0.845	-0.095	-0.282	0.564	0.360	-0.200	0.300	-0.023	0.738
0.454	-0.094	0.262	0.166	0.367	0.845	-0.095	-0.282	0.564	0.360	-0.200	0.300	-0.023
0.835	-0.211	-0.094	0.262	0.166	0.367	0.845	-0.095	-0.282	0.564	0.360	-0.200	0.300
0.384	0.454	-0.211	-0.094	0.262	0.166	0.367	0.845	-0.095	-0.282	0.564	0.360	-0.200
0.230	0.835	0.454	-0.211	-0.094	0.262	0.166	0.367	0.845	-0.095	-0.282	0.564	0.360
0.195	0.384	0.835	0.454	-0.211	-0.094	0.262	0.166	0.367	0.845	-0.095	-0.282	0.564
0.578	0.230	0.384	0.835	0.454	-0.211	-0.094	0.262	0.166	0.367	0.845	-0.095	-0.282
-0.076	0.195	0.230	0.384	0.835	0.454	-0.211	-0.094	0.262	0.166	0.367	0.845	-0.095
0.273	0.578	0.195	0.230	0.384	0.835	0.454	-0.211	-0.094	0.262	0.166	0.367	0.845
-0.150	-0.076	0.578	0.195	0.230	0.384	0.835	0.454	-0.211	-0.094	0.262	0.166	0.367
-0.193	0.273	-0.076	0.578	0.195	0.230	0.384	0.835	0.454	-0.211	-0.094	0.262	0.166
0.366	-0.150	0.273	-0.076	0.578	0.195	0.230	0.384	0.835	0.454	-0.211	-0.094	0.262

(continued)

Table 11-6. (*continued*)

Sliding Windows												
-0.094	-0.211	0.454	0.835	0.384	0.230	0.195	0.578	-0.076	0.273	-0.150	-0.193	-0.400
-0.211	0.454	0.835	0.384	0.230	0.195	0.578	-0.076	0.273	-0.150	-0.193	0.366	0.910
0.454	0.835	0.384	0.230	0.195	0.578	-0.076	0.273	-0.150	-0.193	0.366	-0.400	0.714
0.835	0.384	0.230	0.195	0.578	-0.076	0.273	-0.150	-0.193	0.366	-0.400	0.910	-0.069
0.384	0.230	0.195	0.578	-0.076	0.273	-0.150	-0.193	0.366	-0.400	0.910	0.714	0.151
0.230	0.195	0.578	-0.076	0.273	-0.150	-0.193	0.366	-0.400	0.910	0.714	-0.069	0.220
0.195	0.578	-0.076	0.273	-0.150	-0.193	0.366	-0.400	0.910	0.714	-0.069	0.151	0.389
0.578	-0.076	0.273	-0.150	-0.193	0.366	-0.400	0.910	0.714	-0.069	0.151	0.220	0.874
-0.076	0.273	-0.150	-0.193	0.366	-0.400	0.910	0.714	-0.069	0.151	0.220	0.389	0.673
0.273	-0.150	-0.193	0.366	-0.400	0.910	0.714	-0.069	0.151	0.220	0.389	0.874	0.409
-0.150	-0.193	0.366	-0.400	0.910	0.714	-0.069	0.151	0.220	0.389	0.874	0.673	0.441
-0.193	0.366	-0.400	0.910	0.714	-0.069	0.151	0.220	0.389	0.874	0.673	0.409	0.452
0.366	-0.400	0.910	0.714	-0.069	0.151	0.220	0.389	0.874	0.673	0.409	0.441	0.254
-0.400	0.910	0.714	-0.069	0.151	0.220	0.389	0.874	0.673	0.409	0.441	0.452	0.700
0.910	0.714	-0.069	0.151	0.220	0.389	0.874	0.673	0.409	0.441	0.452	0.254	0.381
0.714	-0.069	0.151	0.220	0.389	0.874	0.673	0.409	0.441	0.452	0.254	0.700	0.672
-0.069	0.151	0.220	0.389	0.874	0.673	0.409	0.441	0.452	0.254	0.700	0.381	0.449

0.415	0.672	0.381	0.700	0.254	0.452	0.441	0.409	0.673	0.874	0.389	0.220	0.151
0.224	0.449	0.672	0.381	0.700	0.254	0.452	0.441	0.409	0.673	0.874	0.389	0.220
0.221	0.415	0.449	0.672	0.381	0.700	0.254	0.452	0.441	0.409	0.673	0.874	0.389
0.414	0.224	0.415	0.449	0.672	0.381	0.700	0.254	0.452	0.441	0.409	0.673	0.874
0.453	0.221	0.224	0.415	0.449	0.672	0.381	0.700	0.254	0.452	0.441	0.409	0.673
0.105	0.414	0.221	0.224	0.415	0.449	0.672	0.381	0.700	0.254	0.452	0.441	0.409
0.349	0.453	0.414	0.221	0.224	0.415	0.449	0.672	0.381	0.700	0.254	0.452	0.441
0.396	0.105	0.453	0.414	0.221	0.224	0.415	0.449	0.672	0.381	0.700	0.254	0.452
0.427	0.349	0.105	0.453	0.414	0.221	0.224	0.415	0.449	0.672	0.381	0.700	0.254
0.591	0.396	0.349	0.105	0.453	0.414	0.221	0.224	0.415	0.449	0.672	0.381	0.700
0.550	0.427	0.396	0.349	0.105	0.453	0.414	0.221	0.224	0.415	0.449	0.672	0.381
0.165	0.591	0.427	0.396	0.349	0.105	0.453	0.414	0.221	0.224	0.415	0.449	0.672
0.459	0.550	0.591	0.427	0.396	0.349	0.105	0.453	0.414	0.221	0.224	0.415	0.449
0.206	0.165	0.550	0.591	0.427	0.396	0.349	0.105	0.453	0.414	0.221	0.224	0.415
0.199	0.459	0.165	0.550	0.591	0.427	0.396	0.349	0.105	0.453	0.414	0.221	0.224
0.533	0.206	0.459	0.165	0.550	0.591	0.427	0.396	0.349	0.105	0.453	0.414	0.221
0.332	0.199	0.206	0.459	0.165	0.550	0.591	0.427	0.396	0.349	0.105	0.453	0.414
0.573	0.533	0.199	0.206	0.459	0.165	0.550	0.591	0.427	0.396	0.349	0.105	0.453
0.259	0.332	0.533	0.199	0.206	0.459	0.165	0.550	0.591	0.427	0.396	0.349	0.105

(continued)

Table 11-6. (*continued*)

	Sliding Windows											
0.349	0.396	0.427	0.591	0.550	0.165	0.459	0.206	0.199	0.533	0.332	0.573	0.380
0.396	0.427	0.591	0.550	0.165	0.459	0.206	0.199	0.533	0.332	0.573	0.259	0.215
0.427	0.591	0.550	0.165	0.459	0.206	0.199	0.533	0.332	0.573	0.259	0.380	0.568
0.591	0.550	0.165	0.459	0.206	0.199	0.533	0.332	0.573	0.259	0.380	0.215	0.327
0.550	0.165	0.459	0.206	0.199	0.533	0.332	0.573	0.259	0.380	0.215	0.568	0.503
0.165	0.459	0.206	0.199	0.533	0.332	0.573	0.259	0.380	0.215	0.568	0.327	0.336
0.459	0.206	0.199	0.533	0.332	0.573	0.259	0.380	0.215	0.568	0.327	0.503	0.407
0.206	0.199	0.533	0.332	0.573	0.259	0.380	0.215	0.568	0.327	0.503	0.336	0.414
0.199	0.533	0.332	0.573	0.259	0.380	0.215	0.568	0.327	0.503	0.336	0.407	0.127
0.533	0.332	0.573	0.259	0.380	0.215	0.568	0.327	0.503	0.336	0.407	0.414	0.334
0.332	0.573	0.259	0.380	0.215	0.568	0.327	0.503	0.336	0.407	0.414	0.127	0.367
0.573	0.259	0.380	0.215	0.568	0.327	0.503	0.336	0.407	0.414	0.127	0.334	0.475
0.259	0.380	0.215	0.568	0.327	0.503	0.336	0.407	0.414	0.127	0.334	0.367	0.497
0.380	0.215	0.568	0.327	0.503	0.336	0.407	0.414	0.127	0.334	0.367	0.475	0.543
0.215	0.568	0.327	0.503	0.336	0.407	0.414	0.127	0.334	0.367	0.475	0.497	0.443
0.568	0.327	0.503	0.336	0.407	0.414	0.127	0.334	0.367	0.475	0.497	0.543	0.417
0.327	0.503	0.336	0.407	0.414	0.127	0.334	0.367	0.475	0.497	0.543	0.443	0.427

0.503	0.336	0.407	0.414	0.127	0.334	0.367	0.475	0.497	0.543	0.443	0.417	0.188
0.336	0.407	0.414	0.127	0.334	0.367	0.475	0.497	0.543	0.443	0.417	0.427	0.400
0.407	0.414	0.127	0.334	0.367	0.475	0.497	0.543	0.443	0.417	0.427	0.188	0.622
0.414	0.127	0.334	0.367	0.475	0.497	0.543	0.443	0.417	0.427	0.188	0.400	0.550
0.127	0.334	0.367	0.475	0.497	0.543	0.443	0.417	0.427	0.188	0.400	0.622	0.215
0.334	0.367	0.475	0.497	0.543	0.443	0.417	0.427	0.188	0.400	0.622	0.550	0.120
0.367	0.475	0.497	0.543	0.443	0.417	0.427	0.188	0.400	0.622	0.550	0.215	0.419
0.475	0.497	0.543	0.443	0.417	0.427	0.188	0.400	0.622	0.550	0.215	0.120	0.572
0.497	0.543	0.443	0.417	0.427	0.188	0.400	0.622	0.550	0.215	0.120	0.419	0.432
0.543	0.443	0.417	0.427	0.188	0.400	0.622	0.550	0.215	0.120	0.419	0.572	0.040
0.443	0.417	0.427	0.188	0.400	0.622	0.550	0.215	0.120	0.419	0.572	0.432	0.276
0.417	0.427	0.188	0.400	0.622	0.550	0.215	0.120	0.419	0.572	0.432	0.040	-0.074
0.427	0.188	0.400	0.622	0.550	0.215	0.120	0.419	0.572	0.432	0.040	0.276	0.102
0.188	0.400	0.622	0.550	0.215	0.120	0.419	0.572	0.432	0.040	0.276	-0.074	0.294
0.400	0.622	0.550	0.215	0.120	0.419	0.572	0.432	0.040	0.276	-0.074	0.102	0.650
0.622	0.550	0.215	0.120	0.419	0.572	0.432	0.040	0.276	-0.074	0.102	0.294	0.404

The sliding window testing dataset is broken in to micro-batch files, and Figure 11-5 shows a fragment of the list of testing micro-batch files.

```
Sample7_Microbatches_Test_Batch_000.csv
Sample7_Microbatches_Test_Batch_001.csv
Sample7_Microbatches_Test_Batch_002.csv
Sample7_Microbatches_Test_Batch_003.csv
Sample7_Microbatches_Test_Batch_004.csv
Sample7_Microbatches_Test_Batch_005.csv
Sample7_Microbatches_Test_Batch_006.csv
Sample7_Microbatches_Test_Batch_007.csv
Sample7_Microbatches_Test_Batch_008.csv
Sample7_Microbatches_Test_Batch_009.csv
Sample7_Microbatches_Test_Batch_010.csv
Sample7_Microbatches_Test_Batch_011.csv
Sample7_Microbatches_Test_Batch_012.csv
Sample7_Microbatches_Test_Batch_013.csv
Sample7_Microbatches_Test_Batch_014.csv
Sample7_Microbatches_Test_Batch_015.csv
Sample7_Microbatches_Test_Batch_016.csv
Sample7_Microbatches_Test_Batch_017.csv
Sample7_Microbatches_Test_Batch_018.csv
Sample7_Microbatches_Test_Batch_019.csv
Sample7_Microbatches_Test_Batch_020.csv
Sample7_Microbatches_Test_Batch_021.csv
Sample7_Microbatches_Test_Batch_022.csv
Sample7_Microbatches_Test_Batch_023.csv
Sample7_Microbatches_Test_Batch_024.csv
Sample7_Microbatches_Test_Batch_025.csv
Sample7_Microbatches_Test_Batch_026.csv
Sample7_Microbatches_Test_Batch_027.csv
Sample7_Microbatches_Test_Batch_028.csv
Sample7_Microbatches_Test_Batch_029.csv
Sample7_Microbatches_Test_Batch_030.csv
Sample7_Microbatches_Test_Batch_031.csv
```

Figure 11-5. Fragment of the list of testing micro-batch datasets

Testing Logic

There are many new coding fragments in this method, so let's discuss them. We load the micro-batch dataset and the corresponding saved network in a loop over the set of testing micro-batch datasets. Remember that we are no longer processing a single test dataset but a set of micro-batch testing datasets. Next, we obtain from the network the input, actual, and predicted price values; normalize them; and calculate the real actual and predicted prices. That is done for all test records for which the saved network records exist.

However, there is no saved network file for the last micro-batch record in the test dataset, simply because the network was not trained for that point. For this record we retrieve its 12 inputPriceDiffPerc fields, which are the keys used during network training. Next we search the keys of all the saved network files that are located in the memory arrays called linkToSaveInputPriceDiffPerc_00, linkToSaveInputPriceDiffPerc_01, and so on.

Because there are 12 keys associated with each saved network, the search is done in the following way. For the micro-batch being processed, we calculate the vector value in the 12D space using Euclidean geometry. For example, for the function of 12 variables y = f(x1,x2,x3,x4,x5,x6,x7,x8,x9,x10,x11,x12), the vector value is a square root of the sum of each x value powered to 2.

$$\sqrt{x1^2 + x1^2 + x1^2 + x1^2 + x1^2 + x1^2 + x1^2 + x1^2 + x1^2 + x1^2 + x1^2 + x1^2} \qquad (11\text{-}1)$$

Then, for each set of network keys held in the linkToSaveInputPriceDiffPerc arrays, the vector value is also calculated. The network keys that closely match the set of keys from the processed record are selected and loaded in memory. Finally, we obtain from that network the input, active, and predicted values; denormalize them; and calculate the real actual and predicted values. Listing 11-7 shows the code for this logic.

Listing 11-7. The Logic of Selecting the Saved Network Record

```
static public void loadAndTestNetwork()
 {
     List<Double> xData = new ArrayList<Double>();
     List<Double> yData1 = new ArrayList<Double>();
     List<Double> yData2 = new ArrayList<Double>();

     int k1 = 0;
     int k3 = 0;

     BufferedReader br4;
     BasicNetwork network;

     try
      {
        // Process testing batches
```

```
maxGlobalResultDiff = 0.00;
averGlobalResultDiff = 0.00;
sumGlobalResultDiff = 0.00;

for (k1 = 0; k1 < intNumberOfBatchesToProcess; k1++)
 {
    br4 = new BufferedReader(new FileReader(strTestingFileNames[k1]));
    tempLine = br4.readLine();

    // Skip the label record
    tempLine = br4.readLine();

    // Brake the line using comma as separator
    tempWorkFields = tempLine.split(cvsSplitBy);

    recordNormInputPriceDiffPerc_00 = Double.parseDouble(tempWork
    Fields[0]);
    recordNormInputPriceDiffPerc_01 = Double.parseDouble(tempWork
    Fields[1]);
    recordNormInputPriceDiffPerc_02 = Double.parseDouble(tempWork
    Fields[2]);
    recordNormInputPriceDiffPerc_03 = Double.parseDouble(tempWork
    Fields[3]);
    recordNormInputPriceDiffPerc_04 = Double.parseDouble(tempWork
    Fields[4]);
    recordNormInputPriceDiffPerc_05 = Double.parseDouble(tempWork
    Fields[5]);
    recordNormInputPriceDiffPerc_06 = Double.parseDouble(tempWork
    Fields[6]);
    recordNormInputPriceDiffPerc_07 = Double.parseDouble(tempWork
    Fields[7]);
    recordNormInputPriceDiffPerc_08 = Double.parseDouble(tempWork
    Fields[8]);
    recordNormInputPriceDiffPerc_09 = Double.parseDouble(tempWork
    Fields[9]);
    recordNormInputPriceDiffPerc_10 = Double.parseDouble(tempWork
    Fields[10]);
```

```
recordNormInputPriceDiffPerc_11 = Double.parseDouble(tempWork
Fields[11]);

recordNormTargetPriceDiffPerc = Double.parseDouble(tempWork
Fields[12]);

if(k1 < 120)
 {
   // Load the network for the current record
   network =
     (BasicNetwork)EncogDirectoryPersistence.loadObject(new
        File(strSaveNetworkFileNames[k1]));

 // Load the training file record
 MLDataSet testingSet =
   loadCSV2Memory(strTestingFileNames[k1],intInputNeuronNumber,
      intOutputNeuronNumber,true,CSVFormat.ENGLISH,false);

// Get the results from the loaded previously saved networks
 int i = - 1; // Index of the array to get results

 for (MLDataPair pair:  testingSet)
  {
    i++;

    MLData inputData = pair.getInput();
    MLData actualData = pair.getIdeal();
    MLData predictData = network.compute(inputData);

    // These values are Normalized as the whole input is
    normTargetPriceDiffPerc = actualData.getData(0);
    normPredictPriceDiffPerc = predictData.getData(0);
    normInputPriceDiffPercFromRecord = inputData.getData(11);

    // De-normalize this data to show the real result value
    denormTargetPriceDiffPerc = ((targetPriceDiffPercDl -
       targetPriceDiffPercDh)*normTargetPriceDiffPerc
        - Nh*targetPriceDiffPercDl + targetPrice
        DiffPercDh*Nl)/(Nl - Nh);
```

```
denormPredictPriceDiffPerc =((targetPriceDiffPercDl -
targetPriceDiffPercDh)*
        normPredictPriceDiffPerc - Nh*targetPriceDiffPercDl +
        targetPriceDiffPercDh*Nl)/(Nl - Nh);

denormInputPriceDiffPercFromRecord =
((inputPriceDiffPercDl -
        inputPriceDiffPercDh)*normInputPriceDiffPercFrom
        Record - Nh*inputPriceDiffPercDl +
            inputPriceDiffPercDh*Nl)/(Nl - Nh);

inputPriceFromFile = arrPrices[k1+12];

// Convert denormPredictPriceDiffPerc and
   denormTargetPriceDiffPerc to real renormalized
// price

realDenormTargetPrice = inputPriceFromFile +
    inputPriceFromFile*(denormTargetPriceDiffPerc/100);
realDenormPredictPrice = inputPriceFromFile +
    inputPriceFromFile*(denormPredictPriceDiffPerc/100);

realDenormTargetToPredictPricePerc = (Math.
abs(realDenormTargetPrice -
    realDenormPredictPrice)/realDenormTargetPrice)*100;

System.out.println("Month = " + (k1+1) +  "  targetPrice =
" + realDenormTargetPrice +
    "  predictPrice =
     " + realDenormPredictPrice + "   diff = " +
     realDenormTargetToPredictPricePerc);

  }  // End of the for pair loop

 } // End for IF
else
 {

   vectorForRecord = Math.sqrt(
   Math.pow(recordNormInputPriceDiffPerc_00,2) +
```

```
Math.pow(recordNormInputPriceDiffPerc_01,2) +
Math.pow(recordNormInputPriceDiffPerc_02,2) +
Math.pow(recordNormInputPriceDiffPerc_03,2) +
Math.pow(recordNormInputPriceDiffPerc_04,2) +
Math.pow(recordNormInputPriceDiffPerc_05,2) +
Math.pow(recordNormInputPriceDiffPerc_06,2) +
Math.pow(recordNormInputPriceDiffPerc_07,2) +
Math.pow(recordNormInputPriceDiffPerc_08,2) +
Math.pow(recordNormInputPriceDiffPerc_09,2) +
Math.pow(recordNormInputPriceDiffPerc_10,2) +
Math.pow(recordNormInputPriceDiffPerc_11,2));

// Look for the network of previous months that closely
   match the
// vectorForRecord value

minVectorValue = 999.99;

for (k3 = 0; k3 < intNumberOfSavedNetworks; k3++)
   {
     r_00 = linkToSaveInputPriceDiffPerc_00[k3];
     r_01 = linkToSaveInputPriceDiffPerc_01[k3];
     r_02 = linkToSaveInputPriceDiffPerc_02[k3];
     r_03 = linkToSaveInputPriceDiffPerc_03[k3];
     r_04 = linkToSaveInputPriceDiffPerc_04[k3];
     r_05 = linkToSaveInputPriceDiffPerc_05[k3];
     r_06 = linkToSaveInputPriceDiffPerc_06[k3];
     r_07 = linkToSaveInputPriceDiffPerc_07[k3];
     r_08 = linkToSaveInputPriceDiffPerc_08[k3];
     r_09 = linkToSaveInputPriceDiffPerc_09[k3];
     r_10 = linkToSaveInputPriceDiffPerc_10[k3];
     r_11 = linkToSaveInputPriceDiffPerc_11[k3];

     r2 = linkToSaveTargetPriceDiffPerc[k3];

     vectorForNetworkRecord = Math.sqrt(
     Math.pow(r_00,2) +
     Math.pow(r_01,2) +
```

```
                  Math.pow(r_02,2) +
                  Math.pow(r_03,2) +
                  Math.pow(r_04,2) +
                  Math.pow(r_05,2) +
                  Math.pow(r_06,2) +
                  Math.pow(r_07,2) +
                  Math.pow(r_08,2) +
                  Math.pow(r_09,2) +
                  Math.pow(r_10,2) +
                  Math.pow(r_11,2));

                  vectorDiff = Math.abs(vectorForRecord - vectorFor
                  NetworkRecord);

                  if(vectorDiff < minVectorValue)
                   {
                     minVectorValue = vectorDiff;

                     // Save this network record attributes
                     rTempKey = r_00;
                     rTempPriceDiffPerc = r2;
                     tempMinIndex = k3;
                   }

     }  // End  FOR k3 loop

   network =
   (BasicNetwork)EncogDirectoryPersistence.loadObject(new
        File(strSaveNetworkFileNames[tempMinIndex]));

    // Now, tempMinIndex points to the corresponding saved network
    // Load this network in memory

   MLDataSet testingSet =
      loadCSV2Memory(strTestingFileNames[k1],intInputNeuronNumber,
         intOutputNeuronNumber,true,CSVFormat.ENGLISH,false);

    // Get the results from the loaded network
    int i = - 1;
```

```
    for (MLDataPair pair:  testingSet)
     {
        i++;

        MLData inputData = pair.getInput();
        MLData actualData = pair.getIdeal();
        MLData predictData = network.compute(inputData);

        // These values are Normalized as the whole input is
        normTargetPriceDiffPerc = actualData.getData(0);
        normPredictPriceDiffPerc = predictData.getData(0);
        normInputPriceDiffPercFromRecord = inputData.getData(11);

// Renormalize this data to show the real result value
        denormTargetPriceDiffPerc = ((targetPriceDiffPercDl -
            targetPriceDiffPercDh)*normTargetPriceDiffPerc
             - Nh*targetPriceDiffPercDl +
            targetPriceDiffPercDh*Nl)/(Nl - Nh);

        denormPredictPriceDiffPerc =((targetPriceDiffPercDl -
        targetPriceDiffPercDh)*
            normPredictPriceDiffPerc - Nh*targetPriceDiffPercDl +
            targetPriceDiffPercDh*Nl)/(Nl - Nh);

        denormInputPriceDiffPercFromRecord =
        ((inputPriceDiffPercDl -
            inputPriceDiffPercDh)*normInputPriceDiffPercFromRecord -
            Nh*inputPriceDiffPercDl +
                inputPriceDiffPercDh*Nl)/(Nl - Nh);

        inputPriceFromFile = arrPrices[k1+12];

        // Convert denormPredictPriceDiffPerc and
            denormTargetPriceDiffPerc to a real
       //renormalized price
        realDenormTargetPrice = inputPriceFromFile +
             inputPriceFromFile*(denormTargetPriceDiffPerc/100);
        realDenormPredictPrice = inputPriceFromFile +
```

```
                    inputPriceFromFile*(denormPredictPriceDiffPerc/100);

            realDenormTargetToPredictPricePerc = (Math.
            abs(realDenormTargetPrice -
                realDenormPredictPrice)/realDenormTargetPrice)*100;

            System.out.println("Month = " + (k1+1) +  "  targetPrice =
            " + realDenormTargetPrice + "
                predictPrice = " + realDenormPredictPrice +
                "   diff = " +
                    realDenormTargetToPredictPricePerc);

            if (realDenormTargetToPredictPricePerc >
            maxGlobalResultDiff)
              maxGlobalResultDiff = realDenormTargetToPredict
              PricePerc;

            sumGlobalResultDiff = sumGlobalResultDiff + realDenorm
            TargetToPredictPricePerc;

          } // End of IF

      }  // End for the pair loop

      // Populate chart elements

      tempMonth = (double) k1+14;
      xData.add(tempMonth);
      yData1.add(realDenormTargetPrice);
      yData2.add(realDenormPredictPrice);

    }   // End of loop K1

  // Print the max and average results

  System.out.println(" ");
  System.out.println(" ");
  System.out.println("Results of processing testing batches");

  averGlobalResultDiff = sumGlobalResultDiff/
  intNumberOfBatchesToProcess;
```

```
      System.out.println("maxGlobalResultDiff = " + maxGlobalResultDiff +
      "  i = " + maxGlobalIndex);
      System.out.println("averGlobalResultDiff = " +
      averGlobalResultDiff);
      System.out.println(" ");
      System.out.println(" ");

  }      // End of TRY
catch (IOException e1)
 {
      e1.printStackTrace();
 }

// All testing batch files have been processed
  XYSeries series1 = Chart.addSeries("Actual Price", xData, yData1);
  XYSeries series2 = Chart.addSeries("Forecasted Price", xData, yData2);

  series1.setLineColor(XChartSeriesColors.BLUE);
  series2.setMarkerColor(Color.ORANGE);
  series1.setLineStyle(SeriesLines.SOLID);
  series2.setLineStyle(SeriesLines.SOLID);

  // Save the chart image
  try
   {
     BitmapEncoder.saveBitmapWithDPI(Chart, strChartFileName,
     BitmapFormat.JPG, 100);
   }
  catch (Exception bt)
   {
     bt.printStackTrace();
   }

  System.out.println ("The Chart has been saved");

} // End of the method
```

Testing Results

Listing 11-8 shows the log of the testing results.

Listing 11-8. Testing Results

```
Month =      1  targetPrice = 1090.81999    predictPrice = 1090.81862
diff = 1.26406E-4
Month =      2  targetPrice = 1133.83999    predictPrice = 1133.84137
diff = 1.21514E-4
Month =      3  targetPrice = 1120.67000    predictPrice = 1120.66834
diff = 1.47557E-4
Month =      4  targetPrice = 957.280000    predictPrice = 957.273196
diff = 7.10741E-4
Month =      5  targetPrice = 1017.00999    predictPrice = 1017.00773
diff = 2.22221E-4
Month =      6  targetPrice = 1098.67000    predictPrice = 1098.66795
diff = 1.86309E-4
Month =      7  targetPrice = 1163.63000    predictPrice = 1163.62063
diff = 8.04467E-4
Month =      8  targetPrice = 1229.22999    predictPrice = 1229.22777
diff = 1.80847E-4
Month =      9  targetPrice = 1279.64000    predictPrice = 1279.63438
diff = 4.38765E-4
Month =     10  targetPrice = 1238.33000    predictPrice = 1238.33288
diff = 2.33186E-4
Month =     11  targetPrice = 1286.37000    predictPrice = 1286.36771
diff = 1.77470E-4
Month =     12  targetPrice = 1335.18000    predictPrice = 1335.18633
diff = 4.74799E-4
Month =     13  targetPrice = 1301.84000    predictPrice = 1301.85154
diff = 8.86728E-4
Month =     14  targetPrice = 1372.70999    predictPrice = 1372.72035
diff = 7.54282E-4
Month =     15  targetPrice = 1328.71999    predictPrice = 1328.70998
diff = 7.53875E-4
```

```
Month =    16  targetPrice = 1320.40999    predictPrice = 1320.40583
diff = 3.15133E-4
Month =    17  targetPrice = 1282.70999    predictPrice = 1282.72125
diff = 8.77519E-4
Month =    18  targetPrice = 1362.93000    predictPrice = 1362.92718
diff = 2.06881E-4
Month =    19  targetPrice = 1388.91000    predictPrice = 1388.89924
diff = 7.74644E-4
Month =    20  targetPrice = 1469.25000    predictPrice = 1469.23911
diff = 7.40870E-4
Month =    21  targetPrice = 1394.46000    predictPrice = 1394.47216
diff = 8.72695E-4
Month =    22  targetPrice = 1366.42000    predictPrice = 1366.41754
diff = 1.79908E-4
Month =    23  targetPrice = 1498.58000    predictPrice = 1498.58325
diff = 2.17251E-4
Month =    24  targetPrice = 1452.42999    predictPrice = 1452.42533
diff = 3.21443E-4
Month =    25  targetPrice = 1420.59999    predictPrice = 1420.60865
diff = 6.09378E-4
Month =    26  targetPrice = 1454.59999    predictPrice = 1454.58933
diff = 7.33179E-4
Month =    27  targetPrice = 1430.82999    predictPrice = 1430.82343
diff = 4.58933E-4
Month =    28  targetPrice = 1517.68000    predictPrice = 1517.66742
diff = 8.28335E-4
Month =    29  targetPrice = 1436.51000    predictPrice = 1436.50133
diff = 6.03050E-4
Month =    30  targetPrice = 1429.40000    predictPrice = 1429.38716
diff = 8.98280E-4
Month =    31  targetPrice = 1314.95000    predictPrice = 1314.95726
diff = 5.52363E-4
Month =    32  targetPrice = 1320.27999    predictPrice = 1320.27602
diff = 3.00856E-4
Month =    33  targetPrice = 1366.00999    predictPrice = 1366.01970
diff = 7.10801E-4
```

Month =   34 targetPrice = 1239.93999   predictPrice = 1239.94653
diff = 5.27151E-4
Month =   35 targetPrice = 1160.32999   predictPrice = 1160.32332
diff = 5.74945E-4
Month =   36 targetPrice = 1249.45999   predictPrice = 1249.45964
diff = 2.80901E-5
Month =   37 targetPrice = 1255.81999   predictPrice = 1255.83124
diff = 8.95371E-4
Month =   38 targetPrice = 1224.37999   predictPrice = 1224.37930
diff = 5.65439E-5
Month =   39 targetPrice = 1211.23000   predictPrice = 1211.23811
diff = 6.70068E-4
Month =   40 targetPrice = 1133.57999   predictPrice = 1133.57938
diff = 5.41728E-5
Month =   41 targetPrice = 1040.94000   predictPrice = 1040.94868
diff = 8.34020E-4
Month =   42 targetPrice = 1059.78000   predictPrice = 1059.78527
diff = 4.98200E-4
Month =   43 targetPrice = 1139.45000   predictPrice = 1139.44873
diff = 1.11249E-4
Month =   44 targetPrice = 1148.08000   predictPrice = 1148.08052
diff = 4.56909E-5
Month =   45 targetPrice = 1130.20000   predictPrice = 1130.19783
diff = 1.91119E-4
Month =   46 targetPrice = 1106.73000   predictPrice = 1106.72432
diff = 5.12476E-4
Month =   47 targetPrice = 1147.39000   predictPrice = 1147.39610
diff = 5.32008E-4
Month =   48 targetPrice = 1076.91999   predictPrice = 1076.91978
diff = 2.00479E-5
Month =   49 targetPrice = 1067.13999   predictPrice = 1067.13933
diff = 6.22573E-5
Month =   50 targetPrice = 989.819999   predictPrice = 989.821716
diff = 1.73446E-4
Month =   51 targetPrice = 911.620000   predictPrice = 911.617992
diff = 2.20263E-4

```
Month =    52  targetPrice = 916.070000    predictPrice = 916.077853
diff = 8.57315E-4
Month =    53  targetPrice = 815.280000    predictPrice = 815.272825
diff = 8.79955E-4
Month =    54  targetPrice = 885.759999    predictPrice = 885.765094
diff = 5.75183E-4
Month =    55  targetPrice = 936.309999    predictPrice = 936.309870
diff = 1.38348E-5
Month =    56  targetPrice = 879.820000    predictPrice = 879.812301
diff = 8.74999E-4
Month =    57  targetPrice = 855.700000    predictPrice = 855.704800
diff = 5.60997E-4
Month =    58  targetPrice = 841.149999    predictPrice = 841.157370
diff = 8.76199E-4
Month =    59  targetPrice = 848.179999    predictPrice = 848.177501
diff = 2.94516E-4
Month =    60  targetPrice = 916.919999    predictPrice = 916.916469
diff = 3.85047E-4
Month =    61  targetPrice = 963.589999    predictPrice = 963.589343
diff = 6.81249E-5
Month =    62  targetPrice = 974.499999    predictPrice = 974.501631
diff = 1.67473E-4
Month =    63  targetPrice = 990.309999    predictPrice = 990.317332
diff = 7.40393E-4
Month =    64  targetPrice = 1008.00999    predictPrice = 1008.01649
diff = 6.44417E-4
Month =    65  targetPrice = 995.970000    predictPrice = 995.962936
diff = 7.09244E-4
Month =    66  targetPrice = 1050.71000    predictPrice = 1050.70415
diff = 5.56362E-4
Month =    67  targetPrice = 1058.19999    predictPrice = 1058.20655
diff = 6.19497E-4
Month =    68  targetPrice = 1111.92000    predictPrice = 1111.91877
diff = 1.10107E-4
Month =    69  targetPrice = 1131.12999    predictPrice = 1131.12013
diff = 8.71747E-4
```

```
Month =    70  targetPrice = 1144.93999    predictPrice = 1144.94455
diff = 3.97919E-4
Month =    71  targetPrice = 1126.20999    predictPrice = 1126.21662
diff = 5.88137E-4
Month =    72  targetPrice = 1107.30000    predictPrice = 1107.30902
diff = 8.15027E-4
Month =    73  targetPrice = 1120.67999    predictPrice = 1120.68134
diff = 1.19709E-4
Month =    74  targetPrice = 1140.83999    predictPrice = 1140.83233
diff = 6.72045E-4
Month =    75  targetPrice = 1101.71999    predictPrice = 1101.72991
diff = 8.99967E-4
Month =    76  targetPrice = 1104.24000    predictPrice = 1104.23781
diff = 1.97959E-4
Month =    77  targetPrice = 1114.58000    predictPrice = 1114.57983
diff = 1.46639E-5
Month =    78  targetPrice = 1130.19999    predictPrice = 1130.19492
diff = 4.48619E-4
Month =    79  targetPrice = 1173.81999    predictPrice = 1173.81767
diff = 1.98190E-4
Month =    80  targetPrice = 1211.91999    predictPrice = 1211.91169
diff = 6.84919E-4
Month =    81  targetPrice = 1181.26999    predictPrice = 1181.26737
diff = 2.22043E-4
Month =    82  targetPrice = 1203.60000    predictPrice = 1203.60487
diff = 4.05172E-4
Month =    83  targetPrice = 1180.59000    predictPrice = 1180.59119
diff = 1.01641E-4
Month =    84  targetPrice = 1156.84999    predictPrice = 1156.84136
diff = 7.46683E-4
Month =    85  targetPrice = 1191.49999    predictPrice = 1191.49043
diff = 8.02666E-4
Month =    86  targetPrice = 1191.32999    predictPrice = 1191.31947
diff = 8.83502E-4
Month =    87  targetPrice = 1234.17999    predictPrice = 1234.17993
diff = 5.48814E-6
```

```
Month =    88  targetPrice = 1220.33000   predictPrice = 1220.31947
diff = 8.62680E-4
Month =    89  targetPrice = 1228.80999   predictPrice = 1228.82099
diff = 8.95176E-4
Month =    90  targetPrice = 1207.00999   predictPrice = 1207.00976
diff = 1.92764E-5
Month =    91  targetPrice = 1249.48000   predictPrice = 1249.48435
diff = 3.48523E-4
Month =    92  targetPrice = 1248.28999   predictPrice = 1248.27937
diff = 8.51313E-4
Month =    93  targetPrice = 1280.08000   predictPrice = 1280.08774
diff = 6.05221E-4
Month =    94  targetPrice = 1280.66000   predictPrice = 1280.66295
diff = 2.30633E-4
Month =    95  targetPrice = 1294.86999   predictPrice = 1294.85904
diff = 8.46250E-4
Month =    96  targetPrice = 1310.60999   predictPrice = 1310.61570
diff = 4.35072E-4
Month =    97  targetPrice = 1270.08999   predictPrice = 1270.08943
diff = 4.41920E-5
Month =    98  targetPrice = 1270.19999   predictPrice = 1270.21071
diff = 8.43473E-4
Month =    99  targetPrice = 1276.65999   predictPrice = 1276.65263
diff = 5.77178E-4
Month = 100  targetPrice = 1303.81999   predictPrice = 1303.82201
diff = 1.54506E-4
Month = 101  targetPrice = 1335.85000   predictPrice = 1335.83897
diff = 8.25569E-4
Month = 102  targetPrice = 1377.93999   predictPrice = 1377.94590
diff = 4.28478E-4
Month = 103  targetPrice = 1400.63000   predictPrice = 1400.62758
diff = 1.72417E-4
Month = 104  targetPrice = 1418.29999   predictPrice = 1418.31083
diff = 7.63732E-4
Month = 105  targetPrice = 1438.23999   predictPrice = 1438.23562
diff = 3.04495E-4
```

```
Month = 106  targetPrice = 1406.82000    predictPrice = 1406.83156
diff = 8.21893E-4
Month = 107  targetPrice = 1420.85999    predictPrice = 1420.86256
diff = 1.80566E-4
Month = 108  targetPrice = 1482.36999    predictPrice = 1482.35896
diff = 7.44717E-4
Month = 109  targetPrice = 1530.62000    predictPrice = 1530.62213
diff = 1.39221E-4
Month = 110  targetPrice = 1503.34999    predictPrice = 1503.33884
diff = 7.42204E-4
Month = 111  targetPrice = 1455.27000    predictPrice = 1455.27626
diff = 4.30791E-4
Month = 112  targetPrice = 1473.98999    predictPrice = 1473.97685
diff = 8.91560E-4
Month = 113  targetPrice = 1526.75000    predictPrice = 1526.76231
diff = 8.06578E-4
Month = 114  targetPrice = 1549.37999    predictPrice = 1549.39017
diff = 6.56917E-4
Month = 115  targetPrice = 1481.14000    predictPrice = 1481.15076
diff = 7.27101E-4
Month = 116  targetPrice = 1468.35999    predictPrice = 1468.35702
diff = 2.02886E-4
Month = 117  targetPrice = 1378.54999    predictPrice = 1378.55999
diff = 7.24775E-4
Month = 118  targetPrice = 1330.63000    predictPrice = 1330.61965
diff = 7.77501E-4
Month = 119  targetPrice = 1322.70000    predictPrice = 1322.69947
diff = 3.99053E-5
Month = 120  targetPrice = 1385.58999    predictPrice = 1385.60045
diff = 7.54811E-4
Month = 121  targetPrice = 1400.38000    predictPrice = 1162.09439
diff = 17.0157

maxErrorPerc = 17.0157819794876
averErrorPerc = 0.14062629735113719
```

Figure 11-6 shows the chart of the testing results.

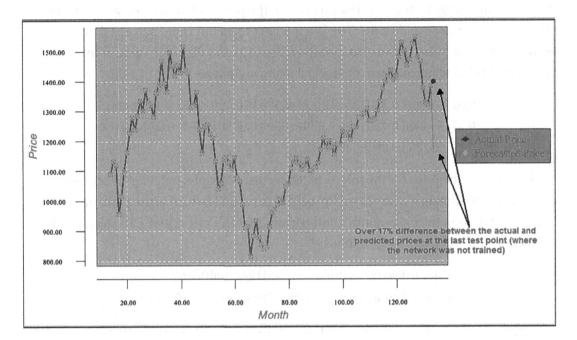

Figure 11-6. *Chart of the testing results*

Analyzing Testing Results

At all the points where the network was trained, the predicted price closely matches the actual price (the yellow and blue charts practically overlap). However, at next month's point (the point where the network was not trained), the predicted price differs from the actual price (which we happen to know) by more than 17 percent. Even the direction of next month's predicted price (the difference from the previous month) is wrong. The actual price is slightly increased, while the predicted price dropped considerably.

With the prices at these points being at around 1200 to 1300, the 17 percent difference represents the error of more than 200 points. This could not be considered as a prediction, and the result is useless for traders/investors. So, what is wrong? We did not violate the restriction of predicting function values outside of the training range (by transforming the price function to be dependent on the price difference between months instead of the sequential months). To answer this question, let's research the issue.

When we process the last test record, we obtain the values of its first 12 fields from the 12 previous original records. They represent the price difference percent between the current and previous months. The last field in the record is the percent difference between the price value at the next month (record 13) and the price value at month 12. With all fields being normalized, the record is shown here:

$$0.621937887 \quad 0.550328191 \quad 0.214557935 \quad 0.12012062 \quad 0.419090615$$
$$0.571960009 \quad 0.4321489 \quad 0.039710508 \quad 0.275810074 \quad -0.074423166$$
$$0.101592253 \quad 0.29360278 \quad 0. \tag{11-2}$$

By knowing the price for the micro-batch record 12 (which is 1,385.95) and obtaining the network prediction as the `targetPriceDiffPerc` field (which is the percent difference between the next month's and current month's prices), we can calculate the next month's predicted price as follows:

$$\text{nextMonthPredictedPrice} = \text{record12ActualPrice}$$
$$+ \text{record12ActualPrice*predictedPriceDiffPerc}/100.00 \tag{11-3}$$

To get the network prediction for record 13 (`predictedPriceDiffPerc`), we feed the trained network the vector value of 12 `inputPriceDiffPerc` fields from the currently processed record (see Listing 10-2). The network returns -16.129995719. Putting it all together, we receive the predicted price for next month.

```
1385.59 - 1385.59 *16.12999/100.00 = 1,162.0943923170353
```

The predicted price for next month is equal to 1,162.09, while the actual price is 1,400.38, so the difference is 17.02 percent. That's exactly the result shown in the processing log for the last record.

```
Month = 121  targetPrice = 1400.3800000016674  predictPrice =
1162.0943923170353   diff = 17.0157819794876
```

The calculated result for next month's price is mathematically correct and is based on the sum of the price at the last training point and the price difference percent between the next and current points returned by the network.

The problem is that the historical stock market prices don't repeat themselves under the same or similar conditions. The price difference percent that the network returns for the calculated vector (10.1) of the last processed record is not correct for calculating the predicted price for the next month. This is the problem with the model that we used in this example, which assumes that the price difference percent for the future month is similar to the price difference percent recorded for the same or close condition in the past.

This is the important lesson to learn. If the model is wrong, nothing will work. Before being involved in any neural network development, the first thing that needs to be done is to prove that the chosen model works correctly. This will save you a lot of time and effort.

Summary

The chapter explained the importance of selecting the correct working model for the project. Prove that the model works correctly for your project before starting any development. Failure to select the correct model will result in an incorrectly working application. The network will also produce the wrong results when it is used to predict the results of all sort of games (gambling, sports, and so on).

CHAPTER 12

Approximation Functions in 3D Space

This chapter discusses the approximation functions in 3D space. Such function values depend on two variables (instead of the one variable that was discussed in the preceding chapters). Figure 12-1 shows the chart of the 3D function we consider in this chapter.

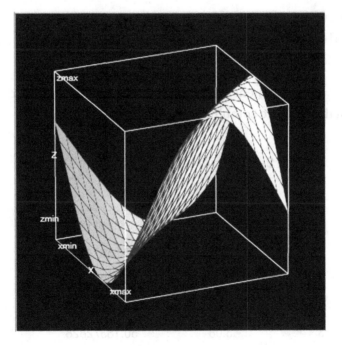

Figure 12-1. *Chart of the function in 3D space*

© Igor Livshin 2022
I. Livshin, *Artificial Neural Networks with Java*, https://doi.org/10.1007/978-1-4842-7368-5_12

Example: Approximation Functions in 3D Space

The function has the following formula: z(x, y) = 50.00 + sin(x*y). But again, we are pretending that the function formula is unknown and that the function is given to us by its values at certain points.

Data Preparation

The function values are given on the interval [3.00, 4.00] with the increment value 0.02 for both function arguments x and y. The starting point for the training dataset is 3.00, and the starting point for the testing dataset is 3.01. The increment for the x and y values is 0.02. The training dataset records consist of three fields, as shown in Listing 12-1.

Listing 12-1. Record Structure of the Training Dataset

```
Field1 - the value of the x argument
Field2 - the value of the y argument
Field3 - the function value.
```

Table 12-1 shows the fragment of the training dataset. The training dataset includes the records for all the possible combinations of the x and y values.

Table 12-1. *Fragment of the Training Dataset*

x	y	z
3	3	50.41211849
3	3.02	50.35674187
3	3.04	50.30008138
3	3.06	50.24234091
3	3.08	50.18372828
3	3.1	50.12445442
3	3.12	50.06473267
3	3.14	50.00477794

(*continued*)

Table 12-1. *(continued)*

x	y	z
3	3.16	49.94480602
3	3.18	49.88503274
3	3.2	49.82567322
3	3.22	49.76694108
3	3.24	49.70904771
3	3.26	49.65220145
3	3.28	49.59660689
3	3.3	49.54246411
3	3.32	49.48996796
3	3.34	49.43930738
3	3.36	49.39066468
3	3.38	49.34421494
3	3.4	49.30012531
3	3.42	49.25855448
3	3.44	49.21965205
3	3.46	49.18355803
3	3.48	49.15040232
3	3.5	49.12030424
3	3.52	49.09337212
3	3.54	49.06970288
3	3.56	49.0493817
3	3.58	49.03248173
3	3.6	49.01906377
3	3.62	49.00917613
3	3.64	49.00285438

(continued)

Table 12-1. *(continued)*

x	y	z
3	3.66	49.00012128
3	3.68	49.00098666
3	3.7	49.00544741
3	3.72	49.01348748
3	3.74	49.02507793
3	3.76	49.04017704
3	3.78	49.05873048
3	3.8	49.08067147
3	3.82	49.10592106
3	3.84	49.13438836
3	3.86	49.16597093
3	3.88	49.2005551
3	3.9	49.23801642
3	3.92	49.27822005
3	3.94	49.3210213
3	3.96	49.36626615
3	3.98	49.41379176
3	4	49.46342708
3.02	3	50.35674187
3.02	3.02	50.29969979
3.02	3.04	50.24156468
3.02	3.06	50.18254857
3.02	3.08	50.1228667
3.02	3.1	50.06273673
3.02	3.12	50.00237796

(continued)

Table 12-1. *(continued)*

x	y	z
3.02	3.14	49.94201051
3.02	3.16	49.88185455
3.02	3.18	49.82212948
3.02	3.2	49.76305311

Table 12-2 shows the fragment of the testing dataset. It has the same structure, but it includes the x and y points not used for the network training. Table 12-2 shows a fragment of the testing dataset.

Table 12-2. *Fragment of the Testing Dataset*

x	y	z
3.01	3.01	50.35664845
3.01	3.03	50.29979519
3.01	3.05	50.24185578
3.01	3.07	50.18304015
3.01	3.09	50.12356137
3.01	3.11	50.06363494
3.01	3.13	50.00347795
3.01	3.15	49.94330837
3.01	3.17	49.88334418
3.01	3.19	49.82380263
3.01	3.21	49.76489943
3.01	3.23	49.70684798
3.01	3.25	49.64985862
3.01	3.27	49.59413779
3.01	3.29	49.53988738

(continued)

Table 12-2. *(continued)*

x	y	z
3.01	3.31	49.48730393
3.01	3.33	49.43657796
3.01	3.35	49.38789323
3.01	3.37	49.34142613
3.01	3.39	49.29734501
3.01	3.41	49.25580956
3.01	3.43	49.21697029
3.01	3.45	49.18096788
3.01	3.47	49.14793278
3.01	3.49	49.11798468
3.01	3.51	49.09123207
3.01	3.53	49.06777188
3.01	3.55	49.04768909
3.01	3.57	49.03105648
3.01	3.59	49.0179343
3.01	3.61	49.00837009
3.01	3.63	49.0023985
3.01	3.65	49.00004117
3.01	3.67	49.00130663
3.01	3.69	49.00619031
3.01	3.71	49.0146745
3.01	3.73	49.02672848
3.01	3.75	49.04230856
3.01	3.77	49.06135831
3.01	3.79	49.08380871

(continued)

Table 12-2. *(continued)*

x	y	z
3.01	3.81	49.10957841
3.01	3.83	49.13857407
3.01	3.85	49.17069063
3.01	3.87	49.20581173
3.01	3.89	49.24381013
3.01	3.91	49.28454816
3.01	3.93	49.32787824
3.01	3.95	49.37364338
3.01	3.97	49.42167777
3.01	3.99	49.47180739
3.03	3.01	50.29979519
3.03	3.03	50.24146764
3.03	3.05	50.18225361

Network Architecture

Figure 12-2 shows the network architecture. The function we are processing has two inputs (x and y); therefore, the network architecture has two inputs.

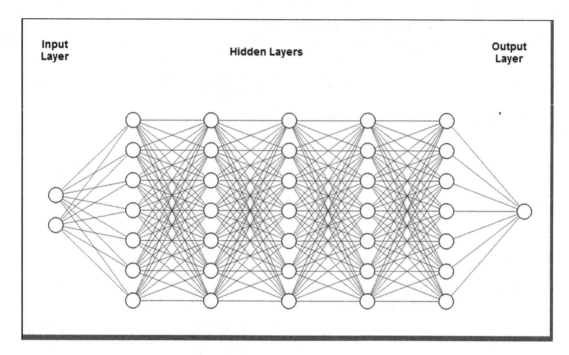

Figure 12-2. *Network architecture*

Both the training and testing datasets are normalized before being processed. We will approximate the function using the conventional network process. Based on the processing results, we will then decide whether we need to use the micro-batch method.

Program Code

Listing 12-2 shows the program code.

Listing 12-2. Program Code

```
// =================================================================
// Approximation of the 3-D Function using conventional process.
// The input file is normalized.
// =================================================================

package sample9;

import java.io.BufferedReader;
import java.io.File;
import java.io.FileInputStream;
```

```java
import java.io.PrintWriter;
import java.io.FileNotFoundException;
import java.io.FileReader;
import java.io.FileWriter;
import java.io.IOException;
import java.io.InputStream;
import java.nio.file.*;
import java.util.Properties;
import java.time.YearMonth;
import java.awt.Color;
import java.awt.Font;
import java.io.BufferedReader;
import java.text.DateFormat;
import java.text.ParseException;
import java.text.SimpleDateFormat;
import java.time.LocalDate;
import java.time.Month;
import java.time.ZoneId;
import java.util.ArrayList;
import java.util.Calendar;
import java.util.Date;
import java.util.List;
import java.util.Locale;
import java.util.Properties;

import org.encog.Encog;
import org.encog.engine.network.activation.ActivationTANH;
import org.encog.engine.network.activation.ActivationReLU;
import org.encog.ml.data.MLData;
import org.encog.ml.data.MLDataPair;
import org.encog.ml.data.MLDataSet;
import org.encog.ml.data.buffer.MemoryDataLoader;
import org.encog.ml.data.buffer.codec.CSVDataCODEC;
import org.encog.ml.data.buffer.codec.DataSetCODEC;
import org.encog.neural.networks.BasicNetwork;
import org.encog.neural.networks.layers.BasicLayer;
```

```java
import org.encog.neural.networks.training.propagation.resilient.
ResilientPropagation;
import org.encog.persist.EncogDirectoryPersistence;
import org.encog.util.csv.CSVFormat;

import org.knowm.xchart.SwingWrapper;
import org.knowm.xchart.XYChart;
import org.knowm.xchart.XYChartBuilder;
import org.knowm.xchart.XYSeries;
import org.knowm.xchart.demo.charts.ExampleChart;
import org.knowm.xchart.style.Styler.LegendPosition;
import org.knowm.xchart.style.colors.ChartColor;
import org.knowm.xchart.style.colors.XChartSeriesColors;
import org.knowm.xchart.style.lines.SeriesLines;
import org.knowm.xchart.style.markers.SeriesMarkers;
import org.knowm.xchart.BitmapEncoder;
import org.knowm.xchart.BitmapEncoder.BitmapFormat;
import org.knowm.xchart.QuickChart;
import org.knowm.xchart.SwingWrapper;

public class Sample9 implements ExampleChart<XYChart>
{
    // Interval to normalize
    static double Nh =  1;
    static double Nl = -1;

    // First column
    static double minXPointDl = 2.00;
    static double maxXPointDh = 6.00;

    // Second column
    static double minYPointDl = 2.00;
    static double maxYPointDh = 6.00;

    // Third  column - target data
    static double minTargetValueDl = 45.00;
    static double maxTargetValueDh = 55.00;
```

```
static double doublePointNumber = 0.00;
static int intPointNumber = 0;
static InputStream input = null;
static double[] arrPrices = new double[2700];
static double normInputXPointValue = 0.00;
static double normInputYPointValue = 0.00;
static double normPredictValue = 0.00;
static double normTargetValue = 0.00;
static double normDifferencePerc = 0.00;
static double returnCode = 0.00;
static double denormInputXPointValue = 0.00;
static double denormInputYPointValue = 0.00;
static double denormPredictValue = 0.00;
static double denormTargetValue = 0.00;
static double valueDifference = 0.00;
static int numberOfInputNeurons;
static int numberOfOutputNeurons;
 static int intNumberOfRecordsInTestFile;
static String trainFileName;
static String priceFileName;
static String testFileName;
static String chartTrainFileName;
static String chartTrainFileNameY;
static String chartTestFileName;
static String networkFileName;
static int workingMode;
static String cvsSplitBy = ",";

static int numberOfInputRecords = 0;

static List<Double> xData = new ArrayList<Double>();
static List<Double> yData1 = new ArrayList<Double>();
static List<Double> yData2 = new ArrayList<Double>();

static XYChart Chart;
```

```java
@Override
public XYChart getChart()
 {
  // Create Chart

  Chart = new  XYChartBuilder().width(900).height(500).title(getClass().
   getSimpleName()).xAxisTitle("x").yAxisTitle("y= f(x)").build();

  // Customize Chart
  //Chart = new  XYChartBuilder().width(900).height(500).
  title(getClass().
  //   getSimpleName()).xAxisTitle("y").yAxisTitle("z= f(y)").build();

  //Chart = new  XYChartBuilder().width(900).height(500).
  title(getClass().
  //            getSimpleName()).xAxisTitle("y").yAxisTitle("z= f(y)").
              build();

  // Customize Chart
  Chart.getStyler().setPlotBackgroundColor(ChartColor.
  getAWTColor(ChartColor.GREY));
  Chart.getStyler().setPlotGridLinesColor(new Color(255, 255, 255));

  //Chart.getStyler().setPlotBackgroundColor(ChartColor.
  getAWTColor(ChartColor.WHITE));
  //Chart.getStyler().setPlotGridLinesColor(new Color(0, 0, 0));
  Chart.getStyler().setChartBackgroundColor(Color.WHITE);
  //Chart.getStyler().setLegendBackgroundColor(Color.PINK);
  Chart.getStyler().setLegendBackgroundColor(Color.WHITE);
  //Chart.getStyler().setChartFontColor(Color.MAGENTA);
  Chart.getStyler().setChartFontColor(Color.BLACK);
  Chart.getStyler().setChartTitleBoxBackgroundColor(new Color(0, 222, 0));
  Chart.getStyler().setChartTitleBoxVisible(true);
  Chart.getStyler().setChartTitleBoxBorderColor(Color.BLACK);
  Chart.getStyler().setPlotGridLinesVisible(true);
  Chart.getStyler().setAxisTickPadding(20);
  Chart.getStyler().setAxisTickMarkLength(15);
  Chart.getStyler().setPlotMargin(20);
```

```
Chart.getStyler().setChartTitleVisible(false);
Chart.getStyler().setChartTitleFont(new Font(Font.MONOSPACED, Font.
BOLD, 24));
Chart.getStyler().setLegendFont(new Font(Font.SERIF, Font.PLAIN, 18));
Chart.getStyler().setLegendPosition(LegendPosition.OutsideS);
Chart.getStyler().setLegendSeriesLineLength(12);
Chart.getStyler().setAxisTitleFont(new Font(Font.SANS_SERIF, Font.
ITALIC, 18));
Chart.getStyler().setAxisTickLabelsFont(new Font(Font.SERIF, Font.
PLAIN, 11));
Chart.getStyler().setDatePattern("yyyy-MM");
Chart.getStyler().setDecimalPattern("#0.00");

try
   {
     // Configuration

     // Training mode
     //workingMode = 1;
     //numberOfInputRecords = 2602;
     //trainFileName =
      "C:/My_Neural_Network_Book/Book_Examples/Sample9_Calculate_Train_
      Norm.csv";
     //chartTrainFileName =
      "C:/My_Neural_Network_Book/Book_Examples/Sample9_Chart_X_
      Training_Results.csv";
     //chartTrainFileName =
     "C:/My_Neural_Network_Book/Book_Examples/Sample9_Chart_Y_Training_
     Results.csv";

     // Testing mode
     workingMode = 2;
     numberOfInputRecords = 2602;
     testFileName =
       "C:/My_Neural_Network_Book/Book_Examples/Sample9_Calculate_Test_
       Norm.csv";
     chartTestFileName =
```

```
    "C:/My_Neural_Network_Book/Book_Examples/Sample9_Chart_X_Testing_
    Results.csv";
   chartTestFileName =
    "C:/My_Neural_Network_Book/Book_Examples/Sample9_Chart_Y_Testing_
    Results.csv";

   // Common part of config data
   networkFileName =
    "C:/My_Neural_Network_Book/Book_Examples/Sample9_Saved_Network_
    File.csv";
   numberOfInputNeurons = 2;
   numberOfOutputNeurons = 1;

   // Check the working mode to run

   if(workingMode == 1)
    {
      // Training mode
      File file1 = new File(chartTrainFileName);
      File file2 = new File(networkFileName);

      if(file1.exists())
        file1.delete();

      if(file2.exists())
        file2.delete();

      returnCode = 0;     // Clear the error Code

      do
       {
         returnCode = trainValidateSaveNetwork();
       }  while (returnCode > 0);
    }
   else
    {
      // Test mode
      loadAndTestNetwork();
    }
  }
```

```
    catch (Throwable t)
      {
         t.printStackTrace();
        System.exit(1);
      }
    finally
      {
        Encog.getInstance().shutdown();
      }

  Encog.getInstance().shutdown();

  return Chart;

}  // End of the method

// ========================================================
// Load CSV to memory.
// @return The loaded dataset.
// ========================================================
public static MLDataSet loadCSV2Memory(String filename, int input, int
ideal, boolean headers,
        CSVFormat format, boolean significance)
  {
     DataSetCODEC codec = new CSVDataCODEC(new File(filename), format,
     headers, input, ideal,
         significance);
     MemoryDataLoader load = new MemoryDataLoader(codec);
     MLDataSet dataset = load.external2Memory();
     return dataset;
  }

// ========================================================
//  The main method.
//  @param Command line arguments. No arguments are used.
// ========================================================
```

```java
public static void main(String[] args)
 {
   ExampleChart<XYChart> exampleChart = new Sample9();
   XYChart Chart = exampleChart.getChart();
   new SwingWrapper<XYChart>(Chart).displayChart();
 } // End of the main method

//=======================================================================
// This method trains, Validates, and saves the trained network file
//=======================================================================
static public double trainValidateSaveNetwork()
 {
   // Load the training CSV file in memory
   MLDataSet trainingSet =
     loadCSV2Memory(trainFileName,numberOfInputNeurons,
     numberOfOutputNeurons,
       true,CSVFormat.ENGLISH,false);

   // create a neural network
   BasicNetwork network = new BasicNetwork();

   // Input layer
   network.addLayer(new BasicLayer(null,true,numberOfInputNeurons));

   // Hidden layer
   network.addLayer(new BasicLayer(new ActivationTANH(),true,7));
   network.addLayer(new BasicLayer(new ActivationTANH(),true,7));
   network.addLayer(new BasicLayer(new ActivationTANH(),true,7));
   network.addLayer(new BasicLayer(new ActivationTANH(),true,7));
   network.addLayer(new BasicLayer(new ActivationTANH(),true,7));

   // Output layer
   network.addLayer(new BasicLayer(new ActivationTANH(),false,1));

   network.getStructure().finalizeStructure();
   network.reset();

   // train the neural network
```

```java
final ResilientPropagation train = new ResilientPropagation(network,
trainingSet);

int epoch = 1;

do
 {
    train.iteration();
    System.out.println("Epoch #" + epoch + " Error:" + train.
    getError());

   epoch++;

   if (epoch >= 11000 && network.calculateError(trainingSet) >
   0.00000091)    // 0.00000371
       {
         returnCode = 1;

         System.out.println("Try again");
         return returnCode;
       }
 } while(train.getError() > 0.0000009);   // 0.0000037

// Save the network file
EncogDirectoryPersistence.saveObject(new File(networkFileName),network);

System.out.println("Neural Network Results:");

double sumNormDifferencePerc = 0.00;
double averNormDifferencePerc = 0.00;
double maxNormDifferencePerc = 0.00;

int m = 0;                      // Record number in the input file
double xPointer = 0.00;

for(MLDataPair pair: trainingSet)
  {
     m++;
     xPointer++;
```

```
//if(m == 0)
// continue;

 final MLData output = network.compute(pair.getInput());

MLData inputData = pair.getInput();
MLData actualData = pair.getIdeal();
MLData predictData = network.compute(inputData);

// Calculate and print the results
normInputXPointValue = inputData.getData(0);
normInputYPointValue = inputData.getData(1);
normTargetValue = actualData.getData(0);
normPredictValue = predictData.getData(0);

denormInputXPointValue = ((minXPointDl - maxXPointDh)*normInpu
tXPointValue -
  Nh*minXPointDl + maxXPointDh *Nl)/(Nl - Nh);

denormInputYPointValue = ((minYPointDl - maxYPointDh)*normInpu
tYPointValue -
  Nh*minYPointDl + maxYPointDh *Nl)/(Nl - Nh);

denormTargetValue =((minTargetValueDl - maxTargetValueDh)*
normTargetValue -
  Nh*minTargetValueDl + maxTargetValueDh*Nl)/(Nl - Nh);

denormPredictValue =((minTargetValueDl - maxTargetValueDh)*
normPredictValue -
  Nh*minTargetValueDl + maxTargetValueDh*Nl)/(Nl - Nh);

valueDifference =
  Math.abs(((denormTargetValue - denormPredictValue)/
  denormTargetValue)*100.00);

System.out.println ("xPoint = " + denormInputXPointValue +
"  yPoint = " +
  denormInputYPointValue + "  denormTargetValue = " +
    denormTargetValue + "  denormPredictValue = " +
    denormPredictValue +
```

```
            "  valueDifference = " + valueDifference);

        //System.out.println("intPointNumber = " + intPointNumber);

        sumNormDifferencePerc = sumNormDifferencePerc +
        valueDifference;

        if (valueDifference > maxNormDifferencePerc)
          maxNormDifferencePerc = valueDifference;

        xData.add(denormInputYPointValue);
        //xData.add(denormInputYPointValue);
        yData1.add(denormTargetValue);
        yData2.add(denormPredictValue);

    }   // End for pair loop

XYSeries series1 = Chart.addSeries("Actual data", xData, yData1);
XYSeries series2 = Chart.addSeries("Predict data", xData, yData2);

series1.setLineColor(XChartSeriesColors.BLACK);
series2.setLineColor(XChartSeriesColors.LIGHT_GREY);

series1.setMarkerColor(Color.BLACK);
series2.setMarkerColor(Color.WHITE);
series1.setLineStyle(SeriesLines.SOLID);
series2.setLineStyle(SeriesLines.SOLID);

try
 {
    //Save the chart image
    //BitmapEncoder.saveBitmapWithDPI(Chart, chartTrainFileName,
    //  BitmapFormat.JPG, 100);

    BitmapEncoder.saveBitmapWithDPI(Chart,chartTrainFileName,BitmapF
    ormat.JPG, 100);

    System.out.println ("Train Chart file has been saved") ;
 }
catch (IOException ex)
```

```java
   {
     ex.printStackTrace();
     System.exit(3);
   }

   // Finally, save this trained network
   EncogDirectoryPersistence.saveObject(new File(networkFileName),
   network);
   System.out.println ("Train Network has been saved") ;

   averNormDifferencePerc   = sumNormDifferencePerc/
   numberOfInputRecords;

   System.out.println(" ");
   System.out.println("maxErrorPerc = " + maxNormDifferencePerc +
   "   averErrorPerc = " +
       averNormDifferencePerc);

   returnCode = 0.00;
   return returnCode;

 }    // End of the method

//===================================================
// This method load and test the training network
//===================================================
static public void loadAndTestNetwork()
 {
  System.out.println("Testing the networks results");

  List<Double> xData = new ArrayList<Double>();
  List<Double> yData1 = new ArrayList<Double>();
  List<Double> yData2 = new ArrayList<Double>();

  double targetToPredictPercent = 0;
  double maxGlobalResultDiff = 0.00;
  double averGlobalResultDiff = 0.00;
  double sumGlobalResultDiff = 0.00;
  double maxGlobalIndex = 0;
```

```
double normInputXPointValueFromRecord = 0.00;
double normInputYPointValueFromRecord = 0.00;
double normTargetValueFromRecord = 0.00;
double normPredictValueFromRecord = 0.00;

BasicNetwork network;

maxGlobalResultDiff = 0.00;
averGlobalResultDiff = 0.00;
sumGlobalResultDiff = 0.00;

// Load the test dataset into memory
MLDataSet testingSet =
loadCSV2Memory(testFileName,numberOfInputNeurons,numberOfOutput
Neurons,true,
   CSVFormat.ENGLISH,false);

// Load the saved trained network
network =
   (BasicNetwork)EncogDirectoryPersistence.loadObject(new
   File(networkFileName));

int i = - 1; // Index of the current record
double xPoint = -0.00;

for (MLDataPair pair:  testingSet)
 {
     i++;
     xPoint = xPoint + 2.00;

     MLData inputData = pair.getInput();
     MLData actualData = pair.getIdeal();
     MLData predictData = network.compute(inputData);

     // These values are Normalized as the whole input is
     normInputXPointValueFromRecord = inputData.getData(0);
     normInputYPointValueFromRecord = inputData.getData(1);
     normTargetValueFromRecord = actualData.getData(0);
     normPredictValueFromRecord = predictData.getData(0);
```

```
denormInputXPointValue = ((minXPointDl - maxXPointDh)*
  normInputXPointValueFromRecord - Nh*minXPointDl +
  maxXPointDh*Nl)/(Nl - Nh);

denormInputYPointValue = ((minYPointDl - maxYPointDh)*
  normInputYPointValueFromRecord - Nh*minYPointDl +
  maxYPointDh*Nl)/(Nl - Nh);

denormTargetValue = ((minTargetValueDl - maxTargetValueDh)*
  normTargetValueFromRecord - Nh*minTargetValueDl +
  maxTargetValueDh*Nl)/(Nl - Nh);

denormPredictValue =((minTargetValueDl - maxTargetValueDh)*
  normPredictValueFromRecord - Nh*minTargetValueDl +
  maxTargetValueDh*Nl)/(Nl - Nh);

targetToPredictPercent = Math.abs((denormTargetValue -
denormPredictValue)/
  denormTargetValue*100);

System.out.println("xPoint = " + denormInputXPointValue +
"  yPoint = " +
    denormInputYPointValue + "  TargetValue = " +
    denormTargetValue + "  PredictValue = " +
    denormPredictValue + "  DiffPerc = " +
      targetToPredictPercent);

if (targetToPredictPercent > maxGlobalResultDiff)
  maxGlobalResultDiff = targetToPredictPercent;

sumGlobalResultDiff = sumGlobalResultDiff +
targetToPredictPercent;

// Populate chart elements
xData.add(denormInputXPointValue);
yData1.add(denormTargetValue);
yData2.add(denormPredictValue);

}  // End for pair loop
```

```java
// Print the max and average results
System.out.println(" ");
averGlobalResultDiff = sumGlobalResultDiff/numberOfInputRecords;

System.out.println("maxErrorPerc = " + maxGlobalResultDiff);
System.out.println("averErrorPerc = " + averGlobalResultDiff);

// All testing batch files have been processed
XYSeries series1 = Chart.addSeries("Actual data", xData, yData1);
XYSeries series2 = Chart.addSeries("Predict data", xData, yData2);

series1.setLineColor(XChartSeriesColors.BLACK);
series2.setLineColor(XChartSeriesColors.LIGHT_GREY);

series1.setMarkerColor(Color.BLACK);
series2.setMarkerColor(Color.WHITE);
series1.setLineStyle(SeriesLines.SOLID);
series2.setLineStyle(SeriesLines.SOLID);

// Save the chart image
try
 {
   BitmapEncoder.saveBitmapWithDPI(Chart, chartTestFileName ,
   BitmapFormat.JPG, 100);
 }
catch (Exception bt)
 {
    bt.printStackTrace();
 }

System.out.println ("The Chart has been saved");
System.out.println("End of testing for test records");
 } // End of the method

} // End of the class
```

Processing Results

Listing 12-3 shows the end fragment of the training processing results.

Listing 12-3. End Fragment of the Training Processing Results

```
xPoint = 4.0  yPoint = 3.3    TargetValue = 50.59207  PredictedValue =
50.58836  DiffPerc = 0.00733
xPoint = 4.0  yPoint = 3.32  TargetValue = 50.65458  PredictedValue =
50.65049  DiffPerc = 0.00806
xPoint = 4.0  yPoint = 3.34  TargetValue = 50.71290  PredictedValue =
50.70897  DiffPerc = 0.00775
xPoint = 4.0  yPoint = 3.36  TargetValue = 50.76666  PredictedValue =
50.76331  DiffPerc = 0.00659
xPoint = 4.0  yPoint = 3.38  TargetValue = 50.81552  PredictedValue =
50.81303  DiffPerc = 0.00488
xPoint = 4.0  yPoint = 3.4    TargetValue = 50.85916  PredictedValue =
50.85764  DiffPerc = 0.00298
xPoint = 4.0  yPoint = 3.42  TargetValue = 50.89730  PredictedValue =
50.89665  DiffPerc = 0.00128
xPoint = 4.0  yPoint = 3.44  TargetValue = 50.92971  PredictedValue =
50.92964  DiffPerc = 0.00131
xPoint = 4.0  yPoint = 3.46  TargetValue = 50.95616  PredictedValue =
50.95626  DiffPerc = 0.00179
xPoint = 4.0  yPoint = 3.48  TargetValue = 50.97651  PredictedValue =
50.97624  DiffPerc = 0.00 515
xPoint = 4.0  yPoint = 3.5    TargetValue = 50.99060  PredictedValue =
50.98946  DiffPerc = 0.00224
xPoint = 4.0  yPoint = 3.52  TargetValue = 50.99836  PredictedValue =
50.99587  DiffPerc = 0.00488
xPoint = 4.0  yPoint = 3.54  TargetValue = 50.99973  PredictedValue =
50.99556  DiffPerc = 0.00818
xPoint = 4.0  yPoint = 3.56  TargetValue = 50.99471  PredictedValue =
50.98869  DiffPerc = 0.01181
xPoint = 4.0  yPoint = 3.58  TargetValue = 50.98333  PredictedValue =
50.97548  DiffPerc = 0.01538
```

xPoint = 4.0 yPoint = 3.6   TargetValue = 50.96565 PredictedValue =
50.95619 DiffPerc = 0.01856
xPoint = 4.0 yPoint = 3.62 TargetValue = 50.94180 PredictedValue =
50.93108 DiffPerc = 0.02104
xPoint = 4.0 yPoint = 3.64 TargetValue = 50.91193 PredictedValue =
50.90038 DiffPerc = 0.02268
xPoint = 4.0 yPoint = 3.66 TargetValue = 50.87622 PredictedValue =
50.86429 DiffPerc = 0.02344
xPoint = 4.0 yPoint = 3.68 TargetValue = 50.83490 PredictedValue =
50.82299 DiffPerc = 0.02342
xPoint = 4.0 yPoint = 3.7   TargetValue = 50.78825 PredictedValue =
50.77664 DiffPerc = 0.02286
xPoint = 4.0 yPoint = 3.72 TargetValue = 50.73655 PredictedValue =
50.72537 DiffPerc = 0.02203
xPoint = 4.0 yPoint = 3.74 TargetValue = 50.68014 PredictedValue =
50.66938 DiffPerc = 0.02124
xPoint = 4.0 yPoint = 3.76 TargetValue = 50.61938 PredictedValue =
50.60888 DiffPerc = 0.02074
xPoint = 4.0 yPoint = 3.78 TargetValue = 50.55466 PredictedValue =
50.54420 DiffPerc = 0.02069
xPoint = 4.0 yPoint = 3.8   TargetValue = 50.48639 PredictedValue =
50.47576 DiffPerc = 0.02106
xPoint = 4.0 yPoint = 3.82 TargetValue = 50.41501 PredictedValue =
50.40407 DiffPerc = 0.02170
xPoint = 4.0 yPoint = 3.84 TargetValue = 50.34098 PredictedValue =
50.32979 DiffPerc = 0.02222
xPoint = 4.0 yPoint = 3.86 TargetValue = 50.26476 PredictedValue =
50.25363 DiffPerc = 0.02215
xPoint = 4.0 yPoint = 3.88 TargetValue = 50.18685 PredictedValue =
50.17637 DiffPerc = 0.02088
xPoint = 4.0 yPoint = 3.9   TargetValue = 50.10775 PredictedValue =
50.09883 DiffPerc = 0.01780
xPoint = 4.0 yPoint = 3.92 TargetValue = 50.02795 PredictedValue =
50.02177 DiffPerc = 0.01236

xPoint = 4.0 yPoint = 3.94 TargetValue = 49.94798 PredictedValue = 49.94594 DiffPerc = 0.00409
xPoint = 4.0 yPoint = 3.96 TargetValue = 49.86834 PredictedValue = 49.87197 DiffPerc = 0.00727
xPoint = 4.0 yPoint = 3.98 TargetValue = 49.78954 PredictedValue = 49.80041 DiffPerc = 0.02182
xPoint = 4.0 yPoint = 4.0   TargetValue = 49.71209   PredictedValue = 49.73170 DiffPerc = 0.03944

MaxErrorPerc = 0.03944085774812906
AverErrorPerc = 0.00738084715672128

We won't be displaying here the chart of the training results, because drawing two crossing 3D charts can get messy. Instead, we will project all the target and predicted values from the chart on a single panel so they can be easily compared. Figure 12-3 shows the chart that illustrates the process of projecting the function values on a single panel.

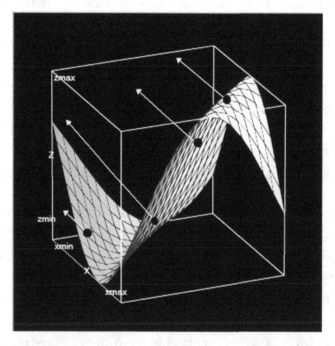

Figure 12-3. *Projection of the function values on a single panel*

Figure 12-4 shows the projection chart of the training results.

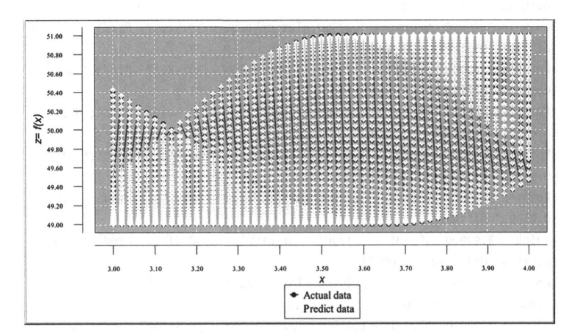

Figure 12-4. *Projection chart of the training results*

Listing 12-4 shows the testing results.

Listing 12-4. Testing Results

```
xPoint = 3.99900  yPoint = 3.13900  TargetValue = 49.98649  PredictValue =
49.98797  DiffPerc = 0.00296
xPoint = 3.99900  yPoint = 3.15900  TargetValue = 50.06642  PredictValue =
50.06756  DiffPerc = 0.00227
xPoint = 3.99900  yPoint = 3.17900  TargetValue = 50.14592  PredictValue =
50.14716  DiffPerc = 0.00246
xPoint = 3.99900  yPoint = 3.19900  TargetValue = 50.22450  PredictValue =
50.22617  DiffPerc = 0.00333
xPoint = 3.99900  yPoint = 3.21900  TargetValue = 50.30163  PredictValue =
50.30396  DiffPerc = 0.00462
xPoint = 3.99900  yPoint = 3.23900  TargetValue = 50.37684  PredictValue =
50.37989  DiffPerc = 0.00605
```

xPoint = 3.99900   yPoint = 3.25900   TargetValue = 50.44964   PredictValue = 50.45333   DiffPerc = 0.00730

xPoint = 3.99900   yPoint = 3.27900   TargetValue = 50.51957   PredictValue = 50.52367   DiffPerc = 0.00812

xPoint = 3.99900   yPoint = 3.29900   TargetValue = 50.58617   PredictValue = 50.59037   DiffPerc = 0.00829

xPoint = 3.99900   yPoint = 3.31900   TargetValue = 50.64903   PredictValue = 50.65291   DiffPerc = 0.00767

xPoint = 3.99900   yPoint = 3.33900   TargetValue = 50.70773   PredictValue = 50.71089   DiffPerc = 0.00621

xPoint = 3.99900   yPoint = 3.35900   TargetValue = 50.76191   PredictValue = 50.76392   DiffPerc = 0.00396

xPoint = 3.99900   yPoint = 3.37900   TargetValue = 50.81122   PredictValue = 50.81175   DiffPerc = 0.00103

xPoint = 3.99900   yPoint = 3.39900   TargetValue = 50.85535   PredictValue = 50.85415   DiffPerc = 0.00235

xPoint = 3.99900   yPoint = 3.41900   TargetValue = 50.89400   PredictValue = 50.89098   DiffPerc = 0.00594

xPoint = 3.99900   yPoint = 3.43900   TargetValue = 50.92694   PredictValue = 50.92213   DiffPerc = 0.00945

xPoint = 3.99900   yPoint = 3.45900   TargetValue = 50.95395   PredictValue = 50.94754   DiffPerc = 0.01258

xPoint = 3.99900   yPoint = 3.47900   TargetValue = 50.97487   PredictValue = 50.96719   DiffPerc = 0.01507

xPoint = 3.99900   yPoint = 3.49900   TargetValue = 50.98955   PredictValue = 50.98104   DiffPerc = 0.01669

xPoint = 3.99900   yPoint = 3.51900   TargetValue = 50.99790   PredictValue = 50.98907   DiffPerc = 0.01731

xPoint = 3.99900   yPoint = 3.53900   TargetValue = 50.99988   PredictValue = 50.99128   DiffPerc = 0.01686

xPoint = 3.99900   yPoint = 3.55900   TargetValue = 50.99546   PredictValue = 50.98762   DiffPerc = 0.01537

xPoint = 3.99900   yPoint = 3.57900   TargetValue = 50.98468   PredictValue = 50.97806   DiffPerc = 0.01297 xPoint = 3.99900 yPoint = 3.59900 TargetValue = 50.96760 PredictValue = 50.96257 DiffPerc = 0.00986

xPoint = 3.99900 yPoint = 3.61900 TargetValue = 50.94433 PredictValue = 50.94111 DiffPerc = 0.00632

xPoint = 3.99900 yPoint = 3.63900 TargetValue = 50.91503 PredictValue = 50.91368 DiffPerc = 0.00265

xPoint = 3.99900 yPoint = 3.65900 TargetValue = 50.87988 PredictValue = 50.88029 DiffPerc = 0.00808

xPoint = 3.99900 yPoint = 3.67900 TargetValue = 50.83910 PredictValue = 50.84103 DiffPerc = 0.00378

xPoint = 3.99900 yPoint = 3.69900 TargetValue = 50.79296 PredictValue = 50.79602 DiffPerc = 0.00601

xPoint = 3.99900 yPoint = 3.71900 TargetValue = 50.74175 PredictValue = 50.74548 DiffPerc = 0.00735

xPoint = 3.99900 yPoint = 3.73900 TargetValue = 50.68579 PredictValue = 50.68971 DiffPerc = 0.00773

xPoint = 3.99900 yPoint = 3.75900 TargetValue = 50.62546 PredictValue = 50.62910 DiffPerc = 0.00719

xPoint = 3.99900 yPoint = 3.77900 TargetValue = 50.56112 PredictValue = 50.56409 DiffPerc = 0.00588

xPoint = 3.99900 yPoint = 3.79900 TargetValue = 50.49319 PredictValue = 50.49522 DiffPerc = 0.00402

xPoint = 3.99900 yPoint = 3.81900 TargetValue = 50.42211 PredictValue = 50.42306 DiffPerc = 0.00188

xPoint = 3.99900 yPoint = 3.83900 TargetValue = 50.34834 PredictValue = 50.34821 DiffPerc = 0.00251

xPoint = 3.99900 yPoint = 3.85900 TargetValue = 50.27233 PredictValue = 50.27126 DiffPerc = 0.00213

xPoint = 3.99900 yPoint = 3.87900 TargetValue = 50.19459 PredictValue = 50.19279 DiffPerc = 0.00358

xPoint = 3.99900 yPoint = 3.89900 TargetValue = 50.11560 PredictValue = 50.11333 DiffPerc = 0.00452

xPoint = 3.99900 yPoint = 3.91900 TargetValue = 50.03587 PredictValue = 50.03337 DiffPerc = 0.00499

xPoint = 3.99900   yPoint = 3.93900   TargetValue = 49.95591   PredictValue =
49.95333 DiffPerc = 0.00517
xPoint = 3.99900   yPoint = 3.95900   TargetValue = 49.87624   PredictValue =
49.87355 DiffPerc = 0.00538
xPoint = 3.99900   yPoint = 3.97900   TargetValue = 49.79735   PredictValue =
49.79433 DiffPerc = 0.00607
xPoint = 3.99900   yPoint = 3.99900   TargetValue = 49.71976   PredictValue =
49.71588 DiffPerc = 0.00781

MaxErrorPerc   = 0.017317654932154674
AverErrorPerc = 0.007356218626151153

Figure 12-5 shows the projected chart of the testing results.

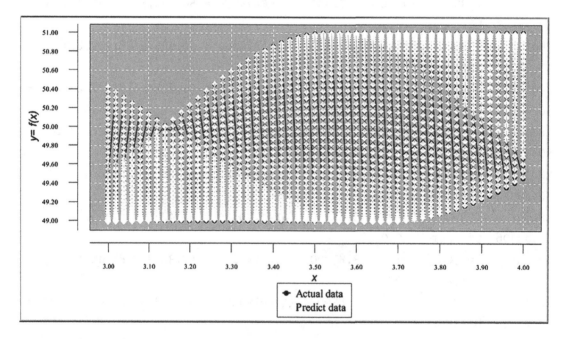

Figure 12-5. *Projected chart of the testing results*

The approximation results are acceptable; therefore, there is no need to use the
micro-batch method.

Summary

In this chapter. we discussed how to use a neuron network for the approximation of functions in 3D space. We learned that the approximation of functions in 3D space (functions of two variables) is done similarly to the approximation of functions in 2D space. The only difference is that the network architecture should include two inputs, and the training and testing datasets should include records of all the possible combinations of the x and y values. These results can be propagated for the approximation of functions with more than two variables.

PART III

Introduction to Computer Vision

CHAPTER 13

Image Recognition

A neural network can also be used to recognize images. Image recognition (image classification) is one of the most important branches of artificial intelligence. Computer vision is actually a visual pattern recognition technology. It is widely used by banks to process checks and by post offices to recognize addresses. There are many areas (self-driving cars, face recognition, and so on) where image recognition is extremely important.

At the same time, image recognition is one of the most difficult disciplines of artificial intelligence. On the surface, it seems that we can reuse all the aspects of neural network processing that we learned in the preceding chapters of this book to recognize images. Each digital image is a set of pixels or dots, so if we create a very large dataset of different images, feed this data to a neural network, and train it, then the network should be able to do the job.

Unfortunately, it is much more complex. We can train the network to recognize various single images and then ask the network to recognize a given image (for example, is it a cat or a dog?). But there are enormous variations of even a single object type (how many dogs are there, their shapes, their fur or hair, their faces, so on). Also, if the dog images show standing dogs, the program won't be able to recognize sitting dogs, moving dogs, dogs shown upside down, or dogs shown from different angles. Some research is underway to build three-dimensional neural networks, and processing colored images adds another dimension of difficulties.

On top of this, real-life images can show a combination of many objects being superimposed on an image. An image can be further complicated by shadows falling on some part of objects or sun glaring on others, such as a cat sitting on a sofa or a dog that is partially shadowed by a car. You get the general idea.

© Igor Livshin 2022
I. Livshin, *Artificial Neural Networks with Java*, https://doi.org/10.1007/978-1-4842-7368-5_13

Classification of Handwritten Digits

In this section, we will discuss the simple task of image recognition, specifically, recognizing handwritten digits. Consider the sequence of handwritten digits shown in Figure 13-1.

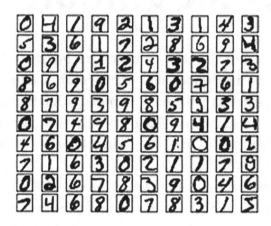

Figure 13-1. *Handwritten digits*

These digits are written by different people. Even the same person can write digits differently, depending on the type of a pen used, whether the person is standing or sitting, and many other factors. See the practically endless variations of the same digits written by people in Figure 13-2.

Figure 13-2. *Variations of handwritten digits*

If we collect thousands (or millions) of handwritten digits and use them to train the neural network, we can build a digit recognizer program.

Preparing the Input Data

To build our input, we will use the MNIST datasets, which contain tens of thousands of scanned images of handwritten digits. MNIST is a modified subset of two datasets collected by the U.S. National Institute of Standards and Technology (NIST). The first dataset includes 60,000 records, and it should be used for network training. The second dataset consists of 10,000 records, and it should be used to test the trained network.

Each record in both datasets represents an image of a digit (28*28 pixels = 784 pixels). The images are black and white. Each record format consists of 785 fields. The first field is a textual representation of the digit (for example, 5). The following 784 fields represent the grayscale number of each pixel intensity in the image. Each pixel value is a single number that represents the brightness of the pixel (pixel intensity) with possible values from 0 to 255, where 0 is white, and the rest of numbers represent darkening shades of gray. Figure 13-3 shows a fragment of the image.

| 5 | 0 | 0 | 0 | 147 | 234 | 253 | 176 | 0 | 0 | 0 | 0 | 0 | 0 | 0 |

Figure 13-3. *Fragment of the record representing an image*

You can get both files by downloading them from the http://yann.lecun.com/ exdb/mnist/ website. However, the data files on this website are formatted for the Python programming language, so downloading them from this site will not do you any good. Instead, we will use files that have been converted to CSV (Excel) format (which we have used in all the examples in this book). You can obtain these files from the GitHub site for this book.

Figure 13-4 shows a fragment of one of the CSV files.

	EN	EO	EP	EQ	ER	ES	ET	EU	EV	EW	EX	EY	EZ	FA	FB	FC	FD	FE	FF	FG
1	0	0	0	0	0	0	0	0	0	0	3	18	18	18	126	136	175	26	166	255
2	0	0	0	0	0	0	0	0	0	0	0	0	48	238	252	252	252	237	0	0
3	0	0	0	0	0	0	0	0	0	0	0	0	0	0	0	0	0	0	67	232
4	0	0	0	0	0	0	0	0	0	0	0	0	0	0	0	0	124	253	255	63
5	0	0	0	0	0	0	0	0	0	0	0	0	0	0	0	0	0	0	0	0
6	0	0	0	0	0	0	0	0	0	0	0	0	13	25	100	122	7	0	0	0
7	0	0	0	0	0	0	0	0	32	237	253	252	71	0	0	0	0	0	0	0
8	0	0	0	0	0	0	0	0	38	43	105	255	253	253	253	253	253	253	174	6
9	0	0	0	0	0	0	0	0	0	5	63	197	0	0	0	0	0	0	0	0
10	0	0	0	0	0	0	0	0	0	0	0	0	0	0	0	0	0	0	0	143
11	0	0	0	0	0	0	0	103	242	254	254	254	254	254	254	66	0	0	0	0
12	0	0	0	0	0	0	0	0	0	0	0	0	0	0	0	0	0	0	0	0
13	0	12	99	91	142	155	246	182	155	155	155	155	131	52	0	0	0	0	0	0
14	0	0	0	0	0	0	0	0	0	38	178	252	253	117	65	0	0	0	0	0
15	0	0	0	0	0	0	0	0	1	168	242	28	0	0	0	0	0	0	0	0
16	0	0	0	0	0	0	0	0	0	0	0	0	0	0	0	0	0	0	0	0
17	0	0	0	0	0	0	0	93	164	211	250	250	194	15	0	0	0	0	0	0
18	0	0	0	0	0	0	0	0	0	0	0	0	0	0	0	0	0	11	203	229
19	0	0	0	0	0	0	0	0	0	0	0	75	247	143	10	0	0	0	0	0

Figure 13-4. *Fragment of the CSV file*

Input Data Conversion

We need to build a program that trains the neural net to recognize (classify) digits. For this, we first need to find a way of coding the digit that each record represents in some digital form that the network understands. We will represent each digit as a ten-field sequence (each field in the sequence has a character value 0 or 1). For example, the digit 5 will be represented by having 1 in the fifth position (field) of the ten-field sequence (with the rest of the fields being set to 0). So, it is a kind of byte-wise representation of a digit.

Figure 13-5 shows an example for the digit 5.

| 0 | 0 | 0 | 0 | 0 | 1 | 0 | 0 | 0 | 0 |

Figure 13-5. *Bytewise representation of the digit 5*

We will put these ten fields of the byte-wise image presentation at the end of each record, and they will be considered as the output fields for the network.

Therefore, we need to convert the records of the original CSV file that consists of 785 fields (the first field is the digit as a letter, and the following 784 fields are the grayscale numbers of each pixel in the image) to the records in a different format. The format of the converted record is as follows: the first 784 fields are the grayscale numbers of each pixel in the image following by 10 fields, the byte-wise presentation of the record's digit.

Figure 13-6 shows the graphical representation of the conversion process.

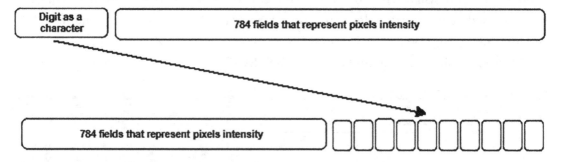

Figure 13-6. *Record conversion*

So, the record will contain the first 784 fields, which are the input fields for the network, followed by the 10 fields that are the target fields for the network. When training the network, we teach the network that if the first 784 fields contain the given grayscale pixel intensity values, then this represents the image of the digit 5 (and so for the rest of images).

While doing this conversion, we also want to normalize the input grayscale field values and the target field values to the interval [-1.00, 1.00].

Building the Conversion Program

The CVS input train dataset is `C:\Image_Recognition\MNIS_Data\mnist_train.csv`. The CVS input test dataset is `C:\Image_Recognition\MNIS_Data\mnist_test.csv`.

These are the corresponding files after conversion:

`C:\Image_Recognition\MNIS_Data\ mnist_train_input_Norm.csv`
`C:\Image_Recognition\MNIS_Data\ mnist_test_input_Norm.csv`

The conversion logic reads all the records from the input dataset. For each record, it takes the first field (which is the character digit) and builds the corresponding target fields (10 fields, the byte-wise representation of the digit). The program puts these 10 target fields at the end of the output record (right after the 784 input fields).

The 784 input fields (located in the input record after the digit field) are put at the beginning of the converted record. Finally, we normalize all fields of the converted record. See Listing 13-1 and Listing 13-2.

Listing 13-1. Program Code for Converting the Input Training Dataset

```
// ================================================================
// The program converts the MNIS CVS input training file that consists of records
// with 785 fields into the CVS normalized training input file.
//================================================================

package numberrecognition_convertinputtrainfile;

import java.time.YearMonth;
import java.awt.Color;
import java.awt.Font;
import java.io.File;
import java.io.FileInputStream;
import java.text.DateFormat;
import java.text.ParseException;
import java.text.SimpleDateFormat;
```

```java
import java.time.LocalDate;
import java.time.Month;
import java.time.ZoneId;
import java.util.ArrayList;
import java.util.Calendar;
import java.util.Date;
import java.util.List;
import java.util.Locale;
import java.util.Properties;
import java.io.BufferedReader;
import java.io.BufferedWriter;
import java.io.File;
import java.io.FileInputStream;
import java.io.PrintWriter;
import java.io.FileNotFoundException;
import java.io.FileReader;
import java.io.FileWriter;
import java.io.IOException;
import java.io.InputStream;
import java.nio.file.*;
import java.util.Properties;

public class NumberRecognition_ConvertInputTrainFile
{

    // Interval to normalize
    static double Nh =  1;
    static double Nl = -1;

    // Input points
    static double minXPointDl = 0.00;
    static double maxXPointDh = 255.00;

    // Target points
    static double minTargetValueDl = 0.00;
    static double maxTargetValueDh = 1.00;
```

```java
public static double normalize(double value, double Dh, double Dl)
 {
    double normalizedValue = (value - Dl)*(Nh - Nl)/(Dh - Dl) + Nl;

    return normalizedValue;
 }
public static void main(String[] args)
 {
    // Normalize train file
    String inputFileName = "C:/Image_Recognition/MNIS_Data/mnist_train.csv";
    String outputNormFileName =
   "C:/Image_Recognition/MNIS_Data/mnist_train_input_Norm.csv";

    BufferedReader br = null;
    PrintWriter out = null;

    String line = "";
    String cvsSplitBy = ",";

     double[] inputXPointValue = new double[784] ;
     double[] targetXPointValue = new double[10] ;

     double[] normInputXPointValue = new double[784];
     double[] normTargetXPointValue = new double[10];

     String[] strNormInputXPointValue  = new String[784];
     String[] strNormTargetXPointValue  = new String[10];;

     String strLabelLine1 = "";

     String fullLine;

     // Build the labelLine1
     for (int m = 0; m < 794; m++)
       if(m == 793)
        strLabelLine1 = strLabelLine1 + Integer.toString(m);
       else
        strLabelLine1 = strLabelLine1 + Integer.toString(m) + ",";
```

```
try
  {
    Files.deleteIfExists(Paths.get(outputNormFileName));

    br = new BufferedReader(new FileReader(inputFileName));
    out = new
     PrintWriter(new BufferedWriter(new FileWriter(outputNormFileName)));

    out.println(strLabelLine1);

    while ((line = br.readLine()) != null)
     {
         // Brake the line using comma as separator
         String[] workFields = line.split(cvsSplitBy);

         for (int k = 0; k < 784; k++)
           inputXPointValue[k] = Double.parseDouble(workFields[k+1]);

         double digitValue = Double.parseDouble(workFields[0]);
         int workIndex = (int) digitValue;

         // First, clear the array targetXPointValue
         for (int v = 0; v < 10; v++)
           targetXPointValue[v] = 0.00;

         targetXPointValue[workIndex] = 1.00;

         // Normalize these fields
         for (int k = 0; k < 784; k++)
           normInputXPointValue[k] =
           normalize(inputXPointValue[k], maxXPointDh, minXPointDl);

         for (int k = 0; k < 10; k++)
           normTargetXPointValue[k] =
           normalize(targetXPointValue[k], maxTargetValueDh,
           minTargetValueDl);

         // Convert normalized fields to string, so they can be
           inserted
         //into the output CSV file
```

```java
        for (int k = 0; k < 784; k++)
          strNormInputXPointValue[k] = Double.toString(normInputX
          PointValue[k]);

        for (int k = 0; k < 10; k++)
          strNormTargetXPointValue[k] = Double.toString(normTargetX
          PointValue[k]);

        // Concantenate these fields into a string line with
        //coma separator

        fullLine = "";

        for (int k = 0; k < 784; k++)
          fullLine  = fullLine + strNormInputXPointValue[k] + ",";

        for (int k = 0; k < 10; k++)
         {
           if(k == 9)
             fullLine  = fullLine + strNormTargetXPointValue[k];
           else
             fullLine  = fullLine + strNormTargetXPointValue[k] + ",";
         }

        // Put fullLine into the output file
        out.println(fullLine);

    }     // end of while

  out.close();
  br.close();
  System.out.println("Convertion completed.");
  System.exit(0);

  } // end of TRY
catch (FileNotFoundException e)
 {
     e.printStackTrace();
     System.exit(1);
 }
```

```
catch (IOException io)
 {
     io.printStackTrace();
 }
finally
 {
   if (br != null)
     {
         try
          {
             br.close();
             out.close();
          }
         catch (IOException e)
          {
             e.printStackTrace();
          }
     }
 }

}

}
```

Listing 13-2. Program Code for Converting the Input Test Dataset

```
// ============================================================
// The program converts the MNIS CVS input test file that consists of a
records
// with 785 fields into the CVS normalized test input file.
// ============================================================

package numberrecognition_convertinputtestfile;

import java.time.YearMonth;
import java.awt.Color;
import java.awt.Font;
```

```java
import java.io.File;
import java.io.FileInputStream;
import java.text.DateFormat;
import java.text.ParseException;
import java.text.SimpleDateFormat;
import java.time.LocalDate;
import java.time.Month;
import java.time.ZoneId;
import java.util.ArrayList;
import java.util.Calendar;
import java.util.Date;
import java.util.List;
import java.util.Locale;
import java.util.Properties;
import java.io.BufferedReader;
import java.io.BufferedWriter;
import java.io.File;
import java.io.FileInputStream;
import java.io.PrintWriter;
import java.io.FileNotFoundException;
import java.io.FileReader;
import java.io.FileWriter;
import java.io.IOException;
import java.io.InputStream;
import java.nio.file.*;
import java.util.Properties;

public class NumberRecognition_ConvertInputTestFile
{

    // Interval to normalize
    static double Nh =  1;
    static double Nl = -1;

    // Input points columns
    static double minXPointDl = 0.00;
    static double maxXPointDh = 255.00;
```

```java
// Target points
static double minTargetValueDl = 0.00;
static double maxTargetValueDh = 1.00;

public static double normalize(double value, double Dh, double Dl)
 {
    double normalizedValue = (value - Dl)*(Nh - Nl)/(Dh - Dl) + Nl;

    return normalizedValue;
 }

 public static void main(String[] args)
  {
     // Normalize train file
     String inputFileName = "C:/Image_Recognition/MNIS_Data/mnist_test.csv";
     String outputNormFileName = "C:/Image_Recognition/MNIS_Data/mnist_
     test_input_Norm.csv";

     BufferedReader br = null;
     PrintWriter out = null;

     String line = "";
     String cvsSplitBy = ",";

      double[] inputXPointValue = new double[784] ;
      double[] targetXPointValue = new double[10] ;

      double[] normInputXPointValue = new double[784];
      double[] normTargetXPointValue = new double[10];

      String[] strNormInputXPointValue  = new String[784];
      String[] strNormTargetXPointValue  = new String[10];;

      String strLabelLine1 = "";

      String fullLine;

      // Build the labelLine1
      for (int m = 0; m < 794; m++)
        if(m == 793)
          strLabelLine1 = strLabelLine1 + Integer.toString(m);
```

```
      else
       strLabelLine1 = strLabelLine1 + Integer.toString(m) + ",";

try
  {
    Files.deleteIfExists(Paths.get(outputNormFileName));

    br = new BufferedReader(new FileReader(inputFileName));
    out = new
      PrintWriter(new BufferedWriter(new FileWriter(outputNormFileName)));

    out.println(strLabelLine1);

    while ((line = br.readLine()) != null)
      {
          // Brake the line using comma as separator
          String[] workFields = line.split(cvsSplitBy);

          for (int k = 0; k < 784; k++)
            inputXPointValue[k] = Double.parseDouble(workFields[k+1]);

          double digitValue = Double.parseDouble(workFields[0]);
          int workIndex = (int) digitValue;

          // First, clear the array targetXPointValue
          for (int v = 0; v < 10; v++)
            targetXPointValue[v] = 0.00;

          targetXPointValue[workIndex] = 1.00;

          // Normalize these fields
          for (int k = 0; k < 784; k++)
            normInputXPointValue[k] =
            normalize(inputXPointValue[k], maxXPointDh, minXPointDl);

          for (int k = 0; k < 10; k++)
            normTargetXPointValue[k] =
            normalize(targetXPointValue[k], maxTargetValueDh,
            minTargetValueDl);
```

```
        // Convert normalized fields to string, so they can be
          inserted
        //into the output CSV file
        for (int k = 0; k < 784; k++)
          strNormInputXPointValue[k] = Double.toString(normInputXPoint
          Value[k]);

        for (int k = 0; k < 10; k++)
          strNormTargetXPointValue[k] = Double.toString(normTargetXPoint
          Value[k]);

        // Concantenate these fields into a string line with
        //coma separator

        fullLine = "";

        for (int k = 0; k < 784; k++)
          fullLine  = fullLine + strNormInputXPointValue[k] + ",";

        for (int k = 0; k < 10; k++)
         {
           if(k == 9)
             fullLine  = fullLine + strNormTargetXPointValue[k];
           else
             fullLine  = fullLine + strNormTargetXPointValue[k] + ",";
         }

        // Put fullLine into the output file
        out.println(fullLine);

     }    // end of while

    br.close();
    out.close();
    System.out.println("Convertion completed.");
    System.exit(0);

   }  // end of TRY
  catch (FileNotFoundException e)
```

```
    {
        e.printStackTrace();
        System.exit(1);
    }
    catch (IOException io)
    {
        io.printStackTrace();
    }
    finally
    {
      if (br != null)
        {
            try
              {
                br.close();
                out.close();
              }
            catch (IOException e)
              {
                e.printStackTrace();
              }
        }
    }

  }

}
```

After running the previous programs, we build the following two files:

- Normalized train file: mnist_train_input_Norm.csv

- Normalized test file: mnist_test_input_Norm.csv

We will use these two files in the next chapter as the input for training and testing the digit recognition program.

Summary

This chapter introduced you to computer vision, a branch of artificial intelligence. It explained the basic concept of the image recognition using artificial neural networks, concentrating on the simplest image recognition job, which is the classification of the handwritten digits. In the next chapter, we will develop a digit recognition program.

CHAPTER 14

Classification of Handwritten Digits

In the previous chapter, we prepared two input files.

- The input file for network training:

  `C:\Image_Recognition\MNIS_Data\ mnist_train_input_Norm.csv`

- The input file for network testing:

  `C:\Image_Recognition\MNIS_Data\ mnist_test_input_Norm.csv`

Just to remind you, the format of the records in both files is as follows: The first 784 fields contain the value of the grayscale pixels' intensity (24*24 = 784 fields). These are the input fields for the network. The next ten fields of the record indicate the image this record represents (coded as the byte-wise digit format). These are the target fields of the record. Correspondingly, we construct the neural network.

Network Architecture

Due to a very large number of neurons, Figure 14-1 shows a conceptual network diagram.

607

© Igor Livshin 2022
I. Livshin, *Artificial Neural Networks with Java*, https://doi.org/10.1007/978-1-4842-7368-5_14

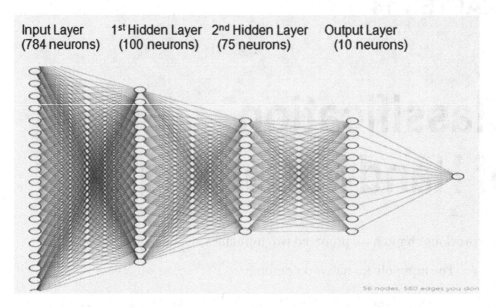

Figure 14-1. *Network architecture*

The number of neurons in the input layer and the number of neurons in the output layer are predetermined by our data model (784 input fields and 10 output fields). But, the number of hidden layers and the number of neurons in the hidden layers are typically determined experimentally, by trying various configurations and selecting the one that produces the best results. For this example, we use the network with two hidden layers. The first hidden layer has 100 neurons, and the second hidden layer has 75 neurons.

Please keep in mind that the networks with more than one hidden layer are considered a deep network. In some complex cases, the deep network can substantially increase the precision of the calculated results. However, quite frequently, developers have difficulties training networks with many hidden layers, and there are cases when the precision of the results for networks with multiple hidden layers is worse than the precision of the network with a single hidden layer (or a flat network).

Also, increasing the number of neurons in the hidden layers and increasing the number of hidden layers typically lead to a substantial increase in the processing volume, requiring more powerful computers. So again, try various configurations and select the one that produces the best results.

Program Code

Listing 14-1 shows the program code.

Listing 14-1. Digit Recognition Program Code

```
/*
 * The program uses training or testing input file, which is a MNIS file
 * of 60,000 (for training) or 10,000 (for testing) images of handwritten
 digits
 * being converted to a CVS file
 * Each string represents a gray-scale image of a picture digit. The image
 size
 * is 28*28 = 784 dots/pixels. Each record includes 784 input fields and 10
 target
 * output fields (the byte wise representation of an image).
 * The converted input file has been already normalized.
 */

package numberrecognition;

import java.time.YearMonth;
import java.awt.Color;
import java.awt.Font;
import java.io.File;
import java.io.FileInputStream;
import java.io.IOException;
import java.io.InputStream;
import static java.lang.Math.abs;
import java.text.DateFormat;
import java.text.ParseException;
import java.text.SimpleDateFormat;
import java.time.LocalDate;
import java.time.Month;
import java.time.ZoneId;
import java.util.ArrayList;
import java.util.Calendar;
```

```java
import java.util.Date;
import java.util.List;
import java.util.Locale;
import java.util.Properties;
import org.encog.Encog;
import org.encog.engine.network.activation.ActivationTANH;
import org.encog.engine.network.activation.ActivationReLU;
import org.encog.ml.data.MLData;
import org.encog.ml.data.MLDataPair;
import org.encog.ml.data.MLDataSet;
import org.encog.ml.data.buffer.MemoryDataLoader;
import org.encog.ml.data.buffer.codec.CSVDataCODEC;
import org.encog.ml.data.buffer.codec.DataSetCODEC;
import org.encog.neural.networks.BasicNetwork;
import org.encog.neural.networks.layers.BasicLayer;
import org.encog.neural.networks.training.propagation.resilient.
ResilientPropagation;
import org.encog.persist.EncogDirectoryPersistence;
import org.encog.util.csv.CSVFormat;

public class NumberRecognition
{
    static int numberOfInputNeurons = 784;
    static int numberOfOutputNeurons = 10;

    // Normalization coefficients

    // Normalizing interval
    static double Nh =  1;
    static double Nl = -1;

    // Normalization range for input fields
    static double imageBitDh = 256.00;
    static double imageBitDl = 0.00;

    // Normalization range for output fields
    static double outputDh = 1.00;
    static double outputDl = 0.00;
```

```java
static String inputFileName;
static String trainFileName;
static String testFileName;
static String networkFileName;

static int workingMode;

static Date workDate = null;
static String strNumberOfMonths;
static String strYearMonth;

static double maxGlobalDiffPerc = 0;
static double averGlobalDiffPerc = 0;

// ========================================================
// The main method.
// ========================================================
public static void main(String[] args)
 {
   // Set program run parameters

   // --- Working mode (0 - training, 1 - testing) --
   workingMode = 0; // Training mode

   // Setting
   trainFileName = "C:/Image_Recognition/MNIS_Data/mnist_train_input_
   Norm.csv";
   testFileName = "C:/Image_Recognition/MNIS_Data/mnist_test_input_Norm.
   csv";
   networkFileName = "C:/Image_Recognition/MNIS_Data/saved_network_file";

   if(workingMode == 0)
    inputFileName = trainFileName;
   else
    inputFileName = testFileName;

  try
    {

      File file1 = new File(networkFileName);
```

```
    if(workingMode == 0)
     {
       if(file1.exists())
         file1.delete();

       // Build the network, train it and test how it works
       trainTestSaveNetwork();
     }
    else
     {

       // Don't save the trained network file. Read it and use it for
         testing
       loadAndTestNetwork();
     }

   }
  catch (Throwable t)
    {
          t.printStackTrace();
    }
   finally
    {
      Encog.getInstance().shutdown();
    }

 Encog.getInstance().shutdown();

 } // End of the main method

//-----------------------------------------------------------------
// Load CSV to memory.
// @return The loaded dataset.
// -----------------------------------------------------------------
public static MLDataSet loadCSV2Memory(String filename, int input, int
ideal, boolean headers, CSVFormat format, boolean significance)
  {
```

```
        DataSetCODEC codec = new CSVDataCODEC(new File(filename), format,
        headers, input, ideal, significance);
        MemoryDataLoader load = new MemoryDataLoader(codec);
        MLDataSet dataset = load.external2Memory();
        return dataset;
    }

//=======================================================================
// This method builds, trains and saves the trained network
//=======================================================================
static public void trainTestSaveNetwork()
 {
    // Prepare the training file by loading the CVS file in memory
    MLDataSet trainingSet = loadCSV2Memory(inputFileName,
    numberOfInputNeurons,numberOfOutputNeurons,true,CSVFormat.ENGLISH,
    false);

    // Create a neural network, without using a factory

    BasicNetwork network = new BasicNetwork();

    // Input layer
    network.addLayer(new BasicLayer(null,true,numberOfInputNeurons));

    // Hidden layer
    network.addLayer(new BasicLayer(new ActivationTANH(),true,100));
    network.addLayer(new BasicLayer(new ActivationTANH(),true,75));

    //network.addLayer(new BasicLayer(new ActivationLOG(),true,3));
    //network.addLayer(new BasicLayer(new ActivationReLU(),true,8));
    //network.addLayer(new BasicLayer(new ActivationSigmoid(),true,3));

    // Output layer
    network.addLayer(new BasicLayer(new ActivationTANH(),false,numberOfOu
    tputNeurons));

    //network.addLayer(new BasicLayer(new ActivationLOG(),false,1));
    //network.addLayer(new BasicLayer(new ActivationReLU(),false,1));
    //network.addLayer(new BasicLayer(new ActivationSigmoid(),false,1));
```

```java
network.getStructure().finalizeStructure();
network.reset();

// Train the neural network
final ResilientPropagation train = new ResilientPropagation(network,
trainingSet);
//Backpropagation train = new Backpropagation(network,trainingS
et,0.7,0.3);
//Backpropagation train = new Backpropagation(network,trainingS
et,0.5,0.5);

int epoch = 1;

do
   {
       train.iteration();
       System.out.println("Epoch #" + epoch + " Error:" + train.
       getError());

     epoch++;
   } while(train.getError() > 0.005);

System.out.println("The network is trained");

for(MLDataPair pair: trainingSet)
{
    final MLData output = network.compute(pair.getInput());
}

// Now test the network. The trained network stays in memory

System.out.println("Testing network");

double[] normImageBit = new double[784];
double[] normTargetImageBit = new double[10];
double[] normPredictImageBit = new double[10];
double[] denormImageBit = new double[784];
double[] denormPredictImageBit = new double[10];
double[] denormTargetImageBit = new double[10];
double[] differencePerc = new double[10];
```

```java
// Load the input CSV file.
MLDataSet testingSet = loadCSV2Memory(inputFileName,numberOfInput
Neurons,numberOfOutputNeurons,true,CSVFormat.ENGLISH,false);

int i = 0;
int numberOfErrors = 0;

for (MLDataPair pair: testingSet)
 {
   i++;

   MLData inputData = pair.getInput();
   MLData actualData = pair.getIdeal();
   MLData predictData = network.compute(inputData);

   // Get the results after optimization

   for (int k = 0; k< 784; k++)
     normImageBit[k] = inputData.getData(k);

   for (int k = 0; k < 10; k++)
     normTargetImageBit[k] = actualData.getData(k);

   for (int k = 0; k < 10; k++)
     normPredictImageBit[k] = predictData.getData(k);

   System.out.println(" ");
   System.out.println("Record = " + i);
   System.out.println(" ");

   //System.out.println("Target =  " + normTargetImageBit[0] + " " +
   normTargetImageBit[1] + " " + normTargetImageBit[2]
   // +
   //          " " + normTargetImageBit[3] + " " +
   normTargetImageBit[4] + " " + normTargetImageBit[5] +
   //          " " + normTargetImageBit[6] + " " +
   normTargetImageBit[7] + " " + normTargetImageBit[8] +
   //          " " + normTargetImageBit[9]);
```

615

```
//System.out.println("Predict = " + normPredictImageBit[0] + " " +
normPredictImageBit[1] + " " + normPredictImageBit[2]
//      +
//            " " + normPredictImageBit[3] + " " +
normPredictImageBit[4] + " " + normPredictImageBit[5] +
//            " " + normPredictImageBit[6] + " " +
normPredictImageBit[7] + " " + normPredictImageBit[8] +
//            " " + normPredictImageBit[9]);

//System.out.println("Compare the record fields after de-
normalization");

//Denormalize point fields
for (int m = 0; m < 784; m++)
 denormImageBit[m] = ((imageBitDl - imageBitDh)*normImageBit[m] -
 Nh*imageBitDl + imageBitDh*Nl)/(Nl - Nh);

// Denormalize Target fields
for (int m = 0; m < 10; m++)
   denormTargetImageBit[m] = ((outputDl - outputDh)*
   normTargetImageBit[m] - Nh*outputDl + outputDh*Nl)/(Nl - Nh);

// Denormalize Predict fields
for (int m = 0; m < 10; m++)
   denormPredictImageBit[m] = ((outputDl - outputDh)*normPredictImag
   eBit[m] - Nh*outputDl + outputDh*Nl)/(Nl - Nh);

System.out.println("Den Target =  " + denormTargetImageBit[0] + " "
+ denormTargetImageBit[1] + " " +
   denormTargetImageBit[2] +
         " " + denormTargetImageBit[3] + " " +
         denormTargetImageBit[4] + " " + denormTargetImageBit[5] +
         " " + denormTargetImageBit[6] + " " +
         denormTargetImageBit[7] + " " + denormTargetImageBit[8] +
         " " + denormTargetImageBit[9]);

System.out.println("Den Predict = " + denormPredictImageBit[0] + "
" + denormPredictImageBit[1] + " " +
```

```
    denormPredictImageBit[2] +
          " " + denormPredictImageBit[3] + " " + denormPredict
          ImageBit[4] + " " + denormPredictImageBit[5] +
          " " + denormPredictImageBit[6] + " " + denormPredict
          ImageBit[7] + " " + denormPredictImageBit[8] +
          " " + denormPredictImageBit[9]);

double r0 = abs(denormTargetImageBit[0]) - abs(denormPredict
ImageBit[0]);
double r1 = abs(denormTargetImageBit[1]) - abs(denormPredict
ImageBit[1]);
double r2 = abs(denormTargetImageBit[2]) - abs(denormPredict
ImageBit[2]);
double r3 = abs(denormTargetImageBit[3]) - abs(denormPredict
ImageBit[3]);
double r4 = abs(denormTargetImageBit[4]) - abs(denormPredict
ImageBit[4]);
double r5 = abs(denormTargetImageBit[5]) - abs(denormPredict
ImageBit[5]);
double r6 = abs(denormTargetImageBit[6]) - abs(denormPredict
ImageBit[6]);
double r7 = abs(denormTargetImageBit[7]) - abs(denormPredict
ImageBit[7]);
double r8 = abs(denormTargetImageBit[8]) - abs(denormPredict
ImageBit[8]);
double r9 = abs(denormTargetImageBit[9]) - abs(denormPredict
ImageBit[9]);

if(abs(r0) < 0.01 &&
   abs(r1) < 0.01 &&
   abs(r2) < 0.01 &&
   abs(r3) < 0.01 &&
   abs(r4) < 0.01 &&
   abs(r5) < 0.01 &&
   abs(r6) < 0.01 &&
   abs(r7) < 0.01 &&
```

```
          abs(r7) < 0.01 &&
          abs(r9) < 0.01)
       {}
     else
      {
        System.out.println("No match");
        numberOfErrors = numberOfErrors + 1;
      }

  } // End of the FOR loop

  System.out.println("Number of errors = " + numberOfErrors);

  // Finally, save this trained network
  System.out.println ("Saving network") ;
  EncogDirectoryPersistence.saveObject(new File(networkFileName),network);
  System.out.println ("Network has been saved") ;

 }   // End of the method

//=======================================================================
// This method loads the previously saved trained network and tests it
//=======================================================================
static public void loadAndTestNetwork()
 {
    System.out.println("Load and test network");

    int numberOfErrors = 0;

    double[] normImageBit = new double[784];
    double[] normTargetImageBit = new double[10];
    double[] normPredictImageBit = new double[10];
    double[] denormImageBit = new double[784];
    double[] denormPredictImageBit = new double[10];
    double[] denormTargetImageBit = new double[10];
    double[] differencePerc = new double[10];

    String[] strNormTargetImageBit = new String[10];
```

```java
//List<Date> xData = new ArrayList<Date>();
//List<Double> yData1 = new ArrayList<Double>();
//List<Double> yData2 = new ArrayList<Double>();

BasicNetwork network =
  (BasicNetwork)EncogDirectoryPersistence.loadObject(new
  File(networkFileName));

MLDataSet testingSet = loadCSV2Memory(inputFileName,numberOfInput
Neurons,numberOfOutputNeurons,true,CSVFormat.ENGLISH,false);

int i = -1;

for (MLDataPair pair: testingSet)
 {
   i++;

   MLData inputData = pair.getInput();
   MLData actualData = pair.getIdeal();
   MLData predictData = network.compute(inputData);

   // Get the data from the network

   for (int k = 0; k< 784; k++)
     normImageBit[k] = inputData.getData(k);

   for (int k = 0; k < 10; k++)
     normTargetImageBit[k] = actualData.getData(k);

   for (int k = 0; k < 10; k++)
     normPredictImageBit[k] = predictData.getData(k);

   System.out.println(" ");
   System.out.println("Record = " + i);
   System.out.println(" ");

   System.out.println("Target =   " + normTargetImageBit[0] + " " +
   normTargetImageBit[1] + " " + normTargetImageBit[2] +
             " " + normTargetImageBit[3] + " " + normTargetImageBit[4]
             + " " + normTargetImageBit[5] +
```

```java
                " " + normTargetImageBit[6] + " " + normTargetImageBit[7]
                + " " + normTargetImageBit[8] +
                " " + normTargetImageBit[9]);

        System.out.println("Predict = " + normPredictImageBit[0] + " " +
        normPredictImageBit[1] + " " + normPredictImageBit[2]
            +
                " " + normPredictImageBit[3] + " " +
                normPredictImageBit[4] + " " + normPredictImageBit[5] +
                " " + normPredictImageBit[6] + " " +
                normPredictImageBit[7] + " " + normPredictImageBit[8] +
                " " + normPredictImageBit[9]);

        // Denormalize input data

        // Denormalize point fields
        for (int m = 0; m < 784; m++)
         denormImageBit[m] = ((imageBitDl - imageBitDh)*normImageBit[m] -
         Nh*imageBitDl + imageBitDh*Nl)/(Nl - Nh);

        // Denormalize Target fields
        for (int m = 0; m < 10; m++)
          denormTargetImageBit[m] = ((outputDl - outputDh)*normTarget
          ImageBit[m] - Nh*outputDl + outputDh*Nl)/(Nl - Nh);

        // Denormalize Predict fields
        for (int m = 0; m < 10; m++)
          denormPredictImageBit[m] = ((outputDl - outputDh)*normPredictImag
          eBit[m] - Nh*outputDl + outputDh*Nl)/(Nl - Nh);

        System.out.println("Den Target =  " + denormTargetImageBit[0] + " "
        + denormTargetImageBit[1] + " " +
          denormTargetImageBit[2] +
                " " + denormTargetImageBit[3] + " " + denormTarget
                ImageBit[4] + " " + denormTargetImageBit[5] +
                 " " + denormTargetImageBit[6] + " " + denormTarget
                 ImageBit[7] + " " + denormTargetImageBit[8] +
                 " " + denormTargetImageBit[9]);
```

```
System.out.println("Den Predict = " + denormPredictImageBit[0] + "
" + denormPredictImageBit[1] + " " +
   denormPredictImageBit[2] +
           " " + denormPredictImageBit[3] + " " + denormPredict
           ImageBit[4] + " " + denormPredictImageBit[5] +
           " " + denormPredictImageBit[6] + " " + denormPredict
           ImageBit[7] + " " + denormPredictImageBit[8] +
           " " + denormPredictImageBit[9]);

double r0 = abs(denormTargetImageBit[0]) - abs(denormPredict
ImageBit[0]);
double r1 = abs(denormTargetImageBit[1]) - abs(denormPredict
ImageBit[1]);
double r2 = abs(denormTargetImageBit[2]) - abs(denormPredict
ImageBit[2]);
double r3 = abs(denormTargetImageBit[3]) - abs(denormPredict
ImageBit[3]);
double r4 = abs(denormTargetImageBit[4]) - abs(denormPredict
ImageBit[4]);
double r5 = abs(denormTargetImageBit[5]) - abs(denormPredict
ImageBit[5]);
double r6 = abs(denormTargetImageBit[6]) - abs(denormPredict
ImageBit[6]);
double r7 = abs(denormTargetImageBit[7]) - abs(denormPredict
ImageBit[7]);
double r8 = abs(denormTargetImageBit[8]) - abs(denormPredict
ImageBit[8]);
double r9 = abs(denormTargetImageBit[9]) - abs(denormPredict
ImageBit[9]);

if(abs(r0) < 0.01 &&
    abs(r1) < 0.01 &&
    abs(r2) < 0.01 &&
    abs(r3) < 0.01 &&
    abs(r4) < 0.01 &&
    abs(r5) < 0.01 &&
```

```
                abs(r6) < 0.01 &&
                abs(r7) < 0.01 &&
                abs(r7) < 001 &&
                abs(r9) < 0.01)
        {}
        else
        {
            System.out.println("No match");
            numberOfErrors = numberOfErrors + 1;
        }

    } // End of the FOR loop

    System.out.println("Number of errors = " + numberOfErrors);

  }  // End of the method

}
```

Programming Logic

This section goes over the settings.

Each record of the input file contains 784 input fields and 10 output fields.

```
static int numberOfInputNeurons = 784;
static int numberOfOutputNeurons = 10;
```

Here is the normalizing interval:

```
static double Nh =  1;
static double Nl = -1;
```

Here is the range of the input field values (maximum and minimum grayscale pixels values):

```
static double imageBitDh = 255.00;
   static double imageBitDl = 0.00;
```

Here is the range of the output field values (maximum and minimum values of the fields that represent the byte-wise presentation of an image):

```
static double outputDh = 1.00;
static double outputDl = 0.00;
```

The program runs in two modes (training mode or testing mode) depending on the value of the workingMode parameter.

```
// --- Working mode (0 - training, 1 - testing) --
workingMode = 0; // Training mode

// Common setting
trainFileName = "C:/Image_Recognition/MNIS_Data/mnist_train_input_Norm.csv";
testFileName = "C:/Image_Recognition/MNIS_Data/mnist_test_input_Norm.csv";
networkFileName = "C:/Image_Recognition/MNIS_Data/saved_network_file";

// Check the workingMode field and run the program in the training or
testing mode

if(workingMode == 0)
   {
      if(file1.exists())
         file1.delete();

      // Build the network, train it and test how it works
      trainTestSaveNetwork();
   }
 else
   {

      // Don't save the trained network file. Read it and use it for testing
      loadAndTestNetwork();
   }

 }
    catch (Throwable t)
      {
         t.printStackTrace();
      }
```

```
finally
 {
    Encog.getInstance().shutdown();
 }
```

Execution

When running in training mode (method `trainTestSaveNetwork` is executed), the logic loads the input file in memory, builds the network, trains the network, and iterates between epochs until the network error becomes less than 0.005.

Finally, we save the trained network to the file on disk, so when running the program in the test mode, we can simply retrieve the saved trained network in memory.

```
"C:/Image_Recognition/MNIS_Data/saved_network_file";
```

When running in the testing mode, the method `loadAndTestNetwork()` is executed. The logic loads the previously saved trained network in memory and tests how it works against the testing dataset used as an input.

We retrieve three groups of fields from the trained network: input data, actual data, and predicted data.

```
MLData inputData = pair.getInput();
MLData actualData = pair.getIdeal();
MLData predictData = network.compute(inputData);
```

Since the input dataset is normalized, the data we retrieve from the network is also normalized, so the next step is to denormalize the input, actual, and predicted data. Finally, we want to check how well the network recognized the handwritten digits. If the digit image is not recognized, we add 1 to the `numberOfErrors` field. This network classifies handwritten digits with about 92 percent accuracy, which is pretty good for this simple program.

Convolution Neural Network

To classify more complex images, researchers currently use a more sophisticated type of artificial neural network called a *convolution neural network*. The neural networks we discussed so far were fully connected networks, meaning that each neuron in the next layer is connected to each neuron of the preceding layer.

In the convolution network, each neuron in the next layer is connected only to a group of closely located neurons of the preceding layer, typically called a *local receptive field* (or a *patch*). Figure 14-2 shows the connections of a hidden neuron to a patch of neurons (5*5).

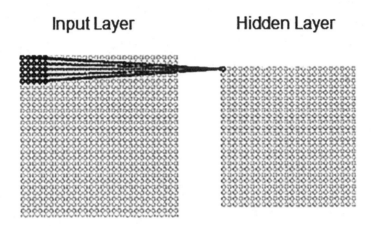

Figure 14-2. *Neuron connections*

The next neuron in the hidden layer is connected to a patch obtained by sliding the patch over by one pixel, and so on. So, each hidden neuron learns to analyze its particular local receptive field, rather than all input neurons. The convolution network structure is much more complex than the fully connected networks and is beyond the scope of this introductory book. More detailed information about convolution networks can be found in the following books:

- *Advanced Applied Deep Learning, Convolution Neural Networks, and Object Detection* by Michelucci Umberto (Apress, 2019)

- *Deep Learning: Fundamentals, Theory, and Applications* by Kaizhu Huang, Amiz Hussain, Qiu-Feng Wang, Rui Zhang (Springer, 2019)

Powerful convolution networks are currently successfully used to process three-dimensional objects differently than flat images. Also, there are attempts to process colored images that have Red-Green-Blue (RGB) encoding (multidimensional images).

Summary

In this chapter, we developed a program able to recognize (classify) handwritten digits with quite good accuracy. We also discussed some basic ideas of different types of neural networks called *convolution networks*.

Index

A

Activation functions, 7–9
Artificial intelligence neural network, *see* Neural network
Artificial neuron, 4

B

Back-propagation pass, 16, 17
Backward pass calculation
    hidden layer, 30
        W^1_{11}, 30, 31
        W^1_{12}, 31
        W^1_{21}, 32
        W^1_{22}, 33
        W^1_{31}, 34
        W^1_{32}, 34
    weight adjustment (output layer), 26
        W^2_{11}, 27
        W^2_{12}, 28
        W^2_{13}, 29
Biological/artificial neuron, 4, 5

C

Complex periodic functions
    chart representation, 168
    code fragment, 198–203
    data preparation, 170, 171
    error limit, 208
    function topology, 172–177

function values, 168, 208
    interval/training process, 208
    network architecture, 178
    program code, 179–198
    sliding windows record, 172–177
    testing output, 206–208
    training processing results, 203–205
Continuous functions/complex topology, 295
    function formula, 295, 296
    micro-batch method
        program code, 321–348
        testing processing results, 344, 345, 347, 348
        training processing results, 317–321
    network architecture, 298, 299
    processing training results, 313–316
    program code, 299–313
    spiral-like functions
        conventional network processing, 370
        conventional processing results, 367
        micro-batch process, 370–400
        multiple function values, 348–351
        network architecture, 352, 353
        program code, 353–393
        testing dataset, 351, 352
        testing results, 397–401
        training dataset, 350
        training processing results, 392–396
    testing dataset, 298
    training dataset, 297

627

© Igor Livshin 2022
I. Livshin, *Artificial Neural Networks with Java*, https://doi.org/10.1007/978-1-4842-7368-5

D

Data preparation
    testing results, 165–167
    training data
        back-propagation
          method, 158
        error message, 159
        fields, 136
        network architecture, 140
        network error, 160
        normalized testing dataset, 139
        normalized training
          dataset, 138
        pair dataset, 161–163
        program code, 141–157
        results, 163, 164
        returnCode method, 158
        transform dataset, 137, 138
Data preparation/transformation, 111
Digging deeper, 40–42
Digit recognition, 609–622

E

Encog software
    datasets
        naming project, 61
        navigation window, 58, 62
        normalization program, 63–67
        project dialog, 60
        Sample1_Norm project, 62
        source code, 63
        testing dataset, 68
        training dataset, 67
    debugging/executing
        program, 101, 102
    function approximation, 55–57
    network architecture, 57

neural network
    global library creation, 79
    import statements, 72
    JAR files location, 74, 75, 78
    navigation window, 70
    project creation, 69
    properties dialog, 73
    source code, 71
    XChart jar files, 76, 77
original/approximated
    functions, 110, 111
program code
    activation function, 97
    back-propagation, 98
    chart file, 100
    code fragment, 95
    code retrieves, 98
    denormalization, 99
    graph element, 100
    network error, 98
    predicted value, 99
    single-variable
      function, 80–94
    training method, 97
    woringMode method, 96–98
    XChart package, 94–96
testing dataset, 57
testing mode
    chart approximation, 109
    chart series, 106
    configuration, 104–108
    output/results, 108, 109
training and testing datasets, 58
training dataset, 56
training processing
    method, 103, 104
Exchange-traded fund (ETF), *see* Stock
    market index

F, G

Forecasting, 111
Forward pass calculation
    hidden-layer, 25
    output-layer, 25, 26
Function topology dataset, sliding
        windows records, 471–479

H

Handwritten digits
    conceptual network diagram, 607, 608
    convolution neural network, 625, 626
    execution, 624
    input files, 607
    local receptive field, 625
    program code, 609–622
    programming logic process, 622–624

I

Image recognition
    conversion process
        byte-wise representation, 594, 595
        graphical representation, 594
        testing dataset, 600–605
        training dataset, 595–600
    handwritten digits, 592
    input data preparation, 593
    MNIST datasets, 593
    record representation, 593
    variations, 592
    visual pattern, 591
Internal mechanics, 9
    actual/target values, 12
    back-propagation, 16, 17
    derivatives, 18, 19
    forward pass calculation, 12, 13

fully connected network, 11
function derivative/divergent, 17, 18
function formula, 9, 10
input record 1, 13
input record 2, 14
input record 3, 14
input record 4, 15
network predicted value, 12
neural network architecture, 11–13
regression, 10
sigmoid activation function, 19

J, K, L

Java environment
    downloads, 48
    Encog frameworks, 51, 52 (*see also*
        Encog software)
    JAVA_HOME environment variable, 50
    properties dialog, 49
    variable dialog, 49
    website, 47
    XChart package, 52, 53
Java/NetBeans environment
    CLASSPATH system variable, 50

M

Manual approximation
    backward (*see* Backward pass
        calculation)
    bias adjustment
        error adjustment, 36, 37
        hidden layers, 36
        output layer, 37
    error function, 24, 41
    forward pass calculation, 24–26
    hidden and output layers, 24

Manual approximation (*cont.*)
    local/global minimum, 41
    matrix/scalar calculations, 39, 40
    mini-batches/stochastic gradient, 43
    network diagram, 22, 23
    neuron presentation, 24
    vector, 22, 23
Micro-batch method
    dataset file, 237
    fragment code, 238, 239
    getChart() method, 262–268
    program code, 239–261
    save-network files, 261, 262
    testing method
        chart representation, 287
        processing code, 282–286
        results, 285–287
    training method
        chart representation, 277
        code fragment 2, 270–276
        fragment dataset, 280, 281
        normalized testing dataset, 279, 280
        output, 275, 276
        record setting, 277
        returnCode (code fragment), 268, 269
        testing dataset, 278–280

N

NetBeans, 47
    IDE process, 69, 75
    user project, 70
    XChart jar files, 76
Neural network
    activation functions, 5–7
    biological/artificial neuron, 4, 5
    human neuron, 3
    learning process, 3

    meaning, 3
    schematic image, 4
    sigmoid function, 6
Noncontinuous functions, 211
    chart representation, 212, 213
    input dataset, 213–215
    micro-batch (*see* Micro-batch method)
    network architecture, 216
    neural network
        error function, 292
        flowchart pattern, 288, 289
        forward pass calculation, 291
        function values, 289, 290
        network architecture, 289, 290
        neurons processing, 292
        processing results, 290
        records errors, 292, 293
        training process, 290, 291
    normalized input dataset, 214, 215
    program code, 216–230
    training method
        fragment code, 230–234
        low-quality function
          approximation, 236
        unsatisfactory code, 234–236

O

Object classification, 401, 402
    data normalization
        program code, 408–412
        testing dataset, 414
        training dataset, 412–414
    program code, 414–433
    records
        network architecture, 407
        testing dataset, 407, 408
        training dataset, 403–407

words–numbers cross-reference, 402, 403

testing method, 440–444

training method, 433–440

validation results

testing code, 454, 455

training code, 444–454

P, Q, R

Periodic functions

complex (*see* Complex periodic functions)

data preparation (*see* Data preparation)

function values, 112–116

network architecture, 116

normalized testing dataset, 115

normalized training dataset, 114

program code, 116–133

testing processing, 134–136

train processing results, 133, 134

S

Stock market index, 457

actual function values, 519

function topology (*see* Function topology)

getError() method, 519

historic monthly prices, 457–460

micro-batch files

network processing program, 485

program code, 479–484

normalized dataset, 466–471

price differences

dataset, 461–466

program code, 485–518

sliding windows, 528–536

SPY monthly chart, 460, 461

testing dataset

analyzing process, 553–555

Euclidean geometry, 537

logical results, 546–553

micro-batch datasets, 536

normalized dataset, 527

price differences, 525–536

saved network

record, 537–546

training method, 519, 520

training results, 521–525

validation results, 524

T, U, V, W, X, Y, Z

Three dimensional (3D) space

chart representation, 557

data preparation, 558–563

network architecture, 563, 564

processing results

projection chart, 583

single panel, 582

testing results, 583–586

training result, 580–582

program code, 564–579

record structure, 558

testing dataset, 561–563

Printed in the United States
by Baker & Taylor Publisher Services

Printed in the United States
by Baker & Taylor Publisher Services